Great Power Competition for Overseas Bases

Pergamon Titles of Related Interest

Douglass SOVIET MILITARY STRATEGY IN EUROPE
Keliher THE NEGOTIATIONS ON MUTUAL AND BALANCED
  FORCE REDUCTIONS
Mroz INFLUENCE IN CONFLICT
Yost NATO'S STRATEGIC OPTIONS

Related Journals*

BRITISH DEFENCE DIRECTORY

*Free specimen copies available upon request.

PERGAMON POLICY STUDIES ON SECURITY AFFAIRS

Great Power Competition for Overseas Bases

The Geopolitics of Access Diplomacy

Robert E. Harkavy

Pergamon Press

NEW YORK • OXFORD • TORONTO • SYDNEY • PARIS • FRANKFURT

Pergamon Press Offices:

U.S.A.   Pergamon Press Inc., Maxwell House, Fairview Park,
                     Elmsford, New York 10523, U.S.A.

U.K.   Pergamon Press Ltd., Headington Hill Hall,
                     Oxford OX3 OBW, England

CANADA   Pergamon Press Canada Ltd., Suite 104, 150 Consumers Road,
                     Willowdale, Ontario M2J 1P9, Canada

AUSTRALIA   Pergamon Press (Aust.) Pty. Ltd., P.O. Box 544,
                     Potts Point, NSW 2011, Australia

FRANCE   Pergamon Press SARL, 24 rue des Ecoles,
                     75240 Paris, Cedex 05, France

FEDERAL REPUBLIC Pergamon Press GmbH, Hammerweg 6
OF GERMANY   6242 Kronberg/Taunus, Federal Republic of Germany

Copyright © 1982 Pergamon Press Inc.
Library of Congress Cataloging in Publication Data

Harkavy, Robert E.
    Great power competition for overseas bases.

    (Pergamon policy studies on security affairs)
    Includes index.
    1. Military bases, American. 2. Military bases,
Russian. I. Title. II. Series.
UA26.A354   1982   /   355.7   82-5374
ISBN 0-08-025089-0   AACR2

Printed in the United States of America

Contents

To Jane and Mike

Acknowledgments

I am indebted to a number of persons and institutions whose contributions to this book were invaluable and who are, of course, excused from its evident shortcomings.

First, I wish to thank the entire staff and collegial ensemble of the Peace Studies Program (PSP), Center for International Studies, Cornell University, where I spent an enjoyable and productive year in 1977/1978, on leave from the U.S. Arms Control and Disarmament Agency, doing research for this work. Particular gratitude is expressed to Franklin Long, then director (who was one of my undergraduate teachers years ago), George Quester, Sean Killeen, Milton Leitenberg, Nicole Ball, Milton Esman, Judith Reppy, David Mozingo, and Colonel Sam Hall, all of whom were unfailingly helpful and encouraging in numerous ways, including their wry tolerance of my peculiar nocturnal working habits. Deborah Ostrander of the PSP was of great assistance with typing and other administrative chores, and Deborah Van Galder did an excellent job typing a first draft manuscript.

Bing West and Hugh Nott of the U.S. Naval War College were helpful in critiquing the first draft of the manuscript, gently persuading me that it needed wholesale revisions. Their reactions initially caused me some anguish, but ultimately served, I hope, to produce an improved version.

Richard Remnek, Robert Weinland, and others at the Center for Naval Analyses were generous with their time in discussing some aspects of my work; likewise, Marguerite King of the State Department's Politico-Military Affairs Bureau, Cmdr. Thomas Mosher of the Defense Department, and Richard Grimmett of the Congressional Research Service. The staff of the Navy and Old Army Branch, National Archives, was very helpful in assisting me to locate materials on basing access in the interwar era in the military intelligence records for that period.

In addition to the Cornell PSP, research and maintenance funds for this project were also provided by the Institute for the Study of World

Politics, and the Advanced Research Council of the U.S. Naval War College (Contract No. N00140-77-M-7075). Typing and reproduction money was provided by the Pennsylvania State University's Political Science Department, headed by John Martz; and by its Liberal Arts Research Office, under Dean Thomas Magner.

A number of my students at Penn State — Chandra Elgin, Randy Dunn, Cathy Gees-Larue, John Messner, Randall Sones, and Alison Doon — assisted me in gathering information and in constructing the tables and bibliography. Donna Harpster did an excellent job of typing the final draft manuscript; Barbara Hendershot and Sue Eberly gave added help. No doubt, others deserve to be mentioned, and they are also thanked, as I here beg forgiveness for the omissions.

During the course of my writing this book, I was also involved in coediting other and related volumes on national security problems with Edward Kolodziej and Stephanie Neuman. Both became close friends in the process and each was of great encouragement and inspiration in many ways felt but not easily measured or expressed.

Finally, love and gratitude are expressed to my wife Jane and son Michael, who are no doubt relieved that this work is finally done, for good or worse. The book is dedicated to them.

1 Introduction

Until very recently, surprisingly scant attention had been paid by international relations scholars either to the policy implications of the major powers' access to overseas facilities or to their theoretical importance for description and analysis of the changing international system itself. This gap has been most pronounced with respect to comprehensive, global analysis and to long-range historical perspective. Indeed, the subject of bases had long been treated as one of the more mundane areas of diplomacy and strategy, visible mostly to readers of dry congressional testimony concerning the minutiae of security agreements, of occasional articles detailing the "legal" aspects of status of forces arrangements with hosts, and of periodic reports of drunken brawls between U.S. servicemen and their hosts' youth.

In recent years, however, there appears to have been a sudden, surprising increase in attention to the geostrategic aspects of basing-access problems. These have been spotlighted by some crucial recent events. Bases, staging points, and overflight corridors have entered the news in the contexts of the role of the Azores Islands in the U.S. arms resupply of Israel in 1973; Soviet utilization of lengthy staging networks for supplying arms to Angola, Mozambique, Ethiopia, and Vietnam; the U.S.-Turkey imbroglio over bases amidst the Cyprus crisis; Arab attempts to nudge the West out of bases in the Azores, Malta, Bahrain, and Oman; Soviet access problems in Egypt, Syria, Libya, Somalia, and Ethiopia; and Israel's use of Kenyan facilities on the way home from Entebbe. In a still broader sense, military access problems have become prominent in a bewildering number of national security and arms-control contexts: arms transfers, nuclear nonproliferation, Indian Ocean demilitarization, SALT verification, raw materials access; and interventions, "surrogate wars," and rescue missions in the Third World. Basing diplomacy had indeed become an important component of "linkage politics," crucially related to numerous other important global regimes and networks of transactions.(1)

1

One recent illustration was provided by the circumstances surrounding the loss to the United States of its long-held intelligence facilities in Iran, deemed crucial for verification of SALT II through the telemetry monitoring of Soviet strategic missile tests. Supporters of the treaty asserted that the Iranian ground facilities could be replaced by U-2 aircraft, flown from a British-controlled base in Cyprus, and rotated over Turkish airspace to provide continuous coverage. There was some irony here, in that the use of Turkish ground facilities earlier used for similar purposes (and many others) had previously been interrupted by the impasse in U.S.-Turkey relations over Cyprus, which then caused the United States to rely on Iranian bases as a backup. The Turkish government was later to claim that it would only allow the United States its U-2 verification flights if Soviet permission for them was granted, demonstrating among other things the long-term divergence of American and Turkish security orientations and the Soviets' success in moving Turkey somewhat toward neutralization. Meanwhile, Norwegian bases were also apparently considered as partial replacements for those in Iran; those reportedly also offered by the People's Republic of China (PRC) were first said not seriously considered, but by 1981, that had changed. American intelligence bases earlier lost in Pakistan, which might have served some of the same purposes, were no longer available – casualties of U.S.-Pakistan strains over the long festering India-Pakistan conflict. Hence, the SALT verification basing issue can be seen to have been enmeshed in a wide swathe of contemporary alignment politics, involving U.S. relations with Turkey and Greece, India and Pakistan, the PRC and Norway, as well as Iran.

The 1973 Middle Eastern war demonstrated the importance of basing diplomacy in some similar but also different ways, here primarily involving lengthy air staging routes and aircraft overflight rights. Soviet supply of arms to Arab clients was eased by the use of staging facilities in Yugoslavia, and of air spaces over Turkey and Yugoslavia. The United States, meanwhile, was denied access to facilities and airspace all over Western Europe on behalf of its arms resupply to Israel, but was able to make crucial use of Portuguese airfields in the Azores Islands. Afterward, in the wake of the Portuguese revolution, the Arabs were to attempt to push the United States out of the Azores with threats and offers of cash, while the United States responded with increased military and economic aid, as well as with a new effort to upgrade the ranges and refueling capabilities of its military aircraft so as to circumvent the restrictions on access imposed during crises, even by formal allies. (For the United States, a variety of other critical military matters were involved, most notably antisubmarine surveillance conducted from the Azores.)

In 1979-1980, meanwhile, in the wake of the crises in Iran and Afghanistan, the focus of attention regarding matters of access centered on American efforts to acquire some new footholds in the Persian Gulf-Indian Ocean area.   Whereas the Carter administration early on in 1977 had attempted to initiate serious negotiations with the

USSR over Indian Ocean demilitarization, it was later prodded by events (Iran and Afghanistan) into seeking new access in Oman, Somalia, Kenya, and Egypt (as well as a further expansion of facilities at Diego Garcia) in conjunction with development of the Rapid Deployment Force (RDF). These moves appeared to signal an American attempt to reverse a long-term decline in the nation's overseas basing assets, a decline which had been in progress for some fifteen years.

A final, additional illustration of the contemporary importance of access diplomacy, and of its political and geographic complexity, has recently been provided by the Iran-Iraq conflict, regarding respective arms resupply to the two combatants. Soviet replacement arms for Iraq were reported transshipped through the Jordanian port of Aqaba, after the closing of access to Basra and also given the necessity for overflying Iranian airspace en route from the USSR to Iraq. Meanwhile, arms reportedly were moved to Iran from its friends in Libya, by Iranian transports traversing Soviet airspace. The Soviet arms resupplied to Iraq, meanwhile, were said to have come from pre-positioned "forward" stocks in South Yemen and Ethiopia, illustrating still one other important aspect of modern basing diplomacy.

In recent years, the United States, with its postwar basing network obviously declining concurrent with an overall contraction of power and responsibility, has been engaged in negotiations over renewal, acquisition, or disgorging of key facilities in a number of dispersed areas in Spain, Greece, Turkey, Thailand, the Philippines, Portugal, and Ethiopia, among others. Even where access has been retained, the economic and political costs have risen dramatically. In what had rapidly become a less permissive environment for U.S. overseas bases, previously obscure place names like Incirlik, Ramasun, Masirah, Kagnew, Cockburn Sound, Ras Banas, Souda Bay, Sigonella, Berbera, and Ascension had become daily fare on the nation's front pages, often in relation to serious crises or national security issues.

The very nature of basing access requirements had also changed in recent years, as new technologies and associated new military requirements created needs for new types of overseas facilities — variously, for intelligence, communications, and ocean and outer space surveillance purposes — and where arms control verification requirements are juxtaposed to those for traditional national security concerns. Less visible, but now often as important as operational or staging bases, these new types of facilities are crucial for antisubmarine warfare (strategic and tactical), telemetry monitoring of rivals' missile tests, electronic (radar) intelligence, detection of nuclear explosions through seismological signals or the gathering of isotopes in air samples, communication with and tracking of satellites, and interception and transmission of a variety of military communications. The competition for access had, in the process, seemed to move from an essentially one-dimensional plane on the surfaces of the earth and oceans to three dimensions, involving also the upper atmosphere, outer space, and the underseas domains.

Also gradually but perceptibly altered over time was the very nature of basing-access diplomacy, historically involving a changing mixture of outright imperial control and various bargains or trade-offs. Of particular note was the apparently growing though much argued nexus between base acquisitions and other types of internation transactions, most notably with the use of arms transfers and military aid as a quid pro quo, explicitly or merely implied. This will be traced in this book through three fairly distinct phases of the twentieth century international system: the interwar, early postwar, and recent postwar periods.

Throughout the period since World War I, and actually on up to the early 1960s, the major powers, with the exceptions of Germany and the USSR, were easily, almost automatically, availed of far-flung basing systems through colonial possessions or functionally equivalent tight spheres of influence. Britain, of course, had its vaunted global network at the zenith of Pax Brittanica, stretching around the world through Gibraltar, Malta, Cyprus, Suez, Aden, Simonstown, Freetown, Mombasa, the Seychelles, Ascension, Ceylon, India, Burma, Singapore, and many, many other places, to support its huge navy. France's smaller but still significant system included outposts in Vietnam, Djibouti, Reunion, Madagascar, Dakar, Bizerte, Martinique, and elsewhere, while even the United States, late getting into the race for imperial strongholds, had facilities in the Philippines, Cuba, and elsewhere, even before World War II.

During the early postwar years, intact but then gradually dwindling colonial remnants – and of equal importance, the permissive basing environment corresponding to the far-flung Western alliances and security commitments around the then Sino-Soviet periphery – allowed Western strategists to take their strategic geographic assets almost for granted. The USSR, although initially boxed in within its own continental empire, meanwhile slowly expanded its network of facilities, most importantly in the Middle East and Cuba during the late 1950s and early 1960s; arms aid and ideological affinities were crucial to these developments, again, with some argument over the mix of cause and correlation. But generally, throughout the early postwar period, the spatial configurations of the big-power conflict remained a faithful reflection of the traditional Mackinderian heartland/rimland paradigm, from which the patterns of basing access naturally followed.

In the past decade or so, the patterns of basing access have changed, and so has the basis for – and modes of – their diplomacy. The earlier geopolitical basis for global conflict had been somewhat altered, and the spatial realities underpinning the West's "containment policy" had significantly disintegrated. The advent of radical and often anti-Western regimes all over the Third World, the claimed lessened importance of a Manichean bipolar capitalist/communist ideological struggle; the annihilation of distance by new weapons and communications technologies; growing fears about serious impending global raw materials shortages; the rise of Eurocommunism; the Sino-Soviet split and a systemic shift toward partial multipolarity; and the Soviets' development of a more global military intervention capability – all had produced a vastly altered global strategic context.

Meanwhile, access rights have increasingly become items of bargained diplomatic exchange, in line with a more symmetrical basis of leverage and influence between the superpowers and some Third World states. As a result, arms sales and military and economic aid have entered the picture in a perhaps far more significant way, though as we shall note, other forms of quid pro quo may also enter into the bargain. Earlier, as it is, before World War II, the arms trade was essentially a free-wheeling, laissez-faire bailiwick of private manufacturers and traders; only after 1945 was the sale of arms to become a really purposive instrument of diplomacy.(2) Gratis military and economic aid before 1945 was nearly nonexistent. And even in the early postwar period, with its tight relationship between military aid and basing access, there was little tension between the two. Recipients welcomed both, assuming them additive and necessary to their own security; indeed, bases on a dependent nation's soil were thought to underpin the credibility of its protectors' security commitments.

In recent years, particularly for the West, alliances and security commitments have become weaker and more tenuous, and as many dependent nations have reoriented their foreign policies, the credibility of the protection formerly thought to derive from a foreign base presence has perhaps receded in importance. And many Third World countries have now simultaneously come to acquire arms from both Western and Soviet-bloc suppliers, utilizing the leverage deriving from the availability of competing sources. Arms-supply competition between the USSR and the Western powers has become fully enmeshed in basing diplomacy, with the former's revisionist drives now underpinned by a more aggressive arms-selling policy, in turn availed by a massive arms-production base which now produces far more planes, tanks, and artillery pieces than its American counterpart.(3)

The Soviet drive for long-sought basing facilities, using arms sales and the prospect for security backing as a leading wedge, has perhaps best been illustrated in Africa, where a network of facilities, port visiting rights, technical installations, and overflight privileges has been acquired in, among others, Algeria, Libya, Mali, Guinea, Guinea-Bissau, Equatorial Guinea (earlier), Congo, Mozambique, Angola, and Ethiopia (the latter now replacing Somalia). In a related manner, Avigdor Haselkorn has detailed the earlier Soviet development of a highly organized security network, involving various levels of access, in the Near East-South Asia region, stretching across Syria, Iraq, India, the Yemens, and Sri Lanka.(4) The United States, meanwhile, its overall geostrategic position long on the wane, had attempted to hang on to some crucial basing points, again almost always with arms transfers as a part of the bargain; 1980, however, saw the beginnings of a more aggressive base-acquisition policy in the wake of the Afghanistan crisis aimed at reversal of these trends.

Essentially, the modern race for bases has remained so far pretty much a two-nation contest, one arena at least which retains a solid measure of bipolarity. France, however, has hung on to outposts in West and East Africa (some recently used in connection with small conflicts), and has apparently sought an additional naval facility in the Mozambique Channel; its greatly expanded arms sales have not, however, been as closely or explicitly linked to such geopolitical considerations as have those of the United States and USSR. Meanwhile, Cuba's use of staging facilities in the Caribbean, Guyana, and West Africa (and perhaps the Azores) for its Angola operations had hinted that future access diplomacy might not be limited solely to the major powers and/or arms suppliers. Further, many small powers have acquired very strong albeit indirect interests in basing matters, in that their arms supplies (and those of rivals) may depend on the access decisions of other small nations en route from major power metropoles. That was one clear lesson of 1973, and also of the Soviet resupply of Vietnam during its conflict with China. Base-denial diplomacy as well as base-acquisition diplomacy has become an important hallmark of contemporary foreign policy.

BASES, GEOPOLITICS, AND GRAND STRATEGY

In the recent past there has been a rising chorus of concern from many scholars and decision makers – mostly but not always on the right of the foreign policy opinion spectrum – about a perceived stasis or even decay in American strategic thought, particularly at the level of what commonly used to be called "grand strategy."(5) There have been calls for new ideas and departures appropriate to "Cold War II," and to counter the still lingering post-Vietnam mood of withdrawal.   By contrast, the Left continues to call for a further abandonment of traditional Cold War strategies, tactics, and rhetoric, but there too one senses a groping for new conceptualizations of a changing global order.

With this sense of strategic malaise, there has been a search for new policies, new definitions, and new global perceptions. In part, the malaise resulted from the suspicion that comprehensive strategic thought had become arrested after the full flowering of nuclear strategic writings in the 1950s and early 1960s. Thus, according to one recent commentary:

> The ideas that developed in the '50s have become part of the common language of world affairs. The balance of terror, mutually-assured destruction and other megadeath concepts are the accepted background to current thinking both within the government and among the general public. . . . There has been a tendency in recent years in both governmental and academic circles to assume that all of the strategic thinking has been done and it is now only necessary to implement ideas from "the golden age" of the '50s and early '60s. Attention is focused on foreign political and military problems in terms of budget cycles plotted against the background of known strategic concepts, without any effort to find fresh ways to approach those problems.

Some of the great names from that golden age, like Kahn and Schelling, think that the ideas that lie behind U.S. security have gotten out of date.(6)

Nuclear deterrence and stability remained, of course, crucially important matters, and the Right had become worried at what it perceived as something more than strategic equivalence to be given the Soviets in the now seemingly aborted SALT II treaty. Short of Armageddon, though, there were serious questions about the implications of a gray area between real parity and Soviet superiority for diplomacy and crisis management short of war, for conflicts between client states of the superpowers, and for conventional stability in Central Europe. These questions involved both "objective" facts of the military balance, but also the often more subjective perceptions of them by nations all around the globe.

The strategic malaise, such as it is, seems centered on the requirement for formulating a comprehensive grand strategy which might encompass the nuclear strategic race, possible limited and/or subnuclear wars, and all of the many other vital economic and political elements of strategy, such as economic growth, human rights, and the promotion of democracy. After Vietnam, of course, "flexible" conventional responses, counterinsurgency, and limited warfare in developing areas involving U.S. forces were no longer in vogue, at least not for the time being.

By the late 1970s, American strategic thought had appeared to have polarized along sharp political/ideological lines, reflecting the breakdown of the once vaunted bipartisan consensus and underscored by the retrospective polemics between "revisionists" and "traditionalists" over the very meaning and origins of the Cold War and its conduct by the United States.

The Carter administration, weighted considerably to the left of the Democratic Party in its top- and middle-level foreign policy appointments, entered office amid a flood of rhetoric about new world orders, abandonment of "rigid, ideological anti-communism," a wholesale shift of emphasis from military to economic strategies for dealing with the developing areas, and an emphasis on "coordinating" more with allies rather than dealing over their heads with the Soviets. The rhetoric and associated actions were later to be somewhat moderated by the usual realities.

On the right, of course, there were heightened worries about a further tendency toward what previously had been suspected was an almost clandestine defeatism under Secretary Kissinger's aegis, an unstated policy of damage limitation and gradual withdrawal from power to cope with the weakening effects of Vietnam. The soaring rhetoric and tepid policies of the Carter administration seemed to them to be merely further covert or even subconscious rationalization to cover objective and growing weakness. Some on the Right who also worried about the decay in strategic thought even came to conclude that not only had the thought atrophied, but the very ends traditionally pursued by strategy – maximization of national interest and power within rational limits of capabilities – had been abandoned.(7) After the 1980 election, of course, the Reagan administration would attempt to translate those views into actual policies in the face of the usual pressures militating toward incrementalism.

The polarization had extended to the rival development of important and significant new perceptual paradigms for assessing the conduct of foreign policy, involving major alterations in ends as well as means. Arms control, for instance, was claimed to have become a virtually dominant "liberal" ideology, superordinate to strategy itself for many allegedly jaded and chastened former Cold War strategists.(8) Others who dealt in new world orders, dependencia, "global issues," and "global consciousness" also seemed to have radically or significantly altered or reversed ends in mind; that is, a wholesale redistribution of power and wealth from north to south.(9) Generally, by the end of the 1970s, a stark cleavage developed over the basic definitions of American national interest – only partly accounted for by arguments over the practical limits of U.S. power – which among other things, had a fault line down the middle of the Democratic Party flanked by its McGovern and Jackson-Moynihan foreign policy wings. That there was an accompanying strategic malaise should not have been a surprise.

Alongside these various connected trends, another one began to loom into view, evidenced both in the press and in scholarly journals, and that had to do with a perceptible recrudescence of interest in the concerns of traditional political geography, a field which long had languished in the shadows since World War II. Some of the reasons for this perhaps surprising reversal have already been surmised or implied: the groping for a truly global strategy to operate under the umbrella of the nuclear standoff; the expansion of U.S.-Soviet political-military rivalry to truly global dimensions, producing a spatially more complex and diffuse competition for influence gradually replacing what earlier had been a closer approximation to a heartland/rimland confrontation; the seeming decline of ideological loci of conflict; and perhaps above all, growing rivalry over raw materials acquisitions in the developing areas.

The latter problem, highlighted by the realization of the West's vulnerability to embargoes and cartels, had focused renewed attention on the protection of sea lanes, control of chokepoints, and access to forward staging areas for possible interventions related to resource requirements. The problem had become even more acute for the West in an era now moving well beyond that of near-global colonial control, and which also witnessed a drastic decline in the power of Western-dominated multinational corporations, now increasingly at the mercy of others' expropriations, to control raw materials sources. And further, the end of territorial colonialism had produced a competition for strategic access based on often tenuous and bargained-for points d'appui, and not on outright, large-scale territorial control.

The foregoing trends had also produced an increased theoretical interest in "cognitive mapping" in connection with geographical rank-orderings of national interests and priorities, including but extending beyond those of strictly traditional military relevance.(10) Previous global cognitions and imagery focused on heartland/rimland or on North Polar projections (or in some cases, on a U.S.-centered world), while still relevant, had begun to give way to new map images highlighting resource locations in Africa, Latin America, and even Antarctica, as well as in resource-laden ocean areas now increasingly subject to closure or restrictions over use and movement.(11)

The renewed interest in the broad, theoretical underpinnings of political geography even appeared to have resulted in a surprising new vogue of "geopolitics," a term rarely heard since the 1940s, but now almost ubiquitously present in the press, albeit with a plethora of vague and ambiguous meanings. Geopolitics, a field of inquiry not easily defined, perhaps part discipline and part ideology in its heyday, was earlier tarred by its commonly assumed association with some of the racist and Social Darwinist theories of the early twentieth century and the interwar period. Not necessarily a "hawkish" term — though often taken as a euphemism for expansionist or at least maximizing balance of power politics — it may merely refer to an emphasis on a geographic basis of power in international relations involving spatial relations and positioning; strategic access, control, and communications; and the relationship between resources and power. There seemed a growing realization that one can learn from studying maps as well as from ideological tracts, technical assessments of weaponry, and the myriad activities and transactions now subsumed under the concepts of "transnational relations" and "global issues".

It is in these numerous but interrelated foregoing contexts that the matter of overseas basing access has received increasing attention. There is, of course, considerable debate about the objective importance of offshore military facilities and related forms of access, revolving about distinctions between objective and subjective power factors. To a degree, some have claimed that what is essentially involved is merely a somewhat symbolic contest, perhaps most analogous to the races for the moon or for Olympic Games medals, with the larger powers vying for proliferated colored, flagged dots on the map. On the contrary, others see an important objective reality to potentially blocked chokepoints, "exposed" forward positions, and "flanked" alliances and trade routes, as well as to others' perceptions of the shifting tides of comparative national power, of momentum toward and away from empire or "Pax X," if not overall influence and at least regional dominance. Thus, some began in the 1970s to attribute great importance to the contrast between the obviously determined Soviet drive for overseas access and the corresponding, ongoing Western contraction of once more far-flung basing networks, with the latter seen at least in part as one price for idealistic arms-control aspirations.

Overall, however, and referring to the previous discussion of the contemporary American strategic malaise, there seemed a need for new general conceptualizations of the present major powers' geopolitical strategies, as importantly though by no means solely reflected in basing policies. One might initially hypothesize, for instance, that whereas earlier, the primitive rimland and heartland theories implied sharp spatial demarcations between the spheres of influence and centers of strength of major antagonists, at present, the newer realities of resource imperatives, insistent new nations' sovereignty, and scattered global enclaves of ideological adherents to major powers have produced a new situation. Both major powers may now be seen seeking well-dispersed points of global access, while still seeking to retain concentrations of uncontested spheres of influence based on proximity to their respective heartlands. The overall strategies (or at least their evolving "outcomes") have come more to resemble Scott Boorman's characterization of the strategic analogy to the ancient Chinese game of wei'ch'i — with its fluid and not very visible "fronts" — than the traditional Western images invoked by analogies to chess or football, as well as Mackinderian geopolitics.(12)

In the following analyses, overlaying the descriptive and historical materials, we shall attempt to tie the great powers' competition for overseas bases to several streams of more or less contemporary international relations theory. That of geopolitical theory has already been bruited, as has that involving definitions and calculi of national interest running along the traditional spectrum from primary to secondary to lesser interests. In dividing the book chronologically between the interwar, early postwar, and recent postwar periods, a framework will be assayed which at least implicitly is based on the "systems" theories or frameworks of Morton Kaplan, Richard Rosecrance, and others.(13) These frameworks, whether essentially deductive or inductive, were earlier intended as initial steps toward what Stanley Hoffmann has called a "sociology of international relations,"(14) and are here applicable to the extent they direct inquiry to the relationships between general characteristics of serial historical eras (polarity, hierarchies of power, ideological or other bases for conflict, extent of maximization or "totality" in war and diplomacy, ethos of elites or "rules of the game," moods, legitimacy of intervention), and such relatively specific functional phenomena (nowadays often called regimes) as arms-transfer patterns — or basing networks.

Another here perhaps tangentially relevant area of international relations theory is that of theories of imperialism (such as Lenin, Hobson, Schumpeter), now recently extended to the almost all-embracing "dependency" theories of Johann Galtung and others.(15) Indeed, present arguments over the meaning of the competition for overseas bases provide some tempting reminders of the earlier debates over imperialism, between economic determinists and those who emphasized the political psychology of expansion and control virtually for their own sakes. On the economic side nowadays, raw materials access undoubtedly outweighs in importance what traditionally have been the two other commonly discussed legs of the imperialist triangle: foreign investment and export markets. Contemporary Marxists, meanwhile, perceive the nexus between arms and bases subsumed beneath the broader asymmetric relationships between "center" and "periphery."

In describing and interpreting the twentieth-century history of the major powers' overseas basing systems, and in relating that analysis to global strategies and changes in the international system, the following progression of chapters will be pursued. Chapter 2 will outline, in a very broad fashion, what is involved in basing diplomacy; that is, the different types or purposes of basing access as they have evolved over the past several decades in response to changes in diplomacy and military technology. Chapters 3, 4, and 5 will describe and analyze the major powers' overseas basing-access networks in the consecutive interwar, early postwar, and recent postwar periods, where fairly clear watersheds are respectively provided for the essentially colonial, bipolar-containment and presently more diffuse-multipolar patterns of access and positioning.

Aside from sheer description, each of these eras will be analyzed loosely according to some crucial systems characteristics; prevailing geopolitical positions, conceptions, and cognitive maps; defensive and offensive access strategies, extant military technology applicable to access problems, and to arms-transfer patterns and practices and other items of quid pro quo which have been the coin of basing diplomacy. The actual use of bases and other forms of access for interventions and other military and political activities in each of the periods will also be reviewed.

Chapter 6 will review the earlier corpus of geopolitical theory — specifically as it relates to basing diplomacy — and will attempt to update it with some modern emendations reflecting contemporary global realities. One emphasis will be on the conflicting assumptions about what reciprocal strategic advantages and disadvantages inhere to the geographic positions of the United States and USSR, again as clearly modified by a host of other political and economic factors.

Chapter 7, by way of summing up, will shift the focus to a number of "functional" areas of world politics which are closely intertwined with basing diplomacy. The competition for facilities will be related, in historical context, to raw materials access, surrogate wars, strategic deterrence, arms control, balances of payments, arms sales and aid, alliances, and other such staple concerns of international relations, as well as to some of the related theoretical concerns enumerated above.

In the process, it is hoped that some small amount of light may be shed on the current American strategic malaise, from a perspective which heretofore has been considerably ignored beneath the shadow of strategic nuclear doctrine, conventional weapons balances, and the recent prominence of formal arms-control and disarmament measures. The acquisition and maintenance of positions of access is only one aspect of grand strategy. But to the extent that these problems may be demonstrated closely to interlock with a number of its other key elements — arms supply and alliance politics, overseas projection of force, nuclear deterrence, resource acquisition — it is hoped that it may provide one vehicle, or one perspective, for an understanding of the broader contours of contemporary strategy and the long-range evolvement of the major powers' global power balance. At the very least, the meaning of the evident simultaneous contraction of Western access and obverse Soviet expansion demands exploration in historical context, for it is now widely perceived as one aspect of a "changing correlation of forces."

NOTES

(1) The term "linkage politics" has come recently to assume two rather distinct meanings. One, associated with Henry Kissinger's diplomacy in the early 1970s, and claimed abandoned by the incoming Carter administration in 1977, involves bargaining across issue areas, as when Soviet "promises" to exercise restraint in the Middle East become part of the "detente process" and even an argument on behalf of SALT. The other, used here and more familiar to the academic international-relations literature, refers to the inextricable, causal interrelationships between domestic and foreign policy, and is habitually discussed in the context of the "levels-of-analysis" problem. Regarding that, see, inter alia, James Rosenau, Linkage Politics: Essays on the Convergence of National and International Systems (New York: The Free Press, 1969).

(2) This point is developed in detail in R. E. Harkavy, The Arms Trade and International Systems (Cambridge, Mass.: Ballinger, 1975), esp. chap. 2. See also Richard Lewinsohn, The Profits of War Through the Ages (London: G. Routledge and Sons, Ltd., 1936); and Otto Lehmann-Russbuldt, War for Profits (New York: A. H. King, 1930).

(3) See, inter alia, "Questions Raised on Army Readiness to Engage in Prolonged Land Conflict," New York Times, September 24, 1980, p. A1; and in particular, R. Burt, "Gearing Up For New Lap in Arms Race," New York Times, January 20, 1980, p. E3, wherein data are provided showing a large Soviet advantage in production of tanks, armored fighting vehicles, combat aircraft, helicopters, etc.

(4) Avigdor Haselkorn, The Evolution of Soviet Security Strategy: 1965-1975 (New York: Crane Russak, 1978).

(5) The multitudinous facets of what is comprised by "grand strategy" are laid out in John Collins, Grand Strategy: Practices and Principles (Annapolis, Md.: Naval Institute Press, 1973).

(6) Quoted from Henry S. Bradsher, "Is the U.S. Surviving on Stale Strategic Concepts?" Washington Star, December 29, 1976, pp. 5-6.

(7) Representative of the literature downplaying the centrality of traditional power politics and stressing, by comparison, a claimed increasing global interdependence are: Robert Keohane and Joseph Nye, Power and Interdependence (Boston: Little, Brown, 1977); Edward L. Morse, Modernization and the Transformation of International Relations

(New York: Free Press, 1976); and Stanley Hoffmann, "Notes on the Elusiveness of Power," International Journal 30, 2 (Spring 1975): 183-184. For an acid rebuke of this mind-set, see Carl Gershman, "The Rise and Fall of the New Foreign-Policy Establishment," Commentary 70, 1 (July 1980): 13-24.

(8) That claim is made in the various recent writings of Colin Gray, for instance, in the opening pages of his The Geopolitics of the Nuclear Era (New York: Crane Russak, 1977).

(9) See Gershman, "Rise and Fall."

(10) See the various contributions in Robert Axelrod, ed., The Structure of Decision: The Cognitive Maps of Political Elites (Princeton: Princeton University Press, 1976), particularly that by Jeffrey Hart, "Geopolitics and Dependency: Cognitive Maps of Latin American Foreign Policy Elites." See also Alan K.   Henrikson, "America's Changing Place in the World: From 'Periphery' to 'Centre'?" in Jean Gottmann, ed., Centre and Periphery: Spatial Variation in Politics (Beverly Hills, Calif.: Sage Publications, 1980).

(11) See, for instance, Geoffrey Kemp, "The New Strategic Map," Survival 19, 2 (March/April 1977): 50-59.

(12) Scott A. Boorman, The Protracted Game: A Wei-chi Interpretation of Maoist Revolutionary Strategy (New York: Oxford University Press, 1969).

(13) See Morton Kaplan, System and Process in International Politics (New York: Wiley, 1957); and Richard Rosecrance, Action and Reaction in World Politics: International Systems in Perspective (Boston: Little, Brown, 1963).   The applicability of "systems theory" to the historical study of arms transfers was discussed in Harkavy, Arms Trade and International Systems; analogously, one can apply such frameworks to the evolvement of strategic basing problems.   A critical analysis of the systems approaches and theories of Rosecrance, Kaplan, Hoffmann, et al. is provided by Kenneth Waltz, Theory of International Politics (Reading, Mass.: Addison-Wesley, 1979), esp. chaps. 2, 3.

(14) Stanley Hoffmann, Contemporary Theory in International Relations (Englewood Cliffs, N.J.: Prentice-Hall, 1960), pp. 174-176.

(15) The various theories of imperialism are summarized and discussed comparatively in E. M. Winslow, The Patterns of Imperialism (New York: Columbia University Press, 1948); Harrison M. Wright, ed., The New Imperialism (Lexington, Mass.:   D. C. Heath, 1961); and David Hoovler, "Structural Theories of Imperialism" (paper delivered at annual meeting of International Studies Assoc., Washington, D.C., Feb. 19-22, 1975). See also Steven Rosen and James Kurth, eds., Testing Theories of Economic Imperialism (Lexington, Mass.: D. C. Heath, 1974).

2 Forms and Functions of Overseas Bases

Presumably, the use of "forward" military bases and the quest for strategic access outside home territories dates far back into the history of warfare.(1) The standard military histories, however, seldom provide a coherent, comprehensive portrayal of earlier basing networks. Detailed historical analysis might be able to reconstruct at least an adequate picture of the naval access utilized by Athens and Phoenicia in the Mediterranean, of Rome's far-flung garrisons and associated supply routes, of the logistical chains and outposts used by Alexander or Ghengis Khan, and the trans-North Atlantic basing network used by the Viking explorers.(2) During the modern era, however, we may trace a gradual evolvement of the characteristic mix of basing functions; paced by a combination of political (systemic) and technological (weapons, communications, transport) factors.

THE FUNCTIONS OF BASES IN THE MODERN PERIOD

Some semantic confusion has been caused by the tendency for the terms "base," "facility," and "access" to be used interchangeably, though the case may also be made for attributing political significance to changing usage here. Though precision of terminology is in this case neither altogether possible nor always important, a few comments will suffice to indicate the usage subsequently to be followed here.

The term "access" normally subsumes all types of bases and facilities (including technical installations), aircraft overflight rights, port visit privileges (often not involving any permanent military presence by the user), and the use of offshore anchorages within sovereign maritime limits. That is what, broadly, is entailed by military access. As it is, many contemporary writers now utilize a much broader construction for what is involved in speaking of strategic access to include, for instance, access to markets, raw materials sources, and/or investments; penetration by radio and television broadcasts; and access for intelligence operations. Hence, too, it has recently become common to discuss the superpowers' "competition for strategic access" in the combined contexts of basing facilities and raw materials and to gauge the

14

strategic value of a small state primarily by the combination of these two criteria, sometimes abetted by others.(3) Hereinafter, our reference to access or strategic access will presuppose a primarily military connotation, referring to bases, overflight privileges, and the like.

More importantly, many recent analyses have insisted upon a strict definitional distinction between "bases" and "facilities," causing considerable semantic confusion, as the scope of what traditionally had been conveyed by the former term was greatly narrowed. What is involved is a continuum describing degrees of sovereign control or exclusive use or access, and perhaps also an inclination to use "base" for major installations and "facility" for smaller, more technical and less obtrusive ones.(4) But it is the former distinction, that dealing with ultimate control, which is central.

A rigid definition of the term "base" concedes the existence of such only where the user has exclusive extraterritorial control, either via compulsion or by treaty. Hence, installations in colonial territories would be, by definition, bases, as would an installation for which a sovereign state had abandoned all control over access and use – as was the case for some American access in the early postwar period and, apparently, for the Soviets' use of the naval base at Alexandria during the early 1970s.

Where the guest power's use of an installation is controlled or merely ad hoc, or where joint access and control is evidenced, it is now common to refer to a "facility." Implied here, of course, is that access to such an installation may be limited or eliminated at any time or for any situation by the host. If one insists upon such a strict definition, of course, almost all overseas access nowadays involves facilities and not bases; indeed, the latter will almost have exited the historical stage with the disappearance of the final remnants of colonial control.

Many commentators, however, continue to use the two terms, "base" and "facility," synonymously and interchangeably, except that major facilities (in the above sense) are more often referred to as bases. Hereinafter, we shall also use both terms rather loosely and interchangeably, if only for variety of usage, and because if the stricter definition were adhered to, the more vivid, familiar, and comfortable meaning conveyed by "bases" would be lost to us. Where necessary, a formal distinction can always be made.

Interestingly, during the interwar period, writers did not concern themselves with this distinction between bases and facilities, no doubt in part because of the prevalence of big-power control in the colonial period. Weigert, however, worrying about definitions along another dimension of current interest, said that

such fallacious thought on the subject results from an uncritical assumption that "base" is more or less synonymous with "port." Thus the term "strategic base" is usually associated with the idea of an insular area, or of a beachhead in foreign territory. But bases are not only overseas but overland, too, as in the important case of what might soon become a vital United States defense frontier in northern Canada.(5)

At any rate, the various types of bases or facilities (here using these terms interchangeably) may be defined according to a spectrum or complex matrix describing their basic justification or purpose, the kinds of military operations conducted from them, and by size, visibility, and military service. Often, a given base complex will be used to serve several functions at once, sometimes spanning the traditional service breakdown between army, navy, and air force. And, over time, the existing characteristic mix of a major power's facilities, their locations, and their numbers, will change in response to technological developments, military requirements, and the patterns of global diplomacy. Further, as we shall see, the functions of many bases are fully explicable only in relation to interlocking regional or global networks where numerous separate elements are needed successfully to perform a mission or continuous operation.

Concerning the general purposes of facilities, a basic breakdown may be made between those providing support for military forces and military operations near the anticipated scene of force deployment, and the providing of a military "presence" at locations critical to national policy and to overall foreign policy credibility.(6) Both of these purposes (involving in part the distinction between defense and deterrence) may be served by some facilities, though one may be primary, or at least initially intended as such. Air and naval bases are perhaps more likely to be used as operational facilities (and are often routinely used for peacetime staging and transit operations involving other countries), whereas ground force facilities are more likely to serve as immediately "nonfunctional" presences involving a visibly ready force, as with U.S. troops in Germany or Korea.

Some scholars, incidentally, prefer virtually to subsume basing matters under the broader heading of logistics, with a heavy emphasis on long-range power projection, and the extension and preservation of empires or global maritime predominance. War-fighting capability is here stressed – along with the associated deterrent threat. Along such lines, Kemp and Maurer have compared the coal- (and later oil-) based logistics of the British navy at the zenith of its power, with recent U.S. experience.(7) Such a focus is, of course, closely intertwined with the heartland-versus-rimland geopolitical perspectives of Mahan and Mackinder – centrally involving comparisons of logistical chains by distance and cost. That focus deals primarily with traditional naval and air transport refueling problems – also with related communications capabilities so central to efficient use of forces – and much less with a variety of now emerging technical basing functions. Then, too, such a focus emphasizes big-power military confrontation contingencies, and much less the capabilities of powers to utilize overseas facilities for military assistance to client states or "surrogates."

One commentator has pointed out that "the distinction as to primary purpose between air and naval bases on the one hand, and ground force bases on the other, is further sharpened by political considerations."(8) Ground force bases are usually not a political problem, as the real political question is whether or not troops are to be stationed at all in a foreign country. If they are there to defend that country – as in Germany or Korea, or as a part of the overall defense of alliance interests – the question of establishing the necessary base support facilities (including air and naval, as well as ground force support) will already have been politically solved in that such facilities are obviously necessary for the extended presence of troops. Naval and air bases, on the other hand, if alone, are not necessarily there primarily to defend the country in which they are located, and may therefore be more vulnerable to political pressures both with respect to their continued existence and to their use outside the host's borders. Hence it may be surmised that bases having the highest probability of retention and the least political vulnerability (where outright control is absent) are those whose primary function is the provision of a military presence or tripwire, particularly if in defense of the host country. However, such a presence may ultimately come to be perceived as a provocation, hence producing vulnerability rather than credible protection, as is now sensed by some U.S. clients in Asia.

Defining bases more narrowly according to specific functions requires elaboration of a long list, by military service and by such categories as tactical air support, submarine warfare, antisubmarine warfare, communications, surveillance, strategic missile deterrence, air transport staging of men and materiel, and many others. We shall here outline what has been involved for some of these, moving back and forth between clear-cut service missions and a range of operational and technical functions which, in varying degrees, span traditional service lines.(9)

The most visible (and potentially most threatening to a host's sovereignty and dignity) type of facility is a large garrison or complex of bases for long-term stationing of troops, aircraft, or naval vessels. These immediately come to mind when we speak of a foreign base, in the broad construction of that term. The permanent stationing of large U.S. Army units in Germany and South Korea, Soviet armored divisions in captive Eastern Europe, large U.S. naval bases in Japan and the Philippines, and U.S. strategic air bases in Spain are some examples. The basis for access in these and other cases does, of course, vary according to degrees of outright or unwanted military occupation, forward positioning of forces by agreement or as part of alliance commitments, or various forms of bargained-for arrangements based on cash rentals, economic or military aid, and so forth. In earlier periods, certainly from the nineteenth century on up to and beyond World War II, most such bases throughout the world were automatically provided by colonial control and were an important aspect and purpose of imperial domination. Here, as far earlier with the Roman Empire, small army garrisons and colocated naval forces were often used to control large captive populations with the provision for quick movement of larger fire-fighting forces from home territory, or from neighboring areas, if control should be threatened by insurrection or foreign incursion.(10)

Depending upon their size, ground forces stationed in a foreign country will often require heavy support facilities, involving barracks and mess halls, storage and maintenance facilities, ammunition and POL storage, hospitals, schools, training areas, and numerous specialized communications and intelligence facilities, as well, often, as nearby air facilities for airlift of replacement personnel or of additional units "earmarked" for military contingencies, as well as of materiel. Access to sea logistics facilities may likewise be important (as it is to U.S. forces in Germany in distinction to Soviet forces in Eastern Europe), given the continuing economies provided by large-scale, bulk, long-distance maritime supplies.

As we shall later further discuss, the long-term "permanent" stationing of large ground forces in other countries, as part of formal negotiated alliance commitments, is rather unique to the postwar period, and even there, significant primarily in the situations of Europe and (for the United States) the Far East.(11) There was nothing remotely equivalent anywhere over a long stretch of several centuries of prior recent history.

In the recent context, the deployment or spread of ground forces has depended on their purposes, whether to defend the host country from invasion, to garrison or occupy a country in the face of possible revolution or irredentism in a postwar occupation, or to provide for military operations outside the country. The U.S. Army in Germany, for instance, while primarily deployed in-line and in-depth to defend against an attack from the East, also earlier had a postwar garrisoning-control function, and also has long had airborne units deployed near major airfields for quick deployment to the Middle East or Africa. Soviet forces in Eastern Europe have had a clearer, longer-term dual purpose, with their deployment both against NATO and against internal insurgencies such as those in Hungary, Czechoslovakia, and Poland in 1956, 1968, and 1981, respectively. Those forces have not been earmarked, for instance, for Middle Eastern contingencies, as that can be more readily handled by quick reaction forces stationed within the USSR. British and French colonial forces both before and after World War II were thinly dispersed throughout various imperial domains, often in traditional "forts," to provide local control. External threats were normally only a subsidiary calculation, though particularly after 1945, these small forces were moved about within and across regions for fighting "brushfire wars" in a futile attempt to halt the inexorable anticolonial tide.

Some permanent facilities — air, naval, and ground — are used primarily for training purposes, often where uncongested space in the air or on the ground, or certain kinds of climate or terrain are required, if not readily available at home or where major forces are permanently stationed. Hence the United States has in the past used areas in North Africa and elsewhere for aircraft gunnery and bombing practice and for unhindered aerial dog-fighting training, because of the restrictions imposed by the heavy volume of air traffic and limited open ground spaces in Western Europe. Locales in Latin America have been used for jungle warfare exercises, those in Norway for cold weather training, and beaches in a variety of climes for amphibious landing practice. The U.S. Marines conduct periodic exercises in the Western Pacific area, in Japan and Okinawa, often involving joint coordinated training with allied forces; more recently, U.S. forces have conducted similar training exercises with Egyptian forces. The Soviets, while incorporating within their own borders most types of climate and terrain, have apparently also used South Yemen's Socotra Island in the Indian Ocean for amphibious assault practice, there being no really equivalent environment within the USSR. The medium NATO powers in Western Europe have used foreign areas for similar purposes, being restricted at home to rather narrow ranges for training experience. In addition, they have utilized overseas facilities for nuclear tests (such as France in Muroroa Island) and for missile tests (Britain in Australia); the United States has done likewise in the Central Pacific. Some training areas, such as that used by U.S. forces at Grafenwohr in West Germany, are used to provide open spaces for extensive maneuvers by troops normally barracked in urban areas, to keep them in a high state of combat preparedness, and to accustom them to bivouacking in the open country.

Regarding ground forces, some pivotal areas are used for logistical support for entire regions, given the need for extensive organizational support and central depots. Germany provides such a function for U.S. forces all over Europe, the Middle East, and Africa; Okinawa and some bases in Japan serve similar purposes for the entire Western Pacific and Southeast Asia regions. Singapore earlier similarly provided a logistics and maintenance hub for British forces in the Far East. In recent years, the United States, disadvantaged by its geographical location in relation to Eurasia and its attendant balance-of-payments problems, has taken to pre-positioning large volumes of combat materiel for forces earmarked for Europe but barracked at home in the United States – this appears a novel and unique historical phenomenon. The USSR pre-positions such materiel in Libya, South Yemen, and Ethiopia for possible operations in the Middle East or Africa; the United States now is moving to counter by stockpiling materiel in Egypt and perhaps Oman.

Air base facilities are used to serve numerous functions aside from the obvious major ones of deploying tactical and strategic combat aircraft. There are also facilities for deploying and staging airlift transports, and for reconnaissance and surveillance aircraft. Many bases, particularly the larger ones, may serve several of these roles simultaneously, though some are primarily specialized for only one. Air base complexes also often house a variety of communications and other technical operations, along with the usual mix of housekeeping units and installations.

U.S. tactical air bases in Germany, the Netherlands, and Turkey (and their Soviet equivalents in Eastern Europe) exist primarily in relation to contingencies for providing ground support and deep interdiction (conventional or nuclear) missions in the case of large-scale conflict in Europe. Those in Japan, Okinawa, and Korea are deployed for similar purposes in the Far East; those in the Philippines are for local defense of an ally, or for contingencies elsewhere in Southeast Asia. American "tactical" aircraft in Europe, often defined as Forward-Based Systems (FBS) in the SALT context, may also be considered part of the strategic nuclear equation vis-a-vis the USSR. Those air facilities deploying combat aircraft are normally "permanent" facilities, often located side-by-side with ground air-defense missile units and large ground forces.

Both U.S. and Soviet forward-based aircraft in Europe and Asia can, if necessary, be shifted to other areas of contention, or even drawn down for arms resupply to allies in crisis situations as an interim measure where speed is essential. The United States has also long deployed tactical aircraft at Canadian bases for air defense; some aircraft elsewhere also are deployed primarily as interceptors in a defensive mode. Recently, the United States has taken to utilizing temporary forward deployments of Airborne Warning and Control (AWACs) as an assertion of "presence," for mild gestures of coercive diplomacy, or to assure allies such as Saudi Arabia.

The United States has also long fielded nuclear attack bombers in forward positions, earlier in Spain, Morocco, and the UK, and continuing to the present in the latter. Other facilities, for instance in Spain, have been intended as recovery bases for SAC bombers in case of all-out war. Cuban bases may be intended by the Soviets for similar purposes with the arrival of the Backfire bomber (this has been much argued over during the SALT II debate), and they also deploy shorter-range aircraft (such as the MIG-23) which could possibly be used by Soviet pilots for nuclear strikes against the United States. Also at the strategic level, there are air base facilities (for the United States, mostly in Arctic regions) for tanker refueling aircraft, which enable great extension of ranges for bombing missions. In the nuclear strategic context, recovery and refueling bases are now of perhaps declining but still residual importance in an era dominated by long-range land- and sea-based missiles.

Staging of transport aircraft for arms supplies, personnel, and other materiel accounts for numerous overseas facilities (sometimes colocated with combat functions), sometimes involving large installations with permanently stationed user personnel, but also often involving joint control or use of client states' facilities on a more or less ad hoc basis.

Some facilities of this type are used on a more or less normal basis during peacetime for routine arms and personnel shipments, while at other times they must be bargained for just before and during crises. Hence, the United States gained the use of Portuguese staging facilities during the 1973 war, but not those of other European allies, while in recent crises in Iran and Nicaragua, the use of nearby bases in Turkey and Costa Rica, respectively, had to be haggled over. Whether or not British permission for staging supplies through Diego Garcia would be granted in the case of another Middle Eastern crisis is an open question. Use of staging facilities in Spain and Italy for arms supplies to Middle Eastern countries other than Israel has also apparently been subject to bargaining. Meanwhile, both the United States and the USSR also have made periodic use of commercial airports throughout the world for various air staging operations, where ad hoc permission during crises may also be at issue.

Many staging bases are also used for ferrying short-range tactical aircraft over long distances, often where time constraints preclude or render less desirable alternate movement by ship. The now longer ranges of such aircraft, and in some cases, their midair refueling capabilities, now render this function somewhat less vital than was the case before and during World War II, when the United States had to utilize numerous short-hop ferrying routes to Europe, Africa, and the Near East. For both staging and ferrying operations, the importance of a given base may be gauged only in the light of regional chains or networks providing routes of access and forward deployment, in conjunction with the availability of overflight corridors.

Recent vast increases in aircraft ranges and in the development of sophisticated in-flight refueling techniques have somewhat lessened the requirements for numerous overseas bases to support a global air staging network. With the interwar period used as a baseline, the change is seen to have been dramatic. Using large numbers of tankers, new cargo aircraft such as the U.S. C-5A may now transport large numbers of troops and massive cargo tonnages throughout the globe with the use of only a small number of well-placed staging and tanker deployment points. Hence, one recent analysis indicated that America's continued use of British-owned Ascension and Diego Garcia islands could alone, in conjunction with tanker refueling, provide the United States the capability for extensive aerial supply to much of Africa and the Middle East.(12) But the trends are still of mixed import. Even with the longer transport ranges, the use of intermediate refueling stops can improve the ratio of cargo to fuel carried, and hence improve the economics of airlift. And the availability of tanker facilities may themselves be in doubt during crises, as were those in Spain in 1973. The now longer ranges of fighter aircraft and their configuration for aerial refueling have somewhat mitigated the need for short-run ferry routes, but not entirely. And the lessened need for strategic air bases may now be balanced somewhat by the increased need for fleet air cover from ground bases (for the Soviets as well as the United States) in a period witnessing the increased vulnerability of surface ship concentrations to interdiction by air- and sea-launched missiles.(13) And, finally, crisis contingencies may require the quick dispatch of aircraft from nearby countries, where movement from the homeland may be prohibitively slow.

On a less visible and hence seemingly less sensitive level, there is the now often crucial matter of aircraft overflight privileges, involving a range of practices and traditions, some altered by time in an era of increasingly "total" warfare, diplomacy, and ideological enmities. Some nations have allowed others more or less full, unhindered, and continuous overflight rights (perhaps involving only pro forma short-term notices), while in other cases, ad hoc formal applications for permission to overfly must be made well ahead of time, which may or may not be granted depending upon the purpose and situation, be it normalcy or crisis.(14) Turkey and Yugoslavia, for instance, granted the USSR overflight rights during the 1973 airlift to the Arabs, while some of America's NATO allies did not grant similar access to the United States on behalf of Israel. The United States has had serious problems with overflights in some Middle Eastern and African corridors, while the Soviets have been availed overflights all up and down both African coasts for airlift of materiel to Angola and Mozambique. Soviet overflight access over some Asian countries was also apparently useful in supplying arms to Vietnam from the eastern USSR during the Vietnam-China war in 1979.

And then, some overflights are made without permission (as with the respective use by the United States and USSR of U-2 and MIG-25 reconnaissance flights), overtly or covertly or with a tacit or resigned wink by the overflown nation. Often a nation whose airspace is violated will not openly complain for fear of international or domestic embarrassment over its impotence, or untoward diplomatic repercussions with a strong power. Hence, the USSR is thought to have overflown Egypt and Sudan, among others, without permission in supplying arms to Ethiopia; earlier, its MIG-25 reconnaissance aircraft apparently flew with impunity over Iran's airspace. The United States is thought to have threatened overflights in some places for future arms resupply of Israel, if it should be utterly necessary.

Covert overflights were probably more frequent before World War II, before the development of radar, when their discovery was pretty much dependent upon visual observation from the ground or from other aircraft. Nowadays, satellite reconnaissance makes such "covert" activities almost impossible, particularly if a small nation has access to information from one of the superpowers.

Nowadays, too, the rather sharp division of the world into hostile ideological camps (and the proliferation of jealous sovereignties produced by decolonization) has made the granting of overflight privileges a more important and sensitive matter than it was during the relatively laissez-faire interwar period, when denial of such rights apparently occurred only in extreme circumstances. Further, various Third World nations have become routinely engaged in pressuring friends to deny overflights from major powers to their neighboring antagonists, rendering the diplomacy of overflights both more important, habitual, and complex. For these reasons, at least one writer has pointed to the "shrinking international airspace as a problem for future air movements."(15)

In a newer area of aerial technological development, facilities for regular or ad hoc staging of antisubmarine surveillance aircraft have become important, involving sonar and other forms of detection from the air and the sowing of sonabuoys in the sea. These aircraft are often based where staging and other facilities are available to the user power. The importance of these bases must be comprehended in connection with complementary terminal and data-processing facilities for hydrophone arrays placed on the seabeds, with the ASW aircraft often being used to fill in gaps not covered by the latter.(16) Underseas surveillance was essentially impossible before the development of sonar, though earlier, aircraft were used to locate diesel submarines when they required frequent battery recharges on the surface.

Use of overseas naval ship facilities by the major powers can assume any of a number of forms across a spectrum describing types of vessels provided access, as well as levels of permitted access, permanence, and use for various contingencies. As catalogued by one recent summary article, the functions served by naval shore facilities can be grouped into four categories: replenishment of consumables, intelligence and communication, repairs, and direct combat support.(17)

The consumable replenishment category involves a wide variety of items, such as water, food, supplies, fuels and lubricants, spare parts, disposable equipment (such as sonabuoys and wing tanks for aircraft), and ordnance, as well as the replenishment of the morale of sailors needing periodic shore leave (rest and recreation). The need for materiel replenishment is paced by the finite storage space on ships (often subject to trade-offs between combat capability and personnel comforts), though the requirements for shore storage facilities can be mitigated by the extensive use of supply ships accompanying the fleet. That is normally considered a fallback expediency where shore bases are not available, as was the case for Soviet operations in many areas prior to the acquisition of newly acquired shore access, and still the case in some areas.

Some of the needed items — such as food and water — are available commercially in all ports, but political contingencies may dictate more permanent and assured sources, as port clearances are subject to denial during crises or even on a more or less permanent basis.

Shore facilities available on a regular basis — at least short of war and crises — are highly sought and are an important aspect of modern naval diplomacy, as witness the U.S. Navy's problems in obtaining even minimal access all around the east-west African littoral in the present political climate, and earlier Soviet efforts at obtaining footholds in the Mediterranean and around the Indian Ocean, after decades of reliance on a combination of shuttling support ships and offshore anchorages.

The arrival of a fleet, even if only for replenishment, can have sensitive political overtones, particularly given the colonial history of gunboat diplomacy, the awesome symbolic display of military might involved, and the always explosive potential for violence when large numbers of sailors are disgorged en masse to roam the local bars.(18) The latter problem earlier caused U.S. access to Turkey to be curtailed, and there have been untoward incidents in the Philippines, Kenya, and elsewhere. Even the close restrictions placed on Soviet sailors in port has not prevented some instances of local resentment, for instance, in Egypt.

Shore facilities at any rate provide convenient and secure places to store often bulky and expensive equipment (missiles, large parts) which could be shipped from home bases, but only at great expense and with a time penalty. Hence, they are one aspect of the major powers' pre-positioning of materiel for conflict contingencies, and it is for that reason that American concerns were raised when the Soviets acquired shore-based missile storage facilities in Somalia, in proximity to potential combat zones in the Indian Ocean-Red Sea-Persian Gulf area.(19) Likewise, the United States has been accorded an advantage in the strategic context by its forward Polaris submarine bases in Scotland, Spain, and Guam, for crew rotation as well as for replenishment and resupply of materiel.

Ship repair facilities abroad – both for minor and preventive maintenance or for major overhauls – are highly sought by all major naval powers, given the enormous costs and time involved in having to bring ships all the way home, and the resulting loss of ship-days on station and readiness for war contingencies.(20) Though some repairs may be done at sea by accompanying tenders (which carry tools and spare parts), and others by tenders in ports, some still will require large drydocks and heavy cranes, necessitating a permanent shore facility. Some commercial yards may be used (as at present in Singapore, and at Shanghai during the interwar period), but again where denial may be subject to diplomatic vicissitudes in an era, contrasting with earlier periods, where all commercial harbor facilities operate under restrictive political controls.

The need for forward repair facilities has long presented a potential disadvantage for the United States in maintaining transatlantic and transpacific fleets far from home. Also, few overseas shipyards can do the sophisticated maintenance and repair required for large warships; building new large repair facilities from scratch is an expensive proposition, and that is not to mention the problem of availability of a necessary skilled labor force. Hence, the United States relies precariously, for its Pacific fleet, on facilities in Japan and the Philippines, and replacing them with new repair facilities, say in Guam, would be very expensive.(21)

Direct combat support facilities involve permanent basing of ships overseas, ranging from individual vessels to small flotillas to large fleets, or smaller units where extensive administrative support is often involved. For the United States nowadays, large fleets are homeported in Japan and Italy, and smaller flotillas, such as that earlier based in Bahrain on the Persian Gulf, may be intended primarily as a "presence" and as a potential nucleus for a buildup in time of crisis. Otherwise, shore facilities may also provide land-based aircraft for defense of fleets – and for attacking rival fleets – as well as for maritime patrol, ASW, reconnaissance, and electronic warfare. Bases deploying aircraft for defense of fleets may be more highly sought where aircraft carriers are not available; hence, this has long been a primary Soviet consideration. The time required to deploy ships to combat in an arc around any forward base is a prime item of calculation in locating bases and in dispersing fleet elements to different bases. Such calculations also may involve the possible use of naval marines in amphibious or helicopter-borne operations.

As noted, many ship support functions can be located either on shore or onboard support ships, involving trade-offs between the greater sophistication and variety afforded by shore facilities (also the absence of adverse weather factors where heavy seas can impede operations) and the freedom from political interference provided by portable shipborne support facilities.(22) Generally, however, shore-based repair shops, warehouses, fuel tanks, magazines, radios, radars, or drydocks can be substituted for afloat, if only at the cost of reallocating naval budgets toward more tail and less tooth, in the form of tenders, repair ships, fuel-tankers or barges, ammunition, storage, communications and electronic ships, hospital vessels and floating drydocks. Many overseas deployments actually make use of both types of facilities. The Soviets have long had to make more extensive use of onboard support ships and offshore mooring points than has the United States (likewise, more use of seaborne intelligence gathering ships in lieu of shore-based facilities), because of the relative lack of overseas bases, a situation which may now, however, be changing.

Generally speaking, extensive naval repair and support facilities provided major powers by smaller or dependent states imply and usually correspond with close security relationships or alliances, while symbolic or routine port visits merely for refueling or showing the flag are often made by navies in countries where there are only weak ties or even a degree of enmity. Soviet and NATO navies have, for instance, made visits to each others' ports in recent years, while reciprocal ship visits between rival navies were virtually de rigeur in the more chivalrous climate prevailing before 1941. Still, the major navies nowadays exert great efforts to persuade smaller countries to allow their fleets short visits, one more aspect of the global "game of nations." Sometimes this is perceived as an opening wedge promising more extensive and militarily significant access, which is why the recent initial Soviet ship visits to Tunisia were greeted with more than idle curiosity in the West.

Of course, purposeful gunboat diplomacy may also be involved in ship visits (as well as with fleet movements toward areas of crisis), either to threaten a host country or to support it in threatening a nearby rival.(23) U.S. fleet support of Turkey after World War II is an oft-cited classic example of such political use of force, in imitation of habitual use of such signaling, coercive behavior by the British navy over a long stretch of time. More recently, the United States has supported Kenya and North Yemen in similar ways when they were threatened by neighbors, while Soviet ship visits to Mozambique have been used to provide long-term warnings to South Africa while also scoring political points for the USSR all over black Africa. Some analysts have relied upon extensive aggregated quantitative data for port visits and also ship-days in various oceans and seas to gauge the long-term tides of superpower influence, presence, and access.(24)

The Soviets, in particular, have also made extensive use of floating anchorages in international waters for refueling, maintenance, and idling and rendezvousing of ships, usually where onshore facilities are not available or where political conditions dictate a low profile. These anchorages, replete with permanent mooring buoys, have been dispersed all over the Mediterranean, the Indian Ocean, and offshore Asia, often barely beyond the traditional three-mile limits demarcating national sovereignty from international waters. Though perfectly "legal," however, the willingness to use anchorages in near proximity to other nations' coastlines may to some extent depend upon the state of political relations – or also asymmetries in coercive power – given the still sensitive symbolic issues involved. These matters have recently been prominent with regard to Soviet naval activities just off the Egyptian coast. And seemingly impending routine global extensions of national control over greater distances from coastlines (most nations now assert 200-mile economic zones on top of 12-mile naval maritime limits) may in the future restrict the use of such anchorages, perhaps creating some serious points of friction.(25) Use of anchorages where port visits are not made available does, of course, carry the disadvantage of precluding shore leave for ship personnel, which may be important both for morale and effectiveness.

Some "traditional" naval and air facilities, or rather modes of access, may fall into a grey area between civilian and military use. The Soviets, for instance, have developed an extensive network of access for their very large fleets of fishing and oceanographic vessels, many of which may have less benign than advertised purposes – such as electronic warfare, military communications relays, shadowing of others' ships, antisubmarine detection, and disruption of and interference with communications cables and underwater sonar arrays.(26) Cuba has made similar use of its extensive fishing fleets. The Soviet merchant marine has also operated as a wing of the Soviet navy, involved in, among other things, the transport of arms and the smuggling of intelligence agents into friendly and neutral ports. Often, the USSR has attempted to use the acquisition of seemingly benign access for its fishing fleets as an opening wedge for broader access, as witness recent bargaining with the Maldives, Mauritius, Tonga, and others. The Soviet national airline, Aeroflot, has similarly been used to acquire "legitimate" grey area access, which has translated into staging points for the movement of troops, "advisors," and materiel in Africa and elsewhere.(27)

In the interwar period, private Western corporations owned or controlled numerous shipyards in less-developed countries – there were several Western shipyards in China – which often served as repair facilities for their own and sometimes other nations' warships.(28) Then too, commercial airlines and their facilities often had functions blurring into the military realm. Before World War II, U.S. intelligence services apparently used Pan-American Airways planes for photo reconnaissance in Latin America; after the war began, numerous Pan Am-owned airports in Latin America became readily available staging points for ferrying materiel to Africa. But American activities of this sort were then overshadowed by the very organized and coordinated use of "commercial" airlines and shipping companies by Germany and Italy, some of which dominated whole regions and transit routes in Latin

America, particularly where ethnic consanguinity was involved.(29) As with Soviet activities later, the formal separation of military and the civilian domains was an only weakly subtle fiction.

THE PROLIFERATION OF ESOTERIC TECHNICAL FACILITIES

Prior to World War II, the subject of overseas bases could nearly have been exhausted by description of traditional naval and air facilities and army troop garrisons. The then underdeveloped state of long-range communications and detection systems and of underseas monitoring technology absented from consideration a large part of what now is discussed within the boundaries of functions requiring overseas access points and networks. Some exceptions, to be discussed in the next chapter, were radio relay stations, terminals for transatlantic communications cables, meteorological stations, and – just prior to World War II – the early forerunners of modern radar.(30)

Nowadays, any discussion of the gamut of functions served by overseas bases must strongly take into account the very important roles of a vast variety of esoteric new military technologies gradually developed since 1945. Little discussed in the press and often shrouded in secrecy, these facilities constitute an important segment of modern basing diplomacy.

The currently important technical facilities can for the most part be broken down into functions relating to intelligence, surveillance, communications, and electronic warfare, and often span or overlap the traditional dividing lines between armies, navies, and air forces; indeed, they are often organizationally located within more comprehensive intelligence services (such as the U.S. National Security Agency under Defense Department control) or within "civilian" organizations such as NASA. Among the numerous activities included here (utilizing current terminology specific to the United States, but duplicated elsewhere) are communications (COMINT), photographic (PHOTINT), and electronic (ELINT) intelligence; naval and presidential or executive communications networks; radar; LORAN and Omega navigational aid systems; high frequency direction finders for aircraft; tracking networks and ground data links for satellites; deep space surveillance; oceanographic surveys; nuclear test detection (seismographic and air sample collections); terminals for underwater hydrophonic submarine detection; and a variety of facilities involved in monitoring both strategic and tactical missile tests.

In similarity to many air staging bases, the functioning and importance of some of these facilities can often only be gauged in terms of global or regional networks, involving matters of complementarity and redundancy again usually beyond the view of casual scholarly observers.(31) The problem of redundancy is also involved in trade-offs across systems and technologies, where more than one alternative technology may be available to serve a given purpose. Hence, newer satellites have begun to supersede the functions earlier served by ground stations for various communications, intelligence, and navigational/positioning purposes, though still other facilities may be required to process and relay data acquired by those satellites.(32) When U.S. ground-based intelligence facilities in Iran were lost for SALT verification of Soviet missile tests, alternatives were sought in satellites and in ground-based U-2 aircraft flights. Underseas areas subject to monitoring by land-anchored hydrophone arrays may also be covered by sonabuoys sowed from aircraft utilizing foreign bases. Surveillance of radars and communications from around the Sino-Soviet periphery may be conducted variously by ground stations, intelligence ships, and aircraft, as well as by satellite. In the absence of land-based facilities, naval vessels (also fishing trawlers and merchant ships) may be used to relay communications, to track satellites, or to monitor missile tests; but for full on-station efficiencies, these vessels may also require port facilities for repairs, replenishment, and crew rotation. Detection of nuclear explosions and analysis of their types and by-products may require a combination of seismological sensing facilities and both ground- and air-based collection of downwind air samples. In short, a full analysis of these functional networks – and of the importance and/or irreplaceability of any one facility – is a very difficult task indeed. A few illustrations may serve to illustrate the point, spanning the key domains of intelligence, communications, satellites, and antisubmarine warfare.

The various American intelligence agencies and armed services (and their Soviet counterparts) operate a large number of systems, utilizing aircraft, ships, satellites, and ground-based equipment, to electronically and visually surveille the world. These activities are primarily directed against the rival superpower, but also against numerous other nations, both foes and friends.   Infrared cameras and televisions onboard satellites or on U-2 or SR-71 "spy planes" monitor Soviet conventional and strategic weapons deployments, watch for missile launches, and observe and detect a variety of other things ranging across industrial plants, wheat crops, and so forth. Radars based on air, sea, and land platforms monitor Soviet ships, planes, and missiles, while SIGINT apparatus, also on various platforms, tunes in on radio transmissions, both encoded and not. ELINT equipment detects and pinpoints Soviet radar emissions, searching for gaps or blind spots as well as what they react to.(33) All of these activities are obviously reliant upon foreign basing access, in networks forming a vast arc around the Eurasian rim of the USSR.

Regarding satellite intelligence, numerous ground facilities are apparently used to query the satellites for information, and to process the information received from TV transmissions, radar reports, ELINT, and SIGINT for nearly real-time transmission to the United States.(34) Detection and early warning of missile launches via observance of missile plumes is also here involved, a crucial aspect of strategic deterrence and, if necessary, nuclear war fighting.   So is ocean surveillance, of surface ships and perhaps also of underseas submarines, if not only of missile firings from under the ocean's surface.

According to one public report, the United States is developing or may already have developed, satellites capable of directly transmitting raw intelligence data to the United States without intermediary overseas data links.(35) But that is apparently not nearly an accomplished fact in all respects and categories, and may be subject to concerns about technical malfunctions and upper atmospheric interference, hence requiring backup and redundant routes of transmissions.

The emergence of satellite technology has also been related to new requirements for overseas bases in connection with weather forecasting, satellite tracking, positional navigational aids for nuclear submarines, and geodetic surveying. The last named, involving the determination of exact positions of points and the figures and areas of large portions of the earth's surface, and variations in terrestrial gravity, apparently requires numerous points of access for measurements by triangulation techniques, and is apparently important for precise targeting of intercontinental missiles to reduce the "bias" factor caused by variations in the earth's shape, atmosphere, and magnetic fields.(36) Tracking of one's own and others' satellites requires near-global coverage from numerous points, and where gaps in coverage may pose disadvantages; that is, one's satellites could be destroyed without one knowing it immediately. As the installations involved are quite small and require global dispersion, access to numerous islands in the world's major oceans may here be important, along with access to countries far removed from cockpits of superpower rivalry, as witness recent location of U.S. satellite tracking facilities in Ascension, Madagascar, Bermuda, Guam, Kwajelein, Canton Island, Tahiti, and in Ecuador and Chile.(37) Shipboard tracking facilities could presumably serve as alternatives to such terrestrial stations; the Soviets may well resort to such expedients.

Global communications facilities constitute a crucial aspect of overseas basing access, and it is in this domain that the importance of technical facilities dates well back into the nineteenth century. What is presently involved stretches across the various service-oriented communications networks, those for diplomatic and intelligence services, and for the United States, a new integrated inter-service Defense Communications System. In this field, as in so many others, ground-, ship-, and aircraft-based facilities are now gradually giving way to satellite technologies, but with the necessity for retention of many terrestrial transmitters, receivers, and relays. Further, command, operational control, and administration of various military activities requires the use of a complex welter of communications modes, along a frequency spectrum running across high frequencies (HF), ultra-high frequencies (UHF), super-high frequencies (SHF), low frequencies (LF), very low frequencies (VLF), microwave, and others.(38) More broadly, one is here dealing with electronic communications, encompassing broadcast radio and TV, telephone, secure voice (electronically scrambled), and teletype and data transmission.

A variety of facilities and corresponding technologies thus comprise the modern global communications networks which require overseas access. A single overseas U.S. naval communications complex might nowadays house, among others, LF and HF radio transmitters and receivers, a microwave link terminal, a multivoice submarine cable terminal, a multichannel troposcatter radio system, an automated digital switch in the worldwide automated digital network (AUTODIN), an automatic voice switch in a worldwide automated voice network (AUTOVON), and still others.(39) Full description of the differing but often overlapping functions of all these systems would be beyond the scope of this work, but their importance and complexity in the context of basing diplomacy deserves highlighting.

Some analyses claim that in the future, satellites will render present terrestrial-based communications facilities essentially redundant, but that many will be retained as backups, or for certain situations where satellites will not be usable. One recent report detailed the impact, for instance, of the U.S. Navy's installation in hundreds of naval vessels and patrol aircraft of UHF transceivers as part of its Fleet Satellite Communications System (FLTSATCOM), which will utilize four geostationary (in sychronous orbit) satellites. Even with completion of this system, however, numerous overseas terminals apparently will be retained to interface with and supplement it. Similarly, the U.S. Navy is now planning to install its (Seafarer) extremely low frequency (ELF) system, with a single huge antenna grid based in the United States, which is designed to contribute to submarine survivability by making it very difficult for the Soviets to track them in a peacetime environment. Despite that, even if Seafarer is authorized, the Navy will apparently still continue to use other means for contacting its nuclear submarines: VLF stations abroad or the Tacamo system utilizing EC-130 "Hercules" aircraft which themselves presumably will continue to require overseas access.

Similar trends, obscure to the prying of academic researchers, presumably characterize Soviet overseas communication requirements, as well as those of the next tier of major powers. Here too, satellite technology is of increasing importance, and for the Soviets, here as in other technical areas, shipborne facilities are of heightened importance because of the dearth of ground facilities.(40) If the Soviet overseas facilities network should continue to expand, however, in consonance with the more wide-ranging movements of its naval and air forces, it too will need to move toward a more diverse and proliferated global communications network.

Recent years have seen some marked developments in antisubmarine warfare, as both the United States and USSR have expended large budgetary funds in trying to find new ways to locate, track, and destroy their rival's nuclear ballistic missile (SSBN) and attack (SSN) submarines. This matter too is deeply enmeshed in access diplomacy. The role of ASW aircraft based around the several oceans has been noted, with the United States now deploying, from foreign bases, numerous computerized S-3A and P-3C aircraft carrying passive and active sonobuoys, whose data acquisitions are processed by the planes to pinpoint submarines, along with Magnetic Anomaly Detectors

(MAD).(41) These aircraft are stationed in, among other places, Iceland, the Azores, Spain, Italy, Thailand, Oman's Masirah Island, Australia, and Kenya, to provide broad coverage of the ocean zones prowled by Soviet strategic missile and attack submarines.

More recently, the United States has moved ahead with passive listening and detection systems involving massive arrays of hydrophones set on the seabed and connected by cable to shore-based data processing systems. This is the basis for the Sound Surveillance System (SOSUS), now apparently being supplemented by the Moored Surveillance System (MSS) and also by the tactical towed sonar (TACTAS), dragged in quiet water well behind ships.(42) SOSUS has produced new needs for overseas access, and the United States apparently uses terminals for it in Iceland (along the route of Soviet submarine egress from the Kola Peninsula) and the Azores, among other places. Such access in some of the Indonesian Straits would appear highly desirable for the United States, along with some other passages en route from Soviet home bases to mid-ocean missile-firing stations, as well as potential combat zones in the Mediterranean and Persian Gulf where SSNs are likely to lurk. Meanwhile, although the United States is considered well ahead of the USSR in this as well as in most other ASW technology, recent reports about Soviet hydrophone arrays washed ashore in Iceland indicated that there is more than one player in this potentially crucial and even destabilizing game.(43) Again, overall, a description of the basing access needed to conduct global ASW – as with communications, satellite tracking, and electronic surveillance – requires delineation of a complex, overlapping system of air, sea, and land facilities adding to an integrated network, not easily discernible to observers not privy to classified information.

Those discussed above, albeit probably in the presently more crucial areas, are only some of the numerous networks of overseas technical facilities required by the competing superpowers. There are others. The U.S. Air Force, for instance, deploys numerous small navigational facilities throughout the world, such as Loran-A, Loran-C, Tacan, and HF/DF, which appear to overlap with some civilian functions. Most are overt and nonsensitive installations, though during the Vietnam war, some navigational aids were apparently planted in Laotian jungles to help guide U.S. aircraft based in Thailand to Vietnamese targets.

There is a global network of some eight VLF "Omega" stations to aid the navigation of, and communications to, ships and aircraft, and for the exact positioning of nuclear missile submarines (in turn aiding their precise targeting), which has rubbed some obvious political sensitivities in Norway and Australia (other Omega stations are in Trinidad, Japan, Liberia, and Reunion Island).(44) Then too, the Voice of America (VOA) deploys numerous broadcasting stations throughout the world as part of its global effort of the dissemination of news and/or propaganda. In all of these areas, the Soviets possess, or have been developing, competing technologies and, hence, have added requirements for overseas access, either on land or for ships performing surrogate functions at sea.

Even foreign embassies have come to house technical facilities which are part of the access game, whether overt or clandestine, and whether with the host's permission and knowledge or not. There have been numerous news reports about Soviet facilities in their Washington embassy which can intercept telephone communications in the United States, and it is presumed that such activities are conducted elsewhere as well. Then, "black boxes" in embassies can apparently be used for air sample collection related to the detection of suspicious upwind nuclear proliferation activities.(45) All of these matters have rendered the subject of basing access more and more complex, albeit not always visible, in recent times.

SUMMARY OF LONG-TERM TRENDS: THE PAST, PRESENT, AND FUTURE OF OVERSEAS BASE FUNCTIONS

Over a broad expanse of history stretching back toward World War I, a number of clearly recognizable trends are evident with respect to the numbers and functions of overseas bases, and the diplomacy of their acquisition and control. Those trends, not entirely linear, nor lacking for alternative explanations, nor, for that matter, necessarily subject to extrapolation to the future, are as follows:

- A decrease in the absolute numbers of air and naval bases required for sustaining a global presence and/or power-projection capability, based on the increased ranges of aircraft and ships, the much fewer numbers of both deployed by major powers, and new refueling techniques; for similar reasons, fewer staging points are required for transporting arms and other purposes. (Conversely, increasing difficulties for the big powers in maintaining access are pacing technological developments which supplant the need for facilities.)
- A vast proliferation of technical facilities' requirements in connection with communications, intelligence, electronic warfare, satellite tracking and data acquisition relay, ASW, navigation aids, geodetics, radar, and so forth.
- Profound alterations of basing requirements to deal with the vast new conflict dimensions of outer space and the underseas.(46)
- The advent of arms control as an institutionalized element of national security strategy, particularly in the United States, and its attendant requirements for new types of foreign facilities concerning missile test verification and nuclear test detections.
- A telescoping of military operational time requirements, requiring bases for real-time intelligence and communication and for quick response to preemptive military contingencies.
- A wholesale alteration of the basis for access from that based on colonial domination to that based on an interrelated mix of ideologically determined alliances, arms supplies, military and economic aid, and other forms of bargained transactions.

As previously noted, the vast proliferation of technical basing requirements has provided a strong lingering – maybe growing – rationale for the maintenance of overseas facilities at a time when some "traditional" combat functions (long-range strategic bombardment, and air staging) are more easily conducted from home bases, at least for the superpowers. But as also noted, this otherwise strong trend has been modified by the continuing need for overseas facilities to serve command, control, and surveillance functions (many related to the underseas and overhead air dimensions), themselves inextricably connected to the conduct of warfare as well as to interventions and coercive diplomacy vis-a-vis both superpower rivals and smaller states.

Many of these new facilities are smaller and less visible than combat support bases or garrisons; indeed, they may be located in remote areas away from the political spotlight of urban centers. As such, they are less blatantly violative of nationalist sensitivities, particularly as they require only small numbers of personnel and perform functions almost obscure to the uninitiated.(47) Many can be located in host countries having only moderately close security relations to major powers, where a major naval or air base might be ruled out by political sensitivities to compromised sovereignty.

Generally, as the instruments of war have become more complex, and as modern war scenarios often envisage hair-trigger time dimensions for long-range preemptive capabilities, the demands for real-time information gathering and processing have increased apace. Overseas installations are therefore essential to a great power to provide a worldwide communications-sensing-navigation complex, to respond instantly, for instance, to ominous large missile launchings, antisatellite activities, or mobilization indicators. The U.S. development in the early 1960s of a global defense communications system under a separate agency, the Defense Communications Agency, was a response to the need for interservice coordination in this environment. The kind of time and space cushion provided in 1941 obviously no longer exists in conditions of modern intercontinental warfare possibilities.

As also noted, the supersession of many ground and sea-based intelligence and communications facilities by satellites has reduced but by no means eliminated requirements for the former. For instance, the continuing use by the United States and USSR of intelligence surveillance aircraft such as the U-2, SR-71, and MIG-25 (the former two U.S. aircraft are usually based abroad) bespeaks a continuing requirement for close-in, quick response, flexible surveillance capability to supplement what can be gleaned by satellites. Similar complex tradeoffs exist with respect to numerous other basing functions. Still, according to some writers, in the long run, as advances in technology overcome the obstacles imposed by geography and physics, these communications and intelligence facilities are likely to decline in importance.(48) To some extent, this has already happened, but not at the rate that was being predicted a few years ago.

Regarding both operational and staging facilities, the greatly increased ranges of aircraft and ships have certainly diminished – in absolute terms — the need for the kind of extensive, interconnected basing networks required only a generation ago merely for airlifting cargo across the North Atlantic from the United States to Britain or from Texas to the Panama Canal Zone. The functions now almost fully served for the United States by Lajes in the Azores, Ascension, Diego Garcia, Guam, and Clark Air Force Base once would have required numerous extra consecutive staging points to provide a viable global system. Hence, there has been a seeming reversal of trends set in motion during the nineteenth century, when the introduction of coal-fired ships created the need for numerous coaling stations; still earlier, the almost limitless ranges of sailing vessels (aside from their need for food and water replenishment) allowed lesser requirements for multiple basing points.(49)

One of the really major changes determining basing needs since World War II has resulted from the decolonization process and the enormous increase in the number of independent nations in the Third World. This in turn has produced, among other things, an enormous increase in the number of — and geographic dispersion of — sovereign arms recipients, and in turn, has enlarged the requirements for staging of war materiel, both during conflicts and in normal peacetime periods. One result has been the emergence of an almost totally new realm of diplomacy dealing with overflight rights, staging facilities, and such in areas once mostly under colonial control and removed from ideological conflicts, but now inordinately jealous of sovereignty and concerned about taking sides in small power conflicts. In this context, the perhaps growing "closure" of overhead air space is becoming a critical matter.

These problems have been well illustrated in recent conflicts involving one or the other of the superpowers as arms suppliers in the Middle East, Angola, Zaire, Vietnam, and the African Horn. Actually, there were few equivalents in the interwar period to the recent surrogate wars fought in outlying regions, and which required arms and spare parts resupply. That was, at any rate, almost entirely a domain of private arms suppliers in the 1920s and 1930s, for instance, in the Chaco War between Paraguay and Bolivia. The Spanish Civil War was perhaps the only really significant exception, a precursor of modern themes, but where arms supply lines were short and only insignificantly subject to basing and overflight restrictions. The then prevailing casual diplomatic practices of the interwar period, which involved normally relaxed constraints on overflights and port visits, effectively precluded equivalents to the diplomatic imbroglios which occurred during the recent Middle Eastern, Horn, and Angolan conflicts.

The enhanced importance of arms control as an aspect of modern diplomacy has also altered some requirements for overseas facilities in a longer-range perspective. As it is, despite the lengthy preparatory efforts for the Geneva Disarmament Conference between 1925 and 1932, there were few concrete, formal arms-control arrangements during the interwar period which might have required facilities for verifying their compliance. The Washington Naval Conference, which established capital ship ratios among the major naval powers and which also limited fortification of some Pacific area naval bases, was essentially the sole exception, and it did indeed produce some thorny verification problems concerning Japanese fortification of some of the League-mandated Pacific islands. The United States and United Kingdom then relied primarily upon human source intelligence (HUMINT) for verification in this case, though there is still the open question, related to the mysterious disappearance of Amelia Earhart's plane, of whether other verification efforts were attempted. In those times, as at present, of course, what had to be done to verify formal controls agreements would had to have been done anyway in the absence of arms control as part of a normal ongoing intelligence effort to monitor rivals' military capabilities.

Nowadays, the SALT and Limited Test Ban arrangements, and also the more globally dispersed requirements for monitoring the nuclear activities of a host of potential additions to the nuclear weapons club, have produced much greater needs for overseas facilities to monitor compliance and to watch for untoward clandestine activities. Indeed, such verification efforts are a key component of the diplomacy of arms control and, to the extent viable, a critical deterrent to violations. In that regard, there are basing requirements for telemetry monitoring of rivals' missile tests; for other related electronics and communications intelligence; for ocean surveillance; and for seismographic detection and measuring of underground nuclear explosions.

As noted, some analysts, in looking to the future, have claimed to perceive a long-range trend toward a lesser overall need for overseas facilities by all of the major powers. Still longer-range aircraft and ships (including nuclear ones) and expanded development of aerial refueling (involving tankers with larger capacities and ranges) are considered gradually to be reducing the number of required forward operational and staging bases. Likewise, the further development of satellite technology and of longer-range communications and navigational systems is thought to promise a diminution of the requirements for many overseas technical facilities. Whether these expectations will at least in part be reversed by new developments in military technology or new military requirements (to cope with resource-related crisis interventions, increased forward troop deployments, needs for land-based aircraft to provide air cover for ships) remains to be seen.

Some writers have speculated about the possibility for greatly increased use of artificial ocean-bases – curiously, there was an earlier flurry of expectation about that in the 1930s when the Germans were thought to be experimenting with artificial bases in the Atlantic corridor between Africa and South America.(50) Of course, the halting, gradual movement toward sea enclosure and internationalization might inhibit such developments. More permanent bases in space and under the seas might also be imagined. Such speculations merely underscore the indeterminacy of the future, where technological surprises and new developments in the international system may produce surprises in requirements for overseas facilities.

NOTES

(1) The obvious though obscure importance of access and logistics over the whole span of military history is stressed in Geoffrey Kemp and John Maurer, "The Logistics of Pax Britannica: Lessons for America" (paper presented at the Fletcher School's Ninth Annual Conference dealing with "Projection of Power: Perspectives, Perceptions and Logistics," April 23-25, 1980).

(2) For one among many examples of much earlier basing problems, see Thucydides, The Peloponnesian War, translated by Rex Warner (Baltimore: Penguin Books, 1954), which discusses the naval conflicts during the era of Demosthenes, around 413 B.C. Hence, on p. 447, in describing his expeditionary force to Sicily:

> They then took the Argive hoplites on board, and sailed to Laconia. First they laid waste part of Epidauras Limera, and then landed in Laconia opposite Cythera, where the temple of Apollo stands. They laid waste part of the country and fortified a sort of isthmus so that the Helots might have a place to which they could desert, and also so that raiding parties, as at Pylos, might have a base from which to operate. When he had helped Charicles to occupy this place, Demosthenes at once sailed on to Corcyra, in order to pick up allied forces from that area and then to cross over to Sicily as quickly as possible.

(3) For one attempt at rigor along these lines, see W. Harriett Critchley, "Defining Strategic Value: Problems of Conceptual Clarity and Valid Threat Assessments," in R. Harkavy and E. Kolodziej, eds., American Security Policy and Policy Making (Lexington, Mass.: D.C. Heath, 1980), pp. 45-65.

(4) These definitional distinctions are discussed in, inter alia, Richard Remnek, "The Politics of Soviet Access to Naval Support Facilities in the Mediterranean," Appendix D of B. Dismukes and J. McConnell, eds., Soviet Naval Diplomacy (New York: Pergamon, 1979); and Herbert Hagerty, "Forward Deployment in the 1970s and 1980s," National Security Affairs Monograph 77-2, National Defense University (Washington, D.C.: 1977). According to the latter (p. 32),

> several distinctions are possible between the words "base" and "facility". The one with which I am most comfortable relates to both size and tenancy; a base is normally a larger complex with both operating and support personnel assigned; a facility tends to be smaller, more limited in function, and with few if any operations personnel regularly resident . . . the word "installation" is generic, it can apply to both.

(5) Hans W. Weigert, "Strategic Bases," in H. Weigert, V. Stefansson, and R. Harrison, eds., New Compass of the World (New York: Macmillan, 1949), p. 222.

(6) Attempts at providing a basic breakdown of types of facilities can be found in Hagerty, "Forward Deployment," and also Richard B. Foster et al., "Implications of the Nixon Doctrine for the Defense Planning Process," Stanford Research Institute, Menlo Park, Calif., 1972, pp. 114-125.

(7) See Geoffrey Kemp and John Maurer, "The Logistics of Pax Britannica: Lessons for America" (paper presented at the Fletcher School's conference on "Projection of Power: Perspectives, Perceptions and Logistics," April 23-25, 1980). Regarding power projection in connection with basing assets, see W. Scott Thompson, Power Projection (New York: National Strategy Information Center, 1978), Agenda Paper no. 7. Among other works dealing with the logistics of the British navy at its peak, see Peter Padfield, The Battleship Era (New York: McKay, 1972); and Bernard Brodie, Sea Power in the Machine Age (Princeton: Princeton University Press, 1941). On earlier U.S. dependence upon the British network of coaling facilities, see John D. Alden, The American Steel Navy (Annapolis, Md.: U.S. Naval Institute, 1972), pp. 333-347; and W.R. Braisted, The United States Navy in the Pacific, 1909-1922 (Austin, Texas: University of Texas Press, 1971), esp. pp. 129-130.

(8) Hagerty, "Forward Deployment," p. 114.

(9) Weigert, "Strategic Bases," p. 223, has a typology of sorts to describe bases, viewed from an earlier perspective.

Our naval and air bases are usually classified in three groups: permanent operational bases which are to be fortified and garrisoned with sufficient strength to hold against a major attack until relieved from the continental United States; limited operational bases, which will be used chiefly for aerial reconnaissance; and emergency bases, which need not be garrisoned in normal times, but which we should be entitled to occupy should an emergency arise.

Note the prescient, contemporary ring of the latter category.

(10) A good picture of how the British utilized an interlocking system of bases for colonial control is in Gregory Blaxland, The Regiments Depart (London: William Kimber, 1971).

(11) Hence, Hagerty, "Forward Deployment," pp. 6-7, quotes Samuel Huntington as saying that "it was not the alliances which were the 'major innovation' in the evolution of U.S. policy; rather it was the

'indefinite' deployment of American forces in Europe, under an international command headed by an American general."

(12) The growing importance of Diego Garcia and Ascension in this sense is highlighted in P.M. Dadant, "Shrinking International Airspace as a Problem for Future Air Movements – A Briefing," Report R-2178-AF, Rand Corp., Santa Monica, Calif., 1978; and Richard G. Toye, "The Projection of U.S. Power by the Air Force in the Western Pacific and Indian Ocean" (paper delivered at the Fletcher School's conference on "Security and Development in the Indo-Pacific Arena," 1978).

(13) This is discussed in Barry M. Blechman and Robert G. Weinland, "Why Coaling Stations are Necessary in the Nuclear Age," International Security 2 (1977): 88-99.

(14) A glimpse at the range of possibilities even among the Western European countries is provided by United States Security Agreements and Commitments Abroad, Hearings before the Subcommittee on United States Security Agreements and Commitments Abroad, of the Committee on Foreign Relations, U.S. Senate, 91st Congress, vol. 2, p. 2378. Some have no special restrictions, whereas some require diplomatic clearance, others diplomatic clearance only for aircraft carrying arms or munitions.

(15) See Dadant, "Shrinking Airspace." Dadant considers not only an increasing trend toward restrictiveness for specific, ad hoc political reasons, but also the anticipated impact of trends toward closure embodied in 200-mile Exclusive Economic Zones (EEZs), and the dilemma of important straits overlapped by 12-nautical-mile territorial seas. See also John R. Pickett, "Airlift and Military Intervention," in Ellen P. Stern, ed., The Limits of Military Intervention (Beverly Hills, Calif.: Sage, 1979), pp. 137-150.

(16) See, for instance, Cmdr. P. Taylor Lonsdale, "ASW's Passive Trap," U.S. Naval Institute Proceedings, July 1979, pp. 35-40.

(17) See Blechman and Weinland, "Why Coaling Stations." The subsequent general discussion of the various functions of naval facilities draws heavily on this article.

(18) For one among many examples of this kind of problem, see "Freeing of Sailor Angers Kenyans," New York Times, October 14, 1980, p. A4., which discusses the turmoil in Kenya over a judge's decision to free a U.S. sailor who admitted killing a Nairobi prostitute in a drunken brawl. Of course, more recently, attention has been directed in reverse to the vulnerability of U.S. military personnel overseas to terrorist actions. See, for instance, "U.S. Revises Rule on Uniforms for Personnel in Turkey," New York Times, December 9, 1980, p. A15.

(19) Further, on the multipurpose Soviet pre-positioning strategy, see W. Scott Thompson, "The Projection of Soviet Power," Rand Corp. report, P-5988 Santa Monica, Calif., August 1977.

(20) For a cataloguing of ship repair facilities' capabilities in the Indian Ocean-Pacific area, see Geoffrey Kemp et al., "Geo-Logistic Constraints on U.S. Mobility in the Indo-Western Pacific Theater" (paper prepared for the conference on U.S. Naval Strategy in the Pacific-Indian Ocean Area 1985-1995, Naval War College, March 24-26, 1977).

(21) See Alvin J. Cottrell and Thomas H. Moorer, "U.S. Overseas Bases: Problems of Projecting American Military Power Abroad," Washington Paper no. 47, Georgetown Center for Strategic and International Studies, Washington, D.C., 1977, pp. 45-54; and "United States Foreign Policy Objectives and Overseas Military Installations," prepared for the Committee on Foreign Relations, U.S. Senate, by the Congressional Research Service, Library of Congress (Washington, D.C., 1979), pp. 134-194. (Hereinafter referred to as The SFR Report.)

(22) For a general but detailed analysis, see Charles C. Petersen, "Trends in Soviet Naval Operations," in Dismukes and McConnell, Soviet Naval Diplomacy, pp. 37-87.

(23) See Charles C. Petersen, "Showing the Flag" (pp. 88-114) and Abram Shulsky, "Coercive Diplomacy (pp. 115-157) in Dismukes and McConnell, Soviet Naval Diplomacy. For a voluminous analysis of the postwar U.S. experience with coercive diplomacy – a mix of events, data analysis, and some case studies – see Barry Blechman and Stephen Kaplan, Force Without War (Washington, D.C.: Brookings Institution, 1978).

(24) See Petersen, "Showing the Flag"; and also Heidi S. Philips, "Host Press Coverage of Soviet Naval Visits to Islamic Countries, 1968-73," Center for Naval Analyses, Arlington, Va., June 1976.

(25) See Dadant, "Shrinking Airspace"; and for more comprehensive analyses, Mark W. Janis, Sea Power and the Law of the Sea (Lexington, Mass.: D.C. Heath, 1976); and Ann L. Hollick and Robert E. Osgood, New Era of Ocean Politics (Baltimore: Johns Hopkins University Press, 1974).

(26) See Michael D. Davidchik and Robert B. Mahoney, "Soviet Civil Fleets and the Third World," in Dismukes and McConnell, Soviet Naval Diplomacy, appendix; and "Soviet Sea Power: The Covert Support Fleet," Conflict Studies, no. 84 (June 1977).

(27) See Davidchik and Mahoney, "Soviet Civil Fleets," pp. 330-355; and Betsy Gidwitz, "Aspects of Soviet International Civil Aviation Policy," Survey, no. 2, 107 (Spring 1979). The latter discusses the Soviet use of

Aeroflot for transport of arms and weapons, for "black box" sur- veillance activities, for special military operations, and for "showing the flag."

(28) See Navy and Old Army Branch, National Archives, Record Group 165 (Records of the War Department, General and Special Staffs), Military Intelligence Division (MID), File No. 2667-D-1061, which discusses the repair of Soviet warships in British-owned Shanghai dockyards. (Hereinafter, citations will be by MID file number only.)

(29) See MID nos. 2670-29, 2657-241, 2657-K-93, 2052-121, which, among other things, detail the control of interior Brazilian air routes by Germany's Condor airline, and Italian dominance of air routes in South America's southern cone.

(30) The major exceptions, involving underseas communications cables networks, is discussed in P.M. Kennedy, "Imperial Cable Communica- tions and Strategy, 1870-1914," The English Historical Review 86, 141 (1971): 728-752. For discussion of some earlier manifestations of electronic warfare during World War I, see John M. Carroll, Secrets of Electronic Espionage (New York: Dutton, 1966).

(31) This point strongly emerges, for instance, from a perusal of the material on various satellite programs (reconnaissance, communica- tions, etc.) in Stockholm International Peace Research Institute (SIPRI), Outer Space - Battlefield of the Future? (New York: Crane, Russak, 1978). For a good analysis regarding communications, ASW, and other technical functions, see Lenny Siegel, "Diego Garcia," Pacific Research 8, 3 (March-April 1977).

(32) See Philip Klass, Secret Sentries in Space (New York: Random House, 1971) for the gradual evolvement of this trend in the 1960s. According to Klass, p. 136,

> the USAF's network of ground stations for receiving satellite pictures and transmitting commands to the spacecraft, originally located along the West Coast of the U.S., has been expanded around the globe and now totals seven stations. These are located in New Boston (near Manchester), N.H., at Vandenberg AFB, Calif., on the Hawaiian island of Oahu, on Kodiak Island in Alaska, on Guam and on the British Seychelles Islands in the Indian Ocean. . . . The seventh station is in an east African country which will not be identified to avoid possible embarrass- ment. Each station has at least one giant 60-foot-diameter antenna to receive picture signals.

(33) See ibid., pp. 185-195. For some interesting material on earlier U.S. ELINT operations, see Patrick McGarvey, CIA: The Myth and the Madness (New York: Penguin, 1972), esp. pp. 49-51.

(34) See Klass, Secret Sentries, chaps. 14, 19; and SIPRI, Outer Space, pp. 147, 158, 178-179. According to Klass, p. 136.

Additionally, there are six shipboard stations, each outfitted with a 30-foot antenna which can be deployed around the globe as needed. Some of them are also used during missile tests to track the weapon. The first of these shipboard stations, the General H.H. Arnold, became fully operational in the fall of 1964. . . . For shipboard stations, the tape-recorded photos can be transferred to a specially outfitted aircraft by playing back and transmitting the signals to the airplane as it circles the ship.

(35) See "U.S. Increases Reliance on Intelligence Satellites," New York Times, December 18, 1979, p. C1, and "Technology is the Key to Arms Verification," New York Times, August 14, 1979, p. C2, for general analyses of satellite capabilities. Siegel, op. cit., claims that "the Pentagon is developing (or has developed) satellites capable of directly transmitting raw surveillance data back to the U.S. for processing."

(36) See SIPRI, op. cit., 158-159, for a brief summary discussion of the military implications of the science of geodesy, defined as "the branch of applied mathematics that deals with the shape of the Earth, its gravitational field, and the exact positions of various points on the Earth's surface." It is further stated that "the Earth's gravitational field is far from uniform since large sections of the Earth's crust have different densities. If the effects of the Earth's shape and its non-uniform gravitational field are neglected, then considerable errors may be introduced in the computations of trajectories and in the inertial guidance systems of missiles and aircraft."

(37) See Erwin J. Bulban, "ASTP Prelude to Space Shuttle Era," Aviation News and Space Weekly, May 5, 1975, pp. 36-43.

(38) See Siegel, "Diego Garcia," p. 6.

(39) Ibid., pp. 6-7. See also the listings of communications installations in the country-by-country analysis in "United States Security Agreements and Commitments Abroad," Hearings Before the Subcommittee on United States Security Agreements and Commitments Abroad, U.S. Senate, Committee on Foreign Relations, 91st Congress, 2nd Session, vols. 1 and 2 (Washington, D.C.: GPO).

(40) Although little is available in the open literature regarding Soviet overseas technical facilities, it is here presumed that such installations are normally – and extensively – colocated with other major Soviet facilities in key client states. Soviet communications facilities in Cuba – along with intercept facilities directed against U.S. communications – have received some press reportage. See, for instance, "Senate Panel Calls a Hearing on Intelligence on Cuba," New York Times, September

7, 1979, p. A6, wherein is referred to "high speed microwave relay systems," and facilities which could "pick up microwave signals from Soviet diplomatic missions." Petersen, "Showing the Flag," p. 71, also notes a formerly important Soviet communications station at Berbera in Somalia. SIPRI, Outer Space, p. 179, reports Soviet satellite tracking facilities are (or have been) located in Egypt, Mali, Guinea, Cuba, and Chad.

(41) See Siegel, "Diego Garcia"; and Lt. David Templeton Easter, "ASW Strategy: Issues for the 1980's," U.S. Naval Institute Proceedings, March 1980, pp. 35-41 for an overview of current ASW technology and tactics. See also R. Garwin, "Anti-Submarine Warfare and National Security," in Arms Control: Readings From Scientific American (San Francisco: W.H. Freeman, 1973).

(42) See Norman Friedman, "SOSUS and U.S. ASW Tactics," U.S. Naval Institute Proceedings, March 1980, pp. 120-122; Norman Palmer, "SURTASS and T-AGOS," U.S. Naval Institute Proceedings, March 1980, pp. 122-123; Capt. Andrew C.A. Jampoler, "ASW for the 1980s," U.S. Naval Institute Proceedings, March 1980, pp. 118-119; and particularly, Thomas S. Burns, The Secret War for the Ocean Depths (New York: Rawson, 1978), pp. 91-94, 154, 158.

(43) Burns, The Secret War, p. 311, refers to Soviet sonar detection devices found on the beaches of Iceland, consisting of a string of 32 hydrophones, 11 feet long, weighing more than a ton. On p. 156, he briefly discusses the prospects for Soviet SOSUS developments. In "A Soviet Sub-Detection System?" Newsweek, September 8, 1980, p. 15, U.S. officials are said to be thinking "the Soviets still lack the land-based technology necessary to make a detection system work properly."

(44) See Frank Barnaby, "On Target with an Omega Station?" New Scientist 109, 993 (March 25, 1976): 671-2; and Albert Langer, Owen Wilkes, and N.P. Gleditsch, The Military Functions of Omega and Loran-C (Oslo: Peace Research Institute, 1976).

(45) Additionally, the United States used its Vela satellites to police nuclear explosions in the atmosphere and in outer space, as discussed in Klass, Secret Sentries, pp. 185-187. After 1970, Vela's mission was taken over by other early warning satellites.

(46) See Geoffrey T.H. Kemp, "Defense Innovation and Geopolitics: From the Persian Gulf to Outer Space," in W. Scott Thompson, ed., National Security in the 1980s: From Weakness to Strength (San Francisco: Institute for Contemporary Studies, 1980), which bruits the advent of a "geopolitics of outer space."

(47) For an analysis of recent trends regarding the impact of facilities on sovereignty, see Richard Remnek, "Is Foreign Military Access

Compatible with Host National Sovereignty?" (paper delivered at the annual meeting of the International Studies Association, Philadelphia, March 19-22, 1980).

(48) This is predicted by Hagerty, "Forward Deployment," p. 26: "We have, of course, been reducing our dependence on overseas basing for more than a decade, principally through the application of new technologies."

(49) This point is developed in Bernard Brodie, Sea Power in the Machine Age (Princeton: Princeton University Press, 1941), in chapter 7, under the heading of "War at Sea under Steam: Strategic Geography and the Fuel Problem." He notes the advent of coal-fired ships also eliminated the earlier important connection between prevailing wind patterns and base locations. Thus (p. 109) "in the Indian Ocean the whole pattern of naval strategy was perforce subservient to the dictates of the monsoons and the anti-monsoons. Bases were chosen and fought for, campaigns were planned and executed, in accordance with the exactions of these peculiar winds."

(50) See James H. Hayes, "Alternative to Overseas Bases" (Santa Monica, Calif.: Rand Corp., August 1975), pp. 3-4; and Hagerty, "Forward Deployment," pp. 26-31. Concerning interwar German activity regarding artificial bases in the South Atlantic, en route from Spain to Brazil, see MID nos. 2082-644 and 2082-825.

3 Bases in the Interwar Period: The Heyday of Colonial Control

BASES AND HISTORY: A LONG-TERM VIEW FROM
THE TIME OF THE SPANISH ARMADA

Broadly speaking, bases and related forms of strategic access may be presumed to have been an element of diplomacy and military strategy stretching well back into the mists of antiquity. However, whereas standard military histories divulge considerable materials on battles, tactics, strategies, and the endless ebbs and flows of offensive and defensive weapons developments, it is rather difficult to obtain a coherent picture of earlier basing networks. Data exist in bits and pieces, but nowhere is there a comprehensive analysis for any given period. Of course, despite the far-flung military adventures of some earlier civilizations – the Phoenicians, Chinese, and Vikings, for example – there were still always serious technological constraints on their projecting of overseas power. Their nature and relationship to acquisition of access from others remains, however, relatively obscure.

However, some works on the origins of European overseas expansion, beginning with those of Spain, Portugal, and Britain at the dawn of the "Columbian Age," do divulge some material on the earlier functions of basing access. It was at this point that the long-range exploratory voyages – first by the Portuguese around the Cape into the Indian Ocean, later by the Spaniards to the Caribbean and South America, and then by the British and French in the Atlantic and Indian Oceans – gave rise to needs for overseas facilities, though similar requirements must have existed, for example, for earlier Arab and Chinese long-range naval ventures in and around the Indian Ocean.

Portugal, in the wake of DeGama's famous voyages in the 1490s, erected what was probably the first really major extraregional, far-flung basing system of the modern era, a precursor to those of the later Dutch and British empires. It was, as Boxer has noted, the first of the empires on which the sun never set.(1) As noted by Wallerstein and others, the Portuguese, taking advantage of then growing naval technological superiority, moved into a virtual political vacuum, taking over a preexisting trade network previously in the hands of Moslem merchants in the Indian Ocean and the Japanese Wako pirates in the China Sea, and following a period of Indian Ocean naval activity by Chinese eunuch admirals who roamed as far as East Africa from 1405 to 1434.(2) Although in a few areas the Portuguese exercised direct sovereignty, their naval dominance was based, per Modelski's model of an "oceanic empire," on a widespread network of points d'appui, where small flotillas were based.(3)

In outflanking the long-held strategic positions of the Ottoman Empire, Venice, and Egypt (the latter along with Russia then had virtually no navy), Portugal set up key bases (for provisioning, refitting, crew rest, and such) at Aden, Hormuz, Goa, Diu, Malacca, and in Mozambique; a fleet was based in Goa which, among other things, was used to cruise the Persian Gulf.(4) The Portuguese eschewed a base at the South African Cape. (Later, the Dutch were to establish one there as a refreshment base for fever-ridden and ill-conditioned vessels which are said to have needed provisions after a month or so, and which could not easily withstand a nonstop voyage of five or six months; also because they failed to capture the Portuguese base at Mozambique.(5)) As an interesting illustration of an earlier example of the changing requirements for bases in response to technological change, it is said that the British later bartered the Cape base after 1795 for Ceylon, because the introduction of coppered bottoms, "Indiamen" and other new warships had resulted in there being less of a need for refit on the voyage to India.(6)

If anything, the Dutch naval basing system associated with its far-flung empire was even more elaborate than that possessed earlier by Portugal.(71) In part, it involved replacing the latter in numerous locales: in India, the Malaccas, Guinea, various Indian Ocean Islands, as well as on the Brazilian coastal promontory at Recife and San Luis do Maranhao. Additionally, the Dutch established new strong points: on Formosa, the South African Cape, and in the West Indies. Portuguese imperial possessions proved easier to overwhelm than those of Spain.(8)

In the early seventeenth century, the Dutch navy fielded some 2,000 warships, of which 40 were deployed in Asia, 20 off the coast of Guinea, and some 100 in the West Indies.(9) These were sizeable overseas fleets, facilities for which enabled rapid deployment to trouble spots or high seas encounters with rival navies.

Outside Europe, Dutch naval basing points were afforded by outright, unchallenged territorial control, in dispersed, key points such as Batavia (Java), Malacca (Malaya), Pulicat (India), and Zeelandia (Formosa).(10) In Europe, more modern basing diplomacy was anticipated by, for instance, a British-Dutch-Portuguese alliance in the war against France (1702-1713) in which Portugal was persuaded to join the Grand Alliance in order that its allies could use Lisbon as a naval base.

Over a period of several centuries, beginning in the late fifteenth century, basing diplomacy was fully enmeshed in the consecutive struggles for naval and colonial supremacy between England and its successive major rivals in Spain, Holland, and France. During Britain's struggle with Spain, there was a political argument within England over Hawkins's strategy for cutting the Spanish treasure route from Latin America, during which Hawkins criticized the monarch for not seizing bases abroad, especially in the Azores, as a step toward complete control of the seas.(11) Later, the Stuart monarchy's naval policy dictated not giving up the Cromwellian conquests of Jamaica and Nova Scotia; both had come to be thought of as important bases. The nature of basing diplomacy then was also illustrated by the marriage of a British king to a Portuguese noblewoman, which was useful for protecting British trade in the Mediterranean by acquiring bases in Portugal, Bombay, and Tangiers. Though some facilities may have been acquired through dynastic marriages, others, anticipating the future, were acquired by formal treaty, for example, the British acquisitions of facilities during the Anglo-Spanish War of 1655-60 in Tetuan and Tangier astride the Gibraltar Straits. Jamaica was a particularly important early British naval base, providing control over trade in the West Indies during the period of intense rivalry with Spain in the Caribbean.

Over a period of several centuries, Britain established dominance of overseas basing points relative to its successive European rivals, and in line with Mahan's classical theory of naval warfare, this became vital to near-global, exclusive sea control, which he and others since have perceived virtually as an all-or-nothing proposition.(12) The expansion extended to all points of the globe, achieved mostly by successful wars, at the conclusions of which some colonies or points of access were often given back to forestall permanent enmities and the development of feared continental coalitions, but while others were retained.

The Peace of Utrecht in 1713 gained Britain Gibraltar, Minorca (long after a key British Mediterranean naval base), Hudson's Bay, Newfoundland, and Nova Scotia.(13) That of Aix-La-Chapelle (1748) brought much of Canada, Cape Breton Island, Florida, St. Vincent, Tobago, Dominica, Grenada, and effective control over all of India.

The Napoleonic Wars saw an epic, though eventually one-sided, duel between France and Britain for overseas bases, colonies, and command of the sea, culminating a century-long race, at the end of which Britain emerged supreme after withstanding the strong pressures of Napoleon's "Continental System." In deciding, as it would in later conflicts, to emphasize sea over land warfare, Britain concentrated on picking off new naval harbors across the globe to gain advantageous positions astride major trade routes.

From 1793 to 1801 Britain took over San Domingo, Pondichery, St. Pierre and Miquelon, Martinique, Guadeloupe, St. Lucia, Ceylon, Malacca, the Cape of Good Hope, Dutch possessions in the East and West Indies, Trinidad, Minorca (Spain), Surinam, Curacao, Malta, and Danish and Swedish islands in the West Indies, while the French colony at Madagascar was destroyed. After, all of these except Ceylon, Trinidad, and parts of India (kept as possessions) were subsequently handed back and Malta "neutralized"; most and still others (Bengal,

Mauritius) were retaken in later phases of the war (some, but not all, again to be disgorged after Waterloo).(14)

The minutiae of the gradual British accretion of overseas bases over several centuries might almost obscure a determined underlying geopolitical strategy which took into account the requirement for judiciously spaced points of access alongside major trading routes (particularly that to India and on to China), and which involved the permanent deployment of naval squadrons in various key areas. Along the 4,600 mile route between the Cape and Bombay, close attention was paid to the key chain of posts running from Madagascar to Mauritius, to the Comoro and Amirante Islands and through the Chagos, Seychelles, and Maldive island archipelagoes. Along the key 1,500-mile route from Colombo to Penang, interest was centered on the Andamans, while further along the 1,500 mile route to Canton, the continuous depredations of Chinese and Malay pirates dictated positions at Singapore and at Labuan in North Borneo. India was, of course, the strategic center of it all, and Ceylon (with its long-held British base at Trincomalee) its spearhead in relation to the great commercial network spanning the Indonesian Straits, China, Australia, Persia, Arabia, Egypt, and East Africa. During the nineteenth century, protective naval squadrons were placed at Bombay, Trincomalee, Singapore, Hong Kong, and elsewhere to protect other trade routes from Bermuda, Jamaica, and the Falkland Islands.(15)

The other major powers, while normally bowing to near comprehensive British sea mastery, were not absent from the game of overseas base acquisition. France, making a comeback from its catastrophic defeat in 1815, slowly reestablished positions in North Africa, along the West African coast, in Reunion, Martinique, and Indo-China, while the Dutch regained their East Indies possessions after their own setbacks in 1815. Spain and Portugal (and also Belgium), while bereft of naval power during the nineteenth century, nevertheless retained key strategic positions, though they were almost completely vulnerable in case of conflict. Germany's efforts at building naval power in the late nineteenth century were paced by acquisition of some bases in Africa and in the Pacific,(16) while before World War I, the United States and Japan vied for some positions in the central and western Pacific, anticipating the later very serious naval rivalry in the partial vacuum created by British weakness in that area after 1918.

In terms of overall geopolitical strategy, the long rivalry over the flanks of the British communications route to India before World War I is of paramount interest, constituting a precursor of the present American concern over lifelines to the Persian Gulf. British fears of French intentions in North Africa, Egypt, and the Levant were later replaced by anxieties over German designs on an overland route to Basra through Turkey, with an eye also kept on Russian strivings for access in Iran, Afghanistan, and the gateways to India.

During the nineteenth century, Pax Britannica depended not only on the British navy itself, but also on Britain's domination over the world's coal trade and its extensive network of overseas coaling stations, unrivaled by any other European power. As Kemp and Maurer have emphasized, this not only enabled rapid and far-reaching British naval movements, but also gave Britain considerable control over the movements of other navies.(17) Dewey's victory over Spain at Manila Bay in 1898 apparently was made possible only through his use of British coaling facilities at Hong Kong. But British (and also German) refusal of similar assistance to Russia apparently delayed the latter's Baltic Fleet en route to the Far East in 1905, contributing mightily to its naval defeat by Japan when it was unable to concentrate its fleets at Port Arthur and Tsushima. This did not go unnoticed later in the writings of Admiral Gorshkov, who in his Sea Power of the State took the Tsarist government to task for not sufficiently understanding the geopolitical basis of seapower:

> The most important of these was the potential need for inter-theatre maneuver by the forces because of the separation of the sea theatres. It was necessary to take into account the absence of possessions and sea routes between the separate theatres equipped with base sites, which was largely the result of the neglect by Czarism of securing for Russia a whole number of islands and overseas territories discovered by Russian seafarers. We should recall, in passing, that the main cause of the loss of these territories was the ingrained misunderstanding of the importance for Russia of sea power.(18)

By contrast, Britain's far-flung basing network enabled it in 1914, as earlier at the outset of the Napoleonic Wars, to quickly clear the oceans outside Europe of German surface vessels, among other things, reinforcing Mahan's thesis about the indivisibility of high seas' control.(19)

Britain had one other major advantage over its rivals in the decades preceding World War I, and that resulted from its vast and unrivaled network of underseas telegraph cables. During this period, all of the key bastions of the British imperial basing system were linked together (and to London) by this network, resulting not only in advantages in early warning and command and control of naval forces, but also in British ability to control the news and hence enhance their influence all over the globe.(20) The submarine cable stations developed at this time were perhaps the first modern examples of what we now call "technical facilities," anticipating the far more varied and complex modern requirements for such access.

British strategists worried endlessly before 1914 about the possible wartime vulnerability of their cable communications system, and also planned the preemptive destruction of potential enemies' less elaborate networks if war should break out. Earlier reliant on cable relay stations in, among other places, Portugal, Spain, Turkey, Iran, Cuba, and the United States, the British strove mightily to develop an "all red" line system which would not rely on basing points in foreign territories, not even in traditionally allied Portugal, nor in the United States.(21) Aside from the fact that Britain deployed far more cable ships than any other power (twenty-eight to second-place France's five) and owned over 60 percent of the world's cables around 1900, she was able to take great advantage of her global island possessions – Mauritius, Seychelles, Maldives, Cocos, Ascension, Malta, Turks, Caicos, and others – which were, of course, so useful as well for well-spaced coaling operations.(22) The British cable line running from Land's End toward the Far East, for instance, was anchored at Gambia, Sierra Leone, Gold Coast, Nigeria, South Africa, Mauritius, Seychelles, and Ceylon; that from Vancouver to Australia across the Pacific ran through Fanning, Fiji, and Norfolk Islands.

Britain was not, of course, alone in constructing an elaborate overseas cable network, nor in its efforts at securing the required access points. According to one source, the United States, in 1898, annexed Guam and Midway for the specific purpose of providing cable stations en route to the Philippines, decades before those islands would become important U.S. air bases.(23) France and Germany also made efforts toward building global systems, but the latter came to rely, before World War I, more on wireless systems, despite the vulnerability of their communications to interception if decoded. By 1914 the Germans had wireless stations in Togoland, Southwest Africa, Tanganyika, Kiung-chow, Yap, Rabaul, Nauru, and Samoa, to abet what they knew would be a very vulnerable cable network if war should break out.(24)

Several points stand out here in providing some historical perspective regarding the diplomacy of access for technical facilities. First, in consonance with the laissez-faire nature of nineteenth-century international economics and the less comprehensive governmental involvement in all areas of national security (note the arms trade was then essentially private-directed), many of the cable networks were privately owned, requiring governments to exert a form of indirect control which could be strengthened in the event of war. Then, in this technical domain, there was a complex diplomacy of inter-nation granting of access, as great powers other than Britain virtually required reliance on basing points in others' territories. The Germans negotiated with the Dutch for access in Sumatra, and the British too, before achieving an "all red" system, utlized terminals in Portuguese-controlled Madeira and Cape Verde Islands and in Cuba en route to Jamaica, where the British Caribbean flotilla was home-ported.(25) France was heavily dependent on British possessions for its cable lines to Vietnam and Madagascar, among other places. All in all, the access diplomacy regarding submarine cables prior to 1914 resembles closely that pertaining currently to the big powers' networks of communications, navigation, and satellite-tracking stations.

At the outset of World War I, Britain was able rapidly to sever all of the German overseas cables, while losing only a couple of its own cable stations temporarily, at Cocos and Fanning islands.(26) The redundancy built into Britain's global system, abetted in 1914 by France's, provided a strong strategic advantage throughout World War I, still one more result of "indivisible" global naval superiority. Later, in 1919, the German cables were divided as war spoils among the allies as part of the Versailles settlement.

In a broadly "functional," comparative sense, one might consider the British concern over the cable communications system prior to World War I as analogous to present U.S. concerns over "early warning." At war's outset, rapid communications could prevent preemptive surprise attacks on naval installations around the globe, just as now satellite relay stations are critical for early warning of missile launches.(27) The time requirements have, of course, narrowed to hair-trigger dimensions.

Clearly, then, the staples of modern basing diplomacy have their roots centuries back. The most profound change has seen the shift from physical, colonial control (either of more coastal points or of more extensive hinterlands) as the primary basis of global access to bargaining between sovereign, if often asymmetrically leveraged, powers, over items of exchange such as rents, security agreements, arms and economic aid, and barter and other government-to-government trading arrangements. Otherwise, the now lesser frequency of actual big-power warfare has perhaps given greater relative importance to the sheer psychological impact of base presences, to implicit or anticipatory conflict, to wars of nerves, and to perceptions of power-in-being in the absence even of anticipated conflict. That contrast with the whole period between the fifteenth and twentieth centuries is quite clear, as witness the then almost constant involvement of Portuguese, Dutch, and British overseas-based naval forces in conflicts, both against rival European and local powers during a period otherwise usually characterized as one of limited wars. Whether there is now a fixed long-term trend to the contrary remains yet to be seen.

WORLD WAR I AND THE MAJOR COMBATANTS' OVERSEAS BASES

At the outset of World War I, the extensive global basing systems of Britain and France provided, of course, a striking contrast to the major overseas positions controlled by Germany in its few colonial outposts in Africa, China, New Guinea, and in the Pacific Islands. This imbalance was a corollary to the vast imbalance in naval strength between the Entente and Central power coalitions. As the war was essentially determined by land power on the European continent, however, overseas bases and naval power in general played only a marginal role in determining its outcome. Britain's superior High Seas Fleet, operating out of Scapa Flow and dominating the exits from the North Sea to the Atlantic, bottled up the German fleet throughout the war, and the UK suffered only some inconsequential bombardments of the British east coast.(28) The British defeated the Germans in the one major fleet battle at Jutland. German naval strategy was hinged upon submarine interdiction of supply lines in the Atlantic and on some commerce raiding, efforts rendered ultimately futile — though not without impact — by overall British control of the seas.

The vast British basing network in the Atlantic and Indian Oceans was one aspect of the almost total control of the seas it had long maintained. Further, British control of a network of land and sea bases in the Mediterranean and throughout the Middle East provided a springboard for multiple offensives against Turkey in the latter stages of the war.

Mahan's thesis about the virtual all-or-nothing character of sea control was borne out by the hopeless vulnerability of exposed German overseas positions at the war's outset. Those in Africa were quickly overrun by the British, while those in China and the Pacific were captured by the Japanese, whose navy virtually took over British responsibilities during the war in the Far East, as well as ranging well into the Indian Ocean and even to the Mediterranean.(29) The one major German overseas naval squadron led by Admiral Spée, operating in the Pacific, had some initial successes, but was later defeated off the Falkland Islands. The fate of German overseas positions was thus reminiscent of that of French outposts during the Napoleonic War, when Britain had earlier taken advantage of stalemated and prolonged continental land warfare to grab up additional overseas possessions from foes unable to match her overseas naval power.

Almost complete control by Britain of a strategic network of bases around the Eurasian heartland was conducive to a fairly successful economic blockade of Germany, albeit of only limited impact in view of the latter's successful efforts at economic autarky and the contributions to its raw materials sources by its European allies and conquered areas. At least according to one source, the blockade was most meaningful with respect to food supply problems in Germany, its economic Achilles' heel, and one which later Nazi strategists would dream of rectifying by occupying the "bread basket" of the Ukraine.(30)

Basing diplomacy played only a small role in the alliance politics of World War I, providing only scattered diplomatic activity worth noting. Uruguayan provision of a communications facility to the British at the time of the Falkland Islands naval battle is said to have given some advantage to the victors.(31) Germany, meanwhile, was at least rumored to have made extensive use of "secret" submarine facilities in various neutral countries, particularly Spain (at Mazarran and in Rio de Oro), Argentina, and even Ireland, some reports of which were probably unfounded.(32) The United States, after its entry into the war, even sent a naval squadron to the Gulf of Fonseca in Central America to check on alleged German submarine activities in Nicaragua and Honduras, and found nothing to substantiate the rumors.(33) Probably the major long-term impact of these German activities was to give strong impetus to contingency planning before and at the outset of World War II to forestall "secret" German and Japanese use of submarine refueling points in a variety of locales within striking distance of the Panama Canal.(34)

Whereas later, the aftermath of World War II would see the victors left in place for a long time in various acquired strategic positions, World War I left few residues of new possessions or retained strategic access positions. Britain's strengthened position in the Middle East – in Palestine and Iraq – was one major exception, as was Japan's occupation under the League Mandate of German possessions in the Pacific, which "legally" were supposed to have been kept demilitarized. Otherwise, France and Britain retained use of air bases at Constantinople and San Stefano in Turkey well into the 1920s, and the United States temporarily retained use of an air base at Ponto Delgado in the Azores.(35) By the early 1920s, with the exception of Japan's greatly expanded access to facilities and the disappearance of Germany's, there was an essential return to the geopolitical status quo ante.

INTERWAR BASING SYSTEMS AND STRATEGIES

In the following sections, the basing systems of the various relevant major powers are discussed in tandem. Table 3.1 summarizes the data covered in these analyses, enumerating the major facilities extant toward the close of the period before the outbreak of World War II, their functions, and the basis for their availability to users, be it colonial control, conquest, or agreement with sovereign host nations.

British Interwar Basing System

At the close of World War I, Britain's empire and far-flung network of bases remained intact; indeed, it had been supplemented in the Middle East, at a time the future importance of that region's oil was first becoming apparent. Otherwise, of course, the massive costs of the war had caused a permanent weakening of Britain's global power, though in retrospect, Britain's imperial and naval decline (currently described as a "climacteric") is now dated from the decades preceding that war, which saw the rise of competing and eventually superior industrial and military power centers in the U.S., Germany, and Russia, and, according to some, an over-reliance by Britain on overseas investment at the expense of domestic manufacturing industries.(36)

For a long time, Britain had relied and insisted upon virtual global sea supremacy and on its fleet being superior to any possible combination of two other navies.(37) During the First World War, however, the dispersion of its global responsibilities and necessity for allocating enormous resources to bolstering the French land-war effort on the western front, had resulted in a de facto parceling out of naval spheres of influence to the U.S. and Japan, respectively in the Western Hemisphere and in the Far East. But, because its primary rival in World War I had, as had France earlier during the Napoleonic Wars, abjured an open fight for sea supremacy and had relied instead on a guerre de course of commerce raiding (surface and submarine), none of its strategic assets had been threatened.(38) But, Britain emerged from that struggle facing enormous internal pressures to cut back on its overseas positions which were about to come under much greater pressure – from rising Japan and from the beginnings of the global anti-colonial reversal of the long expanding imperial tide.

Still, the elaborate basing system remained intact, and a huge navy was maintained. And the old habit of perceiving all other naval powers as potential threats remained, so that perhaps curiously, British diplomacy during the 1920s was seriously concerned about French naval strength in the Mediterranean,(39) and the rise of American naval power and the related question of retention of British naval bases in the Caribbean and in the Western Atlantic and Eastern Pacific areas. Efforts were thus directed at restraining the growth of French influence in the Near East, and strenuous internal debates were conducted over the wisdom of cutting back on the British naval presence in Bermuda, Nova Scotia, Jamaica, and British Columbia.(40)

Some changes in military technology which emerged from World War I also had an impact. Britain, and other major powers, now had to worry about the threat of land-based aircraft against naval concentrations (and hence about its own air as well as naval bases to cope with that), about strategic bombing and deterrence – with its implications for base acquisition and retention – and about submarine strategy. Further, during the interwar period, new developments in communications (and later radar), and long-range flying boats and dirigibles, all produced newly perceived requirements for strategic access, some of which obviously were to be already outdated by the beginning of World War II.(41)

Overall, of course, Britain faced one major generalizable dilemma, in that while its plethora of overseas assets provided advantages for dispatch of forces to trouble spots, far-flung perimeter defense of its empire, and forward positions from which to project power, they also constituted very vulnerable liabilities – and potential traps – to the extent the system was overextended and exposed. The emphasis then became one of concentration on a number of key, fortified positions, which were to become the main bases for overseas fleets and air squadrons, supplemented by a vast network of fueling points, secondary bases (often weakly garrisoned) and contingency bases where fortifications and garrisons might quickly be expanded. There was an analogy to the Maginot Line here (also to the earlier Portuguese imperial strategy) with its weak underlying assumptions about the viability of stationary, well-fortified positions.

The system of British overseas facilities which existed at the beginning of the interwar period, and which was added to in some areas and downgraded in others as the period progressed, can be described geographically, according to: (1) the Far East-South Asia-Pacific region; (2) the basing network stretching across the Mediterranean through the Suez and on to India; (3) West Africa and the South Atlantic; and (4) North America and the Caribbean.

At the close of World War I, with Germany's preexisting position in the Far East demolished and with the United States still deploying only limited naval forces to forward positions, Britain's basing network there and in the Pacific quickly became recognized as highly important in

Table 3.1. Major Powers' Interwar Basing Networks Prior to Outbreak of World War II

User Country	Host	Location/Base	Principal Type Facilities	Basis of Access
U.S.	U.K.	Bermuda	Naval & air, radar	Agreement with U.K. in connection with Lend-Lease
		Bahamas	air, radar	"
		Jamaica/Kingston	air & naval, radar	
		Antigua	air, radar	
		St. Lucia	air reconn. & staging, bombing practice	
		Trinidad/Pt. of Spain	air staging, radar	"
		Brit. Guyana	air staging	"
		Newfoundland/Gander/	air staging	
		Botswood /St. Johns	seaplane base	"
		/Argentia	air staging	"
		/Stephenville	naval air	
		Canada/Halifax	air	
		/Labrador	air & naval	"
		/Northwest River	air staging, ferry	
		/Baffin Bay	air staging, ferry	"
			meteorological	"
	Dutch Guyana	Zandery	air staging	Taken over after fall of Netherlands
	Dominican Repub.	Paramaribo	"	Agreement
	Haiti	Miraflores, Kilbourne	air	
	Mexico	various	"	
		Guaymas, Acapulco, Mazatlan, Manzanillo	air & naval	Agreement
		Tejeria	naval facils.	
	Brazil	Natal-Fortaleza	air staging	
		Belem, San Luis de Maranhao	air staging	Agreement
		Sao Paulo, Bahia, others	naval	

Table 3.1. (Cont.)

User Country	Host	Location/Base	Principal Type Facilities	Basis of Access
U.S.	Ecuador	Galapagos	air staging, reconn.	Agreement
	Cuba	Guantanamo	naval, major	Agreement
	Greenland	Julianhaab, others	air staging, seaplanes, air ferry, meteorology, commo.	Taken over after fall of Denmark
	Portugal	Azores/Terceira, Fayal, San Miguel	air, naval, tech. commo.	Agreement
	Liberia	Jui	flying boats	Agreement
		Monrovia, Marshall	air staging	
	Philippines	Cavite, Subic	naval	Colonial possession
		Clark, etc.	air	"
		Corregidor, etc.	army garrisons	
	Alaska	Dutch Harbor	naval base	Possession
		Unalask Island	air & naval	
		Kodiak, Rat. Is.	various	
	Puerto Rico	Ponce, San Juan	air & naval	Possession
	Panama, C.Z.	various	various, incl. sub bases	Possession
	Virgin Is.	----------	air & naval	Possession
	Pacific Possessions	Wake, Midway, Guam, Samoa, Palmyra, Jarvis, Phoenix, Howland	air & naval	Possession
U.S.S.R.	Mongolia	Urga, Kovdo, others	air & army garrisons	Puppet gov't, "Agreement"
	China	Shanghai	naval repair & replenishment	"
	Czecho-slovakia	various	airfields	Agreement up to 1941–Brit. dockyard
	Bulgaria	Sofia, Bourges	air	Agreement, quiet forward basing, 1936
	Latvia	Liepadja	naval	Agreement, circa 1940
	Lithuania	various	army garrisons	Conquest–1939–40, forward positions
	Estonia	Saaremaa, Hiumaa, Paldiski, Tallinn	air & naval	"
Japan	Manchuria	Harbin, Changchun, etc.	air bases, commo., etc.	Conquest
	Formosa	----------	18 air & seaplane bases	Occupied
	Bonin Isl.	----------	air, seaplane bases, naval anchorage	Possession

Table 3.1. (Cont.)

User Country	Host	Location/ Base	Principal Type Facilities	Basis of Access
Japan	China	Dairen, Swatow, Amoy	naval bases with repair facilities	Occupied
		Hainan Isl.	2 naval bases, 6 air bases, 4 seaplane facils.	Occupied
	Pescadores Isl.	Keino, Bokotad	drydocks, coal yards, submarine mine depot	Occupied
	Indo-China	Camranh, Saigon, Gia Lam, Haiphong, Hanoi, Bien Hoa, etc. Can Tho, Cap St. Jacques, Cat Lai	naval bases air bases	Occupied 1941 " "
		————————	seaplane bases	
	Spratly Is.	————————	seaplane base, naval anchorage, naval commo.	Occupied
	Korea	Chinkai Bay, Pusan	naval bases & air bases	Possession
	Thailand	offshore islands	naval anchorage, approx. 17 air bases	Agreement-1934 Occupied, 1940-1
	Pacific Mandate Islands	Wotje, Bikini Kusaie, Ulithi, Jaluit, Ponape, Truk, Palaus, Saipan, etc.	air, naval, commo, seaplane, meteorological, fuel depots, anchorages, etc.	League Mandate fortifications "legally" prohibited
	Marcus Isl.	————————	air base	Possession
Netherlands	Neth. E. Indies	Java, Sumatra Borneo, Amboina	numerous air bases, army garrisons	Possession
		Soerabaja	main naval base	"
		Lake Tosa	seaplane base	"
		Medan, Batavia	main aerodromes	"
	Neth. W. Indies	Curacao, Aruba, Bonaire	air bases	Possession
	Dutch Guyana	Paramaribo	garrison, air base	"

56

Table 3.1. (Cont.)

User Country	Host	Location/ Base	Principal Type Facilities	Basis of Access
Germany	Spain	Pasages, Marin, Rio de Oro, Cp. Finesterre, Melilla, Ceuta,	sub bases Spanish Civil War Fortifications, troops, aircraft assembly	Agreement-after "
		Malaga, Vigo Canaries/Las Palmas /Gando, Tenerife	sub base air bases	" "
	Portugal/ Africa	Bissagos	Sub, coal & oil depot	Agreement
	Hungary	Budapest, Debrecen, Szeged, etc.	forward air bases	Agreement-1940
	Italy	Rhodes	air staging	Alliance
Italy	Ital Med.	Libya/Cyrenaica	air bases	
		Leros, other Dodecanese Isl.	naval, air, weapons storage, garrisons	Possession "
		Pantelleria	air, naval	
	Albania	Sasseno, others	5 air bases	Pact
	Ital. E. Africa	Abyssinia, Eritrea/Massawa	20+ air bases, garrisons, naval	Conquest
	Libya	Castel Benito, Benghazi, Tobruk, Bardia, Sidi Barrani	air bases	Possession
	Spain	Canaries (Gando) Tetuan, Ifni, Majorca (Palma)	numerous air & sub bases	Agreement-after Span. Civil War
France	Morocco	Alicante, Agadir, Meknes, Fez, 4 others	air bases	Possession
	Tunisia	Tunis, others	air bases, commo., dirigibles, seaplanes	Possession
	Fr. W. Africa	Bizerte Dakar, Bamako, Seguedine, Bafoulable, others	naval base air staging network, garrisons	" Possession
	E. Africa	Djibouti	naval base	Possession

Table 3.1. (Cont.)

User Country	Host	Location/Base	Principal Type Facilities	Basis of Access
	China	Shanghai	naval base-Fr. Asiatic Fleet	Agreement
	Lebanon, Syria	Aleppo, Tripoli, Damascus, Beirut, Rayak	air bases	League Mandates
	Madagascar	Ivato, others Diego Suarez	air staging naval base	Possession "
	Fr. Caribbean	Martinique, Guadeloupe	air, naval, commo., fuel storage, garrisons	Fr. departements
	Indo-China	Saigon, Camranh Bay Bach Mai, Tong, Bien Hoa, Cat Lai	naval bases, Indo-China fleet air bases	Possession-up to 1941 "
U.K.	Ascension Isl.	-------------	air staging	Possession
	Barbados	-------------	naval facils.	"
	Trinidad	Gulf of Paria	naval anchorage, facils.	"
	Falkland Isl.	-------------	air, naval, commo	"
	Jamaica	Kingston	naval base, garrison	"
	Canada	Halifax	naval base, drydocks	Commonwealth
		Esquimalt	naval facils.	"
	Newfoundland	St. Johns, Argentia	air transit, commo.	Possession
	Bermuda	-------------	air & naval drydock, aircraft repair, oil storage	Possession
	Portugal	Azores	naval access	Agreement
	Australia	Melbourne, Sydney, Darwin, Brisbane, Fremantle, Darwin	main naval, air bases	Commonwealth
	New Zealand	Auckland, Pt. Chambers	naval facils.	Commonwealth
	South Pacific Isl.	Fiji, Tonga, W. Samoa	naval facils.	Possession
	N. Borneo	-------------	airfields, naval & materiel storage, garrison	"
	Hong Kong	-------------	main base, China naval sqdrn, fortifications, garrison	Crown Colony

Table 3.1. (Cont.)

User Country	Host	Location/Base	Principal Type Facilities	Basis of Access
U.K.	China	Shanghai; Tientsin, Peking	naval base; garrisons	Agreement-up to late 1930s
	Singapore	Seletar, Tengah, etc.	Main RAF & naval base	Possession
	Malaya	Kluang, Alor Star, Kota Bahru, others	air & seaplane bases	Possession
	Mauritius	———	naval facil.	Possession
	India	Bombay, others; Karachi	main naval base, garrisons, air; naval, dirigible	Possession; "
	Ceylon	Trincomalee	air & naval base	Possession
	Trans-Jordan	Aqaba	naval access	Mandate
	Aden	———	air & naval base	Possession
	Egypt	Suez, Pt. Said, Dehkla, Ismailia, Alexandria, Almaza	naval & air bases, garrisons	Mily Agreement
	Iraq	Basra, Habbaniya	air, dirigible	Mily Agreement
	Sudan	Khartoum, Juba; Pt. Sudan	air staging, ferrying; naval facil.	Possession; "
	S. Africa	Simonstown; Durban; Robbin Island	naval base; air & naval; seaplane base	Commonwealth; "; "
	African Possessions	Lagos, Takoradi, Kano, Freetown, Bathurst, etc., several in Tanganyika	network of air strips	Possession
	Malta	———	main naval base (mostly destroyers)	"
	Cyprus	Akotiri, etc.	air & naval facils.	Possession
	Palestine	Ramleh; Haifa	HQ & armored unit; naval base	Mandate; "
	Gibraltar	———	naval base	Possession
	Greece	Crete, others	air & naval access	Possession ATs, licensed arms prodn.

relation to growing Japanese expansionist aims. These had been under-scored by threats against China (the famous "21 demands") and acquisi-tion of the previously German-held island chains in the Marianas, Carolines, and Marshalls.

Britain's geostrategic position in the Far East, at the outset of the period, was hinged on colonial possessions or Commonwealth ties in Australia, New Zealand, Singapore, Malaya, North Borneo, Hong Kong, Burma, the Andaman and Nicobar Islands, numerous island possessions in the South Pacific, and a few toeholds on mainland China. And, although some small army units were deployed during this period (backed up by the capability for deployment of Australian, New Zealander, and Indian forces in the case of crises), basic reliance was on the deployment of a large and fairly well dispersed group of naval squadrons, increasingly bolstered by aircraft as the period progressed.

With the construction of greatly enhanced fortifications and repair facilities between about 1927 and 1935, the great naval and air base at Singapore became the lynchpin of the British Far Eastern basing system, flanked in all directions by major naval facilities at Hong Kong, Sydney, Trincomalee, and Bombay, and others in Australasia and India (see table 3.1).

The main base at Singapore attracted much attention during the 1920s and 1930s, partly because it was openly declared a provocation by Japan (a matter which entered into the naval arms control discussions surrounding and preceding the Washington and London naval agree-ments), and because the cost, utility, and defensibility of the base were continuous subjects of rancorous political debate within Britain throughout the period. Indeed, in 1929, at the peak of post-World War I optimism about "permanent" peace and disarmament amid the strange euphoria surrounding the Kellogg-Briand Pact, the British actually slowed down base construction at Singapore, pending the outcome of the then ongoing five-power naval disarmament talks.

Later, driven by the Japanese aggression in Manchuria, expansion of the Singapore base was completed around 1935, and became the home of Britain's Far East squadron, which consisted of some fourteen warships. It had extensive wharves, repair dockyards, and fortifications directed against possible seaborne attack, and flying boats were also based there. Nearby were several RAF bases deploying torpedo bombers and reconnaissance and pursuit planes. Slightly further out along the base's periphery were several RAF and Royal Navy aircraft bases in Malaya intended to provide for protection of Singapore.(42)

Britain's Hong Kong base, home of its China squadron which also made frequent visits to major Chinese ports up to the late 1930s, virtually rivaled Singapore in importance. By 1939, it was the home base for a squadron consisting of an aircraft carrier, six cruisers, thirteen destroyers, seventeen submarines, and twenty-four gunboats and torpedo boats, along with support vessels, and several squadrons of torpedo bombers and other aircraft.(43) Other major Pacific bases at Sydney and Auckland deployed a total of seven cruisers, seven destroyers, and escort vessels, in addition to eleven to twelve squadrons of Commonwealth aircraft.(44) As World War II approached, Darwin was built up as an important Royal Navy and RAF fueling station in northern Australia, with docks capable of handling up to cruiser-size ships.(45) Trincomalee in Ceylon, centuries earlier the hinge of the British navy's strategic system directed against Holland and France, was upgraded during the 1930s and became the home port of the East Indies Squadron.(46) It acted as a permanent base for a heavy cruiser, three light cruisers and six escort vessels. Colombo and Bombay served as secondary regional naval bases.

Aside from questions about the match of British naval and air forces to the ominously growing Japanese threat, Britain's Achilles heel — almost unavoidable for a thinly stretched imperial power with a population base of only 50 million — was the small size of its army garrisons in the area. Though there was a sizable mixed British and colonial force in India, and the considerable mobilization potential of the Australian and New Zealander armies, the main bases of the Far East, East Indies, and China naval squadrons were only thinly garrisoned.

There were only 7,000 troops in Singapore in the late 1930s (mostly artillery, antiaircraft, and signal units) along with a small Straits Settlement Volunteer Force; some 6,000 troops dispersed among garrisons in China and some additional but nugatory force elements in North Borneo and British New Guinea.(47) Against the onslaught which was to take place in 1941, these were clearly merely token forces; later, the fortified bastions at Hong Kong and Singapore were exposed as merely highly vulnerable traps, useful primarily as symbolic presences and "trip-wires."

The close of World War I saw Britain's extensive network of bases and access points en route to India via the Mediterranean-Suez-Red Sea route remain intact. Strong-points were maintained at Gibraltar, Malta, Cyprus, in Egypt, and in Palestine. Malta became the primary naval base, home porting a flotilla primarily fielding destroyers and, like Singapore, designed for defense by large air formations.(48) Cyprus was built up as a major air and naval base in the 1930s to counter nearby Italian deployments at Rhodes and Leros; Haifa and Alexandria were auxiliary naval bases; and a complex of air bases was built in Egypt.(49) Close relations with the Greek Air Force (backed up by extensive license production agreements for aircraft) provided additional access on Crete and on the Greek mainland.(50)

Between Egypt and India, the Royal Navy maintained bases at Aqaba and Aden, and was provided additional access at Port Sudan, Basra, Berbera, and in the Seychelles and Maldives Islands. This region remained a virtually fully controlled British naval bailiwick, to be challenged only in the late 1930s by some — ultimately futile — Italian naval and air deployments in Eritrea and Italian Somaliland.

In the vast area encompassing the North Atlantic and the Caribbean, Britain continued to deploy naval forces throughout the interwar period, torn between abandoning the area to hoped-for friendly U.S. control, and enduring the symbolic decline of fully global naval pretensions inherent in withdrawal. For long, British naval power in the area had been based on ship and (more recently) air deployments in Halifax, Bermuda, and Kingston.(51) But in 1929, the newly elected British Labour Party considered virtual abandonment of all of these facilities as a gesture of goodwill to isolationist and pacifist America, but then merely downgraded them de facto, presaging the relinquishing of primary responsibility for naval and air control of the area to the United States in the 1940s.(52) There were, oddly in retrospect, debates in the British Parliament at the time about maintaining naval strength at Kingston because of its proximity to the Panama Canal, reflective of a traditional all-contingencies strategic mentality.

On the other side of North America, Britain retained, well into the interwar period, a naval facility at Esquimalt, British Columbia, which was also a terminal for its Pacific communications cable system. This too was later downgraded to appease American sensibilities.(53)

Not perceived until just before World War II was the vital importance of a chain of facilities on a west-to-east axis running from the Caribbean to the east coast of South America, across the South Atlantic to Africa, and across the latter to Sudan and Egypt. At the outset of the war, they would become vital for ferrying aircraft and other badly needed materiel to the beleaguered British forces in North Africa. The chain began with the Bahamas and various British-owned islands in the West Indies, and continued on through British Guyana, Ascension Island, and a number of access points in West and Central Africa, most notably in Takoradi (now in Ghana), Lagos and Kano, and on to Khartoum and Cairo.

British strategists also foresaw, well before World War II, the importance of north-south staging networks along both the east and west coasts of Africa. Freetown and Bathurst were developed as major air bases in West Africa, while Khartoum, Juba (in Sudan), and a string of staging facilities in Kenya, Tanganyika, and Rhodesia were built to afford a Cairo-to-Capetown air staging route.(54) Around the African littoral, Freetown, Lagos, Simonstown, Durban, Mombasa, and also Mauritius were the principal British naval bases, with only Simonstown possessing major repair facilities.

At the outset of the war, Britain rapidly added to its strategic basing network a number of outposts previously controlled by defeated or still neutral European nations, in effect, repeating the strategy used earlier of utilizing preemptively its sea control to pick off desired new positions. Prior agreements with Portugal were acted upon, and in combination with the United States, the Azores Islands were occupied and an air base (later to become Lajes) was built.(55) Madeira and the Cape Verde Islands, and a Portuguese base in Portuguese Guinea, were "commandeered."(56) Iceland and Greenland were similarly occupied, as were the Dutch possessions in the West Indies and South America and various French overseas possessions.(57) Regarding these latter, there were some problems in overcoming resistance from Vichy French collaborators with the Germans, occasioning some combat in Syria and the sinking of French warships in West Africa.

The French Interwar Basing System

Despite its defeats in wars against Britain in the eighteenth and early nineteenth centuries, in which it lost the race for naval supremacy, France had built an extensive overseas empire in the remainder of the nineteenth century. Correspondingly, it possessed as of 1914 the second most extensive naval basing system in the Far East and the Pacific, Africa, and in the Western Hemisphere. France's navy, though, was far smaller than Britain's, had no pretensions to dominant sea-control capability overseas, and was of necessity concentrated in proximity to its home Atlantic and Mediterranean coasts. This was an inevitable corollary to its concentration of budget resources on land armies, to deter the ever-present German threat.

Yet despite the failure of its guerre de course naval strategy during the Napoleonic Wars, France had never quite abandoned its aspirations for challenging British naval supremacy; indeed, it had engaged Britain in at least two futile naval races during the nineteenth century.(58) Before World War I, of course, the joint Entente naval policy had dictated French concentration of naval forces in the Mediterranean. After, there still remained a strong remnant of traditional Anglo-French naval rivalry, particularly in the Mediterranean.

France's colonial system emerged, even at its zenith, a smaller and geographically more concentrated one than Britain's, and this lent a significantly different character to its basing network and overseas troop deployments. Large French army garrisons were concentrated in North and West Africa, and in Vietnam, in both cases buttressed by native colonial army units. To a great extent, France's basing system was primarily intended for local defense of colonial possessions, with little potential for projection of power into contiguous areas. In areas far from France, there were only weak lines of communication tying the system together.

In the Far East, French naval and air forces were concentrated in Indo-China, where, after a gradual buildup, accelerated to face the Japanese threat in the 1930s, France had major naval bases at Haiphong and Saigon. It was planning at the war's outset an expanded submarine base at a then obscure place called Camranh Bay.(59)

Saigon harbored some eleven surface ships in 1934, mostly gunboats, and some submarines in addition. There were also eight or nine major air bases, but France deployed only some 29,000 men in its Indo-China forces in 1939, clearly insufficient to meet a major Japanese threat.(60) All of the French air and naval bases were taken over by Japan from Vichy France in 1941, and were subsequently utilized for forward deployments next aimed at Singapore, the Dutch East Indies, and the Philippines.(61)

Elsewhere in Asia, France (along with Britain) deployed a small fleet in China, with eleven ships, including two cruisers, operating out of Shanghai until its fall.(62) There was an additional small garrison further south in New Caledonia, which like French possessions elsewhere, was preemptively occupied by the Western allies at the Pacific war's outset, after the fall of France.

France had lost most of its possessions in the Western Hemisphere a century or more before World War I, and afterward possessed only minor basing facilities there. There was a small garrison in French Guyana, and others (totaling only some 1,100 troops) in the West Indies island possessions. Right before the war, the French had planned to enlarge a small and fortified base on Martinique, and to build another on Guadeloupe, but these plans were aborted by France's collapse.(63) France aspired at one point during the interwar period to access at Chimbote, a Peruvian port where French shipbuilders had commercial concessions, but nothing came of it.

The most important French overseas bases were, of course, in its various African possessions: in its vast North, West, and Central African empire; in French Somaliland; and in Madagascar and Reunion. These gave it important naval and air bases which could be used to contest for supremacy in the Mediterranean with Italy and Britain, some capability for reconnaissance and interdiction of shipping in the Atlantic off the African coast, a north-south air logistics network stretching from France itself to Gabon and Congo, and a naval refueling chain running around the Cape en route to Asia.

The main French overseas naval bases were at Bizerte (upgraded during the 1920s), Oran, Dakar, Djibouti, and Diego Suarez; there were also numerous air bases in North and West Africa.(64) There was also a vastly proliferated network of military airstrips and emergency landing fields throughout the region, providing for staging networks on several axes along the Atlantic Coast, south through the Sahara, and eastward from Dakar.(65) Off the east coast of Africa, France deployed combat aircraft on Madagascar.

The remaining points of concentration for French bases were in Syria and Lebanon, which were under French League of Nations mandates during this period. Here, France had air bases, some of which were handed over to the Germans by Vichy forces in 1940, and which menaced British positions at Suez until they were quickly overrun by British forces.(66)

Similar to Britain and other major powers of the period, France had few if any bases outside of its colonial possessions. With Britain, it occupied a couple of air bases in Turkey for several years after World War I. Its naval access in fragmented China has been noted, which was based on the then prevailing state of "capitulations." In the late 1920s there were some negotiations with Greece over access to a port in the Bay of Eleusis, but which seems not to have had significant military implications.(67)

In summary, France's interwar basing network provided somewhat for logistical and combat support in defense of its colonial possessions, but only where forward operations against potential big power antagonists was not really required. The bases later proved irrelevant to its defense against Germany and retained significance only as brief focal points of conflict between British and German forces at the war's outset, when Vichy forces sometimes were pressured to allow the latter access. France's Asia possessions, not dissimilarly to some of Britain's and America's, proved merely vulnerable and exposed hostages, quickly overrun.

THE DUTCH OVERSEAS BASING SYSTEM

Actually, to refer to a Dutch basing "system" by 1919 would be somewhat exaggerated, as Holland's once ambitious empire consisted by then merely of the mineral-rich Dutch East Indies, plus Surinam and the Dutch West Indies in the Caribbean area. The latter were weakly garrisoned at the outset of World War II and were occupied by U.S. forces and held in trust for the war's duration.(68)

The East Indies were another story. There, the Dutch erected an impressive network of bases and fortifications, all the while recognizing the need for U.S. or British assistance if they were to be invaded by Japan. At a late hour, there were some halting attempts at coordinating defense strategy with British forces in Singapore, Malaya, and North Borneo.(69)

As early as 1923, the Dutch built several air bases, a large seaplane base, and even additional "secret" air bases and repair facilities in remote areas.(70) This network was later extended to some twenty airfields – on Java, Sumatra, Borneo, the Celebes, Timor, and New Guinea – which deployed some 200-plus combat aircraft, a motley mixture of U.S. Martin bombers, Curtiss-Wright and Brewster fighters, and ironically, German Dornier bombers.(71) The Dutch army on the islands consisted of some 75,000 troops, concentrated on Java, but with garrisons on Borneo, the Celebes, and Sumatra. The Dutch navy, with its main base at Soerabaya (which had some of the most extensive dockyard facilities in Asia), regularly deployed by 1940 three cruisers, seven destroyers, thirteen submarines, and forty auxiliary ships.

More so than France, Holland's concentrated overseas bases existed solely for local defense. That too, of course, was to prove inadequate after the fall of the homeland and amid the general collapse of allied forces in the early stages of World War II.

THE U.S. INTERWAR BASING SYSTEM

The United States got into the race for overseas empire only very late, with an often noted though much argued reluctance related to its national political origins, and the absence of some of the underlying forces which propelled European imperialism (such as need for raw materials and outlets for surplus population). Overseas expansionism began – and in a sheer territorial sense, more or less ended – only with the Spanish-American War of 1898, which saw the Hawaiian Islands, Guam, Puerto Rico, and the Philippines fall under U.S. control, along with – temporarily – Cuba. Alaska and the Aleutian Islands had previously been purchased from Russia, and the Virgin Islands were later bought from Denmark. American control of the Panama Canal

Zone was achieved after 1900. These several possessions came to incorporate what was to become the rather insignificant overseas basing system available to the United States at the close of World War I and on up to 1940, by which time the United States was already clearly the world's premier potential military power, by any standard of measurement.

The United States had, of course, long eschewed forward peacetime overseas deployment of military forces, excepting some debt-collecting and other military expeditions to the Caribbean and Central America, and far earlier expeditions to combat Barbary Coast pirates. Britain's navy had long allowed for relatively secure U.S. isolationism, and the United States had, despite periodic flurries of concern, long made its vaunted Monroe Doctrine stick with respect to European penetration of Latin America. Its almost absent-minded conquests of 1898 (for which a U.S. president had begged forgiveness from his God) had provided it with a semblance of a geopolitical perimeter defense in the Pacific and naval dominance of the Caribbean. Afterward, with the lessons of the initial setbacks of World War II in mind (including those of the "Battle of the Atlantic" with German submarines), American geopolitical theorists were retrospectively to rue the country's laxity in not providing for a more comprehensive system of access around both of the major oceans.(72) The regrets were to inspire the much more aggressive American policy of base acquisition evidenced immediately after World War II.

At the close of World War I, the United States had withdrawn from some bases utilized during and right after the war, for instance, from a naval base acquired from Portugal at Ponto Delgado in the Azores (although it retained a cable terminal at Aorta).(73) Naval deployments at Rotterdam and Spalato (on the Adriatic) during the postwar reconstruction period were also rapidly withdrawn with the return to normalcy.(74)

Concerning access problems, perhaps the most salient legacy of the war was the near-paranoid fear in 1918 about the activities of German submarines, alleged in some intelligence reports to have operated clandestinely out of Mexico, the Gulf of Fonseca in Central America, Colombia, Venezuela, and Cuba.(75) When another world war began to loom in the late 1930s, fears of a repeat of what was alleged in 1918 were to produce a flurry of diplomatic activity by the United States all over Latin America.

Throughout the 1920s and 1930s, amid very significant changes in military technology — submarines, aircraft, aircraft carriers — the United States did very little to upgrade its overseas facilities or to prepare for the logistical contingencies which would arise at the outset of World War II. Only a handful of overseas bases were fortified or beefed up with deployed naval or air units.

In the Atlantic, the United States continued to rely on British naval power. In the late 1920s, moreover, as noted, Britain downgraded its facilities at Halifax and Kingston, and Jamaica was traded for an at least implicit U.S. signal not to push ahead with a surface fleet which would outpace the Royal Navy.(76) The United States, for its part, in line with an overall strategy basically stressing hemispheric defense, maintained skeletal forces and facilities in the Virgin Islands and at Guantanamo. The major exception was the basing of the "Special Service Squadron" in the Canal Zone at Balboa, consisting of a flagship and some eight cruisers and gunboats, which was used to show the flag and to collect intelligence information throughout Latin America.(77) Designed for rapid deployment, its units were periodically deployed off Mexico, Honduras, and Nicaragua in times of political tension, though the United States appears to have wished to avoid the frictions associated with keeping squadrons in foreign ports for long periods. Some submarines were deployed at Coco Solo in the Canal Zone during this period, for major war contingencies.

There were no U.S. forces or bases in Europe, Africa, or the Middle East during this period, but in Asia there was a "station fleet" at Shanghai, which was larger than the one in the Canal Zone.(78) In 1932 the U.S. Asiatic Fleet consisted of a cruiser, nineteen destroyers, twelve submarines, and nine river gunboats, an assemblage exceeded only by Britain's; some of these units were rotated back and forth to Manila. Originally, these forces were for protection of U.S. lives and business from the chaos of Chinese civilian conflict.

In the Pacific, the United States did carry out a major expansion of its facilities in Hawaii, which became the hinge of the U.S. forward though defensive deployment in the Pacific, supplemented by outlying garrisons at Wake, Midway, Guam, Dutch Harbor, American Samoa, and Howland Island. In addition, there were the fairly extensive though minimally garrisoned facilities in the Philippines, geared primarily to colonial control and reliant upon extensive recruitment of Filipino forces. The main ones were the naval bases at Cavite and Subic Bay, the air base at Clark Field, and the army garrison at Corregidor at the entrance to Manila Bay.(79) As Japan's expansionist aims became more worrisome during the 1930s, these deployments were perceived as a "presence" to deter Japanese aggression, for potential bolstering of British and Dutch forces in the region, and for shadowing the ominous "clandestine" Japanese military buildup in the mandated Pacific islands.

On the eve of World War II, in 1939 and 1940, American anxieties about an impending conflict resulted in a hasty though determined effort at bolstering strategic assets in and en route to both potential theaters of conflict. Primarily, this involved simultaneous efforts at: first, taking over British bases in the Atlantic and Caribbean, to allow for British concentration of effort in Europe and the eastern Atlantic, and to deter possible German penetration in the Western Hemisphere; second, strenuous preemptive diplomacy throughout Latin America to warn off numerous quasi-fascist governments from permitting Axis air and naval access, and to ensure U.S. access in the event of American entry into the war; and third, last-minute upgrading of U.S. facilities in the Pacific to cope with the looming Japanese threat to the mainland United States or at least to its Pacific possessions.

The lend-lease agreement with Britain in 1940 provided for significant U.S. force deployments to a number of British bases in the Atlantic-Caribbean area, and as the base takeovers were later extended beyond World War II, they resulted in the long-term acquisition of important strategic assets. In 1940 and 1941, U.S. forces moved into Bermuda, the Bahamas, Jamaica, Antigua, St. Lucia, Trinidad, British Guyana, Newfoundland, and Labrador, occasioning hasty expansion of existing facilities and construction of new ones.(80) There was also some last-minute negotiating over status-of-forces arrangements, which previewed legal problems negotiated after the war for bases all over the globe.

Bermuda became a U.S. naval base in 1940, with 3,000 personnel deployed, and air units were sent to the Bahamas in 1941.(81) Air and naval bases in Jamaica were occupied by some 1,800 American personnel in 1941. St. Lucia in the same year became a base for U.S. patrol aircraft exercising surveillance over the Caribbean and a staging point for short-range aircraft ferrying from Puerto Rico to Trinidad (later part of a longer staging route to Africa).(82) Port of Spain in Trinidad became a major U.S. air facility, hosting some 15,000 personnel, while British Guyana was then also surveyed for staging points en route to eastern Brazil.(83)

Also in 1941, 5,000 U.S. personnel were deployed to the St. Johns, Argentia, and Stapleville air bases in Newfoundland, and plans were made for use of still others as well as in Nova Scotia.(84) The United States began making use of communications facilities in Newfoundland and began planning for similar facilities on Baffin Island, and also Greenland, where British and German forces were already skirmishing over meteorological installations. Of particular importance was the formation of a staging network for ferrying short-range aircraft to Britain, utilizing bases in Newfoundland, Labrador, Greenland, Iceland, and the Faeroe Islands, the latter two occupied by the UK after the outbreak of war.(85)

Greenland, though not provided as a base to the United States by the 1940 lend-lease agreement, quickly became a focal point in view of its location astride the U.S.-UK air communications network and its importance to hemispheric defense. It became crucial for ferrying short-range aircraft to Britain. In 1941, with the Germans by then driven out, the United States set up there a principal staging airfield at Julianhaab along with radio transmitters and receivers, a meteorological station, and an HF/DF (high frequency direction finder).(86) Elsewhere in the Atlantic, and in collaboration with the UK before the formal U.S. entry into the war, the United States set up a general headquarters and air force reconnaissance base in the Azores and began constructing other bases there.(87)

Presaging the later importance of "technical" facilities in the electronics age, in 1941 the United States set up SCR-70 Ground Control Interceptors (an early radar system) on Newfoundland, Bermuda, the Bahamas, Jamaica, Antigua, Trinidad, and British Guyana, which in addition to similar installations along the U.S. east coast mainland, provided for a rather comprehensive early-warning network directed against a possible German air assault.(88)

As World War II approached, and particularly during and after Hitler's onslaught upon Western Europe in 1940-1941, hemispheric security became a paramount American concern. There were the memories of German submarine activities in the Caribbean and near the Panama Canal in 1918. Further, the United States was faced with the fact that crypto-fascist regimes and pro-Axis sympathies had become widespread throughout Latin America during the late 1930s. Without exception, all of the South American nations – and a couple in Central America as well – were receiving half or more of their arms supplies from Germany and Italy during this period (Panama and Peru were believed to have acquired Japanese small arms as well), and some were acquiring modern German aircraft.(89)

Further, a number of Latin American countries – Brazil, Colombia, Peru, Chile, Uruguay, Paraguay, El Salvador – by then had large German and Italian immigrant populations, many of whom were prominent in commerce and politics. In Brazil, among other places, whole regions were dominated by expatriate Germans, giving rise to fears about "secret" basing facilities and extensive espionage operations and sabotage.(90)

The U.S. military intelligence files from the late 1930s are crammed with (seemingly unsubstantiated) reports about German, Italian, or Japanese purchases of large plantations or jungle tracts along coasts, near key strategic points; in particular, in areas near the Panama Canal and in northern Mexico.(91) These worried about the possibilities of clandestine refueling facilities (using "jerrycans") for Axis submarines, and the sudden and secret deployment of German bombers which might knock out the Panama Canal locks, Pearl Harbor style.

These fears resulted in a strenuous U.S. diplomatic effort, involving both inducements and threats, throughout Latin America, to forestall military connections with the Axis. Démarches were launched in a number of Latin American capitals concerning Axis political penetration, alleged or real; the granting of military basing rights, and the possible grey area military implications of the dominance of Axis-controlled commercial airline and shipping firms.(92) (Some such firms actually owned airports, one of which alone serviced entirely the strategic Galapagos Islands in the Pacific Ocean.(93)) Hurried and determined U.S. military intelligence operations were also launched throughout Latin America, some utilizing clandestine surveillance from commercial aircraft of potential harbors for submarines.(94)

American activities in Latin America during this period were not relegated merely to base denial and political neutralization, though these were important, particularly in view of the possibility of German air bases on the eastern Brazilian coastline which might allow for domination (particularly if combined with German access to West African bases) of large stretches of the Atlantic. The United States was then also involved in acquiring contingency rights for air staging and naval refueling stations all over Latin America (particularly on the northeast coast of South America) to prepare a staging network to and then across Africa, to ease arms supply of embattled British forces in North Africa and the Middle East.

Under some pressure, almost all of the Latin American nations complied with U.S. requests, though in some cases not without serious internal political struggles, and in most only in exchange for weapons supplies to supplant those which would no longer be forthcoming from Germany and Italy. This presented a particularly thorny problem for the United States at a time it was already struggling to arm its own growing forces, not to mention those of Britain.(95)

The American prewar diplomacy in Latin America was successful, in part no doubt because of the stick that might have been invoked if the carrot had failed. Haiti in 1941 revoked a concession for a Vichy France broadcasting station, and then granted the United States unrestricted use of its airfields as well as permission to build a large navy base (Haiti's largest airfield was already controlled by Panair).(96) The Dominican Republic granted the United States access to its two major airports for emergency and "maneuver" landings.(97) Mexico, on poor terms with the United States after the 1938 expropriation of American oil assets, and then under not inconsiderable Axis influence, first granted the United States staging rights for ferrying P-40 fighters to the Canal Zone, and then apparently made a secret arrangement for American use during the war of several ports.(98) Ecuador – under considerable prewar Italian influence – bargained with the United States over basing rights in the Galapagos Islands, deemed important for controlling the western exit lanes from the Panama Canal, which were eventually granted in 1942.(99)

The main U.S. concern, however, was about acquiring a staging network via Brazil to Africa, to supplement already controlled facilities in Puerto Rico, Trinidad, and British Guyana. Negotiations with Brazil resulted in the use of a number of airfields and ports in its northeastern promontory – most notably at Natal, Fortaleza, San Luis de Maranhao, and Belem – after U.S. surveying activities had assured the availability of necessary infrastructure, runway lengths, and repair and refueling facilities.(100) Paramaribo in Dutch Guyana was also then commandeered for a U.S. base, to be held in trust for the defeated Dutch.(101)

By the time of the U.S. entry into the war in late 1941, it had thus achieved agreements with numerous Latin American countries for basing and overflight rights. Many agreements (with Argentina, Bolivia, Brazil, Dominican Republic, Cuba, Costa Rica, Chile, Colombia, Ecuador, El Salvador, Guatemala, Haiti, Honduras, Nicaragua, Paraguay, Peru, Uruguay, Venezuela) provided for open-ended aircraft landings with twenty-four-hour notices, and for naval port staging of up to one division of troops with naval escorts.(102) Although access could have been utilized in numerous places, the main U.S. bases and staging points in Latin America during the crucial period 1941-1943 were at Acapulco, the Galapagos Islands, Guantanamo and Santiago in Cuba, Barbados, Antigua, Martinique, St. Lucia, Trinidad, Puerto Cabello (Venezuela), Georgetown, Paramaribo, Cayenne, and in Brazil.

Related to U.S. diplomacy in Brazil, American military teams were also active in surveying staging areas in Liberia for aircraft to transit the South Atlantic en route to the Middle East. Particular attention was paid to a flying-boat base under construction at Jui and to landing fields and seaplane anchorages in the one African nation long under predominant U.S. influence.(103) Monrovia later became one stopping point on the staging route from Brazil which continued on to Egypt via the British-controlled airfields at Takoradi, Lagos, Kano, and Khartoum.

Otherwise, the United States also made efforts at upgrading its Pacific bases on the eve of Pearl Harbor, but which did not provide the basis for an aerial counterstrike against Japan proper.(104) Further naval bases were planned but never completed in the Philippines, particularly in the south at Malempang.(105) Garrisons and air and naval deployments were increased at Guam, Wake, Midway, Howland, Palmyra, Jarvis, and Baker Islands, in Samoa, and in the northern Pacific, at Dutch Harbor, Unalask Island, and in the Rat and Pribilof Islands.(106) Strangely, in retrospect, during the period of the Nazi-Soviet pact from 1939 to 1941, U.S. defense planners apparently worried profusely about the major U.S. bases in Alaska being within range of Soviet heavy bombers based at Uelen in Siberia.(107)

By 1941, then, the United States had significantly expanded its long weak overseas basing network, though its deployments still bespoke a primarily defensive orientation for hemispheric defense. But at the war's close, there was much less of a temptation to withdraw than there had been in 1919. Extensive manpower demobilization amid the onset of the Cold War went hand in hand with the expansion of a ring of bases all around the Eurasian super-continent; that is, a new basing network reflective of new responsibilities.

ITALY'S INTERWAR BASING SYSTEM

Renascent Italy came late to the race for empire, having been left far behind by rival European powers while consolidating its new-found national status during the last half of the nineteenth century. Its forces were defeated ignominiously by Ethiopia in 1896, when they attempted to expand its small East African empire beyond the enclaves in Eritrea and Somaliland. Over a decade later, Libya was wrenched from the crumbling Ottoman Empire along with the strategic Aegean Dodecanese Islands. These possessions were to form the basis for Italy's overseas basing system before and after World War I.

Italy emerged from that war a frustrated but ambitious revisionist power, feeling that it deserved more extensive spoils as a reward for having weighed in on the winning side, even if belatedly. A few years later, the rise of fascism was accompanied and given impetus by strivings for a more prominent "place in the sun," by dreams of a recrudescent "Roman" empire which might dominate the Mediter-ranean.(108)

Concerning bases, Italian efforts during the interwar period – particularly toward its close – were devoted to projecting air and naval power throughout the Mediterranean, protecting East African holdings, and maintaining an imperial lifeline to the latter despite British control over the interposing,blocking Suez bottleneck.

In the Mediterranean, Italy devoted considerable resources to strengthening outposts on Rhodes and Leros Islands in the Dodecanese group. Naval stations were established in 1919, a first air base in 1923, and there was extensive construction of undergound shelters for ammunition, weapons, and personnel.(109) The clear intent was to construct an Italian equivalent to Malta further east, which might threaten the Suez area, the Levant, Cyprus, and the exit from the Turkish Straits.(110) Later, the Dodecanese bases would be used to attack British bases in Egypt at the outset of World War II and to interdict British shipping in the Mediterranean.

Throughout the period, Italy gradually established a virtual protectorate over Albania; indeed, the latter was eventually bludgeoned into a rather unreciprocal formal defense pact. One result was the establishing of Italian air bases in Albania, including some on the strategic island of Sasseno, which could be used in combination with those on the Italian mainland to dominate the entrance to the Adriatic Sea.(111) To Italy's west, favorable strategic positions were provided by control over Sicily and Sardinia, while in the narrow chokepoint between Sicily and Tunisia, traditional British naval control from Malta was menaced by Italian facilities on the small island of Pantelleria, which were strengthened beginning in 1937.

Libya, of course, was the jewel of the small Italian overseas empire. Well before its oil riches were known, it was conceived by the fascist regime as an important outlet for surplus populations and – despite the desert – for agricultural development. Beginning in 1926, as conflict with Britain and/or France loomed, there was a rapid buildup of military airfields and seaplane bases, greatly accelerated in the mid-1930s. A central air base at Castel Benito near Tripoli was supplemented by several others.(112) And as early as 1939, plans were made for deployment of German aircraft at Libyan air bases to aid the expected onslaught on British positions in Egypt.(113) This was one of only a few examples from this period of basing access being related to formal security alliances.

At the outset of the invasion of Ethiopia in 1935, Italy had several usable airfields and military garrisons in contiguous Somaliland and Eritrea, which formed the basis for its two-pronged assault. Massawa in Eritrea had been developed as a major naval base and port, which, along with Mogadiscio, provided entry points for shipments of war materiel and troops.(114) Britain actually declined to interrupt the Italian logistics line through Suez throughout the war.(115)

During and after the Ethiopian War, Italy greatly expanded its air base network in East Africa, so that by 1939 it comprised some twenty military airfields plus some additional emergency fields.(116) Although these bases (and Italy's deployed army units) flanked British positions in

Egypt and Sudan and also threatened nearby Aden, they quickly fell at the outset of World War II, being immediately and completely cut off from sources of supply from Italy.(117) Here again, British sea control and military preponderance overseas led inevitably to quick collapse of an antagonist's overseas positions which proved merely vulnerable hostages.

Otherwise, and in partnership with its German ally, Italy sought access to bases before World War II in Latin America and in areas flanking the Gibraltar Straits. Heavy arms sales throughout Latin America produced rumors about "secret" submarine and air bases and about long-range logistics networks to potentially friendly Brazil and Argentina, but nought was to come of it.(118) Closer to home, Italian aircraft operated out of the Balearic Islands during the Spanish Civil War, and some quiet access there may have been maintained during the early phases of World War II.(119)

The same was true for Spanish possessions in and offshore from North Africa; in the Canary Islands, Spanish Morocco, and Rio de Oro (in particular, during 1939-1940, Italian aircraft apparently utilized the Spanish base at Gando on Gran Canary Island).(120) British naval control over the region shortly negated these assets, and the Axis air forces quickly were driven from the area.

Concerning the nexus between arms transfers, alliances, and base acquisitions, it is noteworthy that Axis support of Franco Spain was an almost anomalous (in that interwar context) example of a big power translating military aid into strategic access, where a colonial relationship did not exist.

GERMANY'S INTERWAR BASING NETWORK

After its defeat in World War I, Germany was stripped of its few overseas possessions in Africa and the Pacific, and with them went its limited system of overseas strategic access. During World War I, Admiral Spee's squadron had made some use of Germany's Pacific island possessions, but as noted, British naval predominance had precluded significant German surface naval operations based upon overseas possessions.(121) After the war, Germany's previous begrudged sense of having been left behind in the race for overseas possessions and a global basing system was magnified, further fueling a vengeful irredentism.

Despite Tirpitz's vaunted, hurried ambitions for building a German surface fleet to challenge the Royal Navy, German naval strategy during World War I had been constrained to hit-and-run submarine and surface interdiction activities; that is, to a form of naval "guerilla warfare."(122) Though bereft of an overseas basing network to bolster its submarine capabilities, Germany did, however, make some apparent use of refueling points in Latin America, and also in Spain (allegedly using the Spanish submarine base at Mazarran).(123) Hence, it is not surprising that in the diplomacy preceding World War II (and with the comparative strength of the German surface fleet vis-a-vis Britain not substantially altered since 1918), Germany again concentrated on acquiring overseas bases or at least refueling facilities for its submarines and surface raiders(124) or interrupting lines of communication in the Atlantic.

The geographic realities of the distances between the major antagonists in Europe would not have produced extensive requirements for air bases outside of Germany (conquests at the beginning of the conflict did, however, provide additional forward bases for launching air assaults on Britain and the USSR.(125) Otherwise, German basing strategy seems to have concentrated on acquiring air bases from which to control the Gibraltar Straits, for possible assaults upon the Panama Canal and for long-range bombing and reconnaissance missions in the Atlantic to the north of the line running from West Africa to Brazil.

Germany, collaborating with Italy, gave decisive military support to the Nationalist side during the Spanish Civil War, in the forms of arms supplies, advisors, and small units of troops and aircraft.(126) Not surprisingly, a quid pro quo was expected, virtually demanded. Franco eventually declined to enter the war on the Axis side, which, among other things, forestalled an enhanced German threat to Gibraltar and an improved logistical line to Rommel's army in North Africa. Nonetheless, during 1939-1940, western intelligence reported German use of Spanish submarine facilities in an arc around the Gibraltar narrows; at Pasages, El Ferrol, Vigo, Marin, Rio de Oro, in the Canary Islands, and also at Portuguese-controlled Bissagos Island off the West African coast.(127) Further, German personnel were said to have upgraded the fortifications of Spanish military bases at Melilla, Ceuta, and Malaga, and to have installed artillery in Spanish Morocco covering the Gibraltar Straits.(128)

We have previously noted the penetration of Axis arms into South America during the late 1930s, in connection with waxing fascist political influence. Germany during this period supplied first-line combat aircraft to Brazil, Argentina, Chile, Uruguay, and other nations in the region. Also, during a period which saw little outright military grant aid, Berlin offered generous terms on arms sales, often government-to-government barter arrangements involving raw materials.

These growing connections, later thwarted by preemptive U.S. diplomacy, gave rise to reports of impending military access, particularly in Brazil. German commercial air and shipping lines were active there, and as early as 1934, a Zeppelin terminal was installed.(129) At least one German naval surface raider was reported operating out of Recife and Natal, and there were rumors of secret submarine bases.(130)

The prewar German quest for access both along the northwest African coast and in Brazil gave rise to severe British and American anxieties about potential German air and naval domination of the central Atlantic and of wide stretches of the main North Atlantic sealanes. German control of − or influence over − Spain and Portugal might have allowed for basing of aircraft in the Cape Verde, Canary, and Azores Islands, at Madeira, at Bissagos Island, and at Rio de

Oro.(131) There were also fears of German and/or Italian access to the island of Fernando Noronha, 100 miles east of Natal off the Brazilian coast.(132) Further, the Vichy France connection could have resulted in additional Axis access to Senegal, particularly the important French air and naval base at Dakar.(133)

At the then state of the art in bomber technology in the late 1930s, German and Italian aircraft (Heinkel-111, Junkers-88, Savoia-79, Breda-20) possessed ranges of around 2,000 miles with full bomb loads and up to 3,000 miles without bombs. These ranges were expected imminently to be extended by newer aircraft developments.(134) Although the ranges would not have allowed for combat operations in Brazil from West Africa or the Azores, they would have provided air coverage of a line from Newfoundland to French Guyana, across the narrowest part of the Atlantic which runs along a NW-SE axis. The spectre was temporarily a real one for western defense planners, who feared a German air assault on Atlantic shipping to supplement its submarine warfare, and a possible Axis military expedition to Brazil.

Western fears about German access to Spanish, Portuguese, and French facilities later proved greatly exaggerated, of course. Besides, the Axis did not then have the naval power to protect a line of communications to Latin America. Also, much of Germany's air strength had to be concentrated on the Russian front during the early part of the war, not to mention the Battle of Britain, leaving little to be allocated to missions further afield.(135) The threat, nevertheless, prodded the Americans and the British into efforts to control the Natal-Pernambuco area in Brazil, as well as to take preemptive control from Portugal of the Azores, Madeira, and Bissagos.(136)

Prewar German diplomacy did achieve some additional points of strategic military access. Alliances with Hungary, Bulgaria, and Romania allowed for some forward eastern deployments of aircraft vis-a-vis the USSR.(137) That with Italy allowed Germany to launch aerial assaults on British Middle Eastern positions from Libya and the Dodecanese Islands. German submarines reportedly operated sporadically out of Spanish bases at Las Palmas and Tenerife.(138) But attempts at extending the network of German bases failed.

One plan involving arms supplies to Bolivia in exchange for air bases never came to fruition.(139) German construction of airfields in Iran in the late 1930s resulted in stopping points for Lufthansa's Berlin-Kabul commercial route, but ultimately no military air bases from which to threaten the USSR or Britain's Middle East positions.(140) As it was, the reversal of the war's tides in 1942-1943, both in Russia and in North Africa, drove Germany to a close-in perimeter defensive strategy, one absent of hope for utilizing forward bases for offensive operations.

JAPAN'S INTERWAR BASING SYSTEM

Like Italy, late to empire, Japan emerged from World War I in a greatly strengthened position, having taken advantage of the power vacuum in the Far East created by the diversion of British attention, China's then seemingly endemic weakness and fragmentation, and Germany's inability to protect its distant Pacific empire. It had also flexed some long-range muscle in providing ships for the allied Western Mediterranean fleet, and in its postwar incursions into Siberia.

Japan's possession of Korea, Sakhalin, Formosa, the Bonins, Marcus Island, and Port Arthur had already provided some outlying points of access. To this was now added – at least potentially – the sprawling League-of-Nations-mandated island groups in the Marshalls, Carolines, and Marianas. The League mandate for these islands prohibited military bases and fortifications; these prohibitions were supposedly formally reinforced by the 1922 Washington Naval Agreement.(141)

Throughout the interwar period, Japan steadily increased its outlying system of bases; variously, by conquest, buildups in already controlled areas, and by gradual, stealthy fortification of the mandated islands. This expansionist thrust was omnidirectional, providing for both offensive and defensive contingencies in relation to the USSR, China, Southeast Asia, Australia, and the U.S. Hawaiian Islands.(142)

In China, the Japanese gradually expanded their access to strategic facilities, even during the 1920s amid the incredible confusion of China's multisided civil wars, well before the invasion of Manchuria.(143) Tsingtao was taken over from Germany in 1918, but was considered too near Japan to be immediately useful as a naval base. Port Arthur was treated likewise, and only in 1933 was it reestablished as a naval base. During the 1920s, Japan was, however, able to establish a communications net from Port Arthur to Korea through then Chinese-held Manchuria.(144) Some years later, use of the ports of Amoy and Swatow further south was achieved, in the case of the latter involving major drydock facilities. At a time China was a highly vulnerable and "penetrated" nation, there was also extensive multilateral naval access to port and repair facilities, particularly at Shanghai, which had French- and British-owned dockyards, but where Japanese and Soviet vessels were also stationed, repaired, and replenished.(145)

During the 1930s, of course, Japan's conquest first of Manchuria and then of large parts of China proper, provided the springboards for later operations further afield in China, Burma, Indo-China, and against the USSR in the unheralded but sizeable conflict in 1937-1939 along the Manchuria-Siberian frontier.   In connection with the latter, the Japanese by 1941 deployed some 500 combat aircraft at several bases in Manchuria.(146)

With future operations directed against Southeast Asia (including the Philippines) in mind, the Japanese made extensive efforts during the late 1930s at building air and naval facilities on Formosa and the Pescadores Islands, and then, after they were conquered in early 1941, on Hainan Island and the Spratly Islands in the South China Sea.

On Formosa, taken from China in 1895, Japan as early as 1921 possessed a major naval base, radio station, and large army garrisons. By 1941 there were some seventeen military air bases, emergency landing fields, and seaplane bases, providing a major springboard for subsequent operations against Indo-China and the Philippines.(147) Likewise, on the nearby Pescadores Islands, there were drydocks, coal yards, and a submarine mine depot, all geared to establishing control over the Formosa Straits.(148) Hainan, after its conquest, provided major naval ports, a base for eight submarines at Yu-Lin-Kong, anchorages, garrisons, and some ten air bases and seaplane facilities. It became the major springboard for operations against Indo-China.(149)

In 1941, preparatory to the final assault on Singapore, Malaya, and the Dutch East Indies, Japan easily captured French Indo-China, then temporarily controlled by Vichy forces after the fall of France. After some negotiating with Vichy, and in the face of U.S. and British warnings and economic reprisals, the Japanese immediately deployed naval and air forces to the former French bases there. There were several main air bases and seaplane stations, and the naval bases at Haiphong, Camranh Bay, and Saigon.(50) At Camranh in early 1941, Japan deployed seaplanes, flying boats, a battleship, and several gunboats and destroyers. Offshore, menacing the Philippines, a seaplane base and communications facilities were constructed on the main Spratly Island.(151)

Japanese basing diplomacy was also active during this period in Siam, where a pro-Japanese government had for years purchased large amounts of Japanese arms. There were reports as early as 1934 of Japanese use of Siam's naval bases. Later reduced to a virtual puppet state, it then availed the Japanese Air Force of bases in islands off its Indian Ocean coast, which would later be used for operations against Burma and the British-controlled Andaman Islands.(152)

In the Pacific, there were rumors as early as around 1921 of Japanese violations of the mandate provisions proscribing fortifications in the Marianas, Carolines, and Marshalls.(153) As an opening wedge, in a process of gradually escalating violations, communications facilities and fuel depots were apparently set up on several key islands, particularly at Wotje and Mortlock.(154) Later, by around 1933 (and with access to foreigners strictly limited and overhead intelligence very difficult), there were reported unmistakable warlike preparations, involving submarine bases, extensive port visits by large surface ships, and army garrisons.(155) There were also vague U.S. intelligence reports about "midget submarine" bases in the Marshalls and about plans to tow the submarines great distances with "tankers."(156)

By 1941, before the outbreak of World War II, Japan had constructed an elaborate system of Pacific bases. At Pelelieu in the Palaus, which flanked the Philippines, there was a 10,000-man garrison, advanced seaplane facilities, and a naval base capable of accommodating aircraft carriers.(157) There was an advanced submarine base at Truk (a fleet headquarters), and various air and naval facilities on Yap, Ponape, Jaluit, Bikini, Kusaie, Ulithi, and Saipan.(158) Wireless stations were established on at least seven islands.

Hence, by 1941, Japan had a very extensive network of strategic facilities extending in a vast arc through the Pacific, Southeast Asia, and along the East China Coast, as well as in Korea and Manchuria.

These facilities provided forward positions from which to launch sudden air and naval strikes against Hawaii, Wake, Guam, the Philippines, Singapore, and the Dutch East Indies; conversely, for extended defense-in-depth and surveillance-and-warning capability in all directions.

The oft-maligned Japanese preventive war strategy embodying the attack on Pearl Harbor seems to have been predicated on achieving an eventual standoff by maintaining defensive naval superiority within the web of Japanese island facilities in the Pacific, thus presenting the United States with the prospect of an unacceptably long and costly attrition war.(159) The strategy, of course, failed.

THE SOVIET INTERWAR BASING NETWORK

Russia acquired a vast, contiguous empire during the nineteenth century, but was virtually absent from the overseas race for empire. Its earlier possession of Alaska and the efforts of Russian explorers along the U.S. Pacific Coast did not finally prove to be enduring, a point later rued by Admiral Gorschkov, as noted.(160) Russian expansionist drives, in the absence of a first-class navy, were directed at colonizing and consolidating control over Siberia, Muslim Central Asia, and long-contested Turkic areas around the Black and Caspian seas.

What few points of strategic access the USSR achieved before World War II tended to be the result of diplomacy rather than conquest, in contrast to other major powers. Soviet merchant ships, along with others, used repair facilities at British-owned dockyards in Shanghai throughout most of the 1930s.(161) In 1936 there were reports of Soviet aircraft deployed in Czechoslovakia (causing considerable concern in neighboring Hungary), which were apparently later removed after the USSR was unable to organize a joint effort with France and the UK to preserve Czechoslovakia's independence.(162) In 1940 the Soviets were said to be using three forward airfields in Bulgaria, at a time still others there were apparently being used by the Germans.(163)

Further north, Soviet occupation of the three Baltic states after the Hitler-Stalin Pact resulted in the establishment there of army garrisons and forward naval and air bases, most notably with the occupation of naval and air bases on the Baltic islands of Estonia.(164) Soviet forward positions in Eastern Europe were, of course, quickly overrun by German Operation Barbarossa in 1941.

In Asia, the USSR made use of numerous land and air bases in Mongolia (then as now virtually a Soviet puppet state) during its war with Japan in 1937-1939, as well as in its related, then concurrent support to the Chinese Communists.(165) But some limited arms sales to Turkey, Afghanistan, and China were not associated with facility acquisitions, as such sales later would be after 1955 in many places.(166) At any rate, Soviet defense needs at that time (most crucially with respect to repelling German or Japanese invasions) did not require overseas bases.

OTHER NATIONS' INTERWAR BASING FACILITIES

Aside from the major and near-major powers previously discussed, the only others availed of overseas bases (in all cases through colonial possessions) were Belgium, Spain, Portugal, and (if Greenland is thus counted) Denmark. Belgium's position in the Congo and Spanish and Portuguese possessions in Africa did provide the metropole nations some overseas access. As each was bereft of significant naval or air power, and none saw the requirement for force projection outside territories they controlled, what was involved essentially were very limited force deployments in defense of the colonial status quo.

The primary military significance of these possessions lay in their potential for use as bases by other contending, larger powers, either by agreement or through takeover (with or without the fall of the mother country in Europe). Spanish and Portuguese possessions, as noted, became major bones of political contention — before and at the outset of World War II — between the Axis and Western powers. Spanish bases in Africa and in the Atlantic were apparently quietly used by the Germans, while Portuguese facilities in the Azores and in Portuguese Guinea were eventually taken over by western forces, its formal neutrality notwithstanding. Denmark's Faeroe Islands and Greenland were "commandeered" by the West after its fall in 1940, as was Belgium's Congo, which had military significance primarily in regard to its rich raw material resources.

THE RELATIONSHIP OF EPOCHAL CHARACTERISTICS AND BASING NETWORKS IN THE INTERWAR PERIOD

The characterization of discrete — though often fuzzily demarcated — diplomatic epochs by the use of "systems variables" is considered, by some, one of the more useful tools for broad-gauged theorizing in international relations. The approach was first undertaken in a comprehensive way by Morton Kaplan and Richard Rosecrance some years ago, and subsequently there have been further attempts at operationalizing or refining such frameworks with respect to specific eras or types of epochal diplomatic systems, on either a global or a more regional level. Some writers have attempted to analyze and compare such "systems" according to very broad and somewhat abstract criteria, such as the nature of boundaries or dominant types of interactions, while others have brought the analyses down to the more mundane and understandable level of alliance structures, polarity (bipolarity, multipolarity), reigning ideologies, rates of technological change, and others.

The possibilities are endless and much argued over, both with respect to identifying key systems variables and to the demarcation of time periods, over either longer or shorter periods. The extent to which actual empirical measurement is possible and to which causal relationships may be unearthed are also much argued.

Space limitations do not here permit a full analysis of how the basing networks of the interwar period might be said to have reflected the dominant systems characteristics of that period, or how, in a broader sense, the then prevailing nature of strategic access might itself have served to define or characterize that system. Yet, a few comments are in order concerning what, in a general way, stands out in observing the relationship between basing and access patterns, and some of the obvious, dominant characteristics of that period. They are particularly germane regarding system structure, polarity, alliances, the ideological loci of conflict, the state of military technology, and the practices of diplomacy as they were reflected in linkages between certain types of transactions (regimes?), including that of the granting of military access. Many of these points have been foreshadowed in the previous analysis.

The interwar period, in structural terms, may best have been described as a somewhat modified, asymmetric multipolar system, with the United States, the USSR, Japan, the UK-France combination, and the German-Italian duo being its five poles. That, at any rate, is what it evolved into during the latter part of the period.(167) As noted, however, there was very little correlation, as there would later be, between national power and the extent of global military access, the latter having primarily been determined by the then residual facts of colonial empire. The three perhaps strongest powers – United States, USSR and Germany – had very little in the way of overseas facilities.

Alliances during the interwar period were fluid and changing, certainly relative to the period after 1945, if not that before 1914. During the 1920s there was the progression of shifts through the Rapallo and Locarno periods, as Germany maneuvered to escape the shackles of Versailles and its pariah status through alternating tilts between east and west, at a time of considerable hostility between the USSR and Britain and France, and also U.S. isolationism. The brief close collaboration between Italy and the USSR in the early 1930s, the short-lived Stresa Front, the Franco-Soviet pact, and the Hitler-Stalin pact all bespoke a transitory shifting of alignments, with the consolidation of what were to become the World War II alliances occurring only on the very eve of the war.

The very nature of fluid, shifting, interwar alliances may have affected basing-access diplomacy to the extent that it helped to preclude any mutual long-term granting of facilities between alliance partners.(168) There was no real equivalent during that period to the long-term military cooperation, interspersion of forces, interoperability of equipment, and mutual use of facilities which would later become the hallmark of the NATO and Warsaw Pacts (the "Little Entente" was a partial exception to this), as well as of relationships between the postwar superpowers and their numerous allies and clients outside of Europe.(169) Italy's granting of air facilities to Germany in North Africa and the Dodecanese, cooperative German-Italian use of Spanish facilities in the late 1930s, and Britain's use of some Greek airfields seem to have been the only significant exceptions to this generalization, certainly regarding "permanent" long-term use.

And, as noted, the possession of colonial holdings by Britain, France, the United States, Japan, the Netherlands, and others made unnecessary the kind of basing diplomacy and associated payoffs which would also be hallmarks of postwar diplomacy. Still, even the rather long-term Anglo-French interwar alliance, and the then rather close relationship between the United States and the UK, saw very little mutual granting or use of military access, at least until war appeared imminent. At least up to the late 1930s, the absence of rigid ideological lines (the matter of the Soviet-West division aside) seems to have further reinforced these trends.

The facts of colonial control over much of what is now called the Third World had one additional, perhaps ironic, result. As Stephen Roberts has noted, this period saw a contraction of the field of activity for "station fleets." "For as European colonial administrations spread over all of Africa and much of Asia, the seagoing station fleets were no longer needed in these areas to keep order."(170) He goes on to point out that China and Latin America were exceptions where station fleets continued to be maintained. Imputed here is a perception by the major colonial powers (in contrast to earlier experiences) that the likelihood of conflict between them in colonial areas was low, in addition to a perception of the unlikelihood of anticolonial revolts or, at least, the irrelevance of naval forces to their suppression if needed.

In part, what was crucial here was the considerable optimism for over a decade after 1919 about what was thought to be the absence of imminency of major war. While after 1945, the almost immediate onset of the Cold War and its associated rigid bipolar alignments gave rise to tight and structured alliances (and hence to forward garrisoning and use of bases by the United States and USSR), there was no real equivalent to that after 1919, aside from the desultory joint preventive preparations by France, Poland, and Czechoslovakia to forestall a German resurgence.

Besides, the interwar period retained remnants of the nineteenth century's diplomatic casualness, its aristocratic diplomatic "norms," so that the kind of "total war" and "total diplomacy" which was later to be practiced after 1945 did not really then exist.(171) The major powers, during a period of only lazy arms-racing (really crawling) up to the 1930s, seem not to have exerted themselves toward acquiring bases beyond what was provided them by colonial possessions.

As also evidenced in arms trading practices, interwar diplomacy retained a residual "private" quality, reflecting the continuing hold of nineteenth-century laissez-faire practices with their philosophical underpinnings in Adam Smith.(172) Much less could then have been explained by direct government-to-government dealings. Commercial airlines and shipbuilding companies vied for overseas access, in a manner somewhat divorced from the prevailing lines of alliance politics, just as prior to 1914, crucial underseas cable communications were privately built and operated. As a result, access to foreign ship repair facilities and even the use of airports by military aircraft up to the 1930s seem largely to have been determined by essentially private and commercial transactions, all of which provide somewhat of an odd twist to the current literature which trumpets a growing "trans-nationalism."

The spatial (distance) relationships between the then contending great powers – in conjunction with prevailing capabilities of military technology – also played a role in determining basing and access strategies. Britain and France were close enough to Germany (and vice versa) so that forward bases in other countries for strategic deterrence by bombers were not crucially required, although fighter coverage for bombers was, in the British-German pairing, more dependent on such bases.(173) Likewise, that was also the case concerning reciprocal German and Soviet contingency planning, though on the eve of their war they would contend for access to forward positions in Eastern Europe, the Baltic, and in Finland (more significantly related to ground buffers than air bases).

There was no real equivalent to the later race between the United States and USSR for bases around the distant foe's periphery to enable or assist strategic deterrence. The then retarded state of offshore electronics intelligence capability also precluded jockeying for access in areas adjacent to rivals for that purpose. Japan's efforts at extending its basing facilities eastward toward Hawaii were perhaps the one exception where access for strategic deterrence (or offensive strategic capability) was sought in connection with an expected war with another power. That capability related primarily to the major U.S. facilities in Hawaii.

Somewhat of an irony intrudes here. Whereas during the interwar period the ranges of strategic aircraft were much shorter than they would later be (even by 1940, round-trip bomber ranges were around 1,500-2,000 miles; combat radii, half of that, depending upon bombload and flight profile), and aerial refueling still nonexistent, the range requirements were in some cases far less stringent.(174) And then, there was no need for overseas submarine bases for strategic deterrence or compellence. During the very recent period, of course, the kind of critical requirement for overseas strategic bomber and missile bases which existed in the 1950s and 1960s has now greatly evaporated. Generally, however, it should be recalled that strategic deterrence played a less crucial, though still important, role in interwar military considerations, British fears during the 1930s about the poten-tially decisive role of strategic air bombardment notwithstanding.(175)

One other point bears mention here in connection with the then state of military technology. Both air forces and navies during the interwar period were much larger – that is, numerous – than today, as measured narrowly by discrete numbers of aircraft and ships. The major powers had thousands of first-line aircraft, and even modest powers such as Poland, Romania, and Argentina had close to a thousand. The same obtained for navies, where as measured by numbers of ships, the British navy was then far "larger" than any present naval force (the Dutch fleets of the seventeenth century were also "larger").(176) Of course, ships and planes were then considerably cheaper, even discounting for the high rate of inflation since (a first-line fighter aircraft in the 1930s cost some $20,000), and as time went on, more and more capability was built into fewer and fewer systems, which in turn had much shorter production runs as the pace of technological change quickened.

One result, however, of the then far greater number of systems, was the requirement for far more numerous bases and for greater dispersion of them. Whereas today the United States is sufficed by only a small handful of major air bases in Germany and in the Far East, the Japanese in the 1930s and 1940s had many more numerous air bases in Formosa, on Hainan, and elsewhere, as did the Italians in East Africa to accommodate large numbers of planes.(177) These factors, which were evidenced uniformly among the major powers (and in combination with range and other logistics criteria), obviously dictated requirements for more extensive basing systems than are utilized nowadays, and for access in greater numbers of overseas nations. That this was not evidenced as a very crucial problem for competitive big-power diplomacy was, again, largely a function of the then prevailing facts of overseas colonial control.

RAW MATERIALS ACCESS AND STRATEGY DURING THE INTERWAR PERIOD

As Geoffrey Kemp aptly pointed out in one recent article, "history is full of examples of the relationship between military strategy and the need for resources, and for routes and logistical systems necessary for their transportation."(178) He proceeded on in this vein to note such diverse historical examples as Rome's need for Egypt's granaries; Spain's necessity for protecting supply lines from its South American gold and silver mines against British depredations; and the Vikings' search for markets and resources across the North Atlantic, which is said to have resulted in their development of "a blue-water navy to patrol the sea-lanes of empire." Overseas bases were presumably important in connection with each of these, and many similar, situations.

In the interwar period, virtually all of the major powers (with the USSR one possible exception) labored under fears of raw materials shortages or cutoffs in the event of war. The connection with basing and access strategies, however, particularly in comparison with the present, is a bit difficult to pin down.

Probably the most telling point here, but one which must be made with some caution, is that the interwar powers (though in varying degrees among them) perceived the nexus between resource acquisition and basing access almost wholly in terms of the contingency for full-scale warfare. Germany remembered the partially successful allied blockade of World War I (as well as its own only partially successful attempt at cutting off supplies to Britain).(179) Hence, it strove for autarky in food and raw materials, emphasized lebensraum and the drang nach osten (the latter in particular in connection to granaries) and sought bases near the Gibraltar exit from the Mediterranean in preparation for a war of economic attrition with the UK.(180) Chilean nitrates, oil, and tungsten were particularly noticeable and enunciated items of German prewar concern, each deemed vital for the conduct of war.(181)

Britain and France, meanwhile, in contemplating another global struggle, sought to maintain basing networks which would allow for maintenance of the flow of oil and other raw materials from overseas colonies and client states, and which also would allow for rapid occupation of Axis overseas bases which menaced their supply lines. The United States, as for long past, relied on Britain's navy and bases to keep open many of its sources of raw materials, but where much less ominous overall dependence at any rate existed (the primary exceptions were natural rubber, tin, and tungsten from Asia and some metals gotten from Africa).

Although raw materials cutoffs during wartime were a real and seriously considered spectre for each of the major powers, such denial during peacetime — or even the threat of denial — was not nearly as crucial an item of calculation as it would become in the 1970s. There was no OPEC, no North-South division between developed and developing states, with its accompanying overtones of economic warfare, and the term "new world order" had then an entirely different (at least geographic) connotation.

That is not to say that economic warfare during peacetime was entirely absent. Britain's initiation of an imperial preference system after the onset of the Great Depression was in fact precisely so interpreted by the USSR with respect to its timber and other exports.(182) And the situation of blocked currencies and inconvertibility which developed during the early 1930s, along with extensive competitive devaluations and other "beggar thy neighbor" policies, also had overtones of political/economic warfare in some instances. There were also extensive cartel formations in that period — involving industrial as well as mineral products — which were essentially divorced from big-power diplomacy; indeed, the cartels were often comprised of firms spanning the divides of big-power political rivalries.(183)

Generally speaking, however, there were few fears about cutoffs of raw materials from the colonial areas.(184) The raw materials sources were controlled by large corporations which operated in great freedom from home political control, but which were well protected in colonial areas, and they were almost always available to anyone who could pay the going price. Laissez-faire still prevailed here as in other economic domains.

Finally, the whole question of resource shortages and attendant potential economic warfare was then perceived in a somewhat narrower way than it is today. Food supply was never mentioned as a possible item of political warfare. Fisheries were not thought of as on the way to depletion, and there were no calls for extensions of offshore "economic zones." Underwater recovery of minerals and transporting of water from Antarctica were as yet undreamed of. There were no perceived military contingencies equivalent to the present ones involving protection of sea lanes during peacetime around the Cape or through the straits leading from the Persian Gulf. And, of course, there were no questions about subnuclear wars to be fought over resources, beneath the umbrella of a nuclear balance; any serious attempt at interdicting sea lane logistics would have been considered a <u>casus bellus</u>, but without the spectre of immediate escalation to a holocaust.

The one significant exception to the foregoing involved Japan, which began its expansionist drive during the early 1930s in part because of its desire to achieve control over raw materials sources, and which then became the object of threats and some actions directed against its raw materials sources (a classic example of a self-fulfilling prophecy). For whatever reason, the Japanese seem to have been obsessed during the interwar period with the need for a "southward advance" and for control of the raw materials of Southeast Asia (though this was in parallel with a "continental" policy which seems to have been inspired mainly by the desire to stop the march of Communism). From the Japanese perspective, though, the South Seas and Southeast Asia were crucial. The South Seas contained most of the world's hemp and gum supplies, as well as sources of sugar, tobacco, and tea deemed "vital" by the Japanese.(185) They then got much of their petroleum from Borneo and eyed other potential nearby sources in Java, Sumatra, and Sarawak. Coal, iron, copra, and pepper, as well as sugar, tea, and coffee, all were primarily obtained from the Dutch East Indies. And there were the crucial sources of rubber and tin in Malaya. During the 1920s and 1930s, Japan made a strenuous and integrated effort at extending its access to these areas, which involved coordinated policies on shipping lines, development of airlines, a government-sponsored fuel policy, and the utilization of a South Seas Development Company.(186)

Japanese economic expansionism in what later came to be deemed its "Asian Co-prosperity Sphere" did finally provoke gradual economic reprisals, beginning after its much-criticized invasion of Manchuria and heightened after its withdrawal from the League in 1935. In 1936 the Dutch (despite the facts of then existing joint Dutch-Japanese investment projects in iron ore, rubber, and petroleum) placed restrictions on shipments of iron ore to Japan. Later, after Holland was overrun by Germany, the remnant Dutch East Indies regime was to apply a total cutoff, in part because it wished to block retransfer of its iron ore to Germany via Japan. And then, after the Japanese invasion of Indo-China in 1941, there was also the U.S. embargo on oil and scrap iron. In a climate of escalating threats and reprisals, Japan actually justified its invasion of Indo-China — and its occupation there of French air and naval bases — as "defensive" in character, aimed at preventing British and U.S. influence from shutting off supplies of rubber, tin, and rice from Thailand as well as Indo-China.(187)

As noted, however, the Japanese case was the exception. And even here, one cannot really speak of a nexus between bases, political "presence," and raw materials in an entirely peaceful context. Although

Japan was not formally at war with rival powers during the late 1930s, its aggression against neighboring states and its clearly signaled intentions to expand — by war if necessary — produced the threats and reality of raw materials cutoffs in a climate of impending full-scale war.

ARMS TRANSFERS AND BASES DURING
THE INTERWAR PERIOD

As previously noted, the arms trade of the interwar period was somewhat of an atavistic remnant of nineteenth-century laissez-faire practices, with arms having normally been traded by private corporations almost outside of — and often in contradiction to — the prevailing lines of alliances and ideological ties. Numerous nations in the 1930s — including virtually all of the independent states of Latin America, the Middle East, and also Eastern Europe and Scandinavia — received arms supplies simultaneously from both Western and Axis (or sometimes Soviet) sources.(188) Germany sold arms to many of its imminent victims in Europe right up to the eve of the war, while the United States and Britain sold arms to Germany and Japan until very late in the 1930s. By and large, arms supplies were not utilized as a purposeful instrument of diplomatic leverage. Further, gratis arms aid (and also economic aid) was virtually nonexistent from any source.(189) Nor were there any visible trade-offs between arms aid and base rentals.

There were indeed very few instances during this period where base rights were acquired outside the realm of colonial possessions, protectorates, or league mandates. The exceptions, at least some attempts at utilizing such a nexus, were in Latin America. There, during the late 1930s, Germany, Italy, and Japan all appear to have offered arms — under governmental direction — in connection with possible military access rights, as well as with raw materials barter arrangements, investments, tariff reductions, and commercial airline concessions.(190) For the most part, this early "linkage" diplomacy appears utterly to have failed, though it did create sufficient anxieties in the United States to impel counteroffers of arms supplies, albeit in conjunction with veiled threats of reprisals if military access to the Axis was actually granted.

The linked diplomacy involving government-controlled arms aid and base acquisitions in Latin America during the 1930s proved to be a precursor of what was to become the very hallmark of big power diplomacy in the developing areas after World War II, and much more so by the late 1970s. That such practices evolved in Latin America at the very outset of the period in which arms transfers would be used as a purposeful instrument of diplomacy is not surprising. The Latin American republics comprised, of course, the bulk of those areas of the then developing world where full sovereignty existed. There was also Japan's linking of arms aid and bases in Siam at a time the latter almost alone among the smaller nations of Asia maintained some degree of formal independent sovereignty.

SURROGATE WARS AND ARMS STAGING IN THE
INTERWAR PERIOD

In the contemporary period, one of the more crucial aspects of access rights has to do with air and naval staging facilities and overflight rights in connection with the major powers' arms resupplies to client states during small-state "surrogate" wars. Actually, such access may also be at issue even in the absence of armed conflict, but these matters become most urgent and crucial during crises such as those in the Middle East in 1973 and later on in Angola and in the Horn of Africa. It is now de rigeur for nations to deny such access where a major power is attempting to ship arms to a rival or enemy state during a crisis. And, as the events of 1973 proved, even a superpower cannot rely on its alliance partners to provide access during a crisis, if the resupply of an attacked small nation were to result in oil cutoffs or other forms of economic reprisal.

During the interwar period, which saw several "peripheral" conflicts in Eastern Europe, the Far East, Africa, and Latin America, no such impasses over access for staging purposes seem to have occurred. There appear to have been no denials of access for staging arms – on either side – during the conflicts in Poland, Manchuria, the Gran Chaco, Ethiopia, or Spain, though in the latter case there were some interruptions of naval resupply from major powers by both sides in the waters around Spain. The reasons appear to have involved a mixture of then prevailing diplomatic norms, the then "private" nature of the arms trade, the geographical specifics of the locales of conflicts, and again, the impact of the facts of colonial control. Further, the world was not then so rigidly divided between bipolar blocs of nations, which in later times would serve to determine who would be allowed what kinds of access along logistics routes running from arms suppliers to clients engaged in smaller wars. Small powers were not in a position to threaten economic warfare against larger ones if the latter shipped arms to rivals.

As it is, air transport of war materiel was, even in the late 1930s, a very underdeveloped technology, as the carrying capacities and ranges of then state-of-the-art transport aircraft (such as the U.S. DC-3) were but shadows of what they would be a few decades later. Arms supplies, including resupply of equipment, ammunition, and spare parts, were almost entirely carried by ship, and air overflight rights were not, therefore, seriously at issue.(191) As neither side of a conflict pairing might rely on aerial resupply, neither could be relatively disadvantaged, and there was not the kind of hair-trigger-like competitive resupply effort as during the 1973 war. The fact that Britain allowed Italian ships to traverse Suez amid the Italo-Ethiopian War – despite nominal British adherence to the League arms embargo against Italy – bespeaks the extent to which then prevailing diplomatic norms about free transit were adhered to.

As noted, at least up until the very eve of World War II (and with the partial exceptions of the USSR and of the Axis powers late in the period), the arms trade was primarily a private albeit often transnational enterprise, with respect to decisions on the destinations and quantities of arms. Periodic embargoes in extremis and the U.S. attempt at "quarantining" aggressors constituted only minor exceptions and interruptions to the rule. These practices were clearly related to those of the reluctance of nations to refuse overflight rights or to deny air and naval refueling access in connection with arms staging, either with or without ongoing conflict. Besides, in some conflicts (though not all – Spain was an exception) the same private arms traders were selling to both sides, most notably in the cases of the Chinese civil wars of the 1920s, the later Chinese-Japanese War, the Chaco conflict, and even the Russo-Japanese War of the late 1930s. All in all, one of the major issues of present access and basing strategy was virtually absent before World War II.

SUMMARY

Basing systems and military access were, during the interwar period, overwhelmingly a function of colonial control. As some of the really major military powers – the United States, USSR, and Germany – were virtually bereft of overseas empires, while others such as Britain and France had extensive empires, there was little correlation at the big-power level between national and military power on the one hand, and access to overseas facilities on the other.

The fluidity of diplomatic alliances during the period, and the relative absence of an ideological basis for those alignments, resulted in a dearth of long-term, sustained security arrangements (Britain and France were long aligned, but with only minimal joint military coordination) comparable to those of the later NATO and Warsaw Pact alliances. Concomitantly, there were few instances of permanent "forward" garrisoning in preparation for war or the reciprocal allied use of basing facilities.

The sort of competitive global basing diplomacy engaged in at present, primarily by the United States and USSR – hinged upon ideological clientships and military and economic aid – simply did not exist to remotely the same degree in the interwar period. For that matter, gratis military and economic aid was then a virtually non-existent instrument of diplomacy. And in the absence of a global ideological struggle at the contemporary level of intensity (most small "nations" were colonial possessions), few dependent nations would then have perceived a foreign base presence as a credible deterrent to aggression or subversion. There were fears of raw materials cutoffs, but only in the event of full-scale war. There were few facsimiles of the panoply of modern basing and access strategies, which now crucially involve arms support to client states with or without wars, naval access for symbolic and intimidation purposes (though port visits were routine), and positioning for the event of less-than-major wars beneath the umbrella of a potential Armageddon. With the immediate advent of the

Cold War after 1945, all of this was to change in a major way, and the changes would accelerate up to the present.

NOTES

(1) According to C.R. Boxer, The Portuguese Seaborne Empire (New York: Knopf, 1969), p. 51,

> The most striking feature of the Portuguese seaborne empire, as it was established by the mid-sixteenth century, was its extreme dispersion. In the East it was represented by a chain of forts and factories, extending from Sofala and Ormuz on the western side of Monsoon Asia to the Moluccas and Macao (in 1557) on the edge of the Pacific. On the other side of the world it was equally extended with a few strongholds in Morocco (Ceuta, Tangier, Mazagao), with some feitorias and a few forts between Cape Verde and Luanda (in 1575) on the west coast of Africa, with the islands in the Gulf of Guinea, and with some struggling settlements along the Brazilian littoral.

He also points out, however, Portugal's failure to achieve a stronghold at the entrance to the Red Sea, either at Aden or Socotra.

(2) Immanuel Wallerstein, The Modern World System (New York: Academic Press, 1974), pp. 328-329. And, as Boxer (quoted by Wallerstein) notes, "Fortunately for the Portuguese, at the time of their appearance in Asian waters the empires of Egypt, Persia, and Vijayanagar had no armed shipping in the Indian Ocean, if indeed they possessed any ships at all, and Chinese ships were officially confined to navigation along the China coast by imperial decree" (The Portuguese Seaborne Empire note 127, p. 329). Elsewhere (p. 44), Boxer notes Portugal's superiority in naval warships relative to those of the Arab, Gujerati and other Moslem ships which dominated the trade of the Indian Ocean but which had no artillery nor iron construction.

(3) See George Modelski, "The Theory of Long Cycles" in R. Harkavy and E. Kolodziej, American Security Policy and Policy Making (Lexington, Mass.: D.C. Heath, 1980), pp. 14-16, for a comparison of the "imperial model" and the "oceanic model," respectively, involving territorial domination vs. trade and scattered points of access.

(4) See Boxer, Portuguese Seaborne Empire, p. 49, who notes that "Goa was the only Portuguese port in Asia with adequate dockyard facilities."

(5) See Gerald Graham, The Politics of Naval Supremacy (Cambridge: Cambridge University Press, 1965), pp. 38-39.

(6) Thus, according to ibid., p. 39, "The Cape . . . was a useful inter-mediary base in the old days, but with the introduction of coppered bottoms, Indiamen, like men-of-war, had less need to refit on a voyage to India. It had become no more than a 'pleasant' tavern on the passage which often delayed an ordinarily quick through-passage."

(7) For a full analysis, parallel to that for the antecedent Portuguese seaborne empire, see C.R. Boxer, The Dutch Seaborne Empire: 1600-1800 (New York: Knopf, 1965).

(8) See ibid., chap. 1 ("The Eighty Years War and the Evolution of a Nation") and chap. 4 ("Mare Liberum and Mare Clausum"). On pp. 14-15, there is a useful map depicting the Dutch system of global basing access.

(9) Ibid., p. 69.

(10) Ibid., p. 94.

(11) See Paul M. Kennedy, The Rise and Fall of British Naval Mastery (New York: Scribner's, 1976), p. 154; and Graham, Politics of Naval Supremacy, chaps. 1, 2, 3.

(12) See Graham, Politics of Naval Supremacy, p. 112; and Herbert Rosinski, The Development of Naval Thought (Newport, R.I.: Naval War College Press, 1977), pp. 1-19.

(13) Graham, Politics of Naval Supremacy, p. 69, notes that British power in the Mediterranean had been exercised during much of the eighteenth century from Minorca.

(14) Kennedy, Rise and Fall, pp. 86-7.

(15) For good reviews of the British global basing network developed at the zenith of Pax Britannica, see Brig. D.H. Cole, Imperial Military Geography, 12th ed. (London: Sifton Praed, 1956); and Kennedy, Rise and Fall, esp. pp. 154-157. The latter discusses British basing strategy as follows:

> Thus in 1819 Singapore, controlling the main entrance into the China Sea from the west, was taken over; in 1833, the bleak Falkland Islands which overlooked the route around Cape Horn; in 1839 Aden, guarding the southern entrance into the Red Sea; in 1841 Hong Kong, soon to become a great trading port. Further bases, Lagos, Fiji, Cyprus, Alexandria, Mombasa, Zanzibar, and Wei-hai-wei, were acquired later in the century, though possibly none were so important as the earlier ones. In all cases, though, the supremacy of the Royal Navy and the expansion of British commerce made the acquisition of these strategic points both

easy and desirable, while their very possession reinforced this supremacy and furthered the opportunities for economic growth; once again, the mutually-supporting triangle of trade, colonies and navy had worked to Britain's benefit.

Most of these bases were carefully selected for overwhelmingly maritime reasons, even the later ones: Cyprus and Wei-hai-wei were taken to check Russia, for example, while Lagos and Zanzibar were used for the squadrons respectively patrolling the West and East African coasts. There was, in all of this, little sign of what has been called "reluctant imperialism," nor was there any significant "absence of mind" in their acquisition. As such, the bases stood in contrast to the other, more "continental"-style extensions of Crown territory in the half century or so after Waterloo: large parts of India, Canada to the west of the Great Lakes, the vast hinterland behind Cape Town, the unexplored regions of Australia and New Zealand.

(16) See, inter alia, P.M. Kennedy, Rise and Fall, chap. 8. For greater detail, see inter alia, Raymond Sontag, Germany and England: Background of Conflict, 1848-1894 (New York: Russell and Russell, 1964), esp. chaps. 6 and 7, for discussion of German naval and colonial policies at the time of Bismarck, in the context of strategic trade-offs between European and overseas considerations. For a good discussion of later German naval policy and German-British naval rivalry around and after the turn of the century, see V.R. Berglahn, Germany and the Approach of War in 1914 (New York: St. Martin's Press, 1973), esp. chap. 2 ("Tirpitz's Grand Design") and chap. 3 ("The Anglo-German Naval Arms Race").

(17) See the relationship between basing requirements and the transition in the nineteenth century to coal-fired ships as discussed in Bernard Brodie, Sea Power in the Machine Age (Princeton, N.J.: Princeton University Press, 1941), pp. 115-198. The overall impact was seen as mixed. Thus, on p. 30:

Steam increased the degree of control exerted by a superior fleet in the ocean surrounding its base, and even widened the area subject to its immediate intervention, but in introducing dependence upon fuel, it isolated that area regionally to a degree that had not previously been obtained. Whereas under sail the nation with the greatest navy could make its superiority felt practically anywhere in the world, under steam it can do so only within "range" of bases of major proportions.

See also Kemp and Maurer, The Logistics of Pax Britannica, pp. 17-19.

(18) S.G. Gorschkov, The Sea Power of the State (Annapolis, Md.: U.S. Naval Institute Press, 1979), pp. 91-92.

(19) See Herbert Rosinski, The Development of Naval Thought (Newport, R.I.: Naval War College Press, 1977), pp. 10-14.

(20) See Kennedy, "Imperial Cable Communications and Strategy"; and the comments thereon by Kemp and Maurer, The Logistics of Pax Britannica, pp. 21-22. See also Brig. D.H. Cole, Imperial Military Geography, chap. 12, entitled "Cables and Wireless," who indicates that the really crucial British cable bottlenecks were at Porthcurno (UK), Gibraltar, Malta, Alexandria, Pt. Said, Aden, Seychelles, Mauritius, Singapore, Fayal (Azores), St. Vincent (Cape Verde), Ascension, Barbados, and Newfoundland (Avalon Peninsula).

(21) Kennedy, Rise and Fall, p. 731.

(22) Ibid., p. 740.

(23) Ibid., p. 748.

(24) Ibid., p. 749. See also John M. Carroll, Secrets of Electronic Espionage (New York: E.P. Dutton, 1966), pp. 19-21, who notes the Germans' chain of powerful global radio stations hinged on a powerful transmitter at Nauen near Berlin, and key stations at Kamina in Togo, and Windhoek in S.W. Africa. Prior to World War I, the Germans apparently also utilized radio stations in New Jersey and Long Island, in anticipation of British cutting of submarine cables.

(25) Kennedy, Rise and Fall, p. 740.

(26) Ibid., p. 751.

(27) Ibid., p. 752. On the early warning capability developed by the United States through its Midas satellite program, see Klass, Soviet Sentries in Space, chap. 18.

(28) See Rosinski, Development of Naval Thought, p. 81. who notes that

from the outset the sorties of the High Sea Fleet which the German Admirals began to initiate, and gradually to expand, suffered from the hopeless inner contradiction of seeking to bring their opponent to battle, yet having to dread nothing more than to run into his whole force; with the result that between the devil and the deep sea, they found themselves reduced to the desperate expedient of having to seek somehow, by bombardments of British East Coast towns, or by feints against the trade route running through the Skaggerak, to lure part of his forces into a trap.

(29) Michael Howard, The Continental Commitment (London: Temple, Smith, 1972), p. 59; Kennedy, Rise and Fall, pp. 252-3.

(30) See Kennedy, Rise and Fall, pp. 306-12, regarding the blockade strategy vs. Germany, and who notes that Britain too experienced shortages of raw materials because of Japan's conquest of Far Eastern sources and the German "counterblockade" by U-boats.

(31) See Military Intelligence Division 2280-H-3, which notes British use of a wire station at Carrito in Uruguay, said alone among Latin American countries to allow such a thing. It was part of a communications system linking the Admiralty, the British South Atlantic Fleet, and the British naval base in the Falklands.

(32) MID 2266-E-4.

(33) See MID 6370-345, which also reports that the United States considered establishing a naval base on the Gulf of Fonseca in 1917 to forestall German military penetration.

(34) See MID 1766-R-22A, 2082-980, 2538-25, and 2319-206. The latter discusses the possibility perceived in 1941 of German air bases in Ecuador and in its Galapagos Islands.

(35) Regarding British and U.S. access to the Ponta Delgado base in the Azores toward the close of World War II, see MID 2068-27, which discusses Portugal's unhappiness with the prospect of a postwar British Azores base and its suggestion of Madeira as an alternative.

(36) This concept, now commonly used to refer to the zenith of an imperial or hegemonic nation's power and prestige, is elaborated upon in Robert Gilpin, U.S. Power and the Multinational Corporation (New York: Basic Books, 1975), pp. 88-97 (for Britain), and pp. 189-197 (for the United States).

(37) See, in this regard, the discussions of Tirpitz's "risk theory" in Rosinski, Development of Naval Thought, pp. 54-55; and Leonard Wainstein, "The Dreadnought Gap," in Robert Art and Kenneth Waltz, eds., The Use of Force (Boston: Little, Brown, 1971), pp. 153-169. For the impact of World War I on military technology, see Bernard Brodie, Sea Power in the Machine Age (Princeton, N.J.: Princeton University Press, 1941), pp. 248-251, 379-383.

(38) See Rosinski, Development of Naval Thought, chap. 4.

(39) This is discussed in detail in MID 2075-57 and in 265-T-398, wherein is noted the British desire not to see any other nation's naval bases en route from the Mediterranean to India, which required British control over Palestine and a protectorate over Egypt, and restriction of France to a weak presence in Lebanon. The British are here indicated as uneasy over the French presence in Syria under the League Mandate.

(40) See MID 2667-14, which discusses Conservative resistance to Labor Party proposals for closing British bases in the Western hemisphere in 1930. The discussion was related to the then recently consummated Kellogg-Briand Pact intended to "outlaw" war, in which context the Labor government considered dismantling the British naval base at Kingston as a "goodwill gesture."

(41) For instance, MID 2667-H-58 discusses Japanese seaplane facilities' requirements in the Palaus and on Saipan; 2081-1380 discusses a network of French seaplane stations in Indo-China; 272-61 refers to pre-World War II U.S. contingency planning for the use of seaplane facilities for Sikorsky flying boats; 2081-1061 discusses German access in Brazil to a facility for its dirigibles. In 1941, according to 2840-1, the United States was very interested in a flying boat base under construction at Jui in Liberia as a staging point between northeast Brazil and East Africa.
   For a more complete analysis of the basing requirements for airships during the interwar period, crucially involving large mooring masts, see Basil Collier, The Airship: A History (New York: Putnam, 1974). Airships were heavily used in World War I for bombing, ASW, even for transport of arms (the Germans tried thusly during the war to ferry arms to Eire). Collier, pp. 202-203, notes a British mooring mast network en route to Karachi, using facilities at Ismailia, Baghdad, Basra, Athens, and Malta.

(42) MID 2083-1403 and 2714-5.

(43) MID 265-261.

(44) Ibid.

(45) Ibid. Further regarding British interwar basing policies in the Pacific and Indian Ocean areas, see Stephen Roskill, Naval Policy Between the Wars, vol. 1, 1919-1929 (New York: Walker & Co., 1969), chap. 7.

(46) MID 2083-1610.

(47) MID 265-261.

(48) MID 2083-1702.

(49) See MID-2083 for information on the RAF station at Ramleh in Palestine.

(50) During the 1930s, as noted in Harkavy, The Arms Trade and International Systems (Cambridge, Mass.: Ballinger, 1975), p. 153, Greece was producing on license the Atlas Reconnaissance, Avro 626, Avro Tutor, and Blackburn Velos aircraft. See also MID 2017-1270 regarding British use of Greek facilities.

(51) MID 2083-1448, 2083-1573, and 2667-14. Kingston then had considerable naval repair capability; Halifax also had extensive drydocking capability.

(52) MID 2667-14.

(53) MID 2657-122 lists Prince Rupert as well as Esquimalt as a British facility on the western coast of Canada.

(54) See MID-2017-1270/44 regarding British facilities at Freetown; 2083-1731 on British air bases in W. Africa; and 2086-738 regarding British bases in East Africa.

(55) See MID 2667-ZZ-30, 2657-J-27, 2535-28, and 242-96 regarding the Azores facilities. For more extensive detail regarding British and American activities directed at acquiring access to facilities in the Azores in the early phases of World War II, see Kenneth G. Weiss, "The Azores in Diplomacy and Strategy, 1940-1945", Professional Paper 272 (Alexandria, Va.: Center for Naval Analyses, March 1980).

(56) See MID 2840-1 and 183-69 regarding Bolama in Portuguese Guinea.

(57) See MID 2351-272 and 272-61 for a discussion of French bases in the Caribbean area at the outset of World War II – i.e., Martinique, Guadeloupe, and French Guyana.

(58) See Samuel Huntington, "Arms Races: Prerequisites and Results," in Art and Waltz, Use of Force, pp. 365-401, who discusses the Anglo-French naval race between 1840 and 1866, and one pitting England vs. France and Russia from 1884 to 1904.

(59) MID 265-261.

(60) Ibid.

(61) MID 2081-1380, 2714-4, and 2081-1273.

(62) MID 265-261 and 183-167.

(63) MID 2351-7.

(64) See MID 2081-1062 and 2610-E-66 regarding development of air bases at Bizerte and Tunis.

(65) MID 2083-1731, 2081-193, and 2081-1352.

(66) MID 2081/1352.

(67) MID 2084-30.

(68) MID 183-354 and 2657-298.

(69) MID 2657-281.

(70) MID 2087-152 and 2087-207.

(71) MID 2657-81, 2652-298, 2087-211, and 265-261.

(72) See George A. Weller, Bases Overseas: An American Trusteeship in Power (New York: Harcourt, Brace, 1944); and Hans Weigert, "Strategic Bases," in H. Weigert, V. Stefansson, and R. Harrison, eds., New Compass of the World (New York: Macmillan, 1949), pp. 219-237.

(73) MID 2068-136 and 2068-27.

(74) MID 2065-79.

(75) MID 10674-37, 10987-298, and 6370-345. These report on rumors that the Germans were buying up coffee plantations and other such assets in Central America to be used for clandestine military purposes.

(76) MID 2017-1009. Howard, in Continental Commitment, pp. 29-30, notes earlier decisions, in 1902 and 1907, which were precedental in terms of the British Atlantic bases.

(77) See Richard Millett, "The State Department's Navy: A History of the Special Service Squadron, 1920-1940," The American Neptune 35 (1975): 118-138.

(78) Stephen S. Roberts, "The Decline of the Overseas Station Fleets: The United States Asiatic Fleet and the Shanghai Crisis, 1932," Professional Paper no. 208, Center for Naval Analyses (Arlington, Va., November 1977).

(79) See, inter alia, MID 2574-1308 and 300-B-574.

(80) MID 2667-ZZ-27.

(81) Ibid.

(82) MID 2667-ZZ-27.

(83) Ibid.

(84) MID 2667-21 and 2667-ZZ-27.

(85) MID 272-61.

(86) MID 2667-ZZ-28. Then, MID 2257-ZZ-275 and 2257-ZZ-30 report on the importance of Greenland at the outset of World War II for meteorological stations.

(87) MID 2667-ZZ-30.

(88) Regarding early development of radar, prior to and during World War II, see John Carroll, Secrets of Electronic Espionage (New York: E.P. Dutton, 1966), book 2.

(89) See Harkavy, Arms Trade, chap. 4. Ecuador and Paraguay among the Latin American states then acquired the highest proportion of their arms from the Axis Powers.

(90) See MID 2657-K-93, which reports "Teuto-Brazilians" taking jobs as bartenders, etc. around Natal and Fortaleza, and about German control of Brazil's Condor Airline.

(91) MID 2657-241. Regarding possible German U-boat bases, fears were expressed particularly about locales in Peru and Chile.

(92) MID 2657-M-292.

(93) See MID 2665-15, which in particular notes the activities of the German firm, Sedta; and 2667-33-29, which discusses a U.S. offer to build up the Ecuadorean air force in exchange for Galapagos bases at a time when Ecuador was deemed unhappy with the aircraft it had purchased from Italy.

(94) The state of technology for aerial reconnaissance during this period is examined in Glenn B. Infield, Unarmed and Unafraid (London: MacMillan, 1970), chap. 4.

(95) MID 2657-M-292. By August 1940, all Latin American countries except Argentina and Uruguay had agreed to military staff conversations along these lines. For instance, MID 2657-0-188 discusses General Marshall's discussions with Chile about U.S. access to emergency landing fields and POL storage dumps at a time when Chile was looking for the United States to pressure the UK about expedited arms shipments — those arms requests were said to conflict with allied priorities.

(96) MID 183-Z-130 and 10987-73. Herein is related an alleged Nazi plot to take over Vichy French communications facilities, resulting in cancellation of the French concession and subsequent granting to the United States of air and naval access.

(97) MID 2667-ZZ-31.

(98) See MID 2537-103, 183-Z-130, and 10541-1007, the latter reporting on access granted to U.S. mechanics needed for servicing P-40 fighter aircraft being ferried to the Panama Canal via Mexico.

(99) See MID 242-196 for discussion of U.S. consideration of purchase or lease of the Galapagos to preempt similar Japanese designs on them.

(100) MID 2052-121, 2657-M-292, and 10919-48.

(101) See MID 183-354, and 2657-298 which also discusses occupations of Curacao, Aruba, and Bonaire, involving British forces also.

(102) MID 2657-M-292, 183-Z-130, and 2340-64. Mexico was an exception here in requiring special, ad hoc permission for each overflight.

(103) See MID 300-B-572 and 2840-1, discussing among other things clandestine U.S. surveys of possible facility sites, and the possibility of use of a Firestone rubber plantation.

(104) One possible partial exception, noted by Collier, The Lion and the Eagle (New York: Putnam, 1972), p. 336, was the basing of U.S. bombers at Clark Field, intended to knock out Japanese airfields on Formosa in the case of war. This strategy was, of course, preempted by the Japanese raids on the Philippines simultaneous with the assault on Pearl Harbor.

(105) See MID 300-B-574 and 10582-59, which also discuss possible U.S. base sites at Jolo, Halsey Harbor, and Cebu City, the latter deemed important because of its location in relation to the Japanese base at Yap in the Caroline Islands.

(106) MID 2657-298.

(107) See MID 2090-395, which reveals an elaborate Soviet Siberian base structure prior to World War II. See also MID 2667-D-1061, which discusses reports that in 1939, German submarine officers visited Vladivostok, Petropavlovsk, the Kommandorski Islands, and other sites.

(108) See, in particular, Claudio G. Segre, Fourth Shore: The Italian Colonization of Libya (Chicago: University of Chicago Press, 1974).

(109) MID 2086-362 and 2086-635.

(110) MID 2086-460.

(111) MID 2779-2 and 2018-358.

(112) See MID 2086-738 and 2086-527.

(113) MID 2657-V-296 also reports on the Germans' use of air facilities on Rhodes and other Italian-controlled Aegean islands.

(114) MID 2086-847 and 2022-611.

(115) However, as noted in MID 2022-611/28, Britain did refuse over-flights for the ferrying of Italian warplanes from Tripoli over Sudan, after initially permitting some.

(116) See, in particular, MID 2791-8 and 2657-E-336.

(117) MID 2267-A-37 reports the destruction of the Italian Red Sea navy in February 1940 and the shipping of 20,000 Italian prisoners to India.

(118) See MID 2657-241 and 2048-182.

(119) See MID 2657-S-144.

(120) See MID 2657-S-144, 2093-203, and 2093-112. Also, as noted in MID 2657-230, Italy apparently had some air access to the Cape Verde Islands at the war's outset.

(121) See Howard, Continental Commitment, p. 59.

(122) See Rosinski, Development of Naval Thought, chap. 4. Howard, Continental Commitment, p. 67, reports on British fears that Germany would establish submarine bases on the Indian Ocean after gaining control of the Caucasus, Armenia, Persia, and Mesopotamia.

(123) MID 2266-E-4.

(124) The MID files report Allied fears of such German access in numerous places, but particularly in Panama, Venezuela, Ecuador, Colombia, and several other Central American countries, all within close proximity to the Panama Canal. Portuguese and Spanish terri-tories at home and abroad were also very frequently the subjects of speculation and analysis.

(125) See, regarding the importance of the Low Countries for fighter and bomber bases at the outset of World War II, Howard, Continental Commitment, p. 117.

(126) See Harkavy, Arms Trade, chap. 4, for data regarding Axis arms supplies to Nationalist Spain.

(127) MID 2657-230 and 2657-S-144.

(128) Ibid., and MID 2093-191.

(129) MID 2081-1061.

(130) MID 2657-244, 2472-129, and 2459-145.

(131) MID 242-96.

(132) Ibid.

(133) See MID 2504-100, which reports sightings of German seaplanes in Dakar harbor in early 1941.

(134) This is discussed in great detail in MID 242-96.

(135) Ibid., which notes that Germany and Italy, with between them some 15,000 bombers and 8,000 fighter aircraft in 1939, were trying to maintain a 3:2 air superiority ratio over the combined UK-France-USSR air forces.

(136) MID 2052-121 and 2657-J-27, the latter discussing the possibility in 1941 of a German invasion of Portugal to secure bases there and in Madeira, Cape Verde, and Portuguese Guinea.

(137) MID 2677-22 reports on German access to forward air bases in Bulgaria in 1939. In 1940 Germany also apparently acquired access to several forward air bases in Hungary, according to MID 2082-981.

(138) MID 2093-203 and 2072-482, the latter reporting on the use by German submarines and surface raiders of the Bay of El Rio between the islands of Lanzarote and Graciosa. But German requests for a radio facility at Tangiers were apparently denied.

(139) MID 2082-948, referring to a possible German base at Trinidad in Bolivia.

(140) MID 2082-925.

(141) For a review of the provisions of the Washington Naval Agreement regarding military use of the mandated Pacific islands, see, inter alia, Buel W. Patch, "American Naval and Air Bases" (Washington, D.C.: Editorial Research Report), vol. 1, no. 7, February 16, 1939. For a good short summary, see F.L. Benns and M.E. Seldon, Europe: 1914-1939 (New York: Appleton-Century-Crofts, 1965), pp. 155-157, 438-439. See also Basil Collier, The Lion and the Eagle, p. 248, who notes the five basic aspects of the agreement as pertains to bases, really the only such arms control agreement in recent history.

1. The United States would not establish new fortifications for naval bases nor extend existing facilities in its Pacific Island possessions other than in Hawaii (these restrictions not to apply to Alaska or the Panama Canal Zone).

2. Japan would not establish new fortifications or naval bases to extend existing facilities in the Kuriles, Ryukyus, Formosa, or the Pescadores.
3. Britain would be free to develop and fortify Singapore, but not to establish new fortifications or naval bases or extend existing facilities at Hong Kong or in insular possessions east of a line through Hainan and the western extreme of Borneo (not to apply to Australia, NZ, or Canada).
4. The ban on fortification of League-mandated islands would be observed, to apply to Australia's New Guinea holdings and to Japan's mandate over the Caroline Islands.
5. The signatory powers would not be precluded from maintaining existing facilities in a reasonable state of repair.

(142) There were also various reports about Japanese attempts to acquire access in Latin America (Guatemala, Costa Rica, Mexico, Colombia, Nicaragua), even to purchase the Galapagos Islands. Chile was reportedly asked to provide a naval base. See MID 242-96.

(143) MID 2317-H-24.

(144) See MID 2280-J-97.

(145) MID 2667-D-1061, regarding the repair of Soviet merchant ships at British-owned dockyards at Shanghai in 1941 at a time when Soviet diplomacy was steering between a Chinese and Japanese orientation.

(146) MID 2657-166.

(147) MID 2063-357, 2724-H-58.

(148) MID 2667-H-29.

(149) MID 2085-885.

(150) MID 2657-H-528 reports on a Japanese ultimatum to Vichy France in July 1941 regarding eight air bases and two naval bases, which were characterized as "strategically defensive" in character to prevent British and American influence from shutting off supplies of rubber, tin, and rice from Thailand and Indo-China. See also 2081-1380 for an analysis of Japanese plans to use Indo-China bases for an assault against Malaya; as well as Collier, The Lion and the Eagle, p. 335.

(151) MID 2073-673.

(152) See MID 2124-77, which has Siam denying rumors about Japanese use of some of its islands for submarines, ascribing the rumors to the "Third International." See also 2085-898 regarding Japanese aircraft access to Siam.

(153) MID 1766-S-30.

(154) Ibid.

(155) MID 2667-H-58 reports on the informant's role of a Filipino missionary, one of only a few missionaries allowed in the Palau Islands by the Japanese, and who also reported on the dredging of lagoons to allow for mooring of battleships. See also MID 2342-174 and 2657-411 for developments on Mortlock around 1933.

(156) MID 2085-957.

(157) MID 2667-H-58 and 2085-957.

(158) MID 2085-957.

(159) See, among others, John Toland, The Rising Sun, vol. 1 (New York: Random House, 1970), chap. 6, "Operation Z," for an analysis of this strategy, and of Admiral Yamamoto's cautious pessimism regarding its eventual success, even as he enthusiastically planned the Pearl Harbor raid.

(160) See Gorschkov, Sea Power of the State, pp. 79-80:

> Naval ships under the general guidance of the industrialists, Shelekov Baromov and others, perseveringly took control of the coast of North America and of islands from Alaska to St. Elias Cape. However, the further fate of these islands was decided in advance; the Czarist government did not attach due significance to the newly acquired regions which it was impossible to hold without creating strong naval forces in the northern part of the Pacific Ocean.

(161) MID 2667-D-1061.

(162) MID 2090-323 reports on Soviet survey personnel in Czechoslovakia in 1935 and plans to construct there facilities for 1,000 aircraft.

(163) MID 2657-230.

(164) MID 2090-390. Collier, The Lion and the Eagle, p. 313, also states that the Russians gave up 50,000 lives to "get bases on Finnish as well as Estonian soil," implying that such access was a primary rationale for the Winter War.

(165) MID 2657-I-281 reports on Soviet interwar bases in Mongolia and on alleged virtual control of that country by the Soviet military.

(166) See Harkavy, Arms Trade, chap. 4, for discussion of Soviet arms sales policies and patterns during the interwar period. The Soviets did, of course, have some access to shipyards in China as well as to airfields in Czechoslovakia, in both cases concurrent with arms sales to those countries.

(167) Though the distinctions may be more semantic than substantive, it is worth noting that scholars have differed widely over structural descriptions or characterizations of the interwar period. Bruce Russett, in Trends in World Politics (New York: Macmillan, 1965), p. 2, calls the interwar a "balance of power precarious" system; Richard Rosecrance, in Action and Reaction in World Politics (Boston: Little, Brown, 1963), pp. 257-261, sees a bipolar alignment facing off a "status quo, liberal-democratic" bloc against an "expansionist, radical-nationalist" bloc. Some scholars divide the period fore and aft of the advent of Hitler in 1932 into two very distinct periods, as done by S. Michalak, "The United Nations and the League," in L. Gordenker, ed., The U.N. in International Politics (Princeton, N.J.: Princeton University Press, 1971), pp. 60-105.

(168) The more fluid character of alliances during that period relative to the postwar is analyzed in, inter alia, Ole R. Holsti, P. Terrence Hopmann, and John D. Sullivan, Unity and Disintegration in International Alliances: Comparative Studies (New York: Wiley, 1973); and in various of the selections in J.R. Friedman, C. Bladen, and S. Rosen, eds., Alliance in International Politics (Boston: Allyn and Bacon, 1970). For an example from the nineteenth century, see Graham, Politics of Naval Supremacy, pp. 81-82, wherein it is noted the Russians were granted port facilities in Villefranche in 1858, seeming to satisfy the age-old Russian aim of acquiring a naval point d'appui in the Mediterranean. After a lengthy period of only desultory use of the facilities, the Russians did establish a small squadron at Villefranche in 1893 with the right to use Toulon for refitment and repair.

(169) Regarding weapons-production cooperation within the Little Entente as a precursor of modern practices, see Harkavy, Arms Trade, p. 169.

(170) Roberts, "Decline of Overseas Station Fleets," p. 186.

(171) Harkavy, Arms Trade, pp. 30-34. For analyses of various aspects of the "total war" idea, see Robert Osgood, "The Expansion of Force," in Art and Waltz, Use of Force, pp. 29-55; Raymond Aron, The Century of Total War (Garden City, N.Y.: Doubleday, 1954); and J.F.C. Fuller, Armaments and History (New York: Charles Scribner's Sons, 1945), chaps. 2 and 3.

(172) See Harkavy, Arms Trade, esp. pp. 34-41.

(173) See Howard, Continental Commitment, p. 117, regarding the strategic importance of the Low Countries for fighter aircraft bases (in conjunction with then burgeoning radar developments).

(174) MID 242-96 reports that the German He-111 bomber had a range of 2,000 miles, and that it and the Ju-88 could do 3,000 miles without bombs. The Do-17 was said to have a range of 1,050 miles with full bomb load, comparable to the Italian S-79 and Br-20 aircraft. Hence, Germany and Italy could not bomb Brazil from Africa, nor the Panama Canal from Natal. Without bombs, however, it was noted that German air patrols from the Azores, Canaries, Cape Verde, and the Natal/Pernambuco line could operate to a line from St. Johns, Newfoundland to Cayenne, French Guyana, which was a cause for allied concern and a spur to protecting the Natal/Pernambuco area. For greater detail on aircraft ranges in that era, see the serial editions of Jane's All the World's Aircraft (London: Sampson, Law, Marston & Co.), annual, and also the effectively graphic maps and charts in R. Ernest Dupuy, World in Arms (Harrisburg, Pa.: The Military Service Publishing Co., 1939).

(175) See George Quester, Deterrence Before Hiroshima: The Airpower Background of Modern Strategy (New York: Wiley, 1966); and Quester, "Strategic Bombing in the 1930s and 1940s," in Art and Waltz, Use of Force, pp. 184-202.

(176) See Harkavy, Arms Trade, pp. 20-22, for an elaboration of this point.

(177) See the discussion in ibid., p. 22. Among other things, these long-run trends make it very difficult to gauge developments in arms races or arms acquisitions, in the absence of some analogy to an economic "deflator" to compensate for technological development. This point is also made, in a somewhat less general way, in Brodie, Sea Power in the Machine Age (Princeton, N.J.: Princeton University Press, 1941), p. 248, who notes that: "On the strategic side, the consequences of the developments in armor and ordnance have been vast. In the first place, despite the prodigious naval budgets of recent times, the increase in the cost of the individual ship has brought in all navies a decline in the total number of larger units."
MID 2086-738, for instance, reports that the Italian air force in East Africa in 1939 − comprised of some 25 squadrons fielding some 213 aircraft − was based at 11 main air bases but had access to 69 additional airstrips, some intended merely for emergency use. Its 22 squadrons in Libya used 16 air bases. In 1941 (see MID 2085-885), Japan utilized some 17 airfields on Formosa and 5 to 10 more on Hainan including those used solely for seaplanes. And MID 2083-1302 reveals that the RAF utilized some 20 airfields in Tanganyika alone during the 1930s. Part of the explanation here derives from the numbers of planes in service, else, the then (relative to the present) far lesser requirements regarding runway length were presumably germane.

(178) Geoffrey Kemp, "Scarcity and Strategy," Foreign Affairs 56, 2 (January 1978): 397. For a wide-ranging historical analysis of military logistics, see Martin Van Creveld, Supplying War: Logistics from Wallerstein to Patton (New York: Cambridge University Press, 1977).

(179) See Kennedy, Rise and Fall, chap. 11.

(180) For one analysis of British overseas dependence for raw materials and agricultural products at the time of World War II, see Brig. D.H. Cole, Imperial Military Geography, chap. 16.

(181) See MID 242-96, for instance, which reports that in 1938 Germany still had significant dependence on Chilean nitrates even despite its impressive and growing capacity for producing synthetic nitrogen.

(182) See, for instance, Zelda Coates and William P. Coates, A History of Anglo-Soviet Relations (London: Lawrence and Wishart, 1955), esp. pp. 357-532.

(183) One of the best portrayals of the extent of cartel formation during the interwar period, albeit focused primarily on the chemical and related industries, is in U.S. Congress, Senate, Munitions Industry, Report of the Special Committee on Investigation of the Munitions Industry, 73rd Cong. (Washington, D.C.: Government Printing Office, 1936), particularly in the appendix entitled "Evidence Folder on Exhibits 1102 and 1103," which elaborates numerous such intercorporate relationships. For more general context, see also Eugene Staley, Foreign Investment and War (Chicago: University of Chicago Press, 1935); and Raymond Vernon, Sovereignty at Bay (New York: Basic Books, 1971), chap. 2 entitled "The Raw Material Ventures."

(184) For a full analysis of British and French dependence on raw materials during the interwar period in connection with maritime strategies and naval orders of battle, see MID 2657-122/190. French overseas dependence for copper, coal, petroleum, rubber, sulfur, cotton, wool, and cereals is discussed, by sources; likewise, British dependence for wheat, meat, aluminum, antimony, chromium, copper, graphite, iron ore, lead, manganese, mercury, mica, molybdenum, nickel, nitrates, platinum, silver, sulfur, tin, tungsten, zinc, camphor, castor oil, cotton, hemp, silk, and rubber. The British Empire was then noted as having a practical monopoly on rubber, tin, jute, shellac, high grade mica, and nickel.

(185) See MID 2657-H-411 for an extensive analysis of Japanese perceptions of raw materials vulnerabilities right before the outset of World War II, and on its aspirations for a coordinated forward policy in the South Seas region involving shipping lines, airlines, and fuel resources, etc. See also Toland, Rising Sun, chap. 3, for an interesting related analysis, set in the context of 1930s Japanese internal politics and civil-military relations.

(186) Ibid. See also Toland, Rising Sun, p. 108, which reports that Japan's oil stocks still could have lasted two years under peacetime conditions, 18 months under wartime.

(187) Ibid., p. 108, indicates that Japan had actually secured the Indo-China bases through negotiation with Vichy France, but with the latter having capitulated under duress.

(188) Harkavy, Arms Trade, esp. chap. 4, which theorizes that the relatively (compared to the postwar) multipolar and non-ideological character of the interwar system resulted in these cross-bloc acquisition patterns and in arms client relations at variance with other normal measures of association.

(189) This had been the case for a long time. See John M. Sherwig, Guineas and Gunpowder: British Foreign Aid in the Wars with France, 1793-1815 (Cambridge, Mass.: Harvard University Press, 1969), for a review of British military aid to Continental allies during the Napoleonic Wars, preceding the period of private dominance of arms transfers. On the use of subsidies in the seventeenth and eighteenth centuries, including some for arms transfers during the age of dynastic statecraft, see George Liska, The New Statecraft (Chicago: Chicago University Press, 1960), chap. 2.

(190) See, for example, MID 2257-K-30, which notes U.S. and Japanese arms competition in Brazil in 1939, with Japan playing a preemptive arms-selling strategy. Japan pursued similar policies regarding Chile, Peru, Ecuador, and Panama, in the former case apparently involving an aspiration to acquire access to the Chilean-controlled Easter Island, 2,200 miles off the mainland, as noted in MID 242-96. Germany and Italy, meanwhile, attempted during this period to barter directly arms for raw materials all over Latin America.

(191) Overflight restrictions for political reasons were not, however, altogether lacking. Collier, Airship, p. 214, notes that in the 1930s, during the Hitler era, the airship Hindenburg was forbidden to fly over both France and Britain, apparently because it was so symbolic of waxing German military might.

4 Bases in the Early Postwar Period: Bipolarity and the Containment Ring

At the close of World War II the international system familiar to the interwar period was completely and irrevocably shattered. What earlier had been a Eurocentered system altered only in degree from the nineteenth century, even despite the wrench of World War I, had given way to one totally dominated by the preexisting "peripheral" powers, the United States and the USSR.(1) Within a year after the end of the war, there developed an essentially bipolar bloc confrontation, with its harsh ideological conflict overlaying the claimed traditional and near-automatic tendency to rivalry between the world's two leading powers.

Outside the immediate arena of bipolar confrontation in central Europe, there were new stirrings of anticolonial revolt, accelerating a process haltingly underway since 1919. Britain and France, though retaining all of their previous colonial assets and corresponding points of strategic access, emerged from the war with sorely weakened economies, while the former's defeats by Japan earlier in the war had further demythified the symbolic element of the power upon which colonial control was based. The colonial powers, including Britain, had also so nearly been bankrupted by the war that they were left sorely dependent on American aid largesse. Only a couple of years later, the Truman Doctrine, involving a U.S. military commitment to Turkey and Greece, signalled America's replacement of what long had been a British global role in maintaining a Pax Britannica. The United States, despite its extensive postwar demobilization, had determined not to return to traditional isolationism in the face of a newly ominous threat.

In 1948 the fall of China to Communism presented the West with a seemingly greatly enhanced menace. What was to become the Sino-Soviet bloc for some thirteen years contained the population basis for massive land armies, which when juxtaposed to the logistical advantages offered by interior lines emanating from the Eurasian core, made it difficult for the West to match – in general or at specific points – even with a full mobilization. Long after the genesis of Mackinder's geopolitical thesis, his classical heartland-rimland confrontation seemed finally to have come to fruition.(2) For the West, overall strategy came to depend on maintenance of naval and air superiority around and over the rimland and "marginal seas," backed up by an only questionably credible nuclear mass destruction deterrent.

There was an apparently major difference between the denouements of World Wars I and II, which in turn speaks to general questions of spatial conflict alignments and corresponding networks of strategic access. The end of World War I did not immediately give rise to a new threat to the world order; the gradual falling out between Britain and France over reparations, the restraining or even dismembering of Germany, and some tensions over colonial spheres of influence, did not give rise to a really serious confrontation between the victorious major powers. Indeed, the era between 1919 and 1929 was one of considerable optimism, even utopianism, about peace prospects, as evidence the seriousness attributed to the collective security myth embodied by the League of Nations, the Kellogg-Briand Pact, and the lengthy negotiated preparations for the eventual Geneva Disarmament Conference of the early 1930s.(3)

During this period, efforts at constructing elaborate military security alliances were minimal (they violated the new spirit of the League), excepting notably the combination of the Franco-Poland-Czechoslovakia pact directed at forestalling resurgence of German militarism, and the Little Entente, directed against Hungary.(4) As such, and as noted, there were no forward deployments of troops from one ally to another, nor were any permanent air or naval facilities granted among the European powers or to them by sovereign states elsewhere. After the brief roles of occupation forces in Europe were concluded, the victorious powers' military forces were withdrawn to home territories and to overseas colonies.

In the aftermath of World War II, there was no such equivalent withdrawal by the victors from territories held at the close of the war; on the contrary, the war's backwash left the occupying powers in place. The Soviet army came "permanently" to be ensconced in Eastern Europe, while the United States – as well as Britain – maintained forward garrisons and bases in Western Europe.

With respect to overseas military access, the close of World War II had also brought changes in military technology, evolving modes of strategy, and the very basis for basing and access diplomacy. Most notably, the advent of nuclear weapons (superimposed upon the lessons assumed derived from the experience of strategic bombing during World War II) produced new needs for overseas bases, for deterrence purposes, and with a requirement for more or less immediate response. Longer-range bombers and transport aircraft had altered the requirements for basing and staging facilities; air transport of materiel and personnel had assumed greater relative importance by the end of World War II. Developments in radar, communications, and electronic intelligence had also altered basing requirements,(5) and regarding intelligence, there was – for the West – the need to cope with a rather fully "closed" society, one far more impervious to external surveillance than had been Nazi Germany before World War II.

Then, the immediate postwar period saw the emergence of economic and military aid (gratis and on a large scale) as a major instrument of diplomacy, in a manner and of a scope that had altogether been absent prior to 1940. This resulted, at least on the western side, in part from the enormous economic asymmetries between the United States and its European allies which emerged from the war, but also from the rather obvious national security exigencies involved. And as we shall subsequently elaborate upon, there was a tight convergence of perceived interest, ideologically based, at least within the Atlantic alliance (but perhaps also between the USSR and China) which provided a greatly altered basis for alignment diplomacy relative to the interwar period. Economic and military aid came to exist in a quid pro quo relationship with bases within the western alliance (though the rationale for mutual access transcended the matter of aid due to convergent interests). In Eastern Europe, access was imposed, the flow of "aid" went both ways, and the question of mutually perceived convergent interests was effectively moot.(6)

All in all, the global structure of military access which emerged after 1945 was based on a combination of, first, military forces and facilities being retained in place after the war because of the new realities; second, the still strong remnants of colonial control; and third, the evolvement of tight and (as it would turn out) relatively enduring long-term alliances.

This chapter is devoted to describing the competing basing strategies and networks of access which developed in what is referred to here as the "immediate postwar period," with the next chapter moving to the "late postwar period" of the present and more immediate past. Of course, there is no readily defined watershed between the two, either narrowly with respect to basing networks or more broadly. One might claim, however, that during the 1960s a number of interrelated general changes took place, which after gradual evolvement, produced a very altered context for the competition for access between the major powers. Among the most important:

- The near termination of what had been (in Morton Kaplan's terminology) a "tight" bipolar system,(7) caused, inter alia, by the Sino-Soviet split, the partial defection of France from NATO and the rise of a more independent – in some senses – Western European center of power, and the shift toward a north-south locus of conflict superimposed upon the East-West confrontation.
- The rapid and nearly total collapse of European colonial empires, and the movement of many new nations away from Western client status toward anti-western radicalism and "neutralism," underpinning the formation of many Third World arms client relationships with the USSR.
- The evident beginning of the withdrawal and receding of U.S. overseas commitments after Vietnam (paralleled by a vast decline in military and economic grant aid), the onset of the "Nixon Doctrine," and the replacement of the "dollar glut" by the "dollar drain."

- The gradual but significant expansion of Soviet military power in distant overseas areas – in conjunction with the leapfrogging of the containment barrier – resulting in a marked shift in the spatial nature of global conflict away from the earlier heartland-rimland pattern.
- The lessened (but not entirely eliminated) requirement for forward overseas bases in connection with strategic nuclear deterrence.
- The advent of ever-changing new technical functions for overseas bases, related, among other things, to the newly important role of satellites, to telemetry and other intelligence functions, and to advanced antisubmarine warfare.

THE IMPACT OF WORLD WAR II ON SUBSEQUENT POSTWAR BASING STRUCTURES

The foregoing discussion has anticipated that World War II constituted an important watershed demarcating phases of twentieth-century basing structures and related diplomacy. It is important to note in that regard that the course and conduct of the war itself was to have a telling impact here, particularly with respect to U.S. strategic concerns.

As previously noted, the United States entered World War II with an only very limited overseas basing system, and that primarily consisted of outposts both to the east and west which were perceived essentially as perimeter defensive positions, early warnings posts, or "tripwires." It had a small naval station at Guam and maintained limited forces in the Philippines and a flotilla at Shanghai; but it was conceded – though not very openly – that those outposts probably could not be held in the event of a major conflict. The "real" Pacific defense line ran from Alaska to Hawaii to the Panama Canal Zone, the latter deemed especially crucial, and hence heavily fortified.(8) In the Caribbean there were minor bases and naval deployments at Guantanamo, and in Puerto Rico and the Virgin Islands. Before the lend-lease deal with Britain in 1940, protection of the Atlantic rested on the hope of sea control without the aid of outlying bases, and, of course, on the Royal Navy.

In 1940 began the extensive development of American overseas facilities during World War II with the previously discussed acquisition of Atlantic and Caribbean air and naval bases from Britain, then described by President Roosevelt as "the most important action in the reinforcement of our national defense that has been taken since the Louisiana Purchase."(9)

The U.S. Atlantic defense line was further extended even before American entry into the war in 1941. In that year, the United States established a protectorate over Greenland after Denmark's fall to the Nazis, negotiating successfully with the virtually exiled Danish ambassador in Washington for the right to establish air and naval bases there.(10) Shortly thereafter in 1941, the United States also took over from the UK the job of defending Iceland (then owned by Denmark), with the promise to withdraw after the wartime emergency had ended. At the same time, the U.S. Atlantic defenses were strengthened by bases built in cooperation with Canada in its Labrador and Baffin Island.(11)

Negotiations just before and after Pearl Harbor gave the United States rights to use airfields in Mexico and to establish facilities in various places in Latin America, most notably in Brazil, Cuba, Ecuador, and Panama.(12) Additional air bases were built in Cuba in an agreement supplementing the 1903 lease of Guantanamo; numerous facilities outside the Canal Zone were made available by Panama; and a chain of air bases was built in Brazil,(13) which in connection with U.S. use of an air strip on Ascension Island, was vital for ferrying aircraft and other materiel during the war across Africa and on to the Middle East.(14)

Though Portugal had granted the British access to bases in the strategic Azores in 1943, it was not until 1944 that it agreed to construction of an American air base on Santa Maria Island (slightly earlier, the United States was allowed to station a naval air squadron there under British command).(15) By that time, World War II was nearly over, but the U.S. bases in the Azores would later become important in other ways and in relation to newer threats.

In the Pacific, the United States, after losing the Philippines, Guam, and Wake, was forced to rely on its allies' base facilities to conduct its initial campaigns in the Southwest Pacific. American troops moved to Australia in 1942, and extensive use was made of the Free French colony of New Caledonia and of British Dominion controlled Fiji, New Hebrides, and other islands.(16) As the campaign northward and westward proceeded, new installations were built, such as the large base at Manus in the Australian-controlled Admiralty Islands.(17) Later, in 1944-1945, the United States would make extensive use of captured Japanese bases such as Saipan, Palau, Truk, Iwo Jima, and Okinawa for its final onslaught on Japan. The same process occurred, of course, in Europe.

To conduct the wars against Japan and Germany, the United States had to construct an enormous number of facilities, which recalls the almost magical aura which surrounded the Navy's Seabees in those days. According to one source, this involved after 1940, covering only naval and naval air bases,

434 war bases of various dimensions: 195 in the Pacific area, 11 in the Indian Ocean and the Near East, 228 in the Atlantic area, 18 of which are in the North Atlantic, 67 in the Gulf of Panama and the Caribbean, 25 in the South Atlantic, 55 in North Africa and the Mediterranean, 63 in Great Britain, France and Germany.(18)

At its peak during World War II, the Air Force is said to have had no fewer than 1,922 domestic and overseas installations. And as we shall see, the almost immediate onset of the Cold War after 1945 made the United States reluctant, in many cases, to abandon what had been constructed at such a great cost in money and blood.

No other major power acquired and built overseas bases on nearly such a scale during World War II. Britain expanded many of its bases, at least among those not lost at the war's outset. Germany and Japan constructed numerous bases after their initially successful offensives, as springboards for new operations, but then, of course, eventually lost them all to the Allies. And the USSR moved into Eastern Europe in 1944-1945. But it was only the United States that at the close of the war (aside from Britain's temporary recovery of all of its imperial possessions) had possession of a newly massive global basing network, which by 1945 was derived from a combination of conquests, agreements with allies, and temporary arrangements with neutrals and exile regimes that had at least the potential for postwar renewal and extension.

THE DEVELOPMENT OF THE U.S. OVERSEAS BASING STRUCTURE IN THE IMMEDIATE POSTWAR YEARS

When the United States found itself in an almost immediate global confrontation with the USSR after World War II, it moved quickly to consolidate and strengthen the basing assets it had acquired, within the constraints of budgetary limitations and the postwar demobilization and reconversion to "normalcy." Indeed, this became an immediate target of Soviet complaints; in a meeting of the Big Four foreign ministers called for the purpose of "seeking to reduce the existing tensions in Europe," the Soviets insisted that bases – and the newly formed North Atlantic Pact – go on the agenda as "the principal cause of the tense situation in Europe."(19) The three Western powers refused, perceiving the Soviets as having come to complain about a self-fulfilling prophecy.

Even before the coming reality of the Cold War had been fully revealed, the U.S. Congress, remembering the paucity of U.S. basing assets prior to 1941 and the hurried effort which had to be made to correct that deficiency, had begun to insist on permanent retention of many assets acquired and built with American money during the war. An abortive attempt was made to acquire permanent ownership of the British Atlantic bases acquired on a ninety-nine year lease.(20)

As it is, before the Cold War lines hardened and prior to the formation of NATO and the numerous other bilateral and multilateral U.S.-led defense pacts, the United States encountered some considerable diplomatic resistance to its efforts at extending the use of some bases, as wartime allies and dependents sought to regain what they though should have been only temporarily compromised sovereignty. As a result, particularly in the Atlantic, the U.S. basing network was, at least temporarily, cut down in size. The Azores base was returned to Portugal, with an eighteen-month grant of transit rights retained, but which was subsequently extended in 1948 for another five years.(21) Iceland compelled withdrawal of U.S. military personnel in 1946-1947, although it allowed an American commercial airline to continue operation of Keflavik's airfield.(22) Denmark first pressed for termination of the 1941 bases agreement on Greenland, but did not compel American evacuation before a new agreement was completed in 1951.(23) The reflexes from the interwar modus operandus died hard.

In Latin America, the United States turned back most of the facilities it had acquired during the war, though Brazil did agree for some years to retention of the American air bases at Belem and Natal, which were finally deactivated in 1948.(24) And the Panamanian Assembly turned down a tentative agreement which would have provided for continued American use of 13 of 134 installations constructed during the war outside the Canal Zone, including a heavy bomber base at Rio Hato on the Gulf of Panama.(25)

In the Pacific, there was strong sentiment for retaining numerous assets acquired during the war, primarily in the former Japanese mandate islands, but also on some Pacific islands belonging to Australia and Britain. Early heavy funding for some bases, including the one on the Australian-mandated Manus Island, was subsequently cut back. But Australia objected to a permanent American presence in its territories, and it proceeded to construct its own base on Manus, while converting its mandates over New Guinea and the Admiralty Islands into UN Trusteeships, where there were to be no U.S. bases.(26)

As the Japanese mandated islands had been taken by the United States at heavy cost and were considered of vital future strategic value, there was considerable sentiment for their annexation. Still, the United States later got the UN Security Council in 1947 to approve a trusteeship agreement which left the United States as sole administrator of the islands, and which agreement could not be altered without U.S. consent (the Ryukyus and Bonins came under U.S. military occupation). The United States immediately designated some of these islands as "strategic areas" closed to visits and inspections, and maintained numerous bases in Saipan, Tinian, Palau, Eniwetok, and Kwajelein, some of which were to serve as nuclear testing grounds in later years.(27)

The postwar buildup of the American basing network can be divided into two phases, with a watershed around the period 1949-1951, when the grim long-range nature of the struggle with the Soviets had become clear in the aftermath of the Berlin Blockade, the crisis in Greece, the Soviet takeover of Czechoslovakia, the setting up of NATO and, finally, the North Korean invasion of South Korea.

Right after 1945, as noted, the United States was in a much better position than it had been to build up an expanded network of overseas bases by retaining many of its World War II assets and by relying on allies and its own defense positions abroad. It had retained, of course, significant occupation forces abroad in Germany, Italy, Austria, and Japan, and occupied related air and naval bases in those countries. And, the bases acquired from Britain in 1940 had also been retained, though some were reduced virtually to inactive status.

Around 1950-1951, however, the United States moved to expand its facilities in several areas, in many cases by negotiating long-term arrangements to replace those entered into during the war and then only temporarily extended in its immediate aftermath. The U.S. Air

Force obtained permission to expand its already significant facilities at Goose Bay, Labrador. A new defense agreement was entered into with Denmark, to remain operative for the duration of the NATO alliance, which provided for U.S. use of air and naval facilities in Greenland, although Denmark took back control over the former U.S. naval station at Gronnedal.(28) Also in 1951, there was a new agreement with previously recalcitrant Iceland, which made its bases collectively available to NATO and which provided for joint civil and military use of Keflavik.(29)

In the UK, American aircraft continued to use the Sculthorpe bomber base under operational U.S. command, in addition to several other air and logistical bases which were formally kept under British command.(30) Outside of Germany, the United States also obtained "permanent" use of some important facilities, among them a large military supply port at Bordeaux, France (for its forces in Germany), another supply port at Leghorn, Italy (for its forces in Austria), and a NATO southern command headquarters at Naples. In Germany itself, four major air bases initially were set up, along with an important U.S. navy supply entry port at Bremerhaven.

In the Middle East, where the British still retained on behalf of the West a plethora of important air and naval bases (Cyprus, Egypt, Libya, Jordan, Iraq), the United States gained permission to reopen the important Wheelus Air Force Base in Libya. Some use also was made of an air facility at Dhahran in Saudi Arabia.(31) All in all, a fairly extensive though somewhat undermanned basing system was provided up to 1950, for a variety of strategic, staging, garrisoning, and other purposes.

In 1950-1951, the fear of the broader implications of Korea – and also of the now apparent growing Soviet nuclear threat – energized the United States into an enhanced base acquisition effort, later further accelerated once the ring of anti-Soviet alliances around the Eurasian heartland was set up. Primary emphasis was placed on air bases, among other things, to underwrite the emerging nuclear massive retaliation doctrine. In 1951 a $2.2 billion expenditure for overseas construction of facilities was appropriated, divided between the Air Force, Army, and Navy in the respective amounts of $1,487, $478, and $242 millions.(32) The program envisaged adding 77 Air Force bases (71 overseas) to the existing 232 to make a total of 309 installations at home and overseas.

The projects were distributed geographically, and by appropriations, as shown in Table 4.1.

The Alaskan facilities were mostly for the Air Force, those on Guam mostly for the Navy, and those in Hawaii divided between air and naval installations.   Johnston Island Air Force Base was set up as another major Pacific facility to the southwest of Hawaii. Bermuda's Kindley and Puerto Rico's Ramey Air Force bases were to be expanded to provide for enhanced defense of the Atlantic.   Much of the funding in the Pacific Trust Territories was for Kwajalein Island, about to become an important nuclear test facility.(34) Aviation and naval facilities in Cuba, the Philippines, and Newfoundland were expanded, and Yokosuka was to be built up to serve as a major U.S. naval base, which became vital for the conduct of the Korean conflict. In Northern Ireland a major naval communications facility was built at Londonderry.(33) The containment policy, now directed at an at least temporarily cohesive Sino-Soviet bloc, was to be given teeth to undergird a vast rimland defense and deterrence posture.

Table 4.1. Bases on American Territory(33)

Location	Costs
Alaska and Aleutian Islands	$346,700,000
Guam	25,500,000
Hawaii	20,600,000
Puerto Rico	18,300,000
Johnston Islands	5,900,000
Panama Canal Zone	700,000

Bases Overseas – Foreign Territory

Location	
Okinawa	$129,000,000
Philippines	19,000,000
Pacific Tr. Territory	13,700,000
Bermuda	12,400,000
Cuba	5,100,000
Newfoundland	3,300,000
Japan	2,900,000
North Ireland	500,000

Source: Buel Patch, Editorial Research Reports, vol. 2, no. 2 (July 14, 1951), p. 437.

STRATEGIC DETERRENCE AND THE IMMEDIATE POSTWAR U.S. BASING SYSTEM

Between 1945 and the early 1950s, the United States was effectively the only nuclear power, though it is now known that the United States then had only a small handful of atomic weapons – perhaps, in retrospect, not necessarily enough to have been militarily decisive if the requirement had so arisen. But the United States did nevertheless rely during this period somewhat precariously on its nuclear deterrent to counterbalance the enormous Soviet advantage in landpower in central Europe left after the United States had evacuated most of its forces. Soviet activity was relatively restrained, though the Berlin blockade, the Czechoslovak coup, and later the onset of the Korean War demonstrated the finite limits of the "extended deterrence" provided by the small U.S. nuclear arsenal.

The Korean War, with its frustrating stalemate and high casualties, produced determination in the United States to not again get similarly bogged down in land wars in Asia or elsewhere. Then Secretary of State John Foster Dulles enunciated the U.S. "massive retaliation" doctrine, which asserted the United States might react with nuclear weapons even to relatively mild provocations or aggressions, "at a place and time of our own choosing." Almost as soon as the doctrine had been promulgated, however, its very basis came to be threatened. The Soviet tests of hydrogen bombs in 1953-1954, further developments of long-range bombers capable of reaching the United States during 1954-1956, and the initial testing and deployment of ICBMs between 1956 and 1960 progressively called into question the credibility of massive retaliation, certainly for compellence or in less-than-ultimate deterrence circumstances.(36) As the decade progressed, temporary fears about actual Soviet nuclear superiority gave way to optimism about the U.S. deterrent posture, but increasingly in the context of a "balance of terror."

On both sides, the availability — or its lack — of overseas bases was to play a crucial role in calculations about the nuclear balance, mutual deterrence, and fears of first-strike vulnerability. Foreign access was to play a role both for offensive and defensive systems in this context, as well as for crucial intelligence monitoring capability and for related communications. Basically, up to the point of the Cuban revolution, the balance of advantage was all on the American side, given the extensive U.S. ring of bases around the USSR and the latter's complete lack of equivalent access. The advantage was greatest during the early postwar years because of the then relatively limited ranges of aircraft and missiles, and, as we shall see, declined with the advent of ICBMs on both sides, which allowed for a primarily home-based nuclear threat.

Up to around 1952-1953, the United States relied primarily upon the World War II vintage B-29, B-50, and B-36 bombers for nuclear deterrence, utilizing U.S. bases for the long-range B-36, and some in Britain — particularly at Sculthorpe — for the shorter-range aircraft. When these, because of their limited speeds (around 300 mph) became vulnerable to Soviet air defense, the United States began to deploy the pure-jet, 3,000-mile range, 600 mph B-47, which for almost a decade was to be the backbone of SAC. Some 600 were in operation by 1954, a figure which later rose to around 2,000.(37)

Although the ranges of the B-47s were greatly extended by new aerial refueling techniques, the United States determined on forward deployment to enhance their chances for penetration and lessen their vulnerability to a Soviet first strike. The B-47s were constituted as a "reflex" force, rotating between bases in the United States, and in Britain, Morocco, Spain, Greenland, Bermuda, and in the Pacific.(38) A string of SAC bases was also constructed within the United States, most along a swathe of northern territory bordering upon Canada from Maine to Michigan.

Staging of overseas "reflex" flights and refueling of those en route toward the USSR over the Arctic was facilitated by aerial tankers in the series running from KB-50 to KC-97 to KC-135 (the 97 was the backbone of the tanker fleet in the 1950s), based primarily at Thule, Greenland and Goose Bay, Labrador. These bases also provided tankers for refueling the long-range B-52s, once they began entering the American inventory in 1955. With refueling, the B-52s were not in need of forward "reflex" bases, though even a couple of decades later, their later models would require contingent use of post-attack recovery bases in Spain and elsewhere.

The Soviets had no matching forward bases during this period, for strategic deterrence or anything else. Their early bombers, such as the 3,000 mile range TU-4, could only reach the U.S. Pacific Northwest from Siberia, and even then, by giving away some four hours' warning time to presumably alerted U.S. radars, because of their slow speed. That length of time was then considered fully ample to alert and deploy U.S. interceptors as well as to get SAC bombers launched for a counterattack.(39) By around 1955, however, the newer Soviet M-4 bombers, with 600 mph speeds, would cut this radar warning time in half.(40)

As noted, the United States relied on foreign access, primarily in Canada and Greenland, for strategic defense as well as offense during this earlier period. During the early 1950s, the United States and Canada built the $500 million DEW (Distant Early Warning) radar picket line across the Arctic, which the United States relied upon for its two to four hours' warning of a Soviet attack. This capability was an important aspect of American nuclear deterrence. The system was later made three-tiered, added to by the Mid-Canada and Pinetree strings of electronic listening posts, all under the U.S. Air Defense Command, which worked closely with SAC.(41) Some U.S. interceptor aircraft were deployed as well at Canadian bases such as Goose Bay for perimeter early defense.

Beginning around 1955-1956, precocious Soviet missile developments began to erode the hitherto clear U.S. nuclear superiority, leading to the famed "missile gap" scare following upon the leaking of the Gaither Report toward the end of the Eisenhower Administration. In 1955 the Soviets began testing IRBMs with 1,000 mile ranges which could hit Western Europe from the western USSR.(42) By 1956, not only were the IRBMs in full production, but ICBMs were being test-launched by the Soviets down a Pacific range.(43) The launching of the first Sputnik in 1957 gave added credence to growing Soviet missile capabilities. The United States feared a "technological Pearl Harbor," and over the next few years worked feverishly to develop and test the Thor and Jupiter IRBMs, the Atlas and Titan long-range ICBMs, and then the solid-fuel Minuteman ICBM and Polaris submarine missiles which were to become the backbone of its strategic nuclear forces in the 1960s.

As these programs developed, the United States came to foresee in the late 1950s a dangerous period from about 1959 to 1961 (a "window" in current jargon), during which Soviet ICBMs might threaten the U.S. B-52 and B-47 bomber bases, vitiating their deterrent potential. The short-term solution, pending development and deployment of U.S.

ICBMs, was to emplace the shorter-range U.S. Jupiter and Thor IRBMs in the UK, Italy, and Turkey, from where they could reach the major cities of the USSR; this was done around the juncture of 1959 and 1960. Two Jupiter squadrons were deployed in Italy, another in Turkey, and Jupiters and Thors in the UK, to supplement the still considerable deterrence threats of the deployed SAC B-52 and B-47 force.(44) Later during 1960, the United States deployed the first three of its Polaris subs, and almost simultaneously, Atlas and Titan ICBMs were ready-based in the United States, so that the missile gap was quickly on the way to being bridged. The IRBMs nevertheless remained in place for a few years – those in Italy and Turkey were later eliminated after the Cuban missile crisis, their removal having figured in its precarious denouement.(45)

Alongside the importance of the missile and bomber bases provided to the United States overseas was the perhaps equivalently crucial role played by overseas facilities in the surveillance and detection of the Soviet strategic bomber and missile buildup. Specifically, this involved in the 1950s the use of U-2 surveillance flights and the "ferret" activities of electronic surveillance aircraft; later also, the ground activities related to satellite reconnaissance.(46)

The U-2, a high altitude "sailplane" with long, extended wings, began its career in 1956, and its activities were gradually expanded thereafter for the next four years over Soviet airspace. The United States, of course, suffered then as now from a distinct disadvantage vis-a-vis the USSR with respect to strategic intelligence, given the "closed" nature of Soviet frontiers and society and its enormous penchant for security and secrecy, which disadvantage could only in part be made up for by human source intelligence (HUMINT).(47)

In the spring of 1957, U-2 flights operating out of Peshawar, Pakistan, overflew and discovered a new Soviet missile test site at Tyuratam near the Aral Sea, some 700 miles east of the older, main launching site at Kapustin Yar. The flights revealed the progress of the Soviet ICBM program, which earlier had been monitored by a giant radar at Diyarbakir on the Turkish Black Sea coast near Samsun. These flights continued on through 1960, ending that year when Gary Powers's plane, en route from Peshawar to Bodo, Norway (but having originated at Adana, Turkey) was shot down by Soviet missiles near Sverdlovsk.(48) President Eisenhower then had to promise Premier Khrushchev to terminate the U-2 overflights, but not before they had revealed the general outline of the Soviet ICBM buildup as well as other information on bomber deployments and radars.

U-2 flights were flown from a number of bases overseas during this period, primarily in Pakistan, Turkey, Norway, and West Germany (Wiesbaden); additionally, the use of Iranian air space along the southern Soviet frontier was apparently critical. Other U-2s operating out of Atsugi, Japan, were vital to reconnaissance activities in the Far East. Aside from overflights of Soviet territories, these bases also allowed for reconnaissance flights using oblique angle photography from the side windows of high flying planes, which could take pictures of airfields as much as 100 miles distant.(49)

During the late 1950s and early 1960s, the United States and USSR were engaged in parallel development of satellite technology. The first Soviet Sputnik shot had them in the lead by 1957; fifteen months later, in 1959, the United States launched its much smaller Vanguard satellite. But the United States also recognized that the U-2 flights might someday be terminated and that satellite reconnaissance would be needed to fill the gap. As it happened, almost fortuitously, the satellites arrived just in time. By 1961, with the Kennedy administration installed in office after having made an election campaign issue out of the missile gap, the United States was able to obtain satellite photos of Soviet missile sites along the Trans-Siberian railway, only a year after the Powers flight.(50) Those photos resulted in a drastic reduction of estimates of Soviet ICBM strength – by 50 percent – down to about sixty missiles at the time Kennedy was being confronted by Khrushchev over the latter's Berlin ultimatum. Later, the estimates were downgraded still further, and they provided the United States with enormous diplomatic leverage during the confrontations during the early 1960s over Berlin and Cuba.(51) The Soviet Lunik program was soon a virtual match for the U.S. satellites, but of asymmetrically less value, given the open nature of U.S. society which divulged so many of its strategic "secrets" to the casual reader of the daily press, if not military journals.

To recover satellite photos, the United States utilized both radio transmission and midair physical recovery procedures; and as the latter initially encountered difficulties, the former was crucial for rapid and assured transmission of the pictures to analytical laboratories in Washington. For that purpose, the United States deployed ground stations not only in the continental United States (in New Hampshire and California) and in Hawaii, Alaska, and Guam, but also in the British-held Seychelles Islands and in at least one African country.(52) Several shipboard stations with thirty-foot long antennas were used in addition, beginning later in 1964, but these too presumably relied on overseas port facilities for refueling, food, and water.(53) In this area, as in many others, there was a growing need for foreign facilities to provide esoteric technical intelligence activities, at the very time the advent of ICBMs was lessening the need for forward overseas bomber bases.

By the late 1950s, Soviet ICBM developments had rendered somewhat obsolete the three-layered radar early-warning system across the Canadian Arctic, which had been constructed originally to provide several hours' warning of approaching Soviet bombers. To cope with the new missile threat, the United States built, beginning around 1958, the Ballistic Missile Early Warning System (BMEWS), the three hinges of which were in Fairbanks, Thule, and in Yorkshire, UK.(54) Here too, foreign access was crucial to America's nuclear deterrence posture.

Complementary to, and perhaps more important than, BMEWS for warning of an impending missile attack, the United States developed a new class of early-warning satellites which doubled the warning time provided by BMEWS. This involved the MIDAS satellite program, which came to rival in importance the somewhat earlier developed SAMOS satellite reconnaissance system. MIDAS was based on the combined capability of infrared sensors and telephoto lenses to immediately detect missile launching tracks and to transmit this information immediately to U.S. decision makers.(55) The program was apparently immediately successful, despite some initial problems in distinguishing between rocket-engine plumes and sunlight bouncing off clouds.(56) Launched by Atlas/Agena D missiles, advanced MIDAS satellites deployed later in 1969 could be "parked" in synchronous orbits which allowed for continuous coverage of both western Russia and the China-Siberian region, as well as of the Atlantic and Pacific ocean areas where Soviet submarines lurked in firing positions. According to one source, information from the MIDAS satellites' infrared systems is radioed to monitoring stations in Alice Springs, Australia, and in Guam, and then immediately relayed via communications satellites to Washington, NORAD Headquarters in Colorado, and SAC Headquarters near Omaha.(57)

Two other elements of the strategic deterrence system came to depend upon overseas access: fighter interceptor defense, and long-distance and protracted deployment of the Polaris nuclear submarine force. By now, of course, the United States has largely abandoned its air defense system against bombers, having also jettisoned the once complementary ABM system designed to protect the Minuteman missiles against Soviet ICBM attack. But earlier, as implied by the three-tiered radar system in the Canadian Arctic, fighter defense against incoming bombers was deemed both viable and important, echoing earlier geopolitical theories about the crucial nature of air superiority over the Arctic. Fighter-interceptor bases under control of the U.S. Air Defense Command ringed numerous major American cities. Also, they were stationed in Iceland, Greenland, and at various locales in Canada, particularly in Labrador and Newfoundland, along the trans-Arctic route Soviet bombers would have to fly on the way to the United States.(58)

The Polaris subs, as noted, were initially deployed early in the Kennedy administration. The percentage of the fleet which the United States was able to deploy at any given time was enhanced by replenishment and repair facilities at Holy Loch, Scotland; Rota, Spain; and at Guam. Indeed, the asymmetries provided relative to the USSR, once the latter deployed its SSBNs, allowed the United States to negotiate the SALT I treaty which gave the Soviets a 62 to 44 advantage in submarines, but which was claimed nullified by the efficiencies accruing to the United States from its overseas replenishment facilities. Later, the advent of the longer-range Trident submarines would lessen the importance of overseas submarine facilities, allowing the United States to negotiate the closing of the Rota base in Spain.

Throughout the entirety of the early postwar period, the USSR was bereft of overseas access which might have served to rectify the unfavorable strategic balance it faced. As noted, its deterrent capability was long – up to the late 1950s – based upon bombers which might only have been able to achieve one-way missions against the United States.(59) The Soviets also long lagged behind the United States in aerial refueling technology. Early, Soviet development of ICBMs during the late 1950s seemed to augur an at least temporary Soviet strategic advantage, causing the United States to compensate with its hurried overseas deployment of IRBMs while development of the Atlas, Titan, Minuteman, and Polaris programs was hurried along. But what was expected to be a Soviet strategic advantage, at least temporarily around 1960, was quickly turned into a massive U.S. advantage when the aforementioned systems were deployed and while the Soviets still had fewer than 100 ready ICBMs. The shoe was quickly shifted to the other foot, and to compensate, Khrushchev gambled with the introduction of IRBMs into Cuba, hence precipitating the Cuban missile crisis.(60) The rest is history, but it is worth noting that only by 1960 did the Cuban revolution avail the USSR of its first valuable overseas points of access applicable to the strategic nuclear balance. In ensuing years, even despite the forced withdrawal of Soviet IRBMs in 1962, Cuba would become a very valuable Soviet base, its proximity to the United States providing irreplaceable assets related to intelligence, surveillance, and naval replenishment.

During the 1950s and early 1960s, overseas facilities became increasingly important for the United States in relation to other technical operations – again primarily in the areas of surveillance and intelligence – not all of which related solely to the nuclear strategic balance. Again here, the balance of overseas assets was entirely to the favor of the United States, serving to compensate for the closed nature of Soviet society which denied easy surveillance and penetration via open sources or through human-source intelligence. Most notable here was the use of aircraft for electromagnetic reconnaissance and intelligence (ELINT) conducted around the periphery of the USSR, China, and North Korea, as well as of numerous ground-based intercept stations around the Eurasian periphery for communications intelligence (COMINT).(61)

Further in the strategic nuclear arena, both U-2s and other aircraft, primarily the RB-47, were long flown from bases in Europe and Asia to "tickle" Soviet early warning radars; the U-2 flights were used to test radars deep inside the USSR which might be of different types than the Soviets' peripheral early warning systems. By doing so, U.S. planners might ascertain weaknesses, ranges, and scan patterns in the Soviet radar system which could be valuable for planning the penetration routes for a nuclear bomber attack. As time went on, this involved an ever-escalating technological race of reciprocal measures and counter-measures with the use of jammers, antijammers, false image projectors and filters, and so on.(62)

The game of "tickling," begun in the 1950s, even apparently involved mock "raids" mounted by U.S. units in Turkey and elsewhere, which had to penetrate Soviet airspace in order to compel Soviet radar technicians to turn their sets on and hence to reveal their capabilities.(63) These exercises in low-level brinkmanship, all mounted from foreign bases, resulted in some serious incidents in which U.S. ferret aircraft were shot down and their crews killed or captured. Some flights originating at Brize Norton in the UK apparently traversed the entire northern Soviet coastline, emerging at the Barents Sea.(64) According to one source, the United States lost, between 1950 and 1964, 108 airmen killed or captured in this manner, and 26 aircraft shot down or forced to land in incidents over the Baltic, Germany, Czechoslovakia, Hungary, the Adriatic, Black Sea, Armenia, Straits of Taiwan, China Sea, Japan, Korea, and Russia.(65) The area between the Caspian Sea and Sea of Azov was apparently a particular focus of U.S. surveillance, with the United States flying frequent reconnaissance missions over Turkish and Iranian airspace, some staged originally from Germany and Cyprus.(66) Soviet ferrets, on the other hand, mostly operating out of Siberia toward Alaska, are believed rarely to have penetrated U.S. airspace, in part because U.S. radar men apparently kept their sets on at all times.

Later, the use of ferret aircraft for ELINT purposes was apparently replaced in part by large ferret satellites. This function is, however, apparently not easily handled by satellite, due to size and weight problems and the need for human operators in utilizing complex equipment.(67) Still, such activities were apparently begun in around 1962-1963, presumably also requiring overseas facilities for rapid transmission of data to home processing facilities.

In addition to the above, the United States has long made use of numerous facilities for its ground-based radio intercept network (COMINT). McGarvey reports that earlier, this involved some fifty stations in at least fourteen countries, ranging from small mobile field units to sprawling complexes such as the Air Force Security Head-quarters in West Germany.(68) According to him, these facilities have been operated by some 30,000 men worldwide, with a minimum of 4,000 radio intercept consoles in operation in such varied locales as northern Japan, the Aleutian Islands, the Khyber Pass in Pakistan, and an island in the Yellow Sea off the coast of Korea.(69) Further according to him, these COMINT land stations had to be supplemented by numerous flying and seaborne radio intercepts, particularly after Communist military units massively switched to VHF radios during the 1950s, whereinafter complete coverage demanded getting closer to transmitters and circumventing terrain features such as mountains.(70) Early use for this purpose was made of Kimpo airfield in Korea, Clark Field, and many others; at any time, several dozen airborne listening posts were said to have been in intermittent operation. Added to these were some twelve to fifteen spy ships such as the ill-fated Pueblo and Liberty, which also presumably required routine replenishment access to foreign ports.(71) These combined assets were used for interception even of encoded or otherwise unintelligible communications, to monitor merchant shipping, foreign trade, internal transportation, and so forth.

From 1945 to 1960, amid striking developments in electronic and communications intelligence and in side-angle and overhead photography, the United States had an enormous advantage over the USSR due to its strategic overseas assets, with reciprocal access for the Soviets then altogether absent. Later, newer technological advances, particularly in satellites, might somewhat but not altogether reduce the need for these overseas facilities.(72) This was later indicated by the reports about the holes created in the U.S. intelligence effort by the (temporary) loss of Turkish facilities and then of those in Iran, and was also highlighted by the still heavy use of U-2 and SR-71 (successor to the U-2) reconnaissance flights all over the world well after the full development of seemingly sophisticated satellites for reconnaissance and monitoring purposes. And, of course, the U-2 and SR-71 flights also needed overseas staging bases.

The Soviets had, of course, long been aware of and unhappy about the strategic advantage given the United States by its system of overseas access. In 1958, when President Eisenhower first proposed a ban on the use of outer space for military purposes, the Soviets insisted that such a measure be accompanied by "liquidation" of foreign military bases in Europe, the Middle East, and North Africa.(73) At the time, such a mutually agreed upon measure would have been very asymmetrically disadvantageous to the United States, given its strategic reliance on B-47 and related tanker refueling bases, and the whole vast network of facilities devoted to ELINT, COMINT, air sample detection, and what not. But the Soviets would later be much more competitive in acquiring overseas bases for similar functions, and hence also later more reserved about suggesting formal arrangements which might mutually do away with overseas facilities.

THE POSTWAR DECLINE OF THE BRITISH EMPIRE AND ITS IMPACT ON WESTERN BASING ASSETS

In 1945, in the aftermath of victory, Britain recovered and retained, at least for the moment, its vast empire and its accompanying basing facilities. Indeed, many were enlarged and upgraded during the war, and new ones were added. For instance, Britain inherited access to Libya's former Italian air bases at the war's close at Wheelus (Tripoli) and El Adem (Tobruk) and retained access to others, for instance in Bahrain, built in response to wartime contingencies.

Before World War II, most of Britain's overseas army units were deployed in India, Egypt, and Palestine (in 1939, the British Army in India and Burma numbered 45,000 troops).(74) After 1945 occupation forces were left, at least temporarily, in Egypt, Italy, Greece, Germany, Denmark, Italian East Africa, Sudan, Syria, Iraq, Iran, Aden, Burma, Japan, Thailand, Indo-China, and the Dutch East Indies, and air and naval access was correspondingly available to the British in all of these areas, as well as in its colonial possessions.(75) Between 1945 and 1947, the still large British Army deployed some seventy-seven of its own combat battalions abroad, along with eight Ghurka battalions and four additional regiments from the still British-controlled India.(76) There were 10,000 troops in Egypt, thirteen battalions divided between Malaya and Hong Kong; a brigade in Japan; a battalion in Jamaica; nine battalions divided among Greece, Italy, and Austria; a brigade in Cyprus; eighteen battalions and eight armored regiments in Germany, and a major new military command headquarters in Tripoli; and various troop units in Malta, British Honduras, and Somaliland.(77)

Along with the many newly acquired U.S. basing assets, Britain's old and new points of access provided the West during the immediate postwar years with a formidable, integrated global strategic network. Beginning around 1947, however, the British Empire began to unravel in a process which proceeded gradually but remorselessly up to about 1965. As a consequence, the West began to lose one basing asset after another, many of which could not easily be replaced or superseded by new technology, and some of which were ultimately inherited by the USSR on the rebound of postcolonial political radicalization.

The British withdrawal from empire, varying in the extent it was forced or more or less voluntary, began in India and Burma. Amidst the savage communal warfare in the former, all British troops and bases were evacuated by 1948; Burma was similarly withdrawn from in the same year. By contrast with some other British postcolonial experiences, no residual base rights were here granted.(78) And aside from the fact of Britain (and the West) thereby losing a number of important air and naval bases (and shortly thereafter, also, those in Ceylon), the long-held rationale for numerous other British facilities all along the route to India was called into question. As the protracted insurgency in Malaya began almost at the same time as the British withdrawal from India, much of the former British Indian Army, including most of the British-officered Ghurka forces, were moved there, and the Malaya-Singapore area henceforth became the primary British Far Eastern base complex.(79)

During the early Cold War period, up to the early 1950s, British overseas access was diminished or eliminated in a number of other locales. The British had withdrawn from Greece by 1950, after having kept a garrison at Salonika; however, U.S. aid to Greece following the enunciation of the Truman Doctrine allowed for compensatory U.S. air and naval access which would be extended for decades. British troops withdrew from Somaliland in 1950, which many years later would see the (temporary) installation of important Soviet air and naval bases. Sudan was evacuated in 1955. Palestine was abandoned in 1948 after its partition, withdrawing from British control a naval base at Haifa and some airfields, and thwarting an earlier plan to build a massive base complex there if those in Egypt had to be abandoned.(80) In the Far East, the Royal Navy had to give up the China Squadron's old station at the mouth of the Yangtze River when China was overrun by the Communists, forcing withdrawal of remaining British naval units to Hong Kong.(81)

Britain endured a protracted and bitterly contested departure from Egypt between 1945 and 1956, losing a major complex of bases which had been the core of its Middle Eastern military position. Before the war, the 1936 treaty which had assured Egypt virtual independence had provided for the stationing of 10,000 British troops and 400 airmen.(82)

By the war's end, however, Egypt had become a vast British staging and basing center, involving some nine airfields (the main ones at Abu Suweir and Fayid), naval bases at Alexandria and Port Said, a vast ordnance depot at Tel El Kebir, forty miles east of Cairo (which had a seventeen-mile perimeter), several other large army bases and depots, and a general headquarters for the Middle East at Cairo.(83)

As noted, in 1946, under the prod of riots and political pressures in Egypt, the British considered utilizing Palestinian facilities to replace them. That aim thwarted, Britain withdrew from most of Egypt in 1947, but maintained numerous important bases in the Suez Canal Zone. Indeed, there was a proposal in 1949 that the Canal Zone be made into a large NATO base, an idea was turned down flat by Egypt.(84)

After the Egyptian revolution which installed Nasser in power, the British phased out their Egyptian bases over a twenty-month period beginning in October 1954. At that point, Britain had still retained nine air bases, the Tel-el-Kebir repair center for the entire Middle East, various depots around Ismailia and Fayid, army bases at Mouscar and Port Said, and a naval base at the latter.(85) All of these installations were evacuated by 1955, and the Anglo-French-Israeli invasion in 1956 could not bring about a reversal.

Even with the loss of Egypt, Britain retained numerous bases and points of access in the Middle East up to and beyond the mid 1950s. There were the important Libyan air bases at Wheelus and El Adem; a division of British troops was garrisoned in Libya up to 1950.(86) A British garrison was installed at Aqaba in Jordan (which protected the city from Israeli forces in 1948 and then in 1956), which also hosted RAF bases at Amman and Mafraq.(87) Further east, British air bases were retained in Iraq up to 1958 (the most important of which was at Habbaniya), and around the Arabian peninsula, at Aden and Bahrain. Air and naval bases in Malta and Cyprus further served to maintain an integrated, strong British basing structure in the area well into the postwar period.

In the Middle East, as elsewhere, the plethora of British facilities during this period allowed for easy deployment of troops and for staging of air and naval operations at points of conflict. Even as the overall system, once containing considerable redundancy, began to wither, bases in one area or country were available for attempts at stanching the tide of the anticolonialist revolt in others. Britain's military operations in Palestine in 1947-1948 were assisted by nearby and still available staging facilities in Egypt.(88) When trouble erupted in Egypt, troops were sent from Libya.(89) In 1956 the initially successful but ultimately abortive air, land, and sea invasion of the Egyptian Canal Zone was launched primarily from Malta (ground troops and ships) and Cyprus (paratroopers and Valiant bomber sorties) as well as from French bases in North Africa at Algiers and Tyndou.(90) In 1955, when trouble erupted at the Buraimi Oasis on the Arabian Peninsula, British troops from Tobruk were staged there via Jordan and Iraq.(91) The same pattern was repeated in Africa and the Far East, but with an inexorable trend toward almost total elimination of basing assets.

In 1954, after evacuating Egypt, Britain moved its Middle Eastern Land and Air Headquarters to Cyprus, which was to host, for many years, the principal British bases in the region. Cyprus had been acquired in 1878, and was then perceived as a potentially important place d'armes, but had subsequently been eclipsed as Egypt came to house Britain's main Middle Eastern bases.(92) Some twenty-six troop units were deployed there by 1958, among other things, to deter aggression by the then newly formed and assertive United Arab Republic which temporarily fused Egypt and Syria. Troops were moved to Cyprus both from Egypt and Malta, and principal British air bases were developed at Akotiri and Nicosia.(93) From these bases, troops were deployed in times of trouble to Aden and Bahrain, to protect King Idris in Libya, and to defend Jordan in 1958 from a possible Iraqi invasion.(94) The Cyprus bases were perceived as an important back-stopping of British defense treaty obligations to Jordan, Iraq (up to 1958), and also to Greece and Turkey.

However, the EOKA rebellion on Cyprus quickly rendered the new British bases precarious, and after Cyprus became independent in 1960, British troops were physically forced within the relatively small base areas.(95) As it is, the value of the air bases there was greatly diminished by the closure of Arab and Israeli air spaces, so that Britain's Middle Eastern Command was subsequently split in two, with the headquarters on Cyprus renamed Near Eastern Command, and a Middle Eastern Command set up in Aden.(96) Well after Cyprus's independence in 1960, however, its air bases remained valuable for NATO contingencies. In the late 1970s the United States continued to fly U-2 reconnaissance flights from Akotiri over the Sinai, and also considered such Cyprus-based flights for monitoring Soviet missile tests after the fall of Iran's Shah.(97)

In the late 1950s, Britain's Middle Eastern basing structure suffered a number of strong blows, cumulating in a serious diminution of Western strategic access. In 1957 British forces departed Aqaba and the Jordan airfields, and in 1958, after the overthrow of the Iraqi monarchy, Britain lost its important air base at Habbaniya.(98) By 1960 its diminished Middle Eastern basing network was hinged primarily upon Cyprus, Aden, and Bahrain.

In Africa, Britain maintained virtually the entirety of its prewar basing structure throughout the 1950s; only with Ghana's independence in 1957 did the inevitable decolonization process finally begin, with its accompanying implications for Western access rights. As it is, the virtual absence of Soviet penetration into Africa up to 1960 rendered Western bases there essentially only latent assets. Kenya became Britain's primary African basing hub during the 1950s, in part because troops had to be moved there from Egypt, Uganda, Tanganyika, and even from Korea to quell the initial Mau Mau revolts between 1952 and 1956 (Britain had 8½ troop battalions there in 1952).(99) Britain actually considered at one point making Kenya its primary base for the whole southern Middle Eastern region, while developing there the major RAF base at Eastleigh in Nairobi.(100) In the mid-1950s, British troops were deployed variously to Malaya, Aden, and the Persian Gulf from Kenya.

In some cases, the UK tried to write retention of facilities into agreements giving independence to former African colonies. It was given access to airfields and jungle training bases in Nigeria in 1960; but only a couple of years beyond Nigeria's independence, that agreement was quietly voided.(101)

In the Far East during the 1950s, Singapore and Hong Kong continued to serve as the principal British naval and air bases, and housed large garrisons from which troops could be staged to nearby trouble spots. During the Malaya emergency during the 1950s, reinforcements were sent at various times from Kenya, Hong Kong, and the Middle East, and at their peak, British forces in Malaya were comprised of some twenty-four infantry battalions involving British, Ghurkha, Malayan, African, and Fijian forces.(102) Both Hong Kong and Singapore, meanwhile, were used to stage the movement of British forces to Korea from 1950 to 1954.(103)

During the early postwar period, predating the Cuban revolution, British bases in the Caribbean-West Atlantic area were essentially a wasting asset, almost superfluous in light of total and assuredly unmenacing U.S. strategic dominance of the region. Stationing of a small force at Jamaica did, however, allow for rapid deployment of troops to Belize (1948), Grenada and Antigua (1957), and to British Guyana (1953) to quash some early stirrings by leftist political forces under Cheddi Jagan.(104) Britain's assets in the area remained intact up to 1960, however, at which time it still maintained troops and bases in British Guyana, British Honduras, the Bahamas, and Jamaica, all of which reinforced an otherwise strong American-led regional defense structure.

During the 1960s and early 1970s, of course, Britain's former colonial empire was to be reduced near to the vanishing point. However, even during the 1950s, while the United States was constructing an elaborate system of alliances and bases around the southern arc of the Eurasian continent to contain Communist expansionism, the gathering momentum of Britain's imperial collapse was removing numerous points of access for Western military forces.

THE CONTRIBUTION OF OTHER WESTERN EUROPEAN OVERSEAS BASING ASSETS TO THE WEST

In addition to the basing assets amassed by the United States during and after World War II, and to those retained by Britain, the West was initially availed of numerous points of access controlled by other western powers. France, Belgium, Spain, Portugal, and the Netherlands all emerged from the war with their colonial empires intact, at least for the time being. Of course, as was the case for Britain, these assets were gradually diminished as the tide of empire receded. Holland lost the Dutch East Indies shortly after the war, and France later lost its North African empire and then most of its sub-Saharan Africa colonies (in some of which it subsequently retained bases long into the post-independence period). Belgium only later lost the jewel of its empire, Zaire, in the early 1960s. Spain and Portugal lost their respective dominions in Africa (and in the case of Portugal, in Goa and Timor) rather late in the decolonization process, culminating in the divestiture, during the mid-1970s, of Angola, Mozambique, and Spanish Sahara.

Because of the vast basing network controlled by the United States and the UK during the early postwar period, additional points of access provided to the West by other European powers were in most cases virtually superfluous. For instance, Britain's control of a number of Indian Ocean ports and air bases rendered France's control of Djibouti and Diego Suarez somewhat irrelevant, and, indeed, they were of importance primarily for the use of the French themselves.(105)

The principal exceptions involved the U.S. access to strategic bomber bases in French-controlled Morocco up to 1963, and the earlier-discussed American use of Portugal's Azores Islands, the latter very important because of the still limited ranges of state-of-the-art transport aircraft in the immediate postwar period.

In 1950, at a time France was still solidly tied to the U.S.-led Western alliance, the United States obtained its agreement to construct badly needed SAC bomber bases in Morocco, which subsequently were used for the forward deployment of SAC's "reflex" force of B-47s. Bases for them arose at Nouasseur, Sidi Sliman, Ben Guerir, and Bensliman (others were built concurrently in nearby Spain), and a USAF materiel depot along with fighter aircraft units was colocated at the first-named.(106) Additionally, a naval air station and naval communications facility were emplaced at Kenitra, the use of which for the United States was to survive the forced closing of the bomber bases in 1963, some seven years after Morocco's independence.(107) By the time of the base closings, however, home-based U.S. ICBM forces had rendered the forward deployment of B-47s of far lesser importance, and nearby Spanish facilities served, at any rate, as alternatives. Also nearby, the United States had been given access in Spanish-controlled Tangiers to operate a Voice of America transmitter beginning in 1949; it too was removed with Spain's withdrawal in 1962.(108)

For the most part, the gradual dismemberment of the several non-British colonial empires resulted for the West in the loss of a number of points of access which might have been useful for certain specialized contingencies. In 1973, U.S. use of the Azores' Lajes airfield for resupplying Israel was to demonstrate the at least potential importance of such facilities. Of course, as Soviet influence was later to become dominant in numerous ex-French, Spanish, and Portuguese colonies (Algeria, Mali, Guinea-Bissau, Guinea, Angola, Mozambique), the attendant loss of access for the West was to assume a heightened meaning because, in so many places, it was translated into military access for its main rival.

THE ZENITH OF PAX AMERICANA: THE EXPANSION OF THE U.S. ALLIANCE AND BASING STRUCTURE DURING THE 1950s

In the late 1940s and during the 1950s, the United States and its allies constructed a vast global system of alliances and security commitments which were to provide for forward conventional deterrence and for interlocking naval and air logistic capability all around the rim of the Eurasian continent, as well as in more peripheral developing areas. The expansion of these commitments came in response to the hardening of Cold War lines; the events in the late 1940s in Berlin, Greece, and Turkey; the Chinese revolution which produced − at least temporarily − a menacing Sino-Soviet military bloc; and the North Korean aggression against South Korea.

In connection with the alliances constructed in the 1950s, mostly during the Eisenhower-Dulles foreign policy era, the U.S. global system of access reached a high-water mark; subsequently, there was a long-term, gradual constriction produced by the progressive weakening of the alliance system, and defections of formerly pro-Western nations to Communism, anti-Western radicalism, or neutralism. All of these trends were accelerated during the Vietnam War.

During the early postwar period, the United States became involved in eight mutual security treaties involving some forty-two nations, in addition to South Vietnam as a protocol, nonsignatory country under SEATO. These were as follows:

- The Rio Treaty of 1947 and the related Charter of the Organization of American States, involving some twenty Latin American states and including all of the larger nations of South America.
- The North Atlantic Treaty of 1949, ultimately to involve in addition to the United States, Belgium, Canada, Denmark, the FRG, France, Greece, Iceland, Italy, Luxembourg, Netherlands, Norway, Portugal, Turkey, and the UK.
- The Mutual Defense Treaty of 1951 between the United States and the Philippines.
- The Anzus Treaty of 1951 with Australia and New Zealand.
- A 1952 Treaty of Mutual Cooperation and Security with Japan, amended and essentially reiterated by a new treaty in 1960.
- The Mutual Defense Treaty between the United States and South Korea of 1953, signed toward the end of the Korean War.
- The SEATO Treaty of 1954 (signed at the time of the Geneva Accords), involving besides the United States, Australia, France, New Zealand, Pakistan, Philippines, Thailand, and the UK, as well as South Vietnam as a "protocol" country.
- The 1954 Mutual Defense Treaty with Taiwan.(109)

In addition, in the gap in the Eurasian ring around the USSR between Pakistan and Turkey, the United States became involved − though not as a signatory − in the CENTO Treaty arrangement, which originally involved Iraq (which withdrew in 1959 after the 1958 coup), Turkey,

Iran, Pakistan, and the UK. It became involved in CENTO planning and in some of its military exercises and military committees, and virtually committed itself to a military reaction to an attack upon any of its members. With Pakistan a linking hinge between SEATO and CENTO, and Turkey similarly between the latter and NATO, the ring around the Eurasian heartland was made essentially complete, if still subject to the kind of leapfrogging accomplished by the Soviet end-run in Egypt beginning around 1955.

These elaborate and interlocking written defense commitments provided the basis for the expanded American postwar basing system, itself the very physical expression of a "forward" commitment. Otherwise, there were only four countries – Spain, Ethiopia, Morocco, and Cuba – where the United States had major military facilities without formal defense treaties.(110) Spain, of course, was considered for all intents and purposes shielded by the NATO alliance, while the residual U.S. presence in Cuba at Guantanamo after 1959 was an odd anomaly.

Summary data for the U.S. basing system at its postwar zenith – in the early 1960s – is provided in table 4.2, broken down according to hosts, names of major facilities (there were many additional minor ones), the military functions of the installations, and the basis for American access, be it formal alliances, other types of security agreements, or merely the facts of significant arms-transfer relationships.

In the Far East, following the Chinese revolution and the onset of the Korean War, there was a vast buildup of U.S. facilities to form a defensive cordon offshore from Soviet Siberia and China and around Southeast Asia. Japan, Okinawa, South Korea, Taiwan, and the Philippines came to house the bulk of U.S. Far East installations, which provided a full range of naval, air, and various technical functions, as well as forward troop garrisons.

At its peak, the United States had some 3,800 military installations in Japan (reduced by 1970 to 115), of which over thirty were major facilities, including six airfields, two naval bases, two bombing ranges, six ammunition depots, and a maneuver area.(111) By 1970, their operating costs amounted to over a half billion dollars annually, and there were by that time over 40,000 U.S. military personnel in Japan.(112) These bases were vital to the conduct of the Korean War, and were later also important to the logistics for the Vietnam War.

The two major naval bases were set up at Yokosuka and Sasebo, earlier among the major hubs of the former Japanese Imperial Navy. Yokosuka became the home port of the Seventh Fleet and comprised a vast complex including naval ordnance facilities, a naval communications station, and extensive drydocking capacity (six graving docks up to the largest size).(113) The repair capability at Yokosuka covers the full range of shipboard hull, machinery, and electrical and electronic installations, and it became the central U.S. naval maintenance facility in the Western Pacific.(114) Along with Subic Bay, it also became the main U.S. naval basing facility, from which aircraft carriers, cruisers, destroyers, submarines, landing ships, and various other naval units

Table 4.2. The U.S. Primary Base Network at Its Postwar Zenith
1960s

Host	Location/Base	Principal Type/Facilities	Basis of Access: Comments
Japan/Okinawa	Kadena AFB	TacAir, B-52s, tankers	Alliance-agreement
	Camp Schwab	USMC camp	
	Camp Hansen	USMC camp	"
	Camp Courtney	USMC HQ	
	White Beach	USN base	"
	Futenma	USMC air facilities	
	Machinato	USAR logistical depot	"
	Naha	port and air facilities	
	numerous others	incl. nuclear arms & nerve gas depots, special forces units, bombing range, tech. facils., Psyop group, etc.	
Japan/Marcus	Marcus I.	weather station	"
Japan	Atsugi AFB	naval air sta.: electronics, reconn., tact. support, photogr., cargo term., weather, microwave, U-2	"
	Itazuke	AF support base: air range, ammo storage, radar, TACAN, radio relay, troposcatter, AUTODIN, AUTOVON	"
	Tachikawa	AF support base: commands, radio relay, AFCS transmitter, commo, etc.	
	Misawa	AF: F-4, T-33, air range, TACAN, commo, trng.	"
	Yokota	AF, tactical ftrs, transports, weather haven, training, F-4s, B-57s, C-130s	
	Iwakuni	USMC air station, flt. air wing, naval air support, F-4, P-3A, C-54, etc.	"
	Sasebo	USN: drydocks, full repair capability, various tech. functions, sea transp.	"
	Yokosuka	USN: homeport, 7th fleet, marine barracks service, mine flotilla, drydock w. full capab, ordnance, commo trng, etc. - destroyer, cruiser, sub. landing ship units	"

131

Table 4.2. (Cont.)

Host	Location/Base	Principal Type Facilities	Basis of Access: Comments
	Hakata	Security grp. post	Alliance – agreement
	Kamiseya	USN security grp. for flt. support, HF/DF, COMSEC,radio facils, microwave, etc.	"
	Iwo Jima	Loran A master station	"
	Minami Tori	Loran slave station	"
	Tokachibuto	Loran slave station	"
	Wakkonai	commo sta., Hokkaido	"
	Camp Zama	USAR HQ base, US Transport Comm. HQ supply & maint.	"
	Sagami Gen'l Depot		"
	Mito	Bombing range	"
	various	hundreds of small facils	
South Korea	various	USAR-large garrisons, 40,000 troops, whole range of support facils, HAWK, NIKE-Hercules	Alliance-Agreement military aid
	Kimpo AB	USAF base: airlift support	"
	Camp Page	USAR missile command – supports ROK army	"
	Kangnung	n/a – prob. intell, or commo	"
	Pusan	major logistics complex, oil pipeline terminal	"
	Taegu	major USAR depots, HQ	"
	Camp Carroll	support functions, etc.	"
	Camp Humphreys		
	Chinhae	USN advisory grp-security	"
	Suwan	USAF-interceptors, support functs.	"
	Taegu	USAF – tact. air, combat support	"
	Kwang-Ju	USAF – tact. air, reconn, support	"
	Kunsan	USAF – tact. air, support (F-4s), GEODSS	"
	Osan	USAF – tact. air, support, HQ functions, etc.	"

132

Table 4.2. (Cont.)

Host	Location/Base	Principal Type Facilities	Basis of Access: Comments
South Korea	offshore island(n/a)		
Taiwan	Taipeh	NSA Comint Sta. air station, USAF, various support functs.	Alliance-Agreement
	Shou Lin Kae	air station - commo, intell.	"
	Tainan	USAF support for Clark AFB aircraft, war materiel storage	"
	Ching Chuan Kang	USAF: C-130s, KC-135, B-52 weather refuge, commo (AUTODIN), materiel storage	"
	Unkn.	Matador missiles deployed	"
	Keelung	ROC facils used by U.S. forces during Viet war	"
	Koahsiung & others		"
	various	radar sites - 5	"
	Sung Shan	USN: mily cargo, support units, etc.	"
Laos	Phou Pha Ti	Tacan navig. site for Viet bombing	Agreement-pro-U.S. factions-related to SEATO, clandestine milit. support
	Muong Phalane	Tacan navig. site for Viet bombing	"
	Long Tung	T-28 air bases-COIN	
	Luang Prabang	"	
Vietnam	Tan Son Nhut, Bien Hoa, others	USAF-main bases	Agreement-related to SEATO, military aid
	Camranh Bay	USN-logistics	"
	various	USAR-Trng,, support, tech. etc.	"
	Tan My, Con Son Isl.	Loran-C	
Philippines	Clark A.B.	USAF: HQ, base for F-4, F-102, C-130, AD control, commo, SIGINT, MAC staging	Alliance-Agreement military aid, SEATO
			"

133

Table 4.2. (Cont.)

Host	Location/Base	Principal Type Facilities	Basis of Access: Comments
Philippines	Subic Bay	USN: Major base, flt. logistics, full ship repair, supply depot, materiel storage, medical, commo, intell., etc.	"
	Cubi Point	Naval air sta-support for carriers	"
	Sangley Point	Naval air: ASW, Loran, Coast Guard air, air staging, commo, etc.	
	Mactan	USAF: contingency base plus SAC recovery, C-130s, etc.	"
	San Miguel	USN: principal commo base (DCS): microwave, Autodin, LF & HF	"
	Mt. San Rita		"
	Capas	outlying commo sta's, relays	"
	Tarlac		"
	Bataan	Loran A	"
	Tarumpitao, Talampulan	Loran A	"
	Catanduanes, Naulo Pt.	Loran A	"
	Cagayan de Oro	Weather station	"
	Wallace Air Sta	Radar	"
	Camp O'Donnell	commo relay	"
	John Hay AB	Radio (HF), weather, VOA transmitter	"
Thailand	Korat	air base (tact. air & electronics aircraft during Viet	Agreement-also SEATO
	Takhli	air base (F-105, EB-66, KC-135 in Viet)	"
	Udorn	RF-4C, C-130, F-102, radar, Loran-C in Viet	"
	Ubon	radar, F-4D, AC-130 in Viet	"
	Don Muong	F-102, C-130 in Viet	"
	Utapao	B-52, KC-135, A-1, AC-130 in Viet	"

Table 4.2. (Cont.)

Host	Location/Base	Principal Type Facilities	Basis of Access: Comments
Thailand	Sattahip	Loran-C, army supply, logistical command, deepwater port	"
	Green Hill	Army facility	"
	Lapburi	Commo w. numerous outlying stations, special forces	"
	Bangkok	VOA transmitter	"
	Nakhon Phanom	radar, A-1, OV-10 & various prop aircraft	"
	Pitsanuloke, Makdahan	radar facils.	"
	Nam Phong	USAF-"bare base" facil.	"
	Lampong	Loran-C	"
	Ramasun	Major intell. base-NSA	"
	Bang Pla, Camp Narai	Commo	"
	Kohka	Seismic sounding station	"
Micronesia & W. Pacific	Guam	Anderson AFB, naval base, satellite data relay	U.S. possession
	Kwajalein	Terminus-Pacific missile range	"
	Tinian	air & tech. facils.	"
	n/a	Baker-Nunn facil. (deep-space optical tracking)	
New Zealand	Christchurch	logistical support-Antarctica Opn. "Deep Freeze"	ANZUS Treaty, SEATO
Australia	Northwest Cape (Harold Holt)	LF transmitter-link to subs	ANZUS Treaty, SEATO
	Woomera/Nurrungar	Early warning facil-Joint Defense Space Commo Station	"
	Pine Gap/Alice Springs	Commo & intell facil.	
Singapore	Sembawang Naval Basin	MAC transit (later, P-3 ocean surveill. flights) Use of Brit. naval facil.	Agreement
Antarctica	McMurdo, others	various tech. facils.	Occupation-sphere
Pakistan	Peshawar	U-2 staging intell. monitoring	Agreement-CENTO, SEATO
	Khyber Pass		
Seychelles	Mahe	satellite data relay, P-3 staging	Brit. allowed access cont. after independence

Table 4.2. (Cont.)

Host	Location/Base	Principal Type Facilities	Basis of Access: Comments
Maldives	Gan	Air transit	U.S. use of Brit. facil.
Bahrain	Jufair	HQ U.S. Mideast Force, Commo	Brit-allowed access cont. after independence
Iran	Bandar Abbas	ASW patrols	Agreement-Bilat, CENTO
	Tackman I & II	Intell-tech. vis a vis USSR	"
Saudi Arabia	Dhahran	B-52 transit, MAC transit	Agreement-heavy MAP & FMS
Ethiopia	Jidda	USN refueling	"
	Kagnew	Naval commo, HF for DCS	Security Agreement-mily aid "
Kenya	Assab, Massawa	USN refuel, provisioning	
Liberia	Mombasa	USN-limited access	Some ATs
	Roberts Field	USAF staging	Agreement-ATs
	n/a	Omega station, commo	"
	Monrovia	USN access	
Senegal	Dakar	limited air & naval access	French-allowed access cont. after independence
Cyprus	Akotiri, Dhekelia	U-2s, air transit, radar	Access via U.K.
Reunion	------------	Omega station, later	Access via France
Madagascar	n/a	satellite tracking facil	Agreement-from 1963
Oman	Masirah	ASW staging	Brit-allowed, cont. after independence-former RAF base
Libya	Wheelus AFB	USAF transport command, gunnery and trng. base, Loran-C	Acquired from UK, agreement up to Libyan revolution
Morocco	Pt. Lyautey	U-2 flight staging	Orig via agreement w. France, cont. after indep.
	Kenitra	USN-Commo & support for Med. Fleet	MAP, FMS
	Sidi Yahya		"
	Bouknadel		
	Sidi Sliman	SAC bases - B-47s, etc.	
	Ben Guerir	"	
	Bensliman		
	Nouasseur		
	Tangier	VOA relay transmitter	
Cuba	Guantanamo	USN-Training, replenishment	Occupation
Bermuda	Kindley AFB, others	Naval air sta-ASW & ocean surveill.	Rent-free, 99 yr
South Africa	Silvermine	intelligence	Agreement
	Pretoria	missile tracking station	Agreement

136

Table 4.2. (Cont.)

Host	Location/Base	Principal Type Facilities	Basis of Access: Comments
Bahamas		USAF Eastern Test Range, radar	Rent-free, 99-yr. Agreement
Ascension Is.	Wideawake Field	Atlantic Underseas Test & Eval. Center	Access via UK
Antigua	————	Air staging, tech. facils	Access via UK
Trinidad & Tobago	————	Underwater surveillance facil (test) Omega sta., air staging	Access via UK
Grand Turk	————	Testing, radar	Access via UK
Barbados	————	Underwater test facil.	Access via UK
Ecuador	n/a	Space tracking facil.	Agreement
Argentina	n/a	Omega station, later	Agreement
Panama	Canal Zone	U.S. SouthCom (army garrisons, various USAR bases & installations; jungle opns. trng, logistical support school, etc), air bases	U.S. control
			"
Canada	C.Z., Galeta Pinetree, DEW, Mid-Canada lines	Commo facil. Radar picket fence lines Strategic defense	Agreement-NATO
	Goose Bay	SAC base, radars, tankers, interceptors	"
U.K.	Upper Heyford, Greenham Common, Brize Norton, Fairford	SAC B-47 reflex bases	Agreement-NATO
	Welford	USAF, munitions storage	"
	Sculthorpe	USAF-standby base	"
	Mildenhall	USAF-airlift, command & control, logistics	"
	Lakenheath	USAF-fighters, rescue, tact. control	"
	Croughton	Commo relay	"
	Chicksands	technical-security	"
	Holy Loch	Polaris sub base	"
	n/a	Jupiter, Thor launching pads	"
	Yorkshire/Fyling-dale Moor	BMEWS radar	"
	South Ruislip	USAF commo, cmd. & control	"
	Alconbury	USAF-reconn, rescue, C3	"
	Bentwaters/Wood-bridge	USAF-fighters, rescue, C3	"
	Wethersfield	USAF-air base	"

137

Table 4.2. (Cont.)

Host	Location/Base	Principal Type Facilities	Basis of Access: Comments
Iceland	Keflavik	USAF: fighters, air staging, ASW incl. later SOSUS, Loran-C, HF/DF	Agreement-NATO
Netherlands	Soesterberg, other	USAF-air defense fts.	Agreement-NATO
Norway	Bodo	U-2 flights	Agreement-NATO
	n/a and Gamvik	Omega, Loran-C, Caesar	"
	Oslo	USAF-area support	
Denmark/ Greenland	Thule	SAC: bombers, tankers, BMEWs	Agreement-NATO
	Sondestrom	SAC base	
France	Chambley, Chaumont Etain, Laon, Phalsbourg, Evereaux-Fauville, Toul-Rosiere, Captieux-Ord,	USAF bases, various	Agreement-NATO
	Bussac Braconne, Chize, Croix Chapeau, Donges, Ingrande, Saunier, Chinon, Evreaux, St. Andre, LaFerte, Brienne le Chateau, Chalons, Vittry le Francois, Verdun, St. Baussant, St. Mihiel, Nancy, Toul, Metz	USAR depots, various	"
	Chateauroux, St. Mihiel	USAF depots	"
	Bordeaux	U.S. supply port after WW II	"
	Villefranche	USN facil.	"
Italy	n/a	Jupiter IRBM pads	Agreement-NATO
	Gaeta-Naples	USN fleet cmd, flt air facil.	"
	La Maddalena/ Sardinia	Attack sub base	"
	Sigonella/Sicily	USN-ASW, logistics	"
	Aviano	USAF base	"
	Livorno	Supply terminal	"
	Camp Darby	USAR base	"
	Camp Ederle	USAR base	"
	San Vito	Intell. base	"
	various	Radar-early warning	"

138

Table 4.2. (Cont.)

Host	Location/Base	Principal Type Facilities	Basis of Access: Comments
W. Germany	various	7th Army garrisons, HQs, Support facils, etc. - 300,000 troops	Agreement after occupation-NATO
	Spangdahlem	USAF-main bases, various functions	"
	Bitburg	"	"
	Zweibrucken	"	
	Wiesbaden, Sembach, Rhein-Main, Ram-stein, Hahn	"	"
	Hof	Tech. functions	"
	Lindsey, Darmstadt	USAF-C3	"
	Dobraberg	AD control	"
	Frankfurt, Heidelberg Stuttgart	Major HQs	"
Portugal	Lajes	Air staging, ASW, rescue, commo, C3 for subs, naval security	Agreement-NATO
	Terceira	USN-base, hunter-killer subs	"
	San Miguel	Tech. facils-later for SOSUS terminals	"
	n/a on mainland	USAF aircraft maint. facil.	
	Santa Maria	USAF base, early postwar	
Spain	Rota	Polaris sub base, ASW, commo hunter-killer subs, Loran-A, C, logistics, meteorology, etc.	Agreement-econ. & military aid
	El Ferrol	Naval ammo & fuel storage	"
	Cartagena		"
	Moron	SAC B-47 reflex base	"
	Torrejon	USAF - B-47 SAC reflex, tact. air, tankers, transports, commo, logistics, etc.	"
	Zaragoza	SAC reflex - B-47, B-58, refuel, tact. air, staging, trng, etc.	"
	Puig Maior/ Majorca	Air alert radar for SAC bases, one of chain	"

Table 4.2. (Cont.)

Host	Location/Base	Principal Type Facilities	Basis of Access: Comments
Greece	Nea Makri	USN-commo	Agreement-NATO
	Souda Bay/Crete	NATO naval facil	"
	NAMFI/Crete	NATO missile firing station	"
	Iraklion/Crete	Air base	"
	Hellenikon	USAF base-staging, etc.	
	Athens	Various HQ, support facils., destroyer base nearby at Piraeus	"
Turkey	various	Radar, commo	
	Karamursel	Tech-missile telemetry	Agreement-NATO
	Sinop	Tech-intell.-telemetry	"
	Dyarbakir	Space-tracking, missile warning	"
	Adana/Incirlik	USAF-U-2, air staging, tact. air	"
	Belbasi	nuclear test detection	"
	Izmir	HQs, naval facils.	"
	Samsun	Intell. facil.	"
	Cigli	C3, USAF, aircraft	"
	n/a	Jupiter IRBMs, 1959-62	"

140

were deployed. Sasebo became a secondary but still important naval facility, also with full repair capacity.

Six major U.S. air bases set up in Japan provided a formidable forward U.S. air presence in the Far East. Yokota provided a base for a variety of tactical, training, and transport aircraft, at one time deploying B-57 bombers and later a wing of F-4 fighters. Misawa became a principal support base, involving an air range, a TACAN facility, communications facilities and the basing of some 60 F-41s.(115) Itazuke and Tachikawa eventually came to be used as principal support bases and for various technical functions. Iwakuni Marine Corps air station at various times had F-4s, P-3As, A-6s, C-54s, and C-117s stationed there, along with various support functions. The Atsugi Naval Air Station handled a variety of aircraft and was home to a fleet airborne electronics training unit, a fleet air reconnaissance unit, a fleet tactical support squadron, and an air photography unit. As earlier noted, it also earlier served as a U-2 base.(116) Elsewhere on mainland Japan, the U.S. had numerous other facilities spanning a variety of intelligence, navigational, logistical, and training functions.

Okinawa became, after 1945, virtually a vast U.S. island base, involving some 120 military facilities, including 19 major ones.(117) By 1970 it had three major air bases, two maneuver areas, two Marine Corps camps, plus various technical facilities and depots, and also a port and small naval base. The island came to house the largest Marine overseas base, involving a combat division and air wing, some 19,000 personnel in all. Among the major facilities were the large Kadena Air Base (used for B-52s along with KC-135 tankers and later, F-4 fighters beginning around 1967), Naha Air Base, the Futenma Marine Corps air facility, and three large Marine troop bases.(118) Okinawa was also used to store nuclear weapons and nerve gas; before 1969, the U.S. deployed there nuclear-armed Mace B missiles. Given its crucial geographical position, Okinawa became a primary hub of the earlier U.S. deterrence threat vis-a-vis China, as well as a depot and staging base available for contingencies throughout the Far East. The nature of the U.S. presence there also became a divisive issue within Japan, both before and after formal reversion of the island to Japanese control in 1972.

While the United States had originally made scant use of South Korean facilities before the 1950 invasion, the aftermath of the war saw significant forces left in place to deter another, reinforced by the U.S.-ROK Mutual Defense Treaty of 1954. From then until 1971, the United States deployed two army divisions in South Korea backed up by nuclear weapons. This force was reduced in the early 1970s to one division plus supporting units, involving some 40,000 personnel. To back up these forces and those of the ROK, a vast infrastructure was built, involving logistics, communications, major port depots at Pusan and Inchon, and a 155-mile petroleum pipeline from Pohang on the eastern coast to Osan and Seoul.

The U.S. Air Force, meanwhile, became entrenched at six major air bases in South Korea which deployed some 100 combat aircraft.(119) This force was of importance mainly with reference to a possible North

Korean invasion; but when added to those in Japan, Okinawa, and Taiwan, served as a link in the chain of American deterrent power flanking the USSR and China along the Asian pacific coast. Also, some Korean bases could be used to stage COMINT flights off the shores of both Communist powers; generally, South Korea's location made it an excellent intelligence-gathering base.

Access to Korean facilities also provided the United States with an available alternative if political pressures on U.S. bases in Japan and Okinawa were to become unmanageable. The South Koreans, for their own reasons, have been very receptive to U.S. bases and have made a standing offer of Cheju Island off the southern coast for a large base if an alternative to Okinawa became necessary.(120)

At the outset of the Korean War, the United States assumed a defense commitment to Taiwan based on President Truman's declaration that he was interposing the Seventh Fleet in the Taiwan Strait to preclude a Communist Chinese invasion (as well as to blunt Taiwanese threats in the other direction). Later, in 1954, a U.S.-Taiwan Mutual Defense Treaty was signed, underpinned by a congressional joint declaration authorizing the president to use armed forces to protect Taiwan and the Pescadores Islands and also the offshore islands of Quemoy and Matsu.(121) With these arrangements, the United States acquired extensive access to Taiwan, though the basing structure set up was not elaborate, partly because it would have been redundant to that on Okinawa.

Still, the United States stationed several thousand personnel on Taiwan (increased to about 10,000 during the Vietnam War), and deployed there a small number of fighter aircraft up to 1962, as well as some Matador nuclear-armed missiles.(122)

The main U.S. facility set up on Taiwan was the air base at Ching Chuan Kang (CCK), which earlier deployed C-130s for airlift operations and a squadron of KC-135 tankers during the Vietnam War to support air operations in Southeast Asia. Despite some congressional concern over rumors, CCK was not used for mounting B-52 raids during the war. Tainan air base was earlier also used by U.S. aircraft, and there were communications and intelligence bases.(123) Like South Korea, Taiwan served as part of the rimland basing chain facing China (and to a lesser degree, the USSR), and still has the potential for major expansion if there should be a drastic change in the politics of the Western Pacific, such as a reversion to the earlier enmity between the United States and PRC, or a sundering of U.S.-Japanese ties.(124)

The Philippines had, of course, long hosted U.S. basing facilities, and after independence in 1947, an agreement was entered into which gave the United States the right to occupy facilities for ninety-nine years. Their status was further strengthened by the Mutual Defense Treaty of 1951 and by the 1954 SEATO Treaty, to which the Philippines was a signatory.(125) During the 1950s, the vast U.S. basing complex in the Philippines was upgraded, and it became, along with those in Japan and Okinawa, a central element in the peripheral U.S. defense posture around the Asian mainland.

The United States has long had three major bases in the Philippines (along with a host of minor facilities): the Subic Bay navy base, Clark Air Base, and San Miguel Naval Communications Station, all on Luzon.(126) By 1970 the United States had some 18,000 military personnel in the Philippines, and the facilities required an annual operating cost of close to $300 million.(127)

Subic Bay has ranked with Yokosuka as the primary U.S. Asian naval base; at the height of the Vietnam War in 1968, it had some 1,700 annual visits by U.S. naval ships and about half that many by merchant vessels. It provides numerous logistical and support services to the Seventh Fleet.(128) Nearby Cubi Point serves as a supporting air station for carriers in the Southwest Pacific.

Clark Air Base (a primary target in December 1941 for Japanese aircraft, almost simultaneous with the Pearl Harbor strike), has long deployed large numbers of both transports and fighters, and has also served as an air defense control center for the Philippines as well as a hub for some intelligence, navigation, and communications facilities. Earlier, Mactan Air Base on Cebu Island had served as a home for airlift squadrons as well as a SAC recovery base, and some thought was apparently given to basing B-52s there. The navy earlier made extensive use of an air base at Sangley Point, which, among other things, deployed P-3 Orion ASW aircraft assigned to the Seventh Fleet.(129)

Completing the picket line of U.S. facilities along the Western Pacific rim of archipelagos and marginal seas were some limited facilities set up in Australia and New Zealand, both U.S. allies under the ANZUS pact. These were mostly lightly manned technical facilities erected late in the early postwar period; ANZAC sensibilities and the remoteness of the area from major points of confrontation in Asia precluded the permanent deployment of major air and naval facilities, at least up until recently.(130)

In Australia, the United States has used the Harold Holt Naval Communications Station on the Northwest Cape and the Pine Gap facility for naval communications and intelligence, apparently involving Omega communications to and between Polaris submarines operating in the Indian and Pacific Oceans. At Alice Springs there is a jointly operated early-warning communications station, of obvious importance to the U.S. strategic posture.(131) In New Zealand, the United States has had a Baker-Nunn Station devoted to deep-space optical tracking. Only more recently, with "forward" U.S. Asian bases in the Philippines, Thailand, and elsewhere in potential jeopardy, has serious consideration begun to be given to more major operating facilities, for instance, to U.S. use of a major new naval base at Cockburn Sound on Australia's Indian Ocean west coast.(132)

To the east, of course, U.S. control over the former Japanese mandate islands in Micronesia had long provided a formidable net of staging, testing, and technical facilities, some of which could be of still greater importance if U.S. power had to be withdrawn from East Asia. Guam, with its major naval base which has serviced nuclear submarines, and an air base from which B-52s were launched against Vietnam, became the strategic focal point in the West Central Pacific. There were other usable airfields on Midway, Wake, Saipan, and Tinian Islands.(133)

During the 1950s, the buildup of the U.S.-led forward alliance system was concentrated primarily in two regions, in the Far East flanking China and Soviet Siberia, and in Western Europe and the Mediterranean. In part, this was due to the fact that the extensive British basing assets along the vast Eurasian underbelly, stretching from Cyprus to Singapore – and keyed on Iraq, the Persian Gulf, Mombasa in Kenya, the Seychelles, and Mauritius – lessened the need for what then might have been redundant U.S. facilities. The British air and naval bases in and around the Indian Ocean could serve the United States as staging points for movements of personnel and materiel between Europe and the Far East. Later, in the 1960s, as Britain gradually withdrew from the Indian Ocean, the United States would try to compensate by taking over some British facilities (Bahrain, Masirah, Diego Garcia) and by seeking still others as Soviet power moved in to fill the vacuum.(134)

As it is, there was a buildup of U.S. facilities in Southeast Asia beginning around 1961-1962, during the onset of the almost "secret" war in Laos, and several years before the serious beginnings of the U.S. involvement in the major conflict in South Vietnam.(135) Up to 1962, and subsequent to the promulgation of the SEATO Treaty in 1954, the U.S. had expended some $100 million on military construction in Thailand, minimal facilities at seven air bases, and the 450-mile-long Friendship Highway from Bangkok to the Laotian border north of Vietnam.(156) But as the Laotian conflict heated up in 1961-1962, the United States began developing a significant presence in Thailand, involving the deployment of ground personnel and combat aircraft. The buildup escalated gradually up to 1967 – spurred by the heavy utilization of Thai air bases for operations in Vietnam – by which time there were some 33,000 U.S. Air Force and 12,000 U.S. Army personnel in Thailand, and over 500 aircraft.(137)

The United States first stationed interceptor aircraft in Thailand at the Don Muong base beginning in 1961. In 1964, as the Laotian situation deteriorated, F-100s were stationed at Takhli and F-105s at Korat, and some use was made of another base at Nakhon Phanon.(138) Still later, in 1967, the USAF began deploying SAC's B-52 bombers (also A-1 fighter bombers) at Utapao – along with KC-135 tanker refueling craft – from whence bombing raids on Vietnam could be conducted at a far lesser cost and over much less of a distance than from Guam. Also deployed were two squadrons of EB-66 electronic warfare aircraft.

Based on the 1962 Rusk-Thanat communique, which was used to underscore the U.S. commitment to Thailand under the SEATO pact (but without a formal bilateral mutual defense treaty equivalent to those with Taiwan, South Korea, and the Philippines), the United States built an elaborate network of facilities in Thailand besides those directly used for air warfare in Southeast Asia.(139) Various radar, communications, and intelligence facilities were colocated at the seven major U.S. air bases. A major intelligence facility arose at Ramasun, used to monitor Soviet, Chinese, and Vietnamese military communications. Some twenty communications facilities were set up, some for tying in with Special Forces units in Laos and Vietnam, centered on a facility at Lapburi. Finally, at Sattahip, on the southern Thai coast, a major deepwater supply port was constructed, later considered for a major U.S. naval base in Southeast Asia, in part because of fears about the future status of Subic Bay.(140) But these plans were aborted by the denouement of the Southeast Asian conflict and by Thailand's subsequent shift away from close reliance on a U.S. defense commitment.

To complete the picture of U.S. facilities in Southeast Asia during the 1960s, Laos must also be brought into the picture. Beginning in 1961, some 700 CIA and Special Forces troops were deployed there, a number which was to grow in ensuing years. Airstrips were constructed to support the transport aircraft and helicopters of the CIA-sponsored companies Air America and Continental Air Services,(141) and later several navigational aid facilities were installed in Laos to guide American F-4s and F-105s, based in Thailand, to their targets, a couple of which were overrun by Communist forces with the loss of American personnel.(142) The United States also stationed pilots at some five bases in Laos to serve as forward air controllers in small, slow-moving aircraft.(143)

The massive U.S. basing buildup in Southeast Asia from 1964 to 1970 needs no further elaboration here. Its loss, however, after 1972, was to be a part of the degradation of American strategic assets, important not only with respect to Southeast Asia, but also in the context of dwindling assets available for staging routes between the Pacific and Indian Ocean-Near East areas.

As noted, between Southeast Asia and the Mediterranean, and including the eastern coast of Africa, the United States was virtually bereft of significant military facilities during the long buildup of its global basing system during the 1950s and early 1960s. There were a few minor exceptions. Pakistan long provided the United States with a base for its U-2 flights over the USSR from Peshawar, and some intelligence listening posts near the Khyber Pass.(144) Iran, likewise, provided important intelligence facilities (useful among other things for telemetry monitoring of Soviet missile tests) and access to its overhead air space between Pakistan and Turkey, important for surveillance and ferret operations along the southern border of the USSR.(145) Some American use was made of the Saudi air base at Dhahran for staging and refueling, and of the nearby British air base at Bahrain. And in Africa, the United States made use of Kagnew in Ethiopia for communications relays, ship-to-shore communications, and high frequency transmission of diplomatic telecommunications.(146) American use of Kagnew dated from World War II, but its status was formalized in a basing agreement in 1953, which also provided for extensive military assistance to Haile Selassie's regime.

Along with the Far East and Western Pacific, the major expansion of U.S. basing facilities occurred, of course, in Europe and in the

Mediterranean, in connection with NATO's integrated defense structure. The United States retained numerous forces and installations in this area even amidst its demobilization after 1945. But after the promulgation of the Truman Doctrine respecting Greece and Turkey in 1947, the initiation of NATO in 1949, and the onset of the Korean War in 1950, there was a still further expansion of installations throughout the 1950s. During this period, new air and naval installations were developed or reopened in Britain, Spain, Greenland, Canada, Iceland, the Azores, Italy, Greece, and Turkey, and also in nearby French-dominated Morocco.   According to one writer on this period, "So important was the basing impulse that John Foster Dulles, soon to become Secretary of State Dulles and a prime mover in the evolution of our alliance structure overseas, saw basing as the major advantage to the inclusion of Iceland, Denmark, Portugal, and even Italy in the North Atlantic Treaty."(147) The forward deployment of U.S. forces and installations was to make Western Europe the first line of U.S. defenses and to provide credibility for U.S. involvement if Soviet forces were to invade. It also provided for defense-in-depth, early-warning capability, and training operations with allies in areas likely to be contested in any future conflict, and "operational options and dispersion right at the enemy's door."(148) Beyond that, it is also said that "we also learned and appreciated the lesson that overseas bases which support our forward deployment in alliance areas can also be convenient to our general global force posture in time of peace and to our unilateral purposes outside the immediate alliance area, in time of crisis."(149)

In Western Europe, by far the largest deployment of forces and concentration of facilities was in West Germany. Britain, France (up to the mid-1960s), Italy, Spain, Turkey, and Greece also became the locales for large concentrations of U.S. forward facilities; Iceland, Portugal, Netherlands, and Belgium had a smaller number.(150) Among the NATO countries, Norway and Denmark did not become sites for major U.S. installations, in part because of Soviet pressures and proximity (but also because of significant neutralist leanings or an inclination to remain somewhat disengaged) and despite their extreme vulnerability to attack. Norway did, however, allow use of an airfield for terminating U-2 reconnaissance flights,(151) and for some small but important technical facilities (Omega and Transit stations used for precise positioning of nuclear submarines).

Of the 200 or so major complexes which came to form the core of the U.S. postwar overseas basing structure, more than half – 95 Army complexes and 10 air bases – were in West Germany, where they housed the largest concentration of U.S. overseas military manpower. More than half of these complexes were army-related kasernes billeting the several-hundred-thousand-man strong Seventh Army and its supporting units controlled by USAREUR headquarters in Heidelberg and the integrated force command at Stuttgart.(152) The Seventh Army's facilities spanned the whole gamut of functions involved in modern ground warfare, including armor, artillery, infantry, engineering, chemical warfare, missilry, and air defense. Meanwhile – originating in the 1950s – the USAF came to maintain some ten major air bases in the FRG, mostly deploying large numbers of tactical fighter bombers (some nuclear-armed) and interceptors.(153) Still other facilities were hosts to various command and control, management, and technical operations, and there were also USAR installations and a U.S. Army garrison in Berlin. Meanwhile, the northern German port at Bremerhaven, as the main entry point in Europe for troops and materiel, became an elaborate U.S. logistical depot despite its precarious proximity to forward Soviet forces. Later, depots and pipelines built in and through France would provide for a logistical infrastructure with more depth for defense. But after France's divesting of U.S. facilities, the United States was again forced into heavy utilization of supply lines running precariously close to the expected front lines of an hypothetical European war.

It is now often forgotten that France was the site of numerous and costly U.S. military facilities through the 1950s and on up to April 1, 1967, when DeGaulle compelled the United States to withdraw completely. The installations cost about $1 billion (almost none of which was recovered), and as late as 1963, there were some 54,000 U.S. personnel in France, some 32,000 of them uniformed military.(154) Mostly what was involved were U.S.-owned and controlled Army logistics facilities, air bases, and command and control facilities, though the United States also contributed to NATO's jointly funded bases. Crucial was a protected logistics line from Atlantic ports which ran perpendicular to the NATO-Soviet lines of demarcation in central Europe.

At its peak, the U.S. had depot and support facilities at some twenty French locations and a major petroleum pipeline from Donges to Metz – 85 percent of the U.S. military petroleum storage in Europe was located there.(155) There were numerous U.S. Army and Air Force depots and several major USAF air bases.(156) Also, Bordeaux acted as a very major U.S. supply port of entry for many years following World War II, and Villefranche on the Mediterranean was an important Sixth Fleet port.(157) In 1967 the United States and NATO lost a very significant and massive concentration of facilities, some of which could be duplicated elsewhere, but only with considerable losses in dispersion, efficiency, and defensibility.

The Benelux countries (in part because of their location somewhat behind the NATO front lines in central Europe, but also because of local sovereignty issues) have not significantly served as locales for large U.S. military installations. A USAF base in the Netherlands and some U.S. military use of port facilities at Antwerp to supplement those at Bremerhaven have been the exceptions.(158)

After the formation of NATO, Italy rapidly became the site of a number of important U.S. military installations, with its position on the southern flank of the NATO Western European ground front, its earlier importance for supplying U.S. occupation troops in Austria (up to 1955), and most importantly, its crucial relationship to air and naval operations in the Mediterranean. The latter role, of course, became progressively more critical with the growth of Soviet naval strength in the Mediterranean in the 1960s and the increasing precariousness of some other U.S. basing points (Greece, Turkey, Spain) in the 1970s.

In the early postwar period, the United States deployed some ground troops and installations to stiffen the then weak Italian Army, located mostly in northern Italy.(159) Livorno was used as a port of entry for moving materiel to Austria. Also as noted, in the late 1950s, Italy sited two U.S. Jupiter IRBM launching complexes during the brief period between the strategic dominance of the SAC bomber force and the introduction of long-range ICBMs based in the continental United States.(160)

The most important U.S. installations set up in Italy, however, were air and naval, involving a variety of home-porting, submarine, ASW, and some technical functions. Gaeta became the Sixth Fleet's home port, and a large command center in nearby Naples also deployed some U.S. naval aircraft.(161) Later, a base at La Maddalena on Sardinia became a replenishment base for U.S. attack submarines operating in the Mediterranean. Another on Sicily came to deploy U.S. Navy ASW surveillance aircraft, eventually the P-3 Orion. There were also a USAF base and some technical facilities; these were for the most part intended to assist at air and sea control of the western Mediterranean, the Adriatic and Tyrrhenian seas, and the important narrow straits of Otranto, Messina, and Sicily.(162)

Although because of its geographical location, no large U.S. Army combat units have been stationed in the UK since 1945 (and hence, the U.S. presence there has been much smaller and less visible than in West Germany), it has nevertheless all along been the locale for a number of very important facilities. Most important were: the Holy Loch Polaris submarine base in Scotland, the BMEWS terminal in Yorkshire, several forward SAC "reflex" bases for B-47 bombers, and, temporarily, Jupiter and Thor IRBM bases during the late 1950s and early 1960s.(163) The USAF has also deployed tactical fighter bombers and F-111s at these bases and at some others, some of which later were reduced to one degree or another of standby status.(164) These bases also long served as staging points and as homes for a variety of command and control, intelligence, and communications functions.(165) Overseas, of course, the U.S. long made significant use of any number of British-controlled air and naval facilities: at Mahe (Seychelles), Gan (Maldives), Wheelus (Libya), Akotiri (Cyprus), Ascension, Diego Garcia, Antigua, Bahamas, Bermuda, and others, some on the basis of formal rental agreements and others on a less formal, ad hoc basis.

Otherwise, in relation to the northern flank of NATO and to control over the North Atlantic, the United States has long had use of air facilities at Reyjkavik in Iceland (as well as ASW-SOSUS and Loran-C facilities there),(166) and of Danish controlled facilities in Greenland, particularly the SAC base and BMEWS installation at Thule, and another SAC base at Sondestrom.(167)

The Portuguese-owned Azores, with its important Lajes Air Base brought to prominence during the 1973 Middle East airlift, and U.S. air and naval bases leased on British-owned Bermuda, completed the important complex of U.S. facilities developed early in the Cold War on the important North Atlantic sea route, under which Soviet nuclear and attack submarines lurked. In addition to its air transit function, the Azores have also been used to host: some U.S. aircraft; a fixed acoustics range installed on the underwater slopes of islands to acquire submarine "signatures" which are fed into computers on the island of San Miguel (a SOSUS terminal); a USAF maintenance center; a standby NATO naval command center; and some tracking facilities.(168) According to some sources, the air, ground, and sea submarine tracking facilities located in the Azores are near irreplaceable for the United States, as the areas monitored cannot be covered by U.S. aircraft and other facilities from Iceland, Northern Europe, Spain, Bermuda, or North America.(169) Here is also an auxiliary base for U.S. hunter-killer submarines normally stationed at Rota.

Spain, as noted, on the basis of a 1953 agreement, came to provide important SAC forward bases at Zaragoza, Torrejon, and Moron, and also the Polaris sub base at Rota to complement that in Scotland's Holy Loch. The B-47s remained at these bases until 1965, and afterward they continued to be used to deploy B-58 "Hustler" bombers (until 1968), tankers for aerial refueling, and also F-4 and F-100 fighters for local and area defense.(170) Later, Zaragoza and Torrejon would be designated as SAC postattack recovery bases for B-52s, as well as refueling facilities – a purpose also earlier served by bases in Libya (while then still controlled by the United States), Saudi Arabia, and Turkey.   These bases have served a number of other technical, logistical, and command and control functions. Rota came to service both SSBNs and hunter-killer subs and to house a variety of functions including ASW/ocean surveillance operations, logistical airlift, meteorological services, pre-positioning of POL and ammunition, and communications.(171) It became the home for a Naval Security Group listening post, EA3B electronic countermeasure and EC-121 airborne early-warning aircraft, and a supplementary naval communications center, to back up one in Morocco.(172)

The earlier 1953 agreement also involved naval ammunition and fuel storage centers and an air alert radar station on Majorca which was part of a chain of such stations, which earlier served importantly in connection with the SAC bases.(173) Torrejon and Zaragoza have also long been important to the United States for staging military materiel to the Middle East and for other theater airlift operations.(174)

Greek air and naval facilities likewise became important for U.S. military interests in the central and eastern Mediterranean, beginning after the withdrawal of British forces and the promulgation of the Truman Doctrine.(175) The major among the some twenty-six U.S. facilities were the Hellenikon and Athens air bases, an aircraft and intelligence base at Iraklion on Crete, a major naval communications station at Nea Makri, and a navy base at Souda Bay, which is actually under formal NATO aegis.(176) The centrally located island of Crete – with an air and naval base, communications facilities and a missile-firing station – is seen as long having served a crucial role for U.S. sea and air control over the central and eastern Mediterranean.(177) The USAF set up an important headquarters in Athens, meanwhile, which also became a vital staging base. The port of Piraeus also became a favorite rest and recreation spot for Sixth Fleet sailors.

At the eastern end of the Mediterranean, Turkey, which anchored together the NATO and CENTO arrangements, became, beginning around 1950, a very major center of U.S. basing installations. The nature of its critical location along the Black Sea, astride the Bosphorus, and along the border with the USSR needs little elaboration, regarding the obvious ramifications for intelligence, surveillance, and forward strategic deterrence. Here, as in Greece, and in contrast to Western Europe, no U.S. army combat units were deployed, though numerous U.S. advisors gave assistance to the very large and much respected Turkish army.

Over time, the United States came to construct over twenty important facilities in Turkey. Incirlik, near Adana, was earlier used for staging U-2 flights and ferret missions and later for other U.S. air staging activities throughout the Middle East. It also became an important USAF fighter base housing a squadron of F-4s. Jupiter IRBMs were deployed in 1959 and then removed, along with those in Italy, in 1962.

Perhaps most important for the United States, however, were the various sensitive and important surveillance and communications facilities, which in combination came to provide a large share of U.S. intelligence information on Soviet missile (strategic, tactical ship-to-ship in the Black Sea) tests, troop movements within the USSR, and so forth. These facilities came to be crucial to verification and monitoring of strategic arms agreements,(178) and their importance would later be further enhanced by American loss of apparently somewhat complementary facilities in Iran. Some sporadic use of Turkish ports by the U.S. Navy was also important (primarily for showing the flag), though less so than the use of nearby Greek ports.(179)

American use of British-controlled airfields on Cyprus, in close proximity to crucial cockpits of the Middle Eastern conflict areas, completes the picture of an elaborate setup of U.S. installations in the Mediterranean during the zenith period of American power in the 1950s and 1960s.(180)

In the remaining theaters of the globe, in Latin America, including the Caribbean, and in sub-Saharan Africa aside from Ethiopia, the development of U.S. facilities during the height of the Cold War period was much more limited than in Europe and the Far East and Pacific. These areas were not then immediate zones of confrontation with the Soviets, nor were they astride the major air and naval staging routes required by the United States to conduct its rimland strategy of mobile and forward defense and deterrence.

Aside from the SAC bases and technical facilities in Morocco, the USAF's early use of Wheelus in Libya, and the Kagnew commo base in Ethiopia, U.S. military installations essentially were absent from

Africa south of the Sahara. The United States did, however, make some use of Roberts Field in Liberia for staging purposes,(181) and also apparently participated, along with the UK, in the use of the major South African intelligence and communications center at Silvermine near Capetown, astride the Cape of Good Hope.(182) Otherwise, of course, the various ports and airfields in areas under British, French, Belgian, and Portuguese control (as well as the air spaces above them) were routinely available for a variety of American military activities such as refueling, staging, and symbolic courtesy visits. Only well into the 1960s would Soviet penetration into the area and the loss of European control over former colonial areas raise the question of competitive American requests for facilities and access to meet a vastly changed geopolitical context.

In Latin America, the U.S. withdrawal from its World War II air bases in Brazil (and in the Ecuador-controlled Pacific Galapagos Islands) left that entire region also virtually disconnected from the U.S. global basing system. In South America, only a few minor technical facilities (for example, a space tracking station in Ecuador) were utilized.(183) The bulk of U.S. Western Hemisphere military installations were centered in the Panama Canal Zone and in several locations in the Caribbean, which up to the Cuban revolution in 1959, remained a rather securely controlled American lake.

In the Canal Zone, home of the U.S. Southern Command which was set up to deal with all of Latin America, the United States came to deploy some 7,000 army troops, involving an infantry brigade, Special Forces Group, a logistical command, and jungle operations training center. Later, in 1978, an ASW installation at Galeta would become a late rallying point for U.S. conservatives unwilling to abandon not only the canal itself, but some accompanying, multipurpose military installations.(184)

Elsewhere in and around the Caribbean, the United States maintained facilities in Cuba, the Bahamas, Antigua, Trinidad and Tobago, and on Grand Turk Island (all but Cuba were originally British possessions) and with the background here of the 1940 lend-lease trade-off for destroyers.(185)

Guantanamo Bay was a fairly major U.S. naval base up to 1960, and although the United States has maintained control of it ever since in the face of extreme Cuban frustration and some periodic disruptive activities, its status has been reduced to that of a training base. Installations in the Bahamas have been used by the United States for underwater surveillance and testing, radar, and the USAF's Eastern Test Range.(186) The facilities on the other former British-controlled islands have served similar purposes. Trinidad has also hosted one among the eight worldwide U.S. Omega stations utilized in connection with nuclear submarine navigation and positioning.(187)

In standing back from the welter of detail which describes the massive post-World War II elaboration of U.S. bases and other forms of strategic access, it is clear that the regrets expressed by American statesmen in 1940 over the country's lack of immediately ready strategic assets to conduct the war against the Axis powers had led to a far different postwar policy by reaction. During the 1950s, faced by a powerful land-based alliance of the USSR and China, the United States had responded with a classic Mahanian rimland strategy, combining forward-based ready-response ground units, and strong air and naval units with numerous points of access around Eurasia, which provided for ready application of force at almost any point around that periphery. And, as noted, this strategy was underpinned by a network of formal alliances, backed by massive military and economic aid, and by the overwhelming convergence between the United States and its dependent allies on actual perceptions of the nature, source, and strength of the Communist threat. And up until the late 1950s at least, the West's control over the Eurasian rimlands and marginal seas was nearly complete, and its access to and among them by air and sea was secure, routine, and redundant.

Throughout this period, the United States assertedly maintained a force posture corresponding to what was then called, perhaps a bit ambitiously, "a two and one-half war strategy." That entailed at least the aspiration for the simultaneous capability to fight major land wars both in Europe and Asia (against the USSR with its NATO allies and against China with some Asian allies) and against one smaller, nameless foe somewhere in the Third World.(188) Given the massive overall asymmetries of ground troop forces between the United States and its two major rivals, this expressed policy seemed at times a bit quixotic. But yet, as Wohlstetter and others then pointed out, the huge capacity then held by the United States for moving men and materiel by air and sea, combined with the still weak logistical capabilities of the USSR as applicable to Central Asia and the Far East, and of China when applied to Southeast Asia, rendered this a fairly viable posture (more so if one assumed a decent interval for a U.S. buildup similar to the 1940s).(189) The U.S. and British basing systems, in conjunction with tremendous superiority in naval and air transport, were thought to balance off what might otherwise have been the severe penalties of the power-over-distance gradient. And this was indeed borne out in some measure in Korea (1950-54), Lebanon (1958), and later in Vietnam.

And, as we have illustrated, the global basing system amassed by the United States during the 1950s provided it with very favorable advantages over a wide spectrum of military-strategic activities, short of actual major conflict. Nuclear deterrence was aided by aircraft and submarine bases around the USSR, as well as by the surveillance and ferret missions which could be conducted around the latter's borders. The United States was easily provided truly global communications systems (for defense, naval, presidential systems, and so forth), based on numerous points of access for receivers, transmitters, and relays; likewise, it had redundant points of access for navigational facilities such as Loran-A and Loran-C, and later for the global system of Omega stations used to position nuclear submarines. When satellite technology arrived, its optional use was afforded by global systems of communications/data relays, and conversely, there were dispersed global surveillance sites to observe rival Soviet satellites.

Between the U.S.-led alliances and the remnants of European colonial holdings, pro forma port calls and "shows of the flag" were provided Western navies all around the world – at least outside the then circumscribed Soviet bloc – on a routine basis, which served to engender abroad high-value perceptions of Western power and resolve. Likewise, routine overflight privileges and staging and refueling points were provided U.S. and Western aircraft all around the Sino-Soviet rimland and throughout most of the then developing world. There were no discernible problems for the United States during the 1950s in moving its ships and aircraft at will around and over the rimland, nor for moving arms to client states during normal times or even during crises.

During the 1950s and early 1960s, the U.S. basing network reached its zenith (as had those of Portugal, Netherlands, and Britain earlier), while that controlled by the UK began to decline. Altogether, however, there was probably a short-term net expansion. Throughout this period, there was a virtual superfluousness of access in many areas, resulting in some redundancy, but certainly the availability of sufficient fallback options if political problems arose. The Trinidad base leased from Britain in 1940, for instance, was virtually allowed to lapse because of the availability of nearby alternatives. Because of Okinawa and the Philippines, there was no need to turn Taiwan into a major forward U.S. base facing the Chinese mainland, though it could have been done and would have been welcomed by Taiwan. Several training, communications, and SAC bomber facilities in Spain and Morocco came likewise to have virtually overlapping utilities. For the United States during the 1950s, there was undoubtedly and literally an embarrassment de riches regarding overseas facilities.

There was to be little expansion of the U.S. basing network after 1960, with the exceptions – at least temporarily – of the facilities constructed in Vietnam and Thailand to deal with the war in Southeast Asia. Later development of additional facilities in Iran, Diego Garcia, and Australia – and the replacement of the British in Oman and Bahrain – would represent primarily the utilization of fallback positions to compensate for the loss of (or restricted use of) U.S. and British facilities elsewhere.

Concerning the projection of power overseas and the lines of supply to support forward alliances and installations, the heartland/rimland spatial nature of the confrontation with the USSR made, in a way, for a simplified albeit far-flung access strategy. With the "rear areas" of Africa and Latin America relatively secure, emphasis could be focused on the close-in rimland positions and on the primarily east-to-west air and sea lines of communication which linked them into an interlocking network. Only later would the spatial basis of the global conflict become more diffuse and dispersed, with the Soviets' leapfrogging of the old containment rimland line. At that stage, and with the U.S. basing system under pressure (mitigated by some new technological developments), the requirements for U.S. bases would be expanded to a more spatially complex level, to cope with contingencies in areas which had previously been behind the "front lines."

SOVIET EXTERNAL BASES AND ACCESS IN THE IMMEDIATE
POSTWAR PERIOD: A GIANT TEMPORARILY CONSTRAINED

During the first decade of the Cold War, up to the mid-1950s, the
Soviets were almost totally lacking in overseas facilities, corresponding
to their equivalently meager air and naval transport capability. Stalin's
self-perception on behalf of the USSR was still very much that of a
beleaguered nation struggling to unchain itself from "capitalist
encirclement," exacerbated by the looming superior U.S. nuclear force.
Soviet defense doctrine stressed a massive land army (by 1948,
supplemented by the new Red Chinese Army) featuring powerful
armored shock forces, air defense (with heavy reliance on numerous
interceptor aircraft), and a homebound coastal defense navy
(submarines and naval land-based aircraft). There was little prospect
then of long-range projection of power. To the extent there was a
"basing strategy," it was for the most part a base denial strategy
directed against the West's assets through the varied mechanisms of
propaganda and the fomenting of internal political opposition to
Western basing rights through budding anticolonial revolutions. Soviet
propaganda during this period stridently advocated "the elimination of
all foreign bases," a logical strategy for a nation which possessed
virtually no bases.
    The Soviets did, of course, acquire and build a massive structure of
ground and air installations in Eastern Europe, as the Warsaw Pact
became the counterpart and mirror rival to NATO. And unlike NATO –
and despite the problems in Hungary, Poland, and East Germany in
1955-1956 – the Soviets were not seriously subject to any political
problems which might have jeopardized their installations and supply
lines. For the Soviets, there were few serious questions about "status of
forces" agreements; that was settled in a highly characteristic way
whenever nationalist sentiments raised their heads, as in 1956 or 1968.
But even in Europe, with the loss of Yugoslavia during this period after
Tito's defection, Soviet aircraft were virtually imprisoned within
Eastern Europe by the absence of overflight corridors to the
Mediterranean, given the Western hold on Greece and Turkey.
    Outside of the Warsaw Pact, the only significant Soviet facilities
during the early postwar period were the navy bases at Porkalla,
Finland, and at Port Arthur in Chinese-controlled Manchuria, both of
which were returned to indigenous control during the 1950s.(190) Later,
during 1958-1961, some use was made of submarine bases in Albania,
which ended with the Sino-Soviet and Albania-Soviet breaks around
1961.(191) The Soviets were essentially constrained, in terms of
strategic access and overall geopolitical strategy, within the interior
lines of a heartland empire, though some submarines were early
deployed in both major oceans.
    Also, up to around 1955-1956, Soviet arms transfers were limited
primarily to within the Warsaw Pact and to China, i.e., within the then
aptly designated Sino-Soviet bloc. The still relatively weak Soviet arms-
production base was almost entirely occupied with equipping Soviet-

bloc forces, while the United States and United Kingdom controlled most of the arms markets in the developing world, unburdening themselves of massive World War II weapons surpluses. And there were no formal Soviet military alliances beyond the contiguous areas of the Sino-Soviet bloc.

Beginning in the mid and late 1950s, however, the USSR became a weightier factor in the arms markets of the developing world. Arms deals with Egypt and Syria in 1955 were the opening wedges, followed by the initiation of arms relationships with North Yemen (1957), Indonesia (1958), Guinea (1959), India (1961), and indirectly with the Algerian rebels in the late 1950s. Soviet arms supplies tended during this period to be concentrated in large doses in a few key client states which served as initial levers in cracking the iron ring of the interlocked alliances around the USSR.(192) The penetration was paced by ideological affinity, if only through left-leaning neutralism on the part of recipients. Still, although these initial arms-client relationships did not immediately translate into overseas basing facilities for the Soviets in any case, they constituted chips which could later be cashed in when the upgrading of Soviet long-range air and naval capabilities made that a more relevant matter.

In the early 1960s, the Cuban revolution suddenly, no doubt surprisingly, provided the Soviets with a potential large island base right on the American doorstep. It quickly became the locale for numerous Soviet technical facilities; for electronic listening posts which could serve as counterweights to the equivalent, numerous U.S. installations which had ringed the USSR since 1945. Shortly after, the Soviet introduction to Cuba of SAMs and then IRBMs was to trigger off the tense Cuban missile crisis. In terms of overseas access, Cuba became the Soviets' first major leapfrogging of the Western Mahanian rimland strategy. It proved to be merely the first step in what was to become a significant shifting of the global basing "correlation of forces," and of the very spatial basis of superpower political competition which had dominated the early post-war years.

NOTES

(1) This theme of a gradual shift away from Eurocentrism is central to Ludwig Dehio, The Precarious Balance; Four Centuries of the European Power Struggle (New York: Knopf, 1962); and Hajo Holborn, The Political Collapse of Europe (New York: Knopf, 1959).

(2) The assertion of the recently increased relevance of Mackinder's classic thesis is made in Colin Gray, The Geopolitics of the Nuclear Era (New York: Crane, Russak, 1977); and in Robert E. Walters, The Nuclear Trap (Baltimore: Penguin, 1974).

(3) The utopianism of the interwar period, as manifested in collective security myths, is discussed in E. H. Carr, The Twenty Years Crisis,

1919-1939 (London: MacMillan, 1939), esp. chaps. 2-4. See also Joel Larus, From Collective Security to Preventive Diplomacy (New York: John Wiley, 1965), esp. chap. 1.

(4) Basic data on alliances during this period may be garnered from J. David Singer and Melvin Small, "Formal Alliances, 1815-1939," Journal of Peace Research 3, 1 (1966); and an analysis of trends in alliance formation leading into the interwar period may be found in John D. Sullivan, "National and International Sources of Alliance Maintenance" (Dissertation, Stanford University, 1969). On the early France-Poland-Czechoslovakia pact, as typifying the more stable, long-term security alliance to become more familiar later, see Piotr S. Wandycz, France and Her Eastern Allies, 1919-1925 (Minneapolis: University of Minnesota Press, 1962).

(5) A good general analysis of the changes wrought upon basing requirements by the evolving weapons and transport technologies of World War II is in George Weller, Bases Overseas (New York: Harcourt, Brace, 1944), though it was written too soon to incorporate the implications, made clearer a year later, of the advent of nuclear weapons.

(6) See, for a good short summary, Joan Spero, The Politics of International Economic Relations (New York: St. Martins, 1977), Chap. 10.

(7) Morton Kaplan, System and Process in International Politics (New York: Wiley, 1957), part 1.

(8) A review and analysis of the pre-World War II U.S. basing system is in Buel W. Patch, "American Naval and Air Bases," Editorial Research Report 1,7 (February 16, 1939). In an attempt at conceptualization, Weller, Bases Overseas, pp. 128-130, analyzes this system as basically "centrifugal" in nature, one intended "to hold off the potential enemy by a barrier, like the Maginot line or the Great Wall of China." Britain and Japan, by contrast, were perceived as "centripetal" powers, nations which did not possess the complete sustenance of strength within their immediate borders, but which had to go outside, find them, and enclose them in a system of power.

(9) See Basil Collier, The Lion and the Eagle (New York: Putnam, 1972), pp. 312-313; and Buel Patch, "Overseas Bases," p. 442.

(10) Patch, "Overseas Bases," p. 442.

(11) Military Intelligence Division 2667-ZZ-28.

(12) MID 2537-103, 10541-1007, 2657-M-292, and 183-Z-130.

(13) See Patch, "Overseas Bases," p. 444.

(14) Ibid.; Collier, Lion and Eagle, p. 316, also notes the importance of DeGaulle's rallying of French Equatorial Africa to the Allied cause, allowing overflights and staging points en route from Takoradi to Egypt.

(15) Patch, "Overseas Bases."

(16) Ibid.; See also Collier, Lion and Eagle, p. 379, who notes that U.S. operations on Guadalcanal and Tulagi used air support provided by land-based aircraft from New Caledonia, the New Hebrides, Fiji, Samoa, and the Friendly Islands.

(17) Patch, "Overseas Bases," p. 445.

(18) Quoted from a 1945 statement by then Assistant Secretary of the Navy Hensel, in ibid., p. 445.

(19) Ibid., p. 446.

(20) Ibid., quoting from Patch. "The proposal to acquire ownership of the base sites leased from Great Britain was effectively settled soon after the war. When the resolution authorizing the special postwar British loan was before the Senate in May 1946, Sen. McFarland (D., Ariz.) offered an amendment to require Britain to cede the Atlantic bases and grant commercial rights at other American-built bases on British soil. The Senate rejected the amendment only by the relatively close vote of 45 to 40, but thereafter little more was heard of the proposal."

(21) Ibid., p. 446.

(22) Ibid.

(23) Ibid.

(24) Ibid.

(25) Ibid.

(26) Ibid.: "The Australians, while expressing readiness to discuss joint use of bases under a regional defense arrangement, put off the American request for exclusive rights by referring to the Canberra agreement which they had signed wtih New Zealand on Jan. 21, 1944. The agreement had stated that it was 'a recognized principle of international practice that the construction and use in time of war by any power of naval, military and air installations in any territory under the sovereignty or control of another power does not in itself afford any basis for territorial claims or rights of sovereignty or control after the conclusion of hostilities.'"

(27) Ibid., pp. 447-8. For a critical "internationalist" perspective on U.S. policies toward the former Japanese island mandates, see T. Campbell, "Nationalism in America's U.N. Policy, 1944-45," International Organization 27, 1 (Winter 1973): 25-44.

(28)Patch, "Overseas Bases," p. 449.

(29) Ibid., p. 450.

(30) Ibid.

(31) Ibid.; see also for greater detail, James L. Gormley, "Keeping the Door Open in Saudi Arabia: The United States and the Dhahran Airfield, 1945-46," Diplomatic History 4, 2 (Spring 1980): 189-205. This article discusses the Dhahran base issue as crucial to U.S. replacement of British influence in Saudi Arabia during World War II.

(32) Patch, "Overseas Bases," p. 437.

(33) Data are from ibid., p. 437.

(34) Ibid., p. 438.

(35) Ibid.

(36) See, inter alia, Klass, Secret Sentries in Space (New York: Random House, 1971), chaps. 2, 3 for a review.

(37) See Johan Jorgen Holst, "Comparative U.S. and Soviet Deployments, Doctrines, and Arms Limitation" (Chicago: University of Chicago, 1971), Occasional Paper of the Center for Policy Study, pp. 31-32; and Klass, Secret Sentries, p. 30, who notes the B-47 force had grown to 1500 aircraft by 1958, which along with the B-52s, were later supported by a tanker fleet of over 600 KC-135 jet tankers and nearly 200 propeller-driven KC-97s.

(38) Holst, "Comparative U.S. and Soviet Deployments," pp. 35-36; Klass, Secret Sentries, p. 5; and in particular, Clifford B. Goodie, Strategic Air Command (New York: Simon and Schuster, 1965) pp. 12, 14, 24, 42, 52. The requirement for overseas bases for the B-47 resulted from its range of only slightly more than 3,000 miles without refuel. According to Goodie, p. 24, "For many years, until April 1965, B-47 crews flew their planes on a continual shuttle across the Atlantic Ocean to European bases in an operation known as 'Reflex.'" Similar flights were made across the Pacific Ocean to Guam until 1964, when B-52s assumed the Pacific role.

(39) Klass, Secret Sentries, p. 5.

(40) Ibid., pp. 6-8.

(41) See, in particular, Stanley L. Englebardt, Strategic Defenses (New York: Thos. Crowell, 1966), chap. 10. The SFR report, p. 18, lists 21 U.S. DEW line stations in Canada, 31 total in Greenland, Canada, and Alaska, stretching 4,000 miles roughly along the 70N parallel from Alaska to the east coast of Greenland, providing NORAD 40,000-foot high-altitude and 500-foot low-altitude radar surveillance throughout.

(42) Klass, Secret Sentries, p. 15.

(43) Ibid., pp. 15, 20.

(44) Ibid., pp. 17, 42.

(45) See, inter alia, Graham Allison, "Conceptual Models and the Cuban Missile Crisis," American Political Science Review 63, 3 (September 1969): 696.

(46) See Klass, Secret Sentries, chaps. 8, 9, for a discussion of the role of the U-2 during this period; as well as Glenn B. Infield, Unarmed and Unafraid, chap. 10. For a discussion of ferret activities, see Klass, pp. 188-195 and Patrick McGarvey, CIA: The Myth and the Madness (Baltimore: Penguin, 1972), chap. 11.

(47) Infield, Unarmed and Unafraid, chap. 10.

(48) Klass, Secret Sentries, pp. 50-51.

(49) According to Klass, Secret Sentries, p. 84, "In the late 1940s the U.S. had developed the K-30 aircraft camera for oblique-angle photography from the side window of a high-flying airplane, to take pictures of airfields as much as 100 miles distant."

(50) Klass, Secret Sentries, chap. 11. For a discussion of the controversial Gaither Report and the missile scare, see Morton Halperin, "The Gaither Committee and the Policy Process," World Politics 13, 3 (April 1961): 360-384.

(51) Ibid., Klass, Secret Sentries, p. 105, according to which, "Four months later, in June 1961, the U.S. officially reduced its national intelligence estimate of the number of operational Soviet ICBMs by 50 percent." Instead of the 120 missiles that had been forecast to be operational by the summer of 1961, the figure was cut to only 60 missiles. By September 1961, the official count of Soviet ICBMs would be slashed even more sharply.

(52) Klass, Secret Sentries, p. 136.

(53) Ibid.

(54) Ibid., where BMEWs' construction was said to have cost $800 million to provide a 15-minute warning of any Soviet missile attack, which in turn would allow a portion of the U.S. SAC bomber force to become airborne. For further analysis of American BMEWs access outside the United States, see Englebardt, Strategic Defenses, pp. 105-122, which includes, on p. 110B, a map showing the BMEWs, DEW, and Mid-Canada line radar coverages. Here there is a discussion of the choice of the BMEWs site near Thule, Greenland, which was located optimally to meet a variety of combined criteria.

(55) Klass, Secret Sentries, pp. 91, 104-5, 124.

(56) Ibid., p. 175.

(57) Ibid., p. 182.

(58) Ibid., p. 6, which discusses the manner in which F-102 interceptors, by 1954, could be guided by radar and air defense computers on optimum intercept paths for intercepting Soviet bombers.

(59) Ibid., Secret Sentries, pp. 5-6.

(60) Ibid., chap. 12; and Graham T. Allison, "Conceptual Models and the Cuban Missile Crisis," American Political Science Review 63, 3 (September 1969): 689-718.

(61) Klass, pp. 188-195, and McGarvey, CIA, esp. pp. 49-52. According to the latter, "Eighty percent of the take of shipborne and airborne collection platforms is ELINT. . . . War Planners at SAC HQ were concerned with the ability of U.S. bombers to penetrate the Russian radar network undetected. They began to fly missions along the periphery of Russia trying to find the points at which a certain radar set was unable to detect an incoming bomber. Analysis of the pulse rate of the Russian radar would provide data on which the radar set's range and height-finding capability could be estimated. Eventually, war planners made maps pinpointing the location of all Russian radars, and from this were able to project cones or umbrellas of radar coverage outward from the sites. Routes of penetration could then be planned."

(62) McGarvey, CIA, pp. 49-50.

(63) Ibid., p. 50.

(64) See John Carroll, Secrets of Electronic Espionage (New York: Dutton, 1966), p. 175.

(65) Ibid., p. 134.

(66) Ibid., p. 167. See also Klass, Secret Sentries, pp. 51-52.

(67) Klass, Secret Sentries, p. 190. "Aircraft used for this type of ferret work normally carry several human operators whose judgment is needed to operate the complex receiving equipment. Furthermore, aircraft can carry many hundreds of pounds of ferret receivers. In a satellite, space and weight were at a great premium in the early 1960s, and the function of human operators would need to be automated." Pages 190-195 then further discuss the development of the ferret satellite program up to 1971.

(68) McGarvey, CIA, pp. 42-49.

(69) Ibid., chaps. 2, 5.

(70) Ibid., p. 47.

(71) Ibid., p. 49.

(72) Klass, Secret Sentries, pp. 136-7 reports as follows. "For a typical radio-transmission-satellite orbit, with an inclination of approximately 80 degrees, the spacecraft's first daylight pass over Communist territory occurs at the eastern tip of Siberia. Soon the satellite comes within range of the Guam station and can transmit down its photos. Two orbits later, the satellite passes over the east coast of Red China and shortly afterward comes within range of the New Boston, N.H. station. Pictures taken over central Siberia or Red China's missile test range may be radioed to New Boston, or perhaps a shipboard station in the Indian Ocean. As the satellite begins to pass over western Russia, where many of the most important military installations are located, many more photos will be taken and radioed down to stations at Vandenberg, Seychelles and in east Africa. Pictures taken as the satellite passes over Russia's Communist neighbors to the west will be radioed to the stations at Kodiak and Hawaii. . . . The received radio signals are recorded on magnetic tape at the station but are not reconstituted into pictures until they have been flown by special USAF jet courier aircraft to Washington and turned over to the National Photographic Interpretation Center. . . . For shipboard stations, the tape-recorded photos can be transferred to a specially outfitted aircraft by playing back and transmitting the signals to the airplane as it circles the ship."
　　Germane to the question of the extent to which the use of overseas facilities can be circumvented is a note which says that the "Maximum range at which a station can receive transmissions from satellites depends on spacecraft altitude and the topography of ground-station location. For radio-transmission satellites, maximum range is typically about 750 miles."

(73) Ibid., p. 34.

(74) Gregory Blaxland, The Regiments Depart (London: William Kimber, 1971), p. 15.

(75) Ibid., pp. 2-5.

(76) Ibid., p. 9.

(77) Ibid., pp. 12-14, for the distribution of British troops in the immediate wake of World War II.

(78) Ibid., pp. 15-26; and Corelli Barnet, Britain and Her Army: 1509-1970 (New York: William Morrow, 1970), p. 480.

(79) Blaxland, Regiments Depart, pp. 73-90.

(80) Blaxland, Regiments Depart, p. 12, and pp. 217-218.

(81) Ibid., p. 132, wherein it is noted that Hong Kong was reinforced with additional troops to deter a takeover by Mao.

(82) Ibid., p. 215.

(83) Ibid., pp. 215-236, including a map of British installations on p. 216.

(84) Ibid.

(85) Ibid., pp. 234-235.

(86) Ibid., pp. 237, 419. For further information on the British bases in Libya during this period, see William H. Lewis, "How a Defense Planner Looks at Africa," in Helen Kitchen, ed., Africa: From Mystery to Maze (Lexington, Mass.: Lexington Books, 1976), pp. 278-282.

(87) Blaxland, Regiments Depart, pp. 348, 351, also discussing the eventual British withdrawal from Jordan. According to him, p. 219, a British battalion at Aqaba was readied for use in Iran in 1951 during the Mossadegh interregnum, along with another in the Canal Zone, but was not used; later, troops were sent from there to quell riots in Port Said.

(88) Ibid., pp. 48-59.

(89) Ibid., pp. 220-221, which notes British troop movements to Egypt in 1951 from Jordan and Cyprus as well.

(90) Ibid, pp. 236-260. See also Barnet, Britain and Army, p. 486.

(91) Blaxland, Regiments Depart, pp. 352-353.

(92) Ibid., pp. 293-328.

(93) Ibid., p. 310.

(94) Ibid., pp. 349-351.

(95) Ibid., pp. 324-328.

(96) Ibid., p. 293.

(97) See "Cypriot Reds Demand U.S. Halt U-2 Mideast Flight After Crash," New York Times, December 10, 1977, p. 10; and "British-U.S. Intelligence Links are Expected to Become Even Closer," New York Times, March 12, 1979, p. A4, which states that the United States flies about one U-2 mission per week from Akotiri.

(98) Blaxland, Regiments Depart, p. 349.

(99) Ibid., pp. 269-291, 353.

(100) Ibid., p. 324, wherein it is stated that "strategically a ban on air space over Israel and the Arab countries much reduced the value of Cyprus as a base for troops and virtually split Middle East Command in two. Kenya was therefore developed as an alternative." See also pp. 412-413.

(101) Ibid., p. 411. See also John M. Ostheimer and Gary J. Buckley, "Nigerian National Security Policy," in Edward Kolodziej and R. E. Harkavy, eds., Security Policies of Developing States: Implications for Regional and Global Security (Lexington, Mass.: D. C. Heath, 1982), wherein the short-lived, post-independence, Anglo-Nigerian defense agreement is discussed.

(102) Blaxland, Regiments Depart, pp. 91-131.

(103) Ibid., pp. 132-144.

(104) Ibid., pp. 363-374.

(105) But according to Lewis, "How a Defense Planner Looks at Africa," pp. 280-281, stressing the potential in-depth access system for the West, "In North Africa, despite legal precedents to the contrary, the French bases at Casablanca, Mers-el-Kebir, and Bizerte were regarded as informal assets for the NATO command system. British facilities in Libya, notably at Tobruk and El-Adem, had comparable utility. Below the Sahara, from a contingency point of view, the giant Belgium base at Kamina in the Congo, British facilities at Takoradi in Ghana, Kaduna in Nigeria, and Mombasa in Kenya, and French facilities in Somaliland, on Madagascar, and in Dakar were all regarded as being of potential value to Western security interests." Lewis goes on to point out that conferences were held at Nairobi in 1951 and Dakar in 1954 to discuss

coordination of transport and communications facilities among the Western allies.

(106) See, inter alia, Roland Paul, American Military Commitments Abroad (New Brunswick, N.J.: Rutgers University Press, 1973), pp. 192-193; Lewis, "How Defense Planner Looks at Africa," p. 281; Goodie, Strategic Air Command, pp. 24, 42, 52; and in particular, U.S. Senate, United States Security Agreements and Commitments Abroad, Hearings Before the Subcommittee on United States Security Agreements and Commitments Abroad, 91st Congress, vol. 2, parts 5-11, pp. 1961-1962 (hereinafter referred to as USSACA).

(107) USSACA, pp. 1961-1962.

(108) Ibid.

(109) See Paul, American Military Commitments, pp. 14-15.

(110) Ibid., p. 185, notes this fact.

(111) USSACA, vol. 2, p. 1153. For a full analysis of the history of U.S. bases in Japan up to the early 1970s, see USSACA, pp. 1147-1517, especially appendix 1, pp. 1447-1488. See also Paul, pp. 39-50.

(112) Paul, American Military Commitments, p. 40.

(113) USSACA, pp. 1447-1458.

(114) Ibid., esp. pp. 1451-3. See also Alvin Cottrell and Thomas H. Moorer, "U.S. Overseas Bases: Problems of Projecting American Military Power Abroad" (Washington: Georgetown CSIS, 1977), Paper #47, p. 50, wherein it is stated that "Yokosuka has the only aircraft carrier drydock facility capable of handling large attack carriers in the Western Pacific, an installation crucial to the efficient operation of the Seventh Fleet flagship and staff as well as the carrier Midway and a squadron of destroyers, which are homeported in Yokosuka."

(115) USSACA, pp. 1481-83.

(116) Ibid., p. 1454. Infield, Unarmed and Unafraid, pp. 172-73, discusses the use of Atsugi for earlier U-2 flights and the controversy surrounding Lee Harvey Oswald's tour of duty there.

(117) See Paul, American Military Commitments, pp. 50-52.

(118) USSACA, pp. 1513-1514, lists the U.S. facilities on Okinawa, circa 1970.

(119) See USSACA, pp. 1519-1768 for full coverage of the facilities in the ROK, especially pp. 1738-68 and 1629-32. See also Paul, American Military Commitments, pp. 93-104.

(120) Paul, American Military Commitments, p. 97.

(121) Ibid., pp. 30-38.

(122) Ibid., p. 32.

(123) For full coverage of the Taiwan bases, see USSACA, pp. 1061-1141, esp. pp. 1124-1133.

(124) USSACA, p. 1107, also discussed the possibility of relocating Okinawa facilities to Taiwan.

(125) Paul, American Military Commitments, pp. 79-92.

(126) For full coverage of the U.S. bases in the Philippines, see USSACA, pp. 1-362, esp. pp. 82-111.

(127) Paul, American Military Commitments, pp. 82-83.

(128) USSACA, esp. pp. 85-98, wherein the capabilities and location of Subic Bay are compared in detail with various possible alternatives, i.e., Sasebo, Yokosuka, Guam. A more up-to-date analysis of the latter is in U.S. Senate, Committee on Foreign Relations, "U.S. Foreign Policy Objectives and Overseas Military Installations," p. 160, prepared by Congressional Research Service Library of Congress, Washington, 1979, wherein Darwin, Cockburn Sound, Surabaya, Penang and Singapore are considered as alternatives. According to Cottrell and Moorer, "U.S. Overseas Bases," quoting another source, "Subic Bay is a base that has everything a fleet could want: repair shops, an air station that sees 11,000 takeoffs and landings a month, its own mountains reserved for ship-to-shore gunnery practice, enough beaches so that some can be set aside for the Marines to practice amphibious landings," quoted from J. Lelyveld, "U.S. Military Presence in Asia as of old, but justification for it is all new," New York Times, January 26, 1974.

(129) Ibid., pp. 98-99.

(130) See Paul, American Military Commitments, pp. 17-18. Regarding U.S.-Australian frictions over U.S. use of facilities in the immediate aftermath of World War II, see Patch, "Overseas Bases," p. 447.

(131) For a somewhat polemical and perhaps tendentious review of U.S. technical facilities in Australia, see Wiliam Pinwill, "America's Ears in Space Make Australia Prime Nuclear Target But Don't Expect the CIA to Admit It," Australian Penthouse, October 1979, pp. 4-9.

(132) See, inter alia, "Premier's Coalition Trails in Australia," New York Times, October 13, 1980, p. A11; and SFR, "U.S. Foreign Policy Objectives," pp. 159-162.

(133) See Allan W. Cameron, "The Strategic Significance of the Pacific Islands: A New Debate Begins," Orbis 19, 3 (Fall 1975): 1012-1036; and Stephen Ritterbush, "Resources and Changing Perceptions of National Security in the Central and Western Pacific" (delivered at the Fletcher School's Conference on "Security and Development in the Indo-Pacific Arena," April 24-26, 1978), esp. pp. 31-33.

(134) See Lewis, "How a Defense Planner Looks at Africa," pp. 292-295; Barnet, Britain and Army, pp. 480-487; and P. M. Kennedy, The Rise and Fall of British Naval Mastery (New York: Scribner's, 1976), chap. 12.

(135) See Paul, U.S. Security Commitments, pp. 53-78, regarding Laos.

(136) Ibid., p. 108.

(137) Ibid., p. 111.

(138) See Ibid., pp. 105-127 for an overview of U.S. basing activities in Thailand. For a detailed analysis, see USSACA, pp. 607-917, esp. pp. 611-639.

(139) USSACA, pp. 676-77, 685-687; and Paul, U.S. Security Commitments, pp. 105-6 regarding this much disputed communique.

(140) USSACA, pp. 758-761.

(141) For a full review of U.S. facilities in Laos during that period, see USSACA, pp. 364-606. See also Paul, U.S. Security Commitments, pp. 53-78.

(142) USSACA, pp. 470, 489, 490, 499. Herein it is reported that these were TACAN sites which required only periodic maintenance, but which were apparently discovered by the North Vietnamese.

(143) Ibid., p. 509.

(144) See Infield, Unarmed and Unafraid, p. 173; Klass, Secret Sentries in Space, p. 50; and Thomas H. Moorer and Alvin J. Cottrell, "The Search for U.S. Bases in the Indian Ocean: A Last Chance," Strategic Review, Spring 1980, pp. 30-38. McGarvey, CIA, p. 43, notes the earlier existence of a COMINT station on the Khyber Pass, whose activities are typically described, thusly: "All sites maintain a round-the-clock operation, with men sitting at radio recorder consoles monitoring a particular frequency for voice traffic, others watching Morse or tele-

type frequencies, and still others searching a spectrum of the broadcast bands for any unexpected emissions. On the whole, the work is routine, with the daily trivia of a military airfield's training activity or the amblings of a particular Soviet army battalion through a field exercise closely watched from dawn to dusk."

(145) See, inter alia, "U.S. Aides Say Loss of Iran Sites Cuts Test Data on Soviet Missiles," New York Times, April 25, 1979, p. !6. Herein, "According to defense officials, the Iran sites, called Takman I and Takman II had the capability of 'collecting the early stuff' of a missile's launching-data relating to its size, thrust and boost."

(146) For a review of U.S. facilities access in Ethiopia during the Haile Selassie reign, see USSACA, pp. 1881-1958, esp. 1910, 1926-7, 1945, 1953; and Paul, U.S. Security Commitments, pp. 185-192.

(147) See Herbert G. Hagerty, "Forward Deployment in the 1970's and the 1980's," (Washington: National Defense University, 1977), National Security Affairs Monograph 77-2, p. 4, in turn drawn from John F. Dulles, War or Peace (New York: Macmillan Co., 1950), pp. 97-8.

(148) Hagerty, "Forward Deployment," pp. 5-6.

(149) Ibid., p. 6.

(150) For an overview, see Paul, U.S. Security Commitments, pp. 128-184; the SFR report, pp. 12-70; and USSACA, pp. 2015-2301, esp. the appendix, pp. 2277-2295.

(151) Bodo is mentioned as the planned terminus for Gary Powers' flight in, inter alia, Infield, Unarmed and Unafraid, p. 173. The U.S. technical facilities in Norway are discussed in A. Langer, O. Wilkes, and N.P. Gleditsch, The Military Functions of Omega and Loran-C (Oslo: Peace Research Institute, 1976).

(152) The principal USAREUR commands in Germany are listed in the SFR report, p. 37; and in more detail in USSACA, esp. pp. 2281-2291.

(153) SFR report, p. 37.

(154) See U.S. Senate, 90th Congress, 1st Session, Committee on Government Operations, "Disposal of U.S. Military Installations and Supplies in France" (Washington, D.C.: GPO, to January 1967).

(155) Ibid., pp. 6-7, 17.

(156) Ibid., pp. vi, 2, 11, 42-43.

(157) Ibid., p. 7.

(158) According to the SFR report, p. 33, there were later (in the 1970s) U.S. Army facilities at Daumerie Caserne and Chievres Air Base in Belgium to provide logistics and air transportation support for SACEUR, earlier moved from France. In the Netherlands, additionally, were reported communications sites at Hoek Van Holland, Steenwigkerwold, and Tharde, and a logistics center at Schinnen Emmar Mine.

(159) See USSACA, pp. 2278-2294; and the SFR report, pp. 56-58 for reviews of U.S. facilities in Italy. See also Cottrell and Moorer, pp. 21-23, including a discussion of the possible implications of the further growth in strength of the Italian Communist Party for U.S. access there.

(160) See Klass, Secret Sentries, p. 42.

(161) SFR report, pp. 56-58.

(162) Later, p. 56, the SFR report indicated that Italy came to host some 10 separate NATO NADGE (NATO Air Defense Ground Environment) early warning sites and a number of communications sites that are part of the U.S. Defense Communications Systems (DCS).

(163) See the SFR report, pp. 28-30.

(164) By the late 1970s, Lakenheath and Upper Heyford deployed F-111 aircraft; Bentwaters and Woodbridge, F-4Ds; Alconbury, some RF-4Cs and F-5Es; and Mildenhall, C-130s and KC-135s.

(165) The SFR report, p. 30, cites USAF communications sites at Borford St. John, Barkway, Botley Hill, Bovington, Chicksands, Christmas Common, Cold Blow, Croughton, Daventry, Dunkirk, Great Bromley, High Wycombe, Martlesham Heath, Mormond Hill, St. Mawgan, Swingate, and Wethersfield. The U.S. Navy is noted as having communications sites at Edzell, Scotland and at Thurso, GB; an oceanographic observation facility at Brawdy, Wales; and logistics centers at Mildenhall and London; the U.S. Army depot at Burtonwood.

(166) Regarding U.S. facilities in Iceland, see the SFR report, p. 25, wherein it is noted that a P-3 squadron is maintained there (by 1979) on rotation from its home base at Brunswick, Maine. Mention is also made of ground-based radars at Keflavik and at Hofn, as well as air defense provided by a squadron of F-4 interceptors.

(167) See SFR report, p. 23 which, among other things, notes that "Sondestrom serves principally as a logistics staging point in support of the DEW radars in Greenland. Ski-equipped C-130 transports deployed at Sondestrom from Alaska in summer months are the only fixed-wing aircraft in the U.S. inventory capable of landing on the packed-ice

fields adjacent to the two DEW radars built on the Greenlandic icecap. . . . Sondestrom is also an important link in the chain of air bases used to ferry short-range military aircraft across the North Atlantic."

(168) See Cottrell and Moorer, "U.S. Overseas Bases," pp. 12-15; the SFR report, pp. 51-52; and USSACA, pp. 2303-2412 (here, combining analyses of U.S. facilities in Spain and Portugal). The SFR report notes additionally a radio beacon annex used for navigation on Graciosa Island. See also Paul, U.S. Security Commitments, p. 184.

(169) This is discussed in Cottrell and Moorer, "U.S. Overseas Bases," pp. 12-15. According to the SFR report, p. 54, "From facilities in the island chain it is possible to track Soviet submarines operating within a 1,000 mile radius. Thus the Azores bases enable ASW units of the United States stationed there to keep watch over the midpoint of the 4,000-mile sea lane that links the U.S. Sixth Fleet in the Mediterranean with its major supply depots on the American east coast. The Azores installations also permit the United States to maintain extensive surveillance over Soviet activity in and around such a strategic 'choke point' as the Strait of Gibraltar. Furthermore, these installations would enable the United States to conduct specific antisubmarine search and destroy missions which may be necessary in the event of war."

This report also mentioned "a Defense Satellite Communications System earth terminal (near Lajes base) which transmits messages back to the naval air station at Lakehurst, N.J."

(170) See the SFR report, pp. 53-56; and USSACA, pp. 2303-2414, esp. 2402-2405. For general coverage, see also Stephen Kaplan, "The Utility of U.S. Military Bases in Spain and Portugal," Military Review 57, 4 (April 1977): 43-57, and Cottrell and Moorer, "U.S. Overseas Bases," pp. 18-21.

(171) USSACA, p. 2306, notes Loran stations at Estartit and Estacade Vores, and seven communications relay stations.

(172) See Kaplan, "Utility of U.S. Bases," p. 45. Also, according to the SFR report, "The Rota Naval Base is linked with a number of radar and microwave communication stations located throughout Spain. The military communications system in which Rota plays a key part permits continuous contact with the U.S. Sixth Fleet afloat as well as the key DCS centers at Nea Makri and Kato Souli on the Greek mainland as well as with Bouknadel and Sidi Yahia in Morocco. The system in the western Mediterranean is coordinated with NATO's early-warning network through Naples, Italy. Rota further provides storage facilities for POL and ammunition used by the U.S. military forces in the region."

(173) See Kaplan, "Utility of U.S. Bases," p. 47.

(174) Additionally, as pointed out by the SFR report, p. 54, "approximately 70 percent of the air-to-ground and 50 percent of the air-to-air weapons training conducted by USAFE takes place at Zaragoza, and its associated facilities."

Torrejon reportedly was important for ferrying arms to the Shah's Iran and to the Middle Eastern U.S. clients. See "Secret U.S.-Spain Airlift Accord Told," Washington Post, October 11, 1976, p. A24.

(175) For reviews of U.S. facilities in Greece, see the SFR report, pp. 59-61; USSACA, pp. 1769-1880; Paul, U.S. Security Commitments, pp. 163-170; and Cottrell and Moorer, "U.S. Overseas Bases," pp. 23-26.

(176) The SFR report, pp. 59-60, notes also five NATO NADGE sites and other communications facilities spread throughout Greece; also, "nuclear weapons storage sites serving both United States and NATO purposes."

Regarding communications, SFR, p. 61, reports as follows: "A major military communications center which is part of global U.S. Defense Communications System (DCS) is located at Nea Makri, situated near Marathon Bay, 27 miles northeast of Athens. Nea Makri is tied into the Licola terminal of the U.S. military communications complex at Naples, Italy, and the Moron communications terminal in Spain. Kato Souli terminal situated 7 miles northwest of Nea Makri, is linked with the U.S. Sixth Fleet afloat, with the Lago di Patri Naval Base in Spain. Mt. Pateras terminal serves to connect Greece with the Yamanlar terminal near Izmir, Turkey, on the Turkish west central coast. The Mt. Pateras terminal, located 19 miles north of Athens, serves to interconnect a number of U.S. military communications terminals throughout northern and southern Greece."

(177) The SFR report, p. 61, also notes an electronic surveillance station at Iraklion run by NSA, charged with monitoring Soviet military activities in the eastern Mediterranean.

(178) For a summary review, see the SFR report, pp. 62-65. Herein, Sinop is described as a radar monitoring and communications facility manned by NSA, collecting data on Soviet Black Sea air and naval activity and its missile testing. Karamursel is described as a communications and monitoring installation which tracks Soviet naval traffic in the western Black Sea area and around the straits. Diyarbakir is indicated a long-range radar and communications complex in East Central Turkey; Belbasi, a seismographic detection base charged with monitoring Soviet nuclear tests. The report also points to numerous DCS communications terminals, 14 NATO NADGE early warning sites, a Loran site at Kargabarun, and still other facilities.

(179) USSACA, pp. 1864-65, reports semiannual U.S. visits into the Black Sea starting in 1959, the main purpose of which was to "exercise rights" under the Montreux Convention. But according to Cottrell and

Moorer, "U.S. Overseas Bases," p. 26, "even prior to the events of 1974 the United States had no naval facilities in Turkey and was severely restricted in its calls to Turkish ports like Istanbul and Izmir."

(180) Under the 1960 agreement providing for Cypriot independence, Britain maintained two air bases at Akotiri and Dhekelia, which were later used by the United States for intelligence flights. See the SFR report, p. 81.

(181) See Lewis, "How Defense Planner Looks at Africa," p. 279, who notes that "the United States enjoyed special landing and overflight rights in Liberia, where $5.5 million had been disbursed during World War II for the construction of Roberts Field." The SFR report, p. 128, indicates that this base had been replaced for the United States by one at Wideawake Field on Ascension Island.   Silvermine is discussed by Lenny Siegel, "Diego Garcia," Pacific Research, Vol. VIII, no. 3, March-April 1977, pp. 1-11.

(182) Lewis, "How Defense Planner Looks at Africa," p. 294, also notes the United States earlier operated a missile and tracking station at Pretoria, South Africa, later said by the SFR report, p. 128, to have been reduced to standby status.

(183) See the SFR report, 195-205; and Cottrell and Moorer, "U.S. Overseas Bases," pp. 36-44. The latter also discusses the importance for the United States of the Roosevelt Roads naval station in Puerto Rico, in connection with American withdrawal from the Canal Zone.

(184) The SFR report, p. 204, refers to Galeta's purpose as "telecommunications collection," and lists some 17 other CZ facilities, variously involving training, bombing ranges, intelligence, communications, etc. According to Cottrell and Moorer, "U.S. Overseas Bases," p. 43, the purpose of the U.S. naval facilities in Panama, including a ship repair facility and a naval station at Rodman, "is to support U.S. naval units operating in the Caribbean and the Eastern Pacific."

(185) SFR Report, p. 203. Herein are noted oceanographic research facilities at Eleuthra, Grand Turk, Antigua, and Barbados, where various ocean phenomena such as currents are studied, and where acoustic hydrophones are tested. Loran facilities at San Salvador and South Caicos, an underseas ASW test center in the Bahamas, and missile test support facilities in the Bahamas, Grand Turk, and Antigua are also noted.

(186) Ibid., p. 203.

(187) See Frank Barnaby, "On Target with an Omega Station?" New Scientist 109, 993 (March 25, 1976): 671-2, which says the facility in Trinidad was to be moved to Liberia.

(188) Regarding the old 2½ war strategy, see, for a brief summary, James A. Nathan and James K. Oliver, United States Foreign Policy and World Order (Boston: Little, Brown, 1976), in chap. 2 entitled "The Nixon Doctrine and Beyond," esp. pp. 411-413. See also Albert Wohlstetter, "Half Wars and Half Policies in the Persian Gulf," in Scott Thompson, ed., National Security in the 1980s: From Weakness to Strength (San Francisco: Institute for Contemporary Studies, 1980).

(189) For an analysis of this, which tends to downplay traditional notions about a more or less linear "power over distance gradient," see Albert Wohlstetter, "Illusions of Distance" Foreign Affairs 46, 2 (January 1968): pp. 242-255.

(190) See Richard B. Remnek, "The Politics of Soviet Access to Naval Support Facilities in the Mediterranean," in B. Dismukes and J. McConnell, eds., Soviet Naval Diplomacy (New York: Pergamon, 1979), appendix D, p. 359.

(191) Ibid., pp. 362-364. According to Remnek, the Soviets virtually had to "escape" from their Albanian base at Valona in 1961, leaving behind four submarines, a submarine tender, two tugs, and some radar and other military equipment.

(192) This early Soviet pattern of concentrating arms shipments is discussed in Amelia Leiss, Changing Patterns of Arms Transfers, C/70-2 (Cambridge, Mass.: MIT Center for International Studies, 1970), esp. pp. 233-234.

5 Soviet and Western Basing Networks in the Modern Era: The Changing Strategic Map

There is widespread agreement that the United States and its alliance partners maintained a significant edge over the Soviets up until the mid-1960s in available overseas facilities all around the rim of Eurasia and in other major regions of the Third World. And the rapid U.S. nuclear strategic buildup in the early 1960s and the outcome of the Cuban missile crisis in 1962 seemed to promise a long-term, favorable, overall military balance of power for the West.

The seeming auguries of the events and trends of the early 1960s were, however, to prove ephemeral in great measure because the Soviets were then goaded into a maximum reactive effort at creating some new strategic "facts." In the ensuing years, simultaneously, the interminable Vietnam War was sorely to weaken the United States, producing prolonged internal political disarray and weakened foreign policy resolve. There also resulted a gradually lowered defense budget relative to the overall national product, so that by the late 1970s, even in absolute terms, Soviet defense outlays had become comparatively much larger, all the more so in the critical categories of equipment procurement and R&D.(1) By that time, only a decade and a half after the Cuban missile crisis, there had arisen widely shared though not unanimous global assumptions about an already existent or at least impending Soviet edge in strategic nuclear forces, as well as about a considerable conventional force edge applicable certainly to Central Europe. Whether the Reagan Administration's large increases in defense spending, authorized by Congress in the early 1980s, would reverse these trends remained to be seen.

Moving more slowly into the American public consciousness was one other aspect of a changing correlation of forces, and that had to do with the superpowers' relative capability for projecting military force into various contested areas of the Eurasian rimland and the Third World. The near-completion of the protracted decolonization process had, at any rate, opened whole new regions of the globe to two or even three-sided competition for influence and access, variously on the bases of ideological affinity and economic and military support, and where numerous "local" conflicts and historical irredentisms waxed and waned in complex juxtaposition to pro-Western and pro-Soviet ideological orientations.

Amidst these gradual but cumulatively profound changes in the global strategic map, the Soviets had gradually moved toward global maritime equivalence with the United States, and by the late 1970s, fielded an actually much larger navy and "commercial" maritime force, as measured at least by numbers of ships. Indeed, with the exception of the category of aircraft carriers (where also a major expansion was underway, involving several large carriers capable of deploying Fencer fighter-bombers or their equivalents), the USSR had achieved a remarkable quantitative edge over the United States across the board, and it was no longer clear that the United States held an offsetting qualitative advantage.(2) By 1980, the Soviet navy was comprised of over 1700 ships (versus under 500 for the U.S.): only 2 carriers, but 769 surface combat ships (guided missile cruisers, destroyers, frigates), 357 submarines of all sorts (including near 70 SSBNs), 91 amphibious warfare ships, 120 patrol combat ships, 165 mine warfare craft, and 760 auxiliary ships, provoking rueful wisecracks among U.S. naval officials about "the bear having learned to swim."(3) And although the USSR did not yet have the qualitative equal of the U.S. C-141 and C-5 long-range air transports, nor a comparable aerial refueling capability, here too, gradual but unmistakable shifts in the balance of capabilities were increasingly evident, underscored by the Soviet airlifts to Ethiopia, Vietnam, and Afghanistan.(4)

In the most fundamental geopolitical sense, the 1970s saw a gradual but unmistakable shift in the very spatial configurations of the global contest for power and influence. The heartland/rimland basis of that competition had become transformed into something more globally dispersed and diffuse, and less easily characterized, as Soviet centers of influence and military access were acquired in Latin America, the Caribbean, throughout Africa, the Middle East, South Asia, Southeast Asia, and even, prospectively, in the South Pacific. A quest for expanded basing assets to correspond with this newly acquired strategic naval and air reach became an obviously major thrust of Soviet global policy, however muted in public pronouncements.(5)

By the late 1970s the Soviets had achieved in a relatively short period a significant expansion of their once weak system of global facilities, through not without some setbacks. The result was the elaborate global network of facilities outlined in summary form in table 5.1, there broken down by hosts, the military functions of the installa-tions, and the basis for Soviet access, variously, formal defense pacts, informal security relationships, commercial agreements, or merely heavy supplies of military equipment. Simultaneously, once elaborate Western facilities networks were contracting, and what remained was under considerable pressure in almost all areas of the globe, due variously to fragmenting alliances; the defection of previously pro-Western regimes in the Third World; decreased American prestige, will, and military credibility; the policy conflicts created by America's "idealistic" arms control and human rights policies; and the inherent dilemmas produced by the cross-pressures of the Greco-Turkish and Arab-Israeli conflicts, among others. The economic and political costs of American facilities were rapidly escalating, producing a near epidemic of imitative and implicitly competing claims for higher aid compensation or other forms of quid pro quo.(6) On the contrary, however, newer technological developments – in aerial refueling, larger transports, ship containerization, satellite reconnaissance and communications – were thought to have reduced the number and the visibility of overseas facilities required, though also rendering some scattered ocean islands of crucial remaining concern.

Newer debates arose over the nexus between access to raw materials and military facilities, and over levels of basing access required for symbolic threatening shows of force, coercive diplomacy, showings of the flag, demonstrative support for friendly regimes, and the deterrence of small wars; indeed, a significant literature developed concerning the "peaceful uses of force" or "force without war."(7) There was considerable confusion over the very meaning or importance of diplomatic influence in areas removed from the central strategic nuclear balance, and in that context, over how many and what kinds of overseas facilities a big power really needed, and for what. In some minds, a sheer competition for prestige was paramount, even an end in itself, even if its practical ramifications were not clear; in some other minds, there was an insistence that prestige and power could not ultimately be separated, that they were causally and fundamentally related.

THE EXPANSION OF THE SOVIET BASING SYSTEM: THE DRIVE TO GLOBAL DIMENSIONS

As previously indicated, the Soviet Union remained until the early 1960s, or even a half decade or so beyond that point, essentially bereft of overseas strategic assets, still largely constrained to operate within a continental heartland position which, in spatial terms at least, still bore the imprint of the familiar imagery of "capitalist encirclement." This does not, however, mean that the Soviets were then, overall, in such a poor strategic position. As Weigert noted earlier,

We should be dangerously mistaken if, in analyzing the strategic bases of the Soviet Union, we limited ourselves to a discussion of the Kuriles, or her bases in Finland, or Kaliningrad, or to the appraisal of her actual or possible demands for bases in the Dardanelles, in Eritrea and Tripolitania, or on Spitsbergen. To complete the picture of the strategic bases of the Soviet Union we must include Germany east of the Oder-Neisse frontier, as well as northern Korea. We must also include the entire belt of nations within the Soviet sphere of influence, both in Europe and

Table 5.1. The Soviet Facilities Network: Recent Developments

Host	Location/Base	Principal Type Facilities	Basis of Access: Comments
Egypt	Alexandria	Repair facils.-subs and surface ships, auxiliary ships (floating base), storage of ammo, spares, fuel, etc., surf.-surf. missiles	Military alliance, advisors, heavy ATs, terminated fully by 1976
	Port Said	Anchorage, fuel storage, amphib grp. base	"
	Mersa Matruh	Access for subs, support ships, amphib. craft	"
	Aswan, Mersa Matruh	Air facils: ASW, bombers, fighters, etc.	"
	Beni Suef, Cairo West, Inshas, Mansura, Gianaklis	Tu-20, IL-38, ASW craft deployed	"
	Sollum	Naval anchorage, nat'l waters	
	Ras el Kanais	Naval anchorage	
Syria	Tartus	Facil. for minesweepers, AGI's, sub. repair, floating base	Military alliance, heavy ATs, advisors
	Latakia	access for subs & surface vessels	"
	Damascus	Access for Soviet aircraft	"
Yugoslavia	Tivat	Naval repair, incl. subs, floating drydock	Informal arrangements, predom. arms supplier
	Sibenek, Trogir, Bijela	Naval access, repair facils.	
	Pula, Split	Naval access	
Tunisia	Tunis, Bizerte	Ship visits, replenishment, minor repairs	Commercial-no ATs
Greece	Syros Isl.	Commercial ship repair, perhaps some mil. implications	Resumed 1982-political "even-handedness" of new regime

Table 5.1. (Cont.)

Host	Location/Base	Principal Type Facilities	Basis of Access: Comments
Algeria	Annaba Algiers Airfields, various	Sub visits, minor repair Naval visits Transit, staging	Heavy ATs, predom supplier "
Libya	Tobruk Tripoli Wheelus El Adem n/a Bardia	Some sub. access reported Port visits Tu-22, also reconn aircraft, prob. w. Sov. pilots Tech. facils-radar, ELINT, etc. Possible use of naval facils.	Heavy ATs, predom supplier
Spain	Canary Isl.	Replenishment, Sov. fishing trawlers (perhaps military implications)	Commercial agreement
Malta	―――――	Oil storage, commercial & perhaps naval craft	Commercial agreement
Somalia	Berbera	Naval repair (floating drydock), fuel, naval commo,, missile handling & storage, Tu-95	Earlier Treaty of Friendship & Cooperation heavy ATs, terminated 1977-78
	Chisimaio Hargeisa Gallacio, Beledin Amin	naval & air facils. air base – IL-38 ASW, AN-12 reconn. Air facils.	
S. Yemen	Aden	Naval facils., floating dock Air facils. - IL-38, transp. staging	Security tie, heavy ATs, sole supplier
	Khormaskor Socotra Isl.	Air facil. Commo facil. ammo depot, floating drydock, amphib. trng.	
	Ras Karma	Naval access	

Table 5.1. (Cont.)

Host	Location/Base	Principal Type Facilities	Basis of Access: Comments
Mauritius	Port Louis	Port visits, crew rotation, perhaps minor repairs	Commercial, no ATs
Ethiopia	Dahlak Archip.	EW, commo, missile storage, naval anchorage, repair	Security ties, heavy ATs, after 1977
	Massawa, Assab	Naval access	
Iraq	Basra	Naval access - AGIs	Security tie, heavy ATs, weakened after 1980-82 War
	Umm Quasr	Patrol boats	
	Shaiba	Air access	
	Harriyah	Air access, near Mosul	
N. Yemen	Hodeida	Naval access, earlier	Heavy ATs, but cross-pressure of Saudi influence limits access
Sudan	Pt. Sudan	Naval access, earlier	Formerly Soviet & PRC arms client, now U.S. client
Mozambique	Nacala, Beira, Maputo	Naval access reported, perhaps also commo, EW, radar, air reconn.	Predom Sov ATs
Seychelles	-------	Limited naval access reported	Ideological leanings, post-revolution
India	Bombay, Marmagao, Cochin, Vizianagaram, Vishakapatnam	Some naval access	Heavy ATs, security ties licensed arms prodn.
Sri Lanka	Colombo	Naval access earlier reported	Some arms transfers
Tanzania	Dar Es Salaam	Limited air, naval access	Arms transfers, PRC influence superseded
Afghanistan	Kandahar (Char Burjak), numerous others	Air facility access - possible Backfire base re: Persian Gulf	Conquest or puppet state

Table 5.1. (Cont.)

Host	Location/Base	Principal Type Facilities	Basis of Access: Comments
Congo	Brazzaville Pt. Noire	Air staging to Angola Naval access re Angola	Arms transfers, ideological convergence
Uganda	n/a	Satellite ground station, re: Cosmos reconn. craft	Present status, post-Amin, not clear
Angola	Luanda	Reported Bear-D reconn. flights staged	Heavy ATs, backing vs. S. Africa
Mali	Mopti	Earlier reported air staging facil.	Present status not known – Mali polit. orientation recently shifted
	n/a	Satellite tracking facil.	
Guinea	Conakry	Naval flotilla-access (W. Africa patrol), staging, Bear-D reconn, satel. tracking	Heavy ATs, econ. aid for bauxite industry, etc.
Benin	Cotonou	Possible access for trawlers, reported air staging to Angola	Arms & econ. aid
Eq. Guinea	Luba	Air staging, intell. commo. facils.	Reported voided after counter-revolution
Singapore	----------	Ship repairs at Keppel, Sembawang yards	Commercial
Chad	n/a	Satellite tracking facil.	Earlier ATs
E. Germany	various	Massive land, air, naval facils	Warsaw Pact, or empire
Bulgaria	various	" "	

Table 5.1. (Cont.)

Host	Location/Base	Principal Type Facilities	Basis of Access: Comments
Vietnam	Cam Ran Bay	Naval access, support for subs & surface ships	Security ties, heavy ATs, econ. & mil. aid
	DaNang	Naval access	
	Haiphong	Naval access	
	Bien Hoa	Air access	
	Ton Son Nhut		
	various, n/a	Tech facils.	
Cambodia	Kompong Son	Naval access	
Laos	Xieng Khoung	Airbase – MIG-21s	Security ties
Cuba	Cienfuegos	Naval access–repair, replen., attack sub. facil.	Security ties, heavy ATs, commitment vs. U.S.
	Havana	Air facils, naval commo. relay, Tu-95D reconn flights.	
	Mariel	Naval & fishing craft access	
	Antilla	Naval & fishing craft access	
	Lourdes, others	Extensive tech. facils. – microwave commo, ELINT, COMINT, satellite data relay, etc., sat tracking	
Grenada	--------------	Limited air and/or naval access rumored	Ideological convergence
Mongolia	various	Extensive air & ground facils., garrisons	Security tie, quasi-puppet state
Poland	various	Massive land, air, naval facils	Warsaw Pact, or empire
Czechoslovakia	various	" "	
Hungary	various	" "	

Fig. 5.1. Facilities available to United States and Soviet Navies – 1950.
Source: United States Military Posture, An Overview by General
        David C. Jones, USAF, For FY 1982, USGPO.

Fig. 5.2. Facilities available to United States and Soviet Navies – 1980.
Source: United States Military Posture, An Overview by General
        David C. Jones, USAF, For FY 1982, USGPO.

in Asia. To fail to perceive the full meaning of the term "strategic base" is to misjudge completely the relative power positions of the United States and the U.S.S.R.(8)

During the late 1950s and early 1960s, however, the once taut U.S. containment ring began to display some initial cracks as the global decolonialization process accelerated apace, leaving in its wake a host of new regimes in the Third World with radical and/or anti-Western political orientations, or a brand of "non-alignment" which often amounted, de facto, to a markedly pro-Soviet orientation.

Then too, beginning with the East-bloc arms shipments to Egypt and Syria in 1955, the USSR began to play a more aggressive role as supplier of arms to left-leaning regimes, in virtually all cases rooted in ideological affinity. As Soviet arsenals acquired the capacity for churning out planes, tanks, patrol boats, and other systems in numbers well beyond Warsaw Pact requirements (and also well beyond U.S. production figures), it enabled Moscow to target massive and rapid arms deliveries to overseas clients, often then causing sudden shifts in "local" balances of power.(9) The time was now long gone when, as in the 1930s, the Soviets had had to choose, because of limited arms production, between domestic and overseas supply, or between competing overseas clients (as had been the case in the late 1930s when arms deliveries to Loyalist Spain were curtailed because of more urgent requirements in the Far East).(10) It was now the United States and its customers which, post-Vietnam, labored under the constraints of "queuing" and a "critical items list."

The absence of a significant blue-water naval capability and of adequate long-range air transport tended to modify the Soviets' drive for facilities in the period 1955-1965. During this period, acquiring of new overseas arms and economic aid clients did not in most cases result in the establishment of Soviet facilities. In many cases, however, political relationships were established and nurtured which, only later, would allow the Soviets to cash in their chips for military access, often only when naval and air capabilities became commensurate with requirements for bases. Between the late 1950s and the mid-1960s, the Soviets established arms client relationships with, among others, Egypt, Syria, Algeria, Iraq, India, Indonesia, North Vietnam, Ghana, Guinea, Sudan, Somalia, Tanzania, Mali, and of course, Cuba. With the passage of time and the growth of Soviet force projection capabilities, the geopolitical import of these relationships would become clearer even if some – Indonesia, Egypt, Sudan, Somalia – were reversed toward a more pro-Western orientation.

The major burst of Soviet expansion of basing facilities began around 1964-1965, just a couple of years after the Cuban missile crisis. Under Admiral Gorschkov's prod, the Soviets then began to move in earnest toward global naval capability, among other things, so as to reduce the American advantage during "local" crises provided by its sea control beneath the umbrella of the strategic nuclear standoff.(11) As Haselkorn ably has pointed out, however, the growing Sino-Soviet rift (which began to harden at this point) also dictated a Soviet strategy of a collective security framework in South Asia and the Far East with which to meet a growing two-front threat.(12) To this end, Soviet strategy is seen to have moved toward an elaborate, interlocking system of mutual support around the southern Eurasian rim, with numerous inter-and intra-subsystem relationships stretching across the Warsaw Pact, the Middle East, India, and the Far East.

Although the new Soviet forward strategy is said by Haselkorn to have borne some resemblances to its American counterpart, however, one crucial difference is asserted. Thus he says, while

> the United States and its allies have, in general, favored the status quo; its alliances have been defensive. In contrast, the Soviet Union and its allies, at least in the Middle East and South Asia, are trying to change the status quo: India and Afghanistan with respect to Pakistan; Iraq with respect to Kuwait; Somalia with respect to Ethiopia; and so forth. Alliances based on an anti-status quo principle are, on the whole, more unstable, less controllable, and more subject to divergent forces than the defensive alliances that the United States has fostered.(13)

While such interpretations concerning ultimate motives are subject to argument, however, there is little question but that a long-term shift in the geostrategic tide began in the mid-1960s, if then temporarily masked by the post-Cuba American euphoria. This can be portrayed chronologically, and by regions, and involves considerable emphasis on the growing Soviet naval and air capabilities which gradually have rendered the possession of overseas facilities both more feasible and necessary.

Further, it must be kept in mind that the Soviet expansion of an overseas basing network has involved a multiplicity of military functions, somewhat but not precisely paralleling similar U.S. requirements. As the Soviet navy has expanded its size and reach, requirements for shore facilities have arisen in connection with supply replenishment, drydock repairs, crew rest and rotation, housing, communications relays, storage of ammunition and other materiel, aircraft staging, and the like. The Soviet air force, with its expanded capability for long-range staging of arms and personnel, has developed more extensive requirements for staging facilities, overflight corridors, and forward supply depots. And then, in connection with strategic missilry and associated surveillance operations, the USSR has developed growing needs for various overseas technical facilities – such as telemetry monitoring, ASW, nuclear test detection, communications, and satellite tracking – many of which involve interconnected global or regional networks and the possibilities for alternative use of ground stations, ships, and satellites. Constituting a major contrast with the American experience, the Soviets also have pushed for extensive overseas access for their fishing fleets and oceanographic research vessels, where at least in some cases, rather obvious corollary military considerations are involved.(14) Facilities and transit access for Aeroflot and for Soviet merchant vessels have also been sought, where in relative distinction to the United States, military operations may be involved.(15)

Before about 1964-1965, Soviet overseas facilities were significant perhaps only in the case of Cuba (aside from the earlier mentioned but suspended deployments in China, Finland, and Albania). Only in 1964 did the Soviets begin to maintain a continuous naval presence in the Mediterranean, which then began with a small force of surface ships and submarines, but which rose rapidly thereafter. The emphasis early on was on establishing a presence with limited ship deployments and "show-the-flag" port calls.(16) That presence was to expand rapidly after 1967 with the growth of the Soviet Mediterranean squadron, followed in turn by initiation of naval operations in the Indian Ocean in 1968, the beginnings of intermittent deployments to the Caribbean around 1969, the establishment of a naval patrol off West Africa in 1970, and also, far more extensive naval activity throughout the Atlantic and Pacific waters, highlighted by, among other events, the Okean-75 exercise in 1975.(17)

The expansion of Soviet overseas naval activity after 1964 may be measured and illustrated by basic data for port calls and ship-days in various regions, all of which leveled off during the 1970s after stabilizing at a high level. Between 1964 and 1970, for example, Soviet naval ship operating days overseas rose at a rate of over 40 percent per year, from around 6,000 to over 35,000 ship-days (these figures do not include those for SSBNs and oceanographic and space support ships). Broken down by regions, by the mid-1970s, these ship-day figures subsumed around 18,000 in the Mediterranean, 15,000 in the Atlantic, 7,000 in the Pacific, 1,000 each in the Caribbean and in West Africa, and around 7,000 in the Indian Ocean.(18)

In parallel, Soviet diplomatic port visits abroad increased from a nugatory 37 during 1953-1966, to over 170 during the period 1967-1976, coming more and more to focus on the Third World.(19) Regarding operational ship visits for shore support, there was an overall increase of from 55 such visits in 1967 to over 600 by 1974, declining a bit thereafter.(20) As one analyst has noted:

> The leadership of the U.S.S.R. is seriously concerned with projecting an image of formidable military and naval power — one that will impress the governments of the world and those who influence them. To translate the ability to wage war into a psychological "presence" in the minds of the world's leaders requires much more than just building a powerful fleet. Forces must be employed in ways that maximize the likelihood that their strength will be recognized and appreciated.(21)

In recent years, the Soviet navy has gained access for official diplomatic port visits not only in many of its own client states (Cuba, Guinea, Algeria), but also in many Third World nations still basically under Western sway, among them Colombia, Ecuador, Iran (under the Shah), Kenya, Mexico, Pakistan, Tunisia, and Uruguay, as well as in Denmark, France, Italy, and other Western nations.(22)

Naval exercises, sometimes in combination with clients' naval forces, have also been used to show the flag, and to demonstrate prowess, resolve, and political backing. Okean-75, involving some 220 ships and all the major oceans, was the largest naval exercise since World War II, and at its conclusion, post-exercise calls were made by Soviet warships to Morocco, Algeria, Nigeria, Mauritius, Somalia, Iraq, North Yemen, India, Cuba, Yugoslavia, and France, a revealing motley list of audiences targeted for a display of muscle.(23) In the past, combined naval exercises were held with the Egyptian and Syrian and Cuban navies.(24)

In the early phases of Soviet naval expansion, centered on the Mediterranean (and to a lesser but important degree, the Indian Ocean), fleet support was provided by shore facilities, auxiliaries, and merchant fleets. There was heavy reliance on "floating bases" in lieu of permanent shore facilities. This usually involved a group of oceangoing auxiliary vessels — repair ships, oilers, tenders, tugs, replenishment carriers — which operated either in open anchorages in international waters beyond the usual three-mile limits, within the territorial waters close to the shores of a friendly state, or sometimes in a foreign port. In marked contrast to the U.S. experience, the Soviets early relied very heavily on anchorages and in-port use of auxiliaries. This provided a high degree of security and the expression of self-reliance, but involved some serious problems. Major repairs were difficult to accomplish; there was limited storage for spare parts, materiel, and food; and aerial resupply from home Soviet bases was difficult.(25) Anchorages were subject to inclement weather, and Soviet naval personnel had only limited shore leave (though probably also more limited expectations than their American counterparts).

For all of these reasons, Soviet naval deployments in the Mediterranean were limited up to the 1967 war, with ships being sent on station there for only a couple of months at a time, heavily dependent on auxiliaries which shuttled back and forth from the Black Sea with fuel, water, and other consumables. In the eventuality of an actual conflict, there might have been a major problem concerning the resupply of ammunition, spare parts, and other materiel.(26)

After the 1967 war, there was significant change, seeing longer deployments and increasing numbers of ships, hence also greater logistical requirements. This involved some greater use of tankers (heavy use of the Soviet merchant marine's tanker fleet) and other support ships, but also much greater access to foreign ports and offshore anchorages. In a series of quick moves, access was greatly expanded in Egypt, Syria, Yugoslavia, and in North Africa, with some shifting of concentration in response to political vicissitudes and bargaining with various alternative hosts.(27)

Less than a year after the 1967 war, a five-year agreement with then humiliated and highly dependent Egypt provided the Soviets with routine naval access to Alexandria, Port Said, and Mersa Matruh, and the stationing of a naval air unit in Egypt. This access reached its zenith in 1972, at which time Soviet activities were curtailed, most Soviet personnel sent home, and shore installations reverted to Egyptian control.(28) After 1972, the Soviets continued to make use of Egyptian ports on a more limited basis, at which time alternative access was developed in Syria and Yugoslavia.(29) When Soviet-Egyptian relations further worsened in 1975, access was further limited, and in 1976 (after the Soviets had denied Egypt some new arms deliveries and refused to reschedule old debts) was all but eliminated.(30)

Alexandria was the prime focus for Soviet naval activity at the high-water mark of relations with Egypt between 1967 and 1972. Then, the Soviets made extensive use of the Al Gabari shipyard (which they had designed and built for Egypt), and of facilities for crew rest and the on-shore storage of ammunition, spare parts, fuel, and foodstuffs. Crucial was the availability of repair facilities for submarines, surface warships, and auxiliaries. After 1972 and up to 1976, Soviet ships of all sorts were still able to stop at Alexandria for replenishment, and a floating base (a "floating rear") was still maintained at Al Gabari, consisting of a number of auxiliary ships.(31) Access to storage facilities ashore was, however, curtailed. During this period, Soviet F-class submarines were still availed of mid-mission repair and maintenance facilities. After 1976, however, there was a near-complete evacuation of Soviet facilities and personnel, with some elements of the base structure then towed away to a new home in Syria.(32)

During 1967-1972, Port Said was also an important Soviet naval facility, despite its proximity to Israeli Sinai forces; indeed, the Soviet presence there seemed intended to provide a deterrent and "tripwire." Port Said was used by the Soviets for anchorage, fuel storage, and the stationing of a small amphibious group which remained until the 1973 war,(33) but was then moved westward to Mersa Matruh, further from the front lines of the Egyptian-Israeli confrontation. The latter, near the Libyan border, was a third site of significant Soviet naval activity, involving access for submarines, support ships, and an amphibious group. Some Soviet facilities were temporarily moved there as relations with Egypt worsened, presumably to allow for a lower profile, one of lesser political sensitivity.(34)

Additionally, Soviet TU-16 naval reconnaissance aircraft were stationed in Egypt during this period, 1968-1972, used for monitoring U.S. fleet activities in the Mediterranean. As well, there were reports of MIG-25 Foxbats with Soviet pilots and of Yak-28 Brewer light bombers, AN-12 Cub-C transports, and Be-12 Mail amphibious patrol craft; ASW aircraft were staged through Mersa Matruh.(35) By 1970, the Soviet Air Force operated from six airfields in Egypt, and Tu-20 and IL-38 reconnaissance and ASW craft ranged as far as Malta in monitoring the U.S. Sixth Fleet.(36)

In 1972, before Egypto-Soviet relations plummeted, the Soviets also apparently pressed the Egyptians for still newer naval facilities on the Red Sea coast for their Indian Ocean fleet, at Bernis near Ras Banas.

This request was apparently turned down, despite reported Soviet willingness to set up a sophisticated arms-manufacturing complex in Egypt as part of the bargain.(37)

As Soviet access to Egyptian facilities was progressively curtailed, that in Syria was alternatively upgraded. Though some access had previously been granted, after 1973 there began the regular use of Syrian ports at Tartus and Latakia: for minesweepers, intelligence collectors (AGIs) and for submarine repair.(38) Much of the floating base apparatus formerly at Alexandria was moved there along with Soviet amphibious ships. This access was greased by increasingly heavy arms supplies of an increasingly sophisticated nature. Soviet access to Syria was temporarily reduced during the Lebanese crisis in 1977, when Syria temporarily suppressed the PLO, but was later fully restored.(39) Here, as earlier in Egypt, a Soviet presence was intended in part to intimidate and deter Israel, constituting an implicit but visible "tripwire."

Not only Syria, but also Yugoslavia, granted the Soviet navy enhanced access somewhat in lieu of Egyptian ports beginning around 1974, apparently as much for economic as for political reasons, so as to fully utilize the repair capacity of Yugoslav ports.(40) Up to then, Soviet naval access there had amounted merely to periodic ship visits and some repairs of auxiliaries on a more or less ad hoc basis, though Yugoslav yards had long built and overhauled Soviet merchant ships, giving them extensive experience with Soviet maritime technology. Afterward, the Soviets began to make more extensive use of repair facilities at Tivat, Sibenek, Trogir, and Bijela. A floating drydock was installed at Tivat which repaired Soviet submarines. By 1976, however, escalating Soviet requests for access were apparently being stalled, including that for increased Soviet use of Yugoslav overhead airspace.(41) However, Yugoslavia had earlier availed the Soviets use of ports and airfields for their arms resupply of the Arabs in 1973, and Tito had apparently promised a repeat in the case of another Middle Eastern war.(42)

Not only Yugoslavia has apparently given the Soviet navy access to repair facilities for primarily economic reasons, but apparently, or at least briefly, Greece as well. Long a close ally of the United States, at least up until the recent impasse over Cyprus, Greece negotiated for repair and overhaul of Soviet ships at the newly reopened Neorian shipyard at Syros Island in the Aegean (some merchantmen which service the Mediterranean Eskadra had already been serviced there).(43) In 1981, the agreement was apparently voided, but then, after Papandreou's election, it was revived.(44)

Efforts have also been made to extend the Soviet facilities network westwards in the Mediterranean toward Gibraltar. They have met with halting but growing success, paced by broader military relationships.

Over a number of years, the Soviets have reportedly made numerous requests of Algeria for regular use of the formerly important French naval base at Mers El Kebir near Oran in close proximity to the Gibraltar Straits. Up to now, these requests apparently have been turned down by the somewhat radical Algerian regime, which while markedly pro-Soviet, is also jealous of its sovereignty.(45) However, some short port visits have been allowed Soviet ships at Algiers and at Annaba, and the latter port has apparently been used for some minor repairs of submarines. Meanwhile, Soviet aircraft have utilized Algerian airfields for staging arms to Angola, supplying Guinea, and for some transits en route to Cuba.(46) Periodic reports about maritime reconnaissance flights and/or basing of MIG-25s have not yet been borne out. It remains to be seen whether continued Algerian dependence on Soviet arms, and its continuing tensions with Morocco over Spanish Sahara, will lead to enlarged Soviet military access.

Libya and Tunisia have also been involved in recent reports about Soviet efforts at acquiring new facilities, which apparently have had some success in both cases. An agreement with Libya in 1975 – amid massive arms shipments as its relations with Egypt worsened – reportedly involved the development of port facilities at Tobruk, with some limited Soviet naval access.(47) The Soviets were also reported developing the Libyan port of Bardia as a possible future naval facility, and to have operated some transport and naval reconnaissance aircraft from the former Western air bases at Wheelus and El Adem.(48) Finally, as the Libyan-supported insurgency in northern Chad escalated in 1977-1978, there were reports of Soviet construction of air bases in southern Libya, which could also later be used for staging operations to southern Africa.(49) Still, as of 1981, Libya had appeared not yet to have granted the Soviets full use of highly coveted onshore naval facilities.

Tunisia has long been one of the more pro-Western Arab countries, and also had long allowed U.S. port visits. However, in 1977, a visit by Soviet naval chief Gorshkov to Tunis raised speculation about future Soviet access to naval repair facilities at the former French base at Bizerte or in Tunis, and some limited Soviet use of those installations has apparently followed, in large measure because they would otherwise be underutilized.(50) This Soviet move may, however, also have been intended to put pressure on Algeria and Libya concerning enhanced access.

Elsewhere in the Mediterranean, the Soviet navy has also been allowed periodic port visits in Morocco (in the 1960s, a Soviet arms client), in Spain's Algeciras, and Gibraltar, while Soviet fishing vessels have used facilities elsewhere in Spanish territory, and in the Canary Islands.(51) The Soviets were also reported to have pressed Spain for use of Alboran Island, east of Gibraltar, despite Spain's close military ties to the United States and NATO.(52)

As noted, during the long period in which Soviet naval access to Mediterranean ports was restricted, the strategy of self-sufficiency dictated extensive use of offshore anchorages. The Soviets have made far more use of these than has the United States, also of mooring buoys in places relatively sheltered from inclement weather. The mooring areas are spread out all over the Mediterranean, often providing rendezvous points for elements of squadrons en route to or coming from the Black Sea. Their sites also act as points of more or less continuous deployment for ships conducting specific missions; minesweeping, intelligence, submarine support, and the like.

Among the major Soviet Mediterranean anchorages and mooring buoys are those at Kithira (south of Greek Peleponnesus), Hammamet (off the Tunisian coast), Crete East, and in the Alboran Basin some 100 miles east of Gibraltar, off the Chella Bank.(53) Kithira, nearby major U.S. Sixth Fleet bases, often has several warships at anchor, and is used for refueling, replenishment and some repairs. Hammamet is used by submarines and surface combat ships, while anchorages at Alboran allow for support of ships deployed near the strategic Gibraltar exit. That off Crete is used by combat ships during crises in the Middle East.

Numerous other secondary anchorages have been developed by the Soviet navy throughout the Mediterranean: off Cape Andreas near Cyprus; off Limnos Island in the Aegean on the route to and from the Black Sea; at Hurd Bank and Lampedusa Island south of Sicily; off Cape Passero near Sicily, near Gavdos Island south of Crete; and at the Banc le Sec northeast of the Tunisian-Algerian border adjacent to the Tyrrhenian Sea.(54)

The Soviets have made use of anchorages just offshore from NATO countries in an almost brazen, routine manner. Sometimes, however, their use can produce serious diplomatic flaps. When the Soviets were expelled from Egypt, they lost use of a formerly favorite mooring buoy at Ras Al Kanais within the twelve-mile limit, but continued to use one in the Gulf of Sollum just outside that limit.(55) The Egyptians attempted, apparently with eventual success, to move the Soviets' ships away, among other things by conducting live firing exercises in the vicinity.(56) Extensions of national control over offshore waters may create more such problems in the future, and which could asymmetrically disadvantage the Soviets in light of their greater use of them.

The Soviet basing assets around the Indian Ocean littoral developed a bit later than in the Mediterranean, with a major expansion occurring between 1968 and 1974.(57) Up to the 1973 war, of course, the closure of the Suez Canal precluded movement of ships there from the Black Sea, so that Soviet naval deployments had to come all the way from the Siberian naval bases of the Soviet Pacific Fleet.(58) Since then, however, in line with a considerable increase in Soviet naval deployments in the Indian Ocean, access of greater or lesser degree has been achieved in Somalia (earlier) Iraq, South Yemen, India, Mauritius, Ethiopia, and Mozambique, and has doggedly been sought in numerous other places.

The port of Berbera in Somalia became routinely available to the Soviet Navy around 1972, after several years during which the some twenty ships of the Soviet Indian Ocean squadron had relied more or less exclusively on floating bases in international waters. After 1972 there was a major expansion of Berbera (in connection with heavy Soviet arms shipments to irredentist and Marxist Somalia), involving facilities for repairs, fueling, crew rest, and the like, and by 1975, a large floating drydock capable of handling guided missile cruisers and submarines had been delivered.(59) As it happens, the first Soviet ship was repaired there only just prior to the Soviets' expulsion during the Somalia-Ethiopia war. They apparently were allowed to build a naval communications complex at Berbera, and also a widely publicized facility for assembling and storing shipboard missiles.

Somalia came to provide the Soviets other bases as well: several air facilities deploying AN-12 reconnaissance and IL-38 ASW flights, and port facilities at Chisimaio in the south.(60) By 1978, they were apparently planning still additional facilities (a new naval base at Birikao), but the Somalian defection from Soviet clientship abruptly terminated what had become the most important complex of Soviet Indian Ocean bases.

South Yemen, long a radical Soviet arms client state, began in 1978 to replace Somalia as the major site of Soviet basing activities near the Bab El Mandeb, though the United States and Saudi Arabia then jointly made some forestalling diplomatic moves, with the latter attempting to buy out Soviet influence.(61) Soviet ships had used South Yemen ports since 1968 for replenishment (mostly water), refueling, and minor repairs, mostly from offshore anchorages.(62) Further, IL-38 aircraft and some transports have used airfields in Aden, which were particularly useful for staging materiel to Ethiopia during its war with Somalia, and also to Mozambique.(63) By 1974 the Soviets were reported to be building a floating dock at Aden, and an air base at Khormaskor. Then in 1975, there were reports of increasing Soviet activity on the South Yemen-owned island of Socotra, where amphibious landing exercises were apparently conducted, and where a Soviet communications facility and ammunition depot were said to exist.(64) Further reports spoke of possible Soviet plans for additional points of air and naval access along the South Yemen coast to the east of Aden.(65)

After the Soviet reversal of client relationships in the Horn, shifting support to Ethiopia, it was anticipated that the access lost in Somalia could largely be recouped in Ethiopia, and by enhanced access to South Yemen. For some time, however, Soviet use of the naval facilities at Massawa and Assab on Ethiopia's Eritrean coast was restricted because of the Eritrean guerrillas' continuing dominance of nearby areas and the lack of facilities equivalent to those in Berbera. More recent reports have pointed to increased use of Ethiopian facilities as the Eritrean revolt appeared to fade, particularly Ethiopian-controlled islands in the Red Sea in the Dahlak Archipelago.(66) There, the Soviets were reportedly building submarine pens and missile repair and storage silos similar to the ones in Berbera. Electronics communications and surveillance equipment was also reported being set up at Dahlak.

Iraq, increasingly up until recently, had become a major focus of Soviet access activity. After the cooling of relations with Egypt, and also the temporary worsening of ties with Syria during the Lebanese civil war, the Soviets provided newly massive amounts of modern arms to Iraq, and greatly enhanced Soviet military access was an expected quid pro quo.(67) The Soviet Navy had actually begun making calls at the Iraqi ports of Basra and Umm Quasr as early as 1968, and had long trained the Iraqis in using Soviet Osa and Komar missile boats. But the crowded condition of Iraqi ports and their distance from the main Soviet areas of naval operations – primarily in the Gulf of Aden – then seemed to preclude more extensive use.

By 1973, however, the Soviets were reported engaged in improving the facilities at Basra and Umm Quasr, the former housing a large repair ship to support warships on patrol in the Persian Gulf. In 1975, reports of deliveries of Scud SRBMs to Iraq were accompanied by those detailing marine amphibious exercises, the operations of minesweepers and intelligence ships out of Basra, and use of several Iraqi airfields for staging and reconnaissance purposes.(68) The Soviets appeared to have achieved a more solid foothold at one end of the strategic Persian Gulf, that is, until in 1978, when its support of Ethiopia's suppression of the Eritrean revolt, Iraq's crushing of its indigenous Communists, and differences over policies in Yemen had produced a worsening of relations.(69) Iraq began purchasing some arms from France and Italy, and improved its relations with Saudi Arabia, while tensions mounted with the new Iranian revolutionary regime. The future of Soviet air and naval access was, in the process, made somewhat uncertain. Then, the apparent initial denial of Soviet arms resupplies to Iraq during the latter's conflict with Iran in 1980-1982 seems to have worsened rela-tions, presumably resulting in greatly diminished Soviet access to facilities.(70) In late 1981, there were reports of a still newer reversal as the USSR began to resupply arms more heavily to Iraq, but then afterwards, a Soviet "tilt" toward Iran (resulting in its victory) became unmistakable.

Recent years have also seen extensive Soviet efforts at obtaining facilities in a plethora of new locales: Sudan, North Yemen, Tanzania, Mozambique, Mauritius, the Seychelles, the Maldives, India, Pakistan, Sri Lanka, Bangladesh, Afghanistan, Burma, and Singapore. The efforts have been based variously on ideological affinities, military and economic aid, and exploitation of various intraregional conflicts. There have been both successes and failures, but the efforts have been persistent, stubborn, and flexible.

Some reports during 1970, at a time of close ties between the USSR and Sudan underpinned by heavy arms supplies (Sudan was then also supplied by the PRC), spoke of Soviet work on a naval facility near Port Sudan protected by SAM-2 missiles.(71) Relations then soured, however, and Sudan later moved toward an Egyptian/Saudi/Western political orientation, which also entailed acquisition of American weapons. Also during the early 1970s, the Soviets are reported to have worked on possible facilities at Hodeida in North Yemen, but that country also was weaned away, at least temporarily, by Saudi Arabian money, shifting its arms sources accordingly.(72) More recently, a new shift toward Soviet arms has apparently not yet coincided with enhanced Soviet military access.

After Soviet arms had helped achieve independence for Mozambique by 1975, some Soviet-bloc military access was apparently granted there. Soviet arms carriers and other vessels made calls at the Mozambican ports of Lourenco Marques, Nacala and Beira, air facilities were improved, and there were reports of new communications and radar facilities, perhaps manned by East Germans. The Frelimo regime apparently resisted a major Soviet presence even during the Zimbabwean conflict, but the potential for expansion was obvious, particularly if Mozambique should become more seriously involved in confrontation with South Africa. At one point, the Soviets actually mounted a warning naval demonstration in Maputo after a South African raid into Mozambique. By 1981, however, the USSR did not yet appear to have extensive facilities there.(73)

By 1981, the former French naval base at Diego Suarez appeared a primary focus of Soviet attention; it is located astride the Mozambique Channel through which oil tankers must pass en route from the Persian Gulf to Europe, and is also near the potential cockpits in southern Africa. Madagascar had, by 1981, received some arms supplies from the USSR, and its then worsening economic situation was claimed rendering it more vulnerable to Soviet importunings, backed by economic and military aid.(74)

Tanzania had not, by 1982, granted the USSR permanent facilities, but it had become a more solid Soviet arms client after long heavily relying on Chinese weapons. It also appeared the Soviets may have been involved in a Tanzanian effort at consolidating Marxist control over the Seychelles Islands, themselves a potential new Soviet basing point, and later rumored to have serviced some Soviet auxiliary ships.(75) Soviet ships visited Port Louis in Mauritius after the latter's independence, its technicians apparently use Mauritian yards for ship repairs, and there have been persistent reports of plans for more important Soviet naval access.(76) In 1975 and after, there were still other rumors of talks with the Maldives Islands about Soviet fleet operations and air staging, or at least about fishing fleet facilities, following the British withdrawal from the air base at Gan.(77)

India has long been a solid Soviet arms client, going back before its 1965 war with Pakistan, and during Indira Ghandi's split rule, has been involved in a virtual military alliance with the USSR, in great part directed against China. Still, India's insistent "neutralism" has precluded extensive granting of bases to the Soviets. But the latter has made some use of the naval base (which it largely constructed) at Vishakapatnam and of several other ports of call.(78) The Indian facilities are, however, located considerable distances from the major locales of Soviet naval activity in the Indian Ocean. Sri Lanka as well has provided some limited replenishment facilities for Soviet warships, still another case where arms supplies and a degree of ideological convergence earlier bore fruit, but where U.S. ships have also been granted some access. Both India and Sri Lanka, incidentally, have barred ships carrying nuclear weapons.

Considerable recent attention has focused on the possibilities for increased Soviet use of Afghani airfields, either with or without their successfully concluding the present war. Indeed, access to such bases has been speculated as one major rationale for the Soviet invasion. The takeover of airfields around Kandahar in southern Afghanistan is claimed by some to add a new dimension to the military balance in the Persian Gulf area, placing the Straits of Hormuz within range of advanced Soviet fighter bombers.(79) Air bases there could also be used to increase pressures both on Iran and Pakistan, and heightened speculation has arisen about Soviet aspirations for naval and air access in Baluchistan, if it should become detached from Pakistan. Note has also frequently been taken of the possibility of Soviet basing in Afghanistan of Backfire bombers which could range widely across the Indian Ocean.(80)

The USSR has long, of course, applied pressure for a window on the Indian Ocean in this area. Iran, even under the Shah, apparently allowed naval reconnaissance overflights to and from the Indian Ocean, to what extent explained as "under duress" is not clear. Pakistan, while estranged from the United States, is reported to have dickered with the Soviets over a possible submarine base at Gwadar along the Baluchi coast near the Straits of Hormuz and near the then developing Iranian naval base at Chah Bahar.(81) Further east, the Soviets participated in mine-clearing operations off the Ganges Delta in Bangladesh and are even reported to have approached Burma about access to its Coco Islands in the Andaman Sea.(82)

At the juncture of the Indian and Pacific regions, Soviet auxiliary and support ships began around 1968 to call at Singapore for crew rest and replenishment. After 1972, some Soviet ships were repaired at shipyards there, as were vessels of numerous Western nations and Japan where commercial motivations appear paramount.(83) Around 1980, however, Soviet access was apparently ended.

As in the Mediterranean, the Soviets have made extensive use of offshore replenishment anchorages and mooring buoys in the Indian Ocean, which perhaps are now more badly needed after the loss of Berbera, pending future developments in South Yemen and Ethiopia. The main anchorages have been at Socotra (warships and support ships), Cape Guardafui off Somalia, and another southwest of Aden, all concentrated near the crucial Bab El Mandeb. Others used, more widely dispersed around the Indian Ocean, have been off the Chagos Archipelago near Diego Garcia, at Coetivy Island near the Fortune Bank; and also near the Seychelles, at Cargados Carajos in the Persian Gulf, and off the Nicobar and Laccadive Islands.(84)

Though Soviet base expansion was concentrated, from 1964-1977, in the Mediterranean and Indian Ocean areas, more recent developments seem to indicate efforts at expansion in the Pacific and in Africa. They follow the U.S. defeat in Vietnam and the resulting shifts of alignments in Asia; the vastly growing Soviet naval presence in the North Pacific; and some hints of the unraveling of U.S. control over the islands of the central Pacific. The Soviet quest for facilities in this region would presumably involve the entire gamut of functions: air staging, ASW, ocean surveillance, access for fishing fleets and intelligence ships, and so forth. There were familiar adumbrations of a U.S.-Soviet naval access competition in the Pacific by 1980.

The Soviets have, of course, long been availed of Siberian home bases for their Pacific fleet and for naval reconnaissance aircraft. The bases at Vladivostok-Nakhodka, Petropavlovsk, and Sovietskaya Gavan deploy a huge Soviet Pacific fleet, large numbers of surface vessels, SSBNs, and SSNs. A major new base is apparently planned on Sakhalin Island, which would provide for direct passage to the Pacific through the Kurile Islands.

While use of Singaporean facilities for repairs and replenishment has been noted, there had been up to recently a dearth of access to others around Southeast and East Asia, and all across the Pacific, which since 1945 had been virtually an American lake. And, after the Indonesian coup which toppled Sukarno, the Soviets were left without a major client state offshore from Southeast Asia.

The withdrawal of U.S. power from Southeast Asia and the continuing hostility between the USSR and China has propelled the Soviets to search for expanded naval and air access in the Western Pacific and in Asia. Those efforts have been concentrated in Vietnam, Laos, Cambodia, and, more recently and tentatively, in some of the new island nations in the South Pacific.

Since the end of the Vietnam War, there has been much discussion about the possibility of an extensive Soviet takeover of the vast basing infrastructure left by departing U.S. forces; for instance, the naval base at Camranh Bay and the major air bases at Ton Son Nhut and Bien Hoa. And the Soviets have given extensive arms and diplomatic support to Vietnam in connection with the latter's operations in Cambodia and its brief armed conflict with the PRC.(86) Despite U.S. warnings, that has now apparently resulted in extensive access for the Soviet navy at Camranh Bay, and from where Soviet reconnaissance aircraft now operate. A submarine tender at Camranh now apparently serves as a support ship for Soviet submarines operating in the South China Sea near the crucial Malacca Straits; further, this facility apparently is used to service ships in transit between Vladivostok and the Indian Ocean as well as for storing strategic equipment.(87) Some reports claim this enhanced Soviet access is an explicit trade-off demanded in exchange for the Soviets' weapons shipments to Vietnam during and after its small war with China.

Laos also, torn between Chinese and Soviet influence amidst the post-war Indo-Chinese realignments, is claimed to have granted the Soviets access to some facilities; specifically, for electronic listening posts to monitor communications in southern China, radars, and satellite radio-communications. The Soviets are also said to have been utilizing airfields there, particularly one at Xieng Khoun, which might possibly involve military purposes directed against China.(88)

Amid a worsening climate of Soviet-Chinese relations, and the apparent U.S. decoupling from Taiwan, there have been periodic speculations over the years about a Soviet-Taiwanese tie directed against mainland China, often portrayed as Taiwan's "Soviet card." For the Soviets, naval and air bases just offshore China, presenting the latter with a menacing "second front," would be an obvious plum, though maybe less so after the acquisition of facilities in Vietnam. According to one source, the Soviets are understood in 1972 to have approached Taiwan for permission to use the Pescadores Islands in the Taiwan Straits for refueling and repair purposes.(89) Nothing has come of it yet, but the prospect may give some useful leverage both to Taiwan and to the USSR.

Only very recently, the Soviets appear to have undertaken what may eventually be a serious effort at establishing a presence in the South Pacific, a development which has caused periodic concern in Australia and New Zealand, and in France because of the proximity to its nuclear testing facilities at Muroroa. The Soviets are reported to have offered economic and possibly military aid to both Tonga and Western Samoa in exchange for access for their fishing fleets and oceanographic research vessels.(90) Specifically, they are said to have requested an on-shore ship repair and maintenance facility for the former and an airhead for the exchange of Russian crews. Such transactions, if they eventuated, could have broader military implications, for instance, for Soviet ASW and other surveillance activities in the South Pacific. Bases in this area would be in near proximity to the terminal points of the U.S. Pacific Missile Range at Kwajalein and Canton Islands.(91) Earlier, the Soviet development of an arms client relationship with Peru, featuring transfer of Su-22 fighter aircraft, held the hint of an aspiration to set up an aerial staging route to the west coast of Latin America, or at minimum, access for fishing fleets.(92) That apparently has been aborted by recent changes in Peruvian politics, just as earlier Soviet hopes for possible naval access to an Allende-led Chile had been dashed.

Otherwise, a further unraveling of U.S. control over Micronesia could later present the Soviets with still newer targets of opportunity, particularly if negotiated residual long-term rights to bases were to be terminated in changing political conditions. But it is still too early to tell just what will emerge as a "final" political configuration in Micronesia, aside from what clearly will be considerable fragmentation of sovereignty providing extensive opportunities for outside influence.(93)

For the time being, however, the Soviets are constrained to the use of a few offshore anchorages in the Pacific-Southeast Asia area. Those most frequently used are off Pagan Island in the Philippines, not far from Subic Bay, and another south of Singapore. The overall thrust, however, toward a Soviet presence in the Western and South Pacific is rather clear.

The Soviets have also moved toward development of facilities all around the Atlantic Ocean. There have been periodic warship deployments there since 1969 and numerous exercises and show-the-flag ventures, though still generally a low level of deployment.(94) The Soviets do, of course, have numerous SSBNs on station in the Atlantic. And above all, they have large fleets stationed in the Kola Peninsula and in the Baltic (centered respectively at Severomorsk and Kaliningrad) whose primary responsibilities relate to all-out war contingencies in the northern Atlantic. All in all, however, the Atlantic has, for the Soviets, long remained on the nether side of the containment ring.

Cuba and Guinea (and more recently, Angola) have formed the cornerstones of the hitherto rather restricted transatlantic Soviet network of facilities, in cases where Soviet arms have long predominated in correlation to ideological affinity.

The Soviet presence in Cuba dates well back to the immediate aftermath of the Cuban Revolution; in 1962, of course, there was the Soviet attempt at installing IRBMs which triggered the Cuban missile crisis. Though the missiles were withdrawn, Cuba has ever since served as a home for numerous Soviet facilities, running the whole gamut of military functions. As it is the only Soviet client in near proximity to the United States, it has been of immense value for, among other things, intelligence, surveillance, and communications operations which could not now be performed anywhere else.

In the fall of 1970 there was a brief, though quiet, diplomatic skirmish between the United States and USSR over the latter's emplacement of a couple of nuclear submarine support barges at Cienfuegos, clearly intended to allow for Soviet operation of SSNs and perhaps SSBNs out of Cuba. The move was considered by the United States a possible violation of the informal agreements which emerged from the 1962 crisis, and while a U.S. demarche in 1970 was apparently temporarily successful, the issue arose again in 1979-1980.(95) Otherwise, the Soviets have made extensive use of onshore facilities at a number of Cuban ports – Havana, Mariel, Antilla, Cienfuegos – for the whole gamut of naval support functions. Warships and submarines regularly berth at these ports, as do AGIs which range out into the Atlantic and Caribbean.

There are numerous communications and intelligence facilities in Cuba, performing a role for the Soviets equivalent to that served the United States by its technical facilities near the USSR in Western Europe, Greece, Turkey, and Iran (earlier in the latter case). One report, in describing a Soviet electronic surveillance base in Cuba, spoke of "vast antenna farms, big-dish satellite receiver terminals and multichannel high-speed microwave relay stations," which facilities could monitor U.S. missile launchings and satellite communications and pick up microwave signals from Soviet diplomatic posts.(96) Some reports about the 3,000-man Soviet brigade in Cuba speculated that its main purpose was to protect a massive communications intercept facility which allowed the Russians to listen in on American phone conversations as well as to monitor data transmission from satellites and missiles.(97) The Soviets also stage Bear-D reconnaissance flights out of Havana, and across to the Kola Peninsula, which en route, monitor U.S. naval movements along the Atlantic Coast and in the North Atlantic.(98) And, in 1979, amid the controversy over the Cuban brigade, there were reports about Soviet pilots manning MIG-23 fighter bombers in Cuba which could easily be configured with nuclear weapons for strikes against the U.S. mainland.

Guinea was one of the earliest Soviet arms client states in Africa, dating back to around 1960, and has remained so despite periodic ups and downs in Soviet relations with the somewhat unpredictable Sekou Toure regime, which has also flirted with China and the West. In recent years, after a hiatus during the late 1960s, the Soviets began a continuous small naval patrol off the Guinean coast, originally intended to protect Guinea from Portuguese raids from nearby Portuguese Guinea.(100) This Soviet West Africa patrol has normally consisted only of an amphibious ship and oiler, though it can be augmented in crises such as that in Angola in 1975. The ships have anchored off Conakry, which is used for crew rest, minor repairs, and replenishment.

Here also, as in Cuba, Bear-D reconnaissance missions have been launched, and during the 1973 war, those operating out of Conakry were used to monitor the movement of U.S. carriers in the Mediterranean (in the 1962 Cuban missile crisis, however, such access was apparently denied the Soviets). Guinea was also an important staging point for the Soviet airlift to Angola in 1975. However, it has continued to resist Soviet pressures for access to shore facilities, and by 1980 Soviet access seemed jeopardized by what appeared a new tilt by Toure toward a more neutral diplomatic stance.

The Soviets have, however, developed several political/arms client relationships in West Africa which could yet provide some additional points of strategic access. Left-leaning Guinea-Bissau, and also Cape Verde, could become alternate stations for the Soviet West Africa patrol. Benin, Congo, Nigeria, and Equatorial Guinea have all been predominant Soviet arms recipients at times, and some apparently allowed Soviet staging operations en route to Angola.(101) Nigeria now appears tilting to a more moderate stance,(102) while Equatorial Guinea, which according to some reports, earlier had given the Soviets important access for air staging, intelligence, and communications, had undergone an anti-Soviet counterrevolution.(103) Angola itself, though resisting up to now full Soviet access to its airfields and ports, is reported to have allowed Soviet Bear-D reconnaissance flights out of Luanda which have probed around the South African cape.(104) In the West African interior, Mali, which also apparently participated in the Angola staging operation, earlier was reported allowing the Soviets to build a large air base intended for future staging contingencies further south, but the status of that development is now unclear as Mali too may have shifted alignments.

Further north along the Atlantic, the Soviets earlier are reported to have attempted to exploit the earlier radical phase of the Portuguese revolution, pressing for port facilities for their Atlantic fishing fleet. And, of course, the Soviets also then had their eyes on the strategic Azores Islands, where U.S. basing rights then appeared temporarily jeopardized by the early phases of the Portuguese revolution and by associated Arab preemptive diplomacy.

In the Caribbean, the recent radicalization of Grenada may have opened one additional possibility for the Soviets, whether or not entirely superfluous to the Cuban facilities. Despite rumors, there is no evidence yet of Soviet military access to Grenada, nor to Nicaragua since the Sandanista takeover, though Cubans have been reported constructing a large civilian airport in the former with obvious potential military implications.(105)

SOVIET GREY AREA ACCESS:
MILITARIZATION OF CIVILIAN FUNCTIONS

Heretofore, we have concentrated our attention primarily upon the elaboration of Soviet facilities for explicitly military purposes, ranging across the traditional functions of garrisoning, staging, surveillance, communications, and so on. Recalling our earlier extended (political plus economic) definition of the concept of "access," however, it must be stressed that the Soviet quest for overseas access also encompasses a broader range of purposes; specifically, involving its by now huge fishing and commercial vessel fleets, and also Aeroflot, the government-controlled Soviet airline, as well as oceanographic research. In all of these areas, it is a widely shared assumption that the lines between military and civilian purposes are somewhat blurred, given the obvious intelligence capabilities of fishing trawlers and ocean transports, the potentialities for transporting human intelligence operatives by aircraft, and the relationship of oceanographic research to ASW and the optimal positioning of strategic nuclear submarines, and so forth.

In great measure because of the interminable failures of Soviet agriculture, the diets of Soviet citizens have long heavily depended on the protein which comes with fish – relative to U.S. and European experience.(106) A vast Soviet fishing fleet has been developed which roams many of the world's most promising fishing grounds, and has often been criticized for depleting them by huge annual catches. That fleet grew from 358 units in 1950 to 4,363 by 1975, and now accounts for about 60 percent of the world's fishing fleet tonnage, if only some 12 percent of the annual fishing catch, still trailing Japan in the latter category.(107)

Soviet "factory ships" which can process and preserve large numbers of fish accompany the fishing fleets, which are comprised of large modern trawlers which sweep the oceans with huge nets. These craft are claimed often to carry sophisticated intelligence-gathering gear, radars, and perhaps ASW equipment, and as such, are virtual adjuncts of the Soviet navy. Because of their ostensible peaceful purposes, however, the Soviets have often been able to gain access for them in places where overt military access would probably be denied (Spain's Canary Islands, for example), and in other cases, the Soviets have apparently requested such access to provide an opening wedge for the later granting of access to naval units.(108)

The Soviet fishing fleet, believed coordinated by a centralized command and control system, conducts near-global operations.(109) In the Atlantic, it has concentrated in the North Sea, the English Channel, in the Great Sole Bank, and off the Shetland Islands; off the United

States and Canada, in the Grand, Sable Island, and Georges Banks. Other more recent favorite fishing grounds have been off the west coast of Africa, near Walvis Bay, the Gulf of Guinea, the Cape Verde area, and the Canary Islands; in the South Atlantic, Soviet fishing boats prowl near the Falkland Islands and South Georgia.(110) Whaling fleets operate off Antarctica. In the Indian Ocean, the Soviets exploit fisheries near Farquhar Island, near the Seychelles and Mauritius, near Kerguelen Island on the Madagascar plateau, in the Mozambique Channel, and off the Australian Northwest Cape. In the Pacific, fishing operations used to be concentrated in the Bering Sea and off the U.S. West Coast, but are now diminished.

The new 200-mile economic zones (now enforced by the United States and Canada, along with many other nations) have forced the Soviets out of some formerly favorite fisheries and have compelled a search for new ones, in some cases at great distances from Soviet home ports. Most notable in this respect is the expanded Soviet interest in the still relatively unexploited fishing areas in the Southwest Pacific; near New Zealand, Tonga, and Samoa.(111)

The size of the Soviet fishing fleet, its far-flung operations, and the demands for its efficient utilization, have dictated requirements for replenishment, repairs, and rotation of crews, so as not to have to bring the fishing ships all the way home. Such access has been granted by a number of Soviet client states, and others (such as Spain) as well. A large Soviet fishing fleet operates, for instance, out of the Cuban port of Mariel, and another out of Basra in Iraq. The Soviets have also offered fisheries aid to some thirty-six countries, and have engaged in joint fishing ventures with some twenty others.(112) Their fishing fleets are often accompanied by research vessels, some with small submersibles aboard for underwater investigations.

The now huge Soviet merchant marine fleet has often been used to support the Soviet navy; according to one source, it is "under central naval control ultimately directed by Admiral Gorschkov."(113) Soviet merchant ships participated in Okean-75 and have been used to monitor Western naval operations. The Soviet navy, in particular, has made extensive use of merchant tankers, which may provide as much as one half of the fleet's fuel requirements.(114) Soviet merchant ships have greatly increased their calls to Third World ports in recent years, not only in client states, but significantly in countries such as Brazil, Tunisia, Malaysia, Spain, Greece, Singapore, and India. Otherwise, joint maritime firms have been established with India, Sri Lanka, Egypt, Spain, the Philippines, Iraq, and Somalia.(115)

Aeroflot, the Soviet government's own airline, has been used a number of times in relation to military operations, for instance, in resupplying Egyptian and Syrian forces after the 1967 war and in ferrying Cuban troops to Angola in 1975-1976. According to one source, Aeroflot also has been used frequently to move weapons to the Third World, and its "routes to Cairo, Damascus, Conakry, Aden and Mogadiscio have played an important role in supporting Soviet military operations in Africa and the Middle East."(110) Access for its planes clearly may be important for a wide variety of purposes and, it is noted, recent years have seen its regular service extended to Greece, Mozambique, Thailand, Guinea-Bissau, India, Bangladesh, Kuwait, Peru, Portugal, Angola, Equatorial Guinea, Chad, Mauritania, and Chile, not to mention the United States.(117)

CONTINUING SOVIET QUEST FOR ACCESS

Amidst this welter of detail describing the expansion, mostly since the mid-1960s, of Soviet overseas access, a number of general points may be made. These relate to the purposes of that expansion – the extent to which a range of military-related functions may thereby be served, and what can be inferred from its gradually evolving spatial patterns. Given the relative dearth of Soviet writings or pronouncements on its overseas bases, comments on their intentions must, however, remain tentative and speculative. What is hardly to be denied is a major, energetic, purposeful Soviet thrust toward a global network of bases. More arguably, the purposes of this expansion can be attributed to a variety of offensive, defensive, and symbolic aims (or various combinations of these), such as strategic and conventional warfare contingencies and a possible ambition to deny the West critical raw materials and sea lines of communication. And as Haselkorn has ably demonstrated, the Soviet basing expansion can by now be attributed to strategies vis-a-vis both the Western powers and China.(118)

On a more specific plane, the Soviet expansion can be analyzed according to the various types and functions of facilities, ranging across forward "defense" garrisons, staging, and various technical facilities. As with their American counterparts, many of the Soviet facilities must be comprehended in terms of the complementarity and possible redundancy of networks spanning whole regions, oceans, and lengthy sea and air routes.

Noticeably, the Soviets have as yet not achieved nor made extensive use of overseas "forward" garrisons, involving the large-scale stationing of combat troop units and the inevitably associated infringements upon hosts' sovereignty. The exceptions have been in the contiguous allied states of Eastern Europe, and in Mongolia, where large Soviet army and missile units are deployed vis-a-vis China.(119) In numerous other places, past and present, Soviet "advisors" (sometimes in fairly large numbers) have been involved in manning aircraft or air defense weapons, while interspersed with "indigenous" forces. Their role in Egypt between 1967 and 1972 was one example, and there have been others in Cuba, Syria, Iraq, Libya, Ethiopia, and perhaps Angola. Nonetheless, the contrast in experience with the American forward garrison structure in Western Europe and the Far East is clear.

The development of extensive aerial staging networks to allow for rapid movement of men and materiel to far-flung clients, and in support of small surrogate wars, has been an obvious paramount aim of Soviet access strategy. The use of such air routes involves, of course, both facilities for refueling and access to overhead air space. Here, the Soviets have concentrated primarily on development of two perceptible major routes, one involving a north-south axis over the Mediterranean and south into Africa, and the other an east-west route connecting its client states from Algeria to India along the Mediterranean-Red Sea-Indian Ocean littorals.

Concerning the former, it is recalled that for a long period, the ring of western alliances around the southwestern rim of the USSR (and also intermittently strained relations with Tito's Yugoslavia) had rendered precarious and tentative the extensive Soviet utilization of long-range air transport. In 1973, however, Turkey and Yugoslavia both granted the Soviets overflight rights for flying materiel to Arab clients.(120) Likewise, Yugoslavia has apparently allowed the Soviets extensive overflights en route to other arms clients in North Africa and sub-Saharan Africa, at least when convergent political interests in the Third World have obtained. Further east, it has been pointed out that the Shah's Iran also apparently availed the Soviets of some authorized overflights of reconnaissance aircraft en route to the Indian Ocean, though still other reports spoke of unauthorized MIG-25 Foxbat flights. All in all, the availability of overflight routes in a southerly direction has improved of late for the Soviets, though remaining potentially precarious for as yet unforeseen future situations. Its burgeoning security relationship with Iran's Khomeini regime could result in some fallout in this regard.

Once south across the Mediterranean, the Soviets may now make use of a fairly extensive pattern of regularly authorized air access stretching all the way to southern Africa. This has been well demonstrated by their use of staging networks en route to clients in Angola, Mozambique, Tanzania, and Ethiopia, though at least in the case of arms supply to the latter, some problems apparently arose.

In the massive airlift to Angola, which peaked in 1975, the Soviets were at various times and by a variety of sources reported to have used air staging facilities in Algeria, Libya, Mali, Guinea, Benin, Nigeria, Equatorial Guinea, and Congo; and a quick glance at the map reveals the likelihood that the air spaces of several other nations were involved, whether authorized or not.(121) Here, not only "pro-socialist" ideological considerations, but also the anticolonial sentiments of many moderate African nations were brought into play. In moving arms to Mozambique, Zambia, and Tanzania in support of black guerrillas in Zimbabwe, many of the same staging and overflight patterns were apparently used, and in addition, perhaps others in South Yemen, Uganda, Ethiopia, and Somalia (earlier).

In airlifting arms to Ethiopia in the wake of its abandonment of Somalia (the latter had generally widespread support in the Arab world, Libya and South Yemen excepted), the Soviets apparently encountered some troublesome overhead access problems. Arms were staged through Aden (and arms prepositioned there were apparently moved in addition to those newly originating in the USSR), but some press reports referred obliquely to unauthorized overflights, perhaps involving Egypt and Sudan (with Libya as a point of origin) and maybe Iran as well if Iraq had been used en route to Aden.(122) There was at least one diplomatic incident involving Pakistan in this regard.

Given the almost monolithic support of Arab, North African, and black African states for liberation movements in southern Africa, the Soviets seem assured of later access to staging and overflight rights en route to possible future combat zones in that area. Overall, the system of access now available to the Soviets in Africa, for most conceivable purposes, is both more extensive and of far greater utility than that available to the West, to a degree a direct correlate of the by now more extensive Soviet network of arms supply client relationships.

Cutting across the north-south Soviet staging network to the Middle East and Africa, is an equally important system of communications along a discernible east-west axis running across North Africa, through the Middle East and on to India, which also involves a relatively integrated security system and the extensive pre-positioning of war materiel. Haselkorn, examining this in great detail, noted the earlier mutually interlocked system of support among Soviet client states in Egypt, Syria, Iraq, both Yemens and India.(123) Recent shifts in alignments have removed Egypt from this system. Still, the belt of states which includes Algeria, Libya, South Yemen, Syria, Iraq, and Afghanistan provides the Soviets with an effective "lateral" staging network for the movement of men and materiel; a portion of it, apparently involving Iraq, was used to stage arms to Vietnam during the latter's conflict with China.(124)

Elsewhere around the globe, some of the basing points available to the Soviets provide for still other long-range staging networks, and they clearly intend to develop still others. Guinea, assuming its Soviet tie does not further weaken, affords a stopping point on a cross-Atlantic route to Cuba, and might, at any rate, be replaced by another West African state, say Guinea-Bissau, Cape Verde, or Benin; South Vietnam provides a potentially important staging point en route to Southeast Asia, reachable either from Siberia or perhaps via India. In the Indian Ocean, the Soviets clearly desire to acquire facilities in one or another of the new island nations – Maldives, Seychelles, Mauritius – both for naval and air staging purposes, as well as to shadow U.S. naval operations out of Diego Garcia and Mombasa.

Similar considerations apparently drive the Soviet quest for new available naval ports of call. Long reliant on offshore anchorages and floating repair facilities, the Soviets obviously would prefer to obtain a more extensive system of "permanent" onshore facilities. The loss first of Alexandria and then of Berbera has created the need for alternatives both in the Mediterranean and in East Africa, respectively, to serve the Mediterranean and Indian Ocean eskadras, now only partially served in the former case by access to Syrian and Yugoslav facilities, and in the latter by those in South Yemen and Ethiopia. In the future, the Soviets may be expected to push hard for increased onshore access in Libya, Algeria, and Ethiopia to allow for lengthier ship deployments in proximity to the crucial Gibraltar and Bab El Mandeb Straits. Access to at least one South American country, and to one or more in the South Pacific, would also appear obvious future goals, to fill out a still less than totally global web of naval access.

Less clear to a casual observer availed only of open sources is the extent to which the Soviets perceive the necessity for expanded access to a range of technical facilities, some of which might require transnational networks. The present existence or status of such Soviet facilities is not easily ascertained. Only bits and pieces of information may be gleaned from occasional press reports, for instance, those claiming Soviet communications and surveillance facilities in India, Laos, Mozambique, and in particular, Cuba; sowing of ASW hydrophones in the Gulf of Suez during canal-clearing operations,(125) or their use of satellite communications stations in Amin's Uganda and satellite tracking facilities in Guinea, Chad, Mali, and Cuba.(126) Then too, perhaps more than has been the case for the United States, the Soviets have made extensive use of intelligence-gathering ships (AGIs) in lieu of ground-based facilities, so that port call facilities for them have been of utmost importance.

Generally speaking, the Soviets would appear to require, in particular, added ground-based facilities for tracking U.S. submarines in all three major oceans, and perhaps in addition, a more global system for submarine-related navigational and positioning facilities equivalent to the U.S. Loran and Omega stations. Additional radar, communications, and satellite-tracking stations may also be highly sought after. As is the case for the United States, such requirements may dictate an ever-escalating quest for new points of overseas access, even if and when those for aerial staging and naval replenishment should reach the point of virtual global redundancy.

One other point bears mention here, and that has to do with the extensive Soviet network of available ports which serve its vast fleet of arms-carrying ships, which transport some 90 percent of its weapons shipments.(127) As the number of Soviet arms client states has risen, particularly in Africa, these ships (mostly from the Soviet merchant fleet) have established rather regular routes of call, carrying tanks, crated MIGs and Sukhois,etc. to several countries in sequence. A Soviet arms-laden ship may leave Odessa, and then make consecutive stops to deliver arms at, for instance, Algiers, Conakry, Luanda, and Nacala before heading home. Maintenance of such a network provides efficiencies in Soviet arms deliveries and helps to cement growing intra and interregional ties between Soviet Third World allies and friends.

In summary, it must be emphasized that in a short span of time, in little more than a decade, the Soviets have achieved a massive and elaborate development of global air and naval facilities, usable for a wide range of military, quasi-military, and political purposes. Without a significant forward deployment posture outside of Eurasia, they have achieved the beginnings of a global air and naval facilities network which might, with some additions, rival that of the United States. These facilities have successfully been used to assist client states in conflict – Algeria, the Arab confrontation states, India, South Yemen, Ethiopia,

Angola, Mozambique, and others. They have also helped to reinforce the perception in the Third World and elsewhere of growing Soviet power and momentum, of credibility to friends and foes, and the prestige that goes with a truly visible global presence.

THE CONTRACTION OF THE U.S. BASING SYSTEM, POST 1965

Beginning in the 1960s, and accelerating throughout the 1970s, the United States experienced a progressive constriction in the once elaborate basing infrastructure that long had sustained the forward deployments which had compensated for inherent geographical disadvantages. At the same time, the near-final collapses of former European colonial empires removed still additional points of access once routinely available to the United States and the Western alliance.

The magnitude of the decline of the U.S. basing structure and its practical implications are much argued over. Cottrell and Moorer, in a lengthy and (from the perspective of the United States) pessimistic analysis, measured the decline in gross quantitative terms to illustrate the basic trends involved. According to them, "from 1953 to the present, the United States has seen its overseas naval and air bases decline in actual numbers from 150 to approximately 30."(128) They go on, pointing to an accompanying chart, to assert that "the Soviets during the same period have increased their facility arrangements abroad to a point where they are roughly equal to the United States in terms of access to foreign facilities and their requirement for bases and facilities will grow as they continue to project themselves on a global scale."(129) Their analysis then proceeds in detail on a region-by-region basis.

One should, of course, view the raw numbers involved with some caution, in the light of several related criteria. First, as noted, there has been an overall decline in the number of facilities reasonably required by major powers (perhaps except in the Soviet case because they only recently began building an overseas basing structure almost from scratch) caused by the progressively fewer numbers of ships and aircraft in their inventories, an unmistakable, secular long-term trend which has seen more and more capability packed into fewer discrete weapons platforms. Then, too, the United States came out of World War II with a vast surfeit of available facilities, which then provided considerable redundancy in some regions, which has by now evaporated. There has also been, of course, an economic component to these matters, with budgetary constraints causing base closures both at home and abroad.

Finally, the development of aircraft of greater ranges and carrying capacity, and of aerial refueling, along with parallel technological developments on the naval side, have lessened the overall U.S. requirements for bases. Likewise, the increased ability to move troops overseas quickly and in large numbers from the continental United States has reduced somewhat the requirements for forward garrisoning.

As noted, however, seemingly increased overall requirements for basing some newer technical facilities may have militated against the grain of these trends. Then, too, critics on the left, in the wake of Vietnam, argued that the United States required fewer bases simply because it had to pull in its horns to more prudently match its goals to its capabilities, and had to stop trying to be the "world's policeman."(130)

Given all of these caveats, however, the pessimism of Cottrell and Moorer, and of other like-minded analysts, seems not altogether unwarranted. Over the past fifteen years or so, the United States has lost altogether or nearly so, its former facilities in a number of places: France, Libya, Iran, Pakistan, Ethiopia, Thailand, Laos, South Vietnam, the Seychelles, and others. As a result of the British, Portuguese, and Spanish withdrawals from empire, still other potential, usable points of access have been lost: Malta, the Maldives, Angola, Mozambique, Cape Verde, Mauritius, and others. Denial of access to South Africa has been more or less self-imposed, for the time being at least. And for a variety of political and economic reasons, access has been restricted, become more costly, or been at least threatened in Portugal, Spain, Italy, Greece, Turkey, Iceland, the Philippines, Taiwan, Japan, Okinawa, Micronesia, Panama Canal Zone, and Morocco. In a trend approaching crescendo in the late 1970s, it appeared that nearly all of the U.S. overseas facilities, with some very few exceptions, had become nagging issues of one sort or another, so that in numerous cases, their future availability —either in general or for specific contingencies – was to one degree or another in doubt. And as Cottrell and Moorer ably pointed out, these trends had ramifications not only for specific, potential military contingencies, but also, more subtly, for the perceptions of numerous nations – friends, foes, and neutrals – about American prestige, resolve, and credibility.(131)

At a very broad level of generality, one can cite a number of explanations for these trends, applicable to greater or lesser degree in specific cases. The decolonization process and the anti-Western ideological antipathy of many new nations have had their impacts, in many cases where Soviet military and economic aid has filled the resulting void, leading to replacement of Western access by that for the USSR. Then, the Vietnam denouement severely damaged U.S. prestige and credibility, causing many former clients to drift toward neutralism, one or another form of "Finlandization," and the recognition that a U.S. base presence, while not offering credible protection, might further provoke Soviet-bloc enmity or aggression.(132)

Then too, there is the widespread assumption that there is no longer such a near-automatic convergence of security perspectives between the United States and many of its allies as existed in the first two decades of the postwar period; variously, because of growing multi-polarity, the increased importance of north-south issues to rival east-west ones, the lessened salience of traditional ideological conflict, and in some cases, because of lessened fears of actual communist military aggression leading in turn to one or another form of "Finlandization." These trends were by no means restricted to within Europe.

In line with these changed perspectives, many countries still hosting U.S. facilities have begun to insist on more explicit and increased quid pro quo, particularly as many have come to the assessment that such use may not correspond with their own interests, or may incite hostility from potential adversaries, thus placing a heavier defense burden on them. Domestic pressures, the recognition that dwindling facilities are so important to the United States that more extensive quid pro quo can be demanded and gotten away with, and escalating expectations aroused by the magnitude of compensation paid for bases elsewhere, have all also been major factors.(133) The U.S. has found itself in a worsening position to bargain over those facilities which it still retains.

Varying general perspectives have come to clash on the meaning of these trends for U.S. security interests. Some maintain the continued necessity for forward deployments and facilities in Western Europe (and perhaps also in Japan and South Korea), but downplay the need for those usable for interventions in the Third World, mirroring related views about the role and makeup of the U.S. Navy which peaked during the Carter administration. At the other end of the spectrum, some would prefer to hang on to every point of access possible, to retain the capability for dealing with all imaginable contingencies, including numerous worst-case scenarios; for instance, interventions in the Persian Gulf, southern Africa, or South Asia. Some critics of the American basing structure maintain that reasonable requirements ought first be set forth (perhaps on a region-by-region basis), and that basing assets then be tailored specifically to those requirements. Others claim to the contrary that there must necessarily be a mixed cause and effect between basing and overall military requirements, and that political/psychological factors require stanching of further hemorrhaging of U.S. facilities assets at almost any cost. Between the poles of these arguments, there are serious disagreements about the real needs for specific facilities – in the Philippines, Diego Garcia, the Azores, Oman, and Kenya, for example – which involve a mixture of politico-military and budgetary considerations.

For one overall summary of recent trends, the following statement taken from Cottrell and Moorer may serve as a point of departure, again, from a relatively pessimistic perspective, which comes down on one end of the opinion spectrum:

The deterioration in the U.S. overseas base structure has been worldwide, but nowhere has it been more drastic than in the western Pacific (in the wake of the U.S. disengagement from Southeast Asia) and in the Mediterranean Sea. The Mediterranean served as the pivotal area of the postwar U.S. strategy of containment; for two postwar decades it was an uncontested "American Lake" patrolled by the Sixth Fleet. Today, deep and widening cracks have opened in the once solid logistics chain stretching from the Azores Islands to Turkey. The cracks have reached the point where the effective projection of U.S. power to the Middle East and in support of NATO's southern flank is subject to growing doubt. And uncertain political trends in such key countries as Spain, Italy, Greece, and Turkey point to an even more somber future in this critical region. In short, the Mediterranean is a salient area which today offers the United States no politically "hard bases," i.e., bases safely under U.S. control. Even future access to "semi-hard" bases, namely, those under the sovereignty of old allies such as Spain, Italy, Turkey and Greece, is in doubt.(134)

The Far East and Western Pacific

In the vast area encompassing the Far East, Southeast Asia, and the Western Pacific, the United States suffered a severe degradation of its basing assets during the 1970s, and some current trends seemed to augur further losses. The importance of these trends, again, has been much contested. Those in the United States not inclined to dismay argue that the reduction of U.S. defense commitments in the area (the unlikelihood anytime soon of another U.S. war of intervention like Vietnam) and the changed relationship with China enable the United States safely to reduce its presence, and to worry less about deployments from the United States in the event of new crises. Those more inclined to worry argue the necessity for maintaining some irreducible commitments, the importance of perceptions of U.S. power and resolve by various regional actors (Japan, South Korea, China, USSR, and others), and the relationship between U.S. access to Asian facilities and possible staging requirements to the Indian Ocean/Middle East area. The possibilities for nuclear proliferation in South Korea, Taiwan, and Japan (in the former two cases considered quite serious if now abated), and these nations' dependence on sea lines of communication for virtually all of their oil, are related desiderata.(135)

The U.S. withdrawal from Southeast Asia resulted, of course, in complete loss of bases in South Vietnam and Laos, most critically involving the large naval base at Camranh Bay and the air bases at Danang, Bien Hoa, and Ton Son Nhut. These, however, had only become significantly part of the U.S. basing structure in response to the Vietnam crisis itself, and their loss did not immediately have important broader ramifications to the U.S. security posture, except in that they became Soviet bases. Overall, however, the loss of the Vietnam war did have a broader impact insofar as long-term U.S. allies such as Thailand and the Philippines were nudged toward degrees of disengagement from U.S. clientship, that is, toward accommodation with new realities of regional power.

Thailand reacted to the U.S. withdrawal from Indo-China by rapidly moving toward a somewhat more neutral posture, and new leftist political currents almost immediately jeopardized U.S. facilities. A subsequent rightist coup seemed first to augur a partial return to the status quo ante of 1972, but by 1978 it appeared that U.S. basing rights in Thailand were on the way to near-complete elimination. The U.S. had abandoned there several important air bases, apparently retaining some use of the facility at Utapao for staging operations, including P-3 flights. The status of the formerly important intelligence facility at Ramasun was unclear (it was earlier described as a critical link in the U.S. global strategic network, used to monitor Soviet, PRC and Vietnamese electronic military communications), but appeared to have been closed down, and the earlier broached possibility of building a major naval base at Sattahip, either to replace or supplement that at Subic Bay, was in abeyance.(136) However, in 1980 Vietnamese incursions across the Thai border from Cambodia had engendered increased U.S. military aid to Bangkok, and it appeared possible that resumed U.S. access to their facilities might be made part of the bargain.(137) Nearby, and Soviet propaganda to the contrary, little more was heard of the possibility of U.S. facilities in Indonesia, despite mounting U.S. arms sales to that strategically vital OPEC nation which, along with the other members of ASEAN, became increasingly concerned about Vietnamese expansionism in Southeast Asia.(138) There were (unsubstantiated) rumors about U.S. SOSUS terminals astride the crucial Indonesian Straits transited by Soviet as well as American nuclear submarines.(139)

By 1977-1978, however, even the long-term U.S. presence in the Philippines – based on a mid-1960s renegotiation of the 1947 agreement which gave the United States the right to retain use of twenty-three naval and air facilities rent-free for ninety-nine years – had become more questionable, certainly subject to harder bargaining. At one point, Philippine President Marcos actually threatened a closedown of all of the U.S. facilities. Actually, by the late 1970s the U.S. retained only six of its original bases, but those included the elaborate naval base at Subic Bay and the important Clark Air Force Base. Subic was widely considered a key to U.S. naval operations in the Western Pacific, particularly for the South China Sea, and its facilities were assumed not easily, if at all, replaceable by Yokosuka in Japan, or Guam. Its importance was highlighted by the crisis in North Yemen and then in Iran, during both of which U.S. naval units were deployed all the way across the Indian Ocean from Subic Bay.

After three years of talks and hard bargaining (also threats by the U.S. Congress to abort the U.S. presence in the Philippines if the costs were to become too high), a new four-year agreement was reached in 1979 which assured the United States relatively unhampered continued use of the facilities.(140) It reaffirmed the old U.S. security commitment to the Philippines, and also involved $500 million of U.S. military and economic aid stretched out over five years, roughly similar to the costs of continued use of bases in Turkey, Greece, and Spain.(141) Then, there were changes in the nature of U.S. access to the Filipino bases. The land areas under U.S. control at Subic and Clark were reduced substantially, and the physical security of the new base perimeters became the responsibility of the Philippines. And it was assumed that use of the facilities by U.S. forces for specific missions would be subject to a Filipino veto. Such use might not at all be automatic, say, if the United States were to request use of Clark Air Base for resupply of arms to Israel during a new Middle Eastern crisis. There were, incidentally, indications that the Philippines had used the base negotiations to pry qualitatively more sophisticated aircraft transfers from the United States at a time the Carter administration was attempting to control such transfers in the Southeast Asia region, was also remonstrating with the Filipinos over human rights problems, and was abjuring direct assistance to their counterinsurgency effort against Muslims in the country's southern areas. Finally, it remained to be seen whether the essentials of the 1979 agreement would be retained when its renewal came up in 1983.(142)

Further north along the Pacific littoral, constriction of U.S. access to Taiwan, Japan (including Okinawa), and South Korea was also at least brought into question. The United States itself, by the late 1970s, had apparently virtually ended the use of most if not all facilities in Taiwan, in line with the withdrawal of diplomatic recognition and the establishment of new relations with the PRC. Whether use of some technical facilities on Taiwan was to be retained was not clear, for instance, electronic listening posts and SOSUS terminals.(143) Bases in South Korea were retained (primarily useful in relationship to deterring or fighting a new Korean War) after the Carter administration's reversal of its initial plans for a phased, near-complete withdrawal of U.S. forces.(144) Japan and Okinawa had become, meanwhile, even more than before, the vital hinge of the remnant U.S. basing structure in Northeast Asia, even as signs of an eventual large-scale Japanese rearmament loomed.

As of the late 1970s, the United States retained its huge naval base at Yokosuka, its importance now increased with the near close-down of U.S. use of Sasebo. It also retained the use of several air bases utilized for a variety of purposes (ASW and intelligence, for example), most notably those at Misawa and Yokota, though the Tachikawa base, once the USAF's chief logistical center, had been deactivated. At least one publication also cited Japan as a terminal for U.S. SOSUS arrays, important in light of the continuing Soviet naval buildup at Vladivostok and Petropavlovsk.(145)

But, there were now new restrictions. Leftist and pacifist political forces in Japan had been somewhat mollified by the earlier reversion of Okinawa to Japan; but in its aftermath, American use of Okinawa was supposedly to be restricted to use only in defense of Japan. U.S. facilities in Japan proper apparently retained a wider mandate, but the United States had agreed to "prior consultation" – a Japanese veto – before making major changes in deployments there, introducing nuclear weapons, or launching combat operations. It is not clear what that might mean for future operations in Korea, the Taiwan Straits, or for support of possible military operations in Southeast Asia or in the Indian Ocean.

Also not clear is what the impact of a U.S. military withdrawal – partial or full – from South Korea might be on the future of U.S. bases in Japan, not to mention the broader context of U.S.-Japanese security relationships; that is, whether or not the Japanese might then drift toward a form of neutrality. That, by 1981, seemed a far less likely eventuality under the Reagan administration than it did at the outset of its predecessor. Restriction of U.S. basing rights in the Philippines, seemingly less imminent after the agreement of 1979, might also yet impact on the use of those in Japan – and their use might then become more crucial. And finally, as Cottrell and Moorer point out: "a potential socialist victory in Japan – a likelihood which cannot be discounted, given the tenuous position of the present government with its small majority in parliament – could well at some future time create political conditions that would bar Japanese territory and facilities to U.S. military forces."(146) That fear was not borne out by the 1980 elections in Japan and the change of premiership, but remained a future possibility, in connection with either increased Japanese neutralism and disengagement or with Japanese rearmament.(147)

Running somewhat counter to trends elsewhere in the region, the U.S. facilities structure in Australia has seemed somewhat more secure in recent years, because of the coming to power of the conservative and pro-American government headed by Prime Minister Malcolm Fraser. Earlier, the Labour government under Gough Whitlam had taken a progressively dimmer view of U.S. bases, most notably of the critical technical facilities at Pine Gap (Alice Springs) and Woomera (Nurrungar), and the naval communications station at Northwest Cape.

During Fraser's tenure, there has been considerable talk about the expansion of American use of Australian facilities, first in connection with the possibility of U.S. loss of its Philippine bases, but then later amid the U.S. buildup in the Indian Ocean in the wake of the Iran and Afghanistan crises. The United States seemed assured of continued use not only of the aforementioned technical facilities, but perhaps also of enhanced use of a new naval base being constructed at Cockburn Sound on the western coast, perhaps both for surface ships and submarines.(148)

Also seriously bruited was the possibly increased U.S. use of air staging facilities en route from the Pacific to the Indian Ocean, even if it involved a somewhat longer route than one where Clark Field or Thailand's Utapao were available.(149) Indeed, recent reports indicated tentative Australian approval of U.S. staging of B-52 flights between the Pacific and Diego Garcia through Darwin. However, as of 1981 the negotiations were stalled over the issue of notification of flights carrying nuclear weapons. The Fraser regime appeared, overall, particularly in the wake of the Afghanistan crisis, favorably inclined to a continued U.S. presence in the Indian Ocean (at Diego Garcia) and in Southeast Asia, but there was still the question of what would be entailed by a reversal of Australian political tides which might bring Whitlam or someone of similar views back to power. Among other things, there were still rumblings from the Australian left about the U.S. facilities (satellite data relays for early warning and ELINT, submarine communications and navigation) related to nuclear deterrence, which could make Australia a logical Soviet target in the event of a full-scale nuclear war.

Otherwise, there were also growing questions about the future availability to the United States of its earlier seemingly assured access to bases in the Micronesian islands. Guam, of course, long a U.S. territory, would remain indefinitely available with its elaborate naval complex which could, at great expense, be expanded. It cannot now, however, handle the repair of large ships, and it has only a small harbor.(150) Though it could hypothetically serve as a fallback position if Subic Bay and Yokosuka were lost to the United States, its capabilities are limited, its labor costs are high, and, of course, its geographic position is not altogether favorable for operations along the Asian coast, not to mention longer-range deployments to the Indian Ocean.

There has been some talk of the United States building a large naval base in the Palau Islands, at Kossol Reef, once a major Japanese naval anchorage, and favored by closer proximity than Guam to Southeast Asia and the important sea lanes of communication through the Indonesian Straits. Here too, however, the expense of building a new base from scratch might be prohibitive. Additional air bases could, meanwhile, be constructed on Saipan or Tinian as well as in the Palau's on Babeldgup Island.(151)

By 1980 U.S. hopes for maintaining continued military access in Micronesia were enmeshed in some complex negotiations over independence or various degrees of autonomy for the several groupings of islands comprising the UN Trusteeship. The Northern Marianas Islands elected to become a U.S. Commonwealth, like Puerto Rico, hence presumably maintaining U.S. military access for the time being in Saipan and Tinian. In 1980 the Marshall Islands group attained limited independence but where exclusive U.S. military rights were assured for at least fifteen years.(152) In exchange for payments of $9 million a year, the United States thereby retained use of its base in Kwajalein, the terminus of its Pacific missile range. A similar agreement was completed when the Palau Islands became the new Republic of Belau. Still to be completed was an expected similar agreement with the Federated States of Micronesia, comprising the islands of Truk, Yap, Ponape, and Kusaie.

Whether further constraints on U.S. use of facilities in Japan and the Philippines will later eventuate, and if they do, whether the U.S. will then wish to bear the cost of constructing fallback bases in Micronesia, is not yet clear. Given the history of the threat mounted against the United States at the outset of World War II, American planners may actually assign more weight to the "strategic denial" side of this problem, hoping for long-term arrangements which would ensure at least that no foreign bases are built in Micronesia, which could be particularly important for ASW purposes, as well as providing proximity to U.S. missile range terminals on Kwajelein and Canton Islands and the French nuclear testing facility on Muroroa.(153) Soviet overtures to Tonga and Western Samoa have already raised that specter.

Loss of forward naval bases in the Western Pacific would seriously handicap the American ability to project force over a wide expanse of strategic territory, extending all the way to the eastern coast of Africa. For instance, American ability to support Kenya in a recent crisis with Uganda depended on movement of a carrier task force westward from Subic Bay; likewise, U.S. support for North Yemen when it was threatened by its southern neighbor. Concerning aerial staging for possible contingencies in Korea and Taiwan, loss of presently available facilities in the Philippines and/or Japan might be less crucial, though not unimportant. Thus, according to one recent paper,

> even if Clark and Kadena were not available; if F-4's were based on Guam, they could be flown to Taiwan or Korea with two aerial refuelings and C-130's would be able to carry full loads. If, however, there were a need to perform the counter-air or interdiction missions to protect the aircraft flying to the contingency area, Clark and Kadena became more important because of the more limited range of armed fighter aircraft.(154)

Access to overhead air space for the United States is a less critical matter in the Western Pacific than elsewhere, given the obvious fact of an unimpeded all-ocean route from Hawaii to all of the important littoral states. On the naval side, however, there has been some concern about the future of U.S. transit rights for warships and submarines through the several Indonesian straits, in the context of the new, evolving Law of the Sea regime, as Indonesia has threatened to enlarge its span of sovereign control.(155) Indeed, maintenance of those rights by constant testing is perhaps one major rationale for continued U.S. rotation of naval vessels from the Pacific to the Indian Ocean.

Further degradation of U.S. basing rights in the Far East and Western Pacific would, of course, bear heavily on a range of crucial technical functions, even despite their gradual supersession by satellite technology. Ocean surface reconnaissance, ASW, communications, and various intelligence facilities are located in South Korea, Japan, the Philippines, Australia, and perhaps still to some extent in Thailand and Taiwan. Though some use of fallback positions might be available in the case of one or more defections, loss of the entire system would clearly reduce American regional, if not global, capabilities in a number of functional areas. Guam, for instance, would presumably be considerably limited for ASW operations in the South China Sea or the Sea of Okhotsk; and some intelligence and communications facilities clearly depend on near proximity to Asia not availed by fallback positions in Micronesia, nor perhaps either by extant satellite technology.(156) But on the reverse side of the coin, there was the U.S. acquisition of intelligence monitoring stations within the PRC, one important aspect of "the China Card." That became an important consideration during the first year of the Reagan administration, as it wrestled with its "Two-Chinas" policy.(157)

Latin America and the Caribbean

With the exception of a few minor technical functions, the United States has made little use of bases in South America since the immediate aftermath of World War II. The progress of the global geopolitical competition had not, until recently, raised new requirements, though the seemingly new-found importance of the South Atlantic has at least aired the matter of future use of Brazilian air bases.(158) But with the weakening U.S. influence in South America, earlier exacerbated, for good or worse, by the Carter administration's human rights policies – and reflected in a dramatic drop in the U.S. share of Latin American arms markets – there seemed, until recently, little prospect of expanded U.S. basing assets in that area. For the most part, the primary U.S. interest has remained that of strategic denial; that is, an informal extension of the Monroe Doctrine.

The main area of U.S. access problems in the Western Hemisphere (assuming those in Canada to be secure for the near future) is in the Caribbean. For a long time, U.S. access in that area was predicated on the need to protect the Panama Canal, and its naval dominance had been almost uncontested since Britain's withdrawal from Jamaica. More recently, of course, the extensive Soviet presence in Cuba, the coming to independence of several new radical or near-radical states in the Caribbean (first Jamaica, then Grenada) and revolutionary ferment in Central America (the Nicaraguan revolution, civil war in El Salvador, troubles in Guatemala) have brought that region into the realm of big-power competition for access. Over it all looms the hugely growing importance of new oil fields in Mexico and Guatemala, whose reserves may yet rival those of the Persian Gulf. In 1982, as the U.S. embroilment in El Salvador's problems continued, there were reports that the U.S. was seeking new points of access for staging military aircraft, in Colombia and Honduras.(159)

Though the United States maintains naval training facilities at Roosevelt Roads in Puerto Rico, it has insisted on holding on to its base at Guantanamo Bay. Here too, the motive of strategic denial vis-a-vis the USSR is presumably important, as the United States does not wish to hand the Soviets excellent harbor facilities to supplement those at Havana, Mariel, and Cienfuegos. Whether the United States will maintain its hold on Guantanamo, or whether it will eventually be traded off for Cuban concessions or in connection with a U.S.-Cuba detente remains to be seen.

Otherwise, the recent Panama Canal Treaty now appears to augur eventual jeopardization of U.S. facilities in the Canal Zone. The treaty appears to envisage a gradual reduction of the U.S. presence up to the year 2000, followed by complete elimination. In Panama also, the strategic denial question is of utmost importance in the face of a possible radicalization of Panamanian politics, as already adumbrated by Panama's military support for the Sandanistas.(160)

The extent to which continued U.S. access, even in areas long under close-by military sway is now under severe political pressure was illustrated during the Nicaraguan civil war, during which the U.S. was ordered "within 24 hours" to withdraw a small Air Force contingent and its two helicopters from Costa Rica.(161) The latter were initially allowed to enter Costa Rica to be available if an evacuation of U.S. citizens from Nicaragua became necessary. Costa Rica, along with Mexico and Panama, was backing the Sandanistas, and its refusal of access to a U.S. rescue contingency unit was echoed later by Turkey's restriction of similar American access to Incirlik during the Iranian revolution.

Elsewhere in the Caribbean region, there are increasing pressures on continued United States use of long-held technical facilities in formerly British-owned but now independent Barbados, Bermuda, Antigua, and the Bahamas, some of which may now be relatively superfluous.(162) Negotiations over base rentals are impending or ongoing in each of these cases. Others on Grand Turk and Caicos Islands, still associated with the UK, appear relatively more secure, but the U.S. Omega station in Trinidad (one of eight such worldwide low-frequency navigation systems for ships and aircraft) will probably be closed and replaced by another in Liberia. As elsewhere, the overall regional trend for U.S. access rights has seemed downward (whether to be reversed by new access to Colombia and Honduras remains to be seen) mitigated somewhat by the availability of fallback facilities in nearby areas of the continental United States. Even in Puerto Rico, continued U.S. use of, for instance, its Sabana Seca Communications Center, appeared jeopardized by violent revolutionary activity, and subject in the long run to the uncertain future of Puerto Rico's political status.

Not altogether to be precluded for the future, of course, are changes in political rivalries in Latin America which might prod the United States toward enhanced access there. The turmoil in Central America at least raises the question of bolstered U.S. access to neighboring states or perhaps Britain's Cayman Island. And the Reagan administration's evident inclination to improve relations with South America's conservative regimes (increased arms sales, relaxed human rights pressures) might yet raise the issue of facilities, particularly if the Soviet presence in the South Atlantic or South Pacific should loom larger.(163) Then too, the United States might later require more technical facilities in Latin America (space-tracking facilities, for instance), the acquisition of which might be eased by closer military and political cooperation. These questions are subject to great uncertainties amidst the unfolding of the Falkland Islands crisis, which may — temporarily or for a longer period — result in a worsening of U.S. ties throughout Latin America.

The Indian Ocean/Middle Eastern Area

Until recently, the United States has had limited accessibility to facilities around the crucial Indian Ocean littoral. The American presence was earlier withdrawn from Pakistan and also, for the most part, from Thailand. The U.S. Navy's access to Bahrain, also, was somewhat reduced from that of a home-port naval station to one more readily characterized as access for periodic visits. The earlier availability of British facilities in Mauritius, the Seychelles, and Maldives had also evaporated (though a tracking facility in the second-named yet remained); likewise, U.S. use of the former French naval base at Diego Suarez in Madagascar (though U.S. use of Djibouti appeared to increase).

By the late 1970s, with the major facilities in Diego Garcia still under construction, the United States was forced to mount naval demonstrations of resolve, on behalf of North Yemen and also (futilely) for the Shah of Iran, all the way from Subic Bay. Almost the entire littoral of South Asia and East Africa had become closed to American naval access, certainly for crises or coercive diplomacy, while aerial staging to the Indian Ocean had become critically dependent on the British islands of Diego Garcia and Ascension, rather a necessary bare minimum.(164) Low profile P-3 flights staged through Masirah, Kenya, Diego Garcia, Singapore, Thailand, and Australia's Learmouth and Cocos Islands appeared a dwindling remnant of a once far more formidable system of Western access, though still providing at least an ASW surveillance network over the northern Indian Ocean.

By 1980, U.S. use of some important technical facilities in this area had also been reduced − to what extent entirely compensated for by satellites and other new technologies was not clear. The close-down of the communications base at Kagnew after Haile Selassie's fall was apparently not crucial, its installations being superseded by satellites and perhaps (only temporarily, as it turned out) by Bandar Abbas in Iran. The United States also appeared on the verge of losing its space-tracking station at Mahe in the Seychelles (after the latter's coup which apparently was supported by Tanzania, if not overtly by the USSR itself), as it earlier had lost a satellite-related facility in Madagascar.(165) The implications of these losses, on top of self-denial of access to South Africa's intelligence and communications installation near Capetown, was, however, not readily apparent.

What was apparent was that many U.S. basing functions, those not replaceable by satellites, ships, or aircraft, were being concentrated at Diego Garcia, which had come to assume vast importance even before the traumatic events of 1979-1980 in Iran and Afghanistan. For that reason, it became a major object of Soviet propaganda, as well as a target of numerous regional radical and "neutral" states anxious to force a complete withdrawal of the U.S. presence from the region.

Completion of the U.S. base on Diego Garcia was due in 1981, some ten years after work on it began. It was then to have a 12,000-foot runway, on which P-3s are already based, but which would then be able to accommodate large transport aircraft and tankers, and also B-52 bombers.(166) A mile-long jetty would allow a carrier task group to be based in the lagoon which forms the island's heart. Numerous technical facilities − communications, satellite data relays − are also apparently to be based on Diego Garcia, replacing those lost in nearby areas. One report cited, among others, facilities for real-time transmittal of satellite intelligence (TV transmissions, radar reports, ELINT, SIGINT); relays of similar information from SR-71 aircraft; and HF, VHF, SHF, LF and VLF (Omega) communications.(167) Particularly important, it was said, was Diego's role in the Navy's new Fleet Satellite Communications System, which utilizes four geostationary satellites, and for which Diego was to provide backup; interface with other communications systems; and "data processing and switching support."(168) The same report claimed that later, Diego would have lesser value as a communications station as soon as this new system was fully operational.

Even before the events of 1980, Diego was perceived as crucial for contingencies in East Africa and the Persian Gulf; one expert referred to it as "the key to projecting Air Force power onto the Indian Ocean littoral and, in the event of a European war, into the Gulf."(169) As it was, even with the availability of Diego and of Clark Air Base in the Philippines, extensive refueling would be required to bridge the long 3,250 mile air route between them via the Straits of Malacca.(170)

Some reports also claimed that later, Diego Garcia might assume a role in support of U.S. SSBNs, if they should be put on station in the Indian Ocean with the deployment of the Poseidon C-4 missile and the new Trident submarine. That might merely entail stationing of a submarine tender at Diego. No information about this has emerged, and some analyses claim that the long-range Tridents will not utilize the Indian Ocean, because they can patrol near the United States and still be in range of their prime targets.(171)

In the late 1970s, there were some desultory discussions about Indian Ocean demilitarization, which if brought to fruition, would probably have involved respective U.S. and Soviet withdrawals from Diego Garcia and Berbera.(172) The Soviets lost their bargaining chip, of course, and moved to replace it in nearby Ethiopia and South Yemen. The U.S. Congress placed some restrictions, meanwhile, on U.S. development of Diego, about which there were questions at any rate, of whether British permission would be given for use in certain circumstances; for instance, assistance to Israel in a new Middle Eastern crisis.

The entire situation regarding U.S. access to facilities in the Middle East-Indian Ocean area underwent a dramatic change, at any rate, with the events surrounding the Iranian revolution and Soviet invasion of Afghanistan. What previously had been considered by many primarily an arms-control problem — Indian Ocean demilitarization — was transformed suddenly into a strong consensus in Washington about the need for improved basing access for possible force projection into the Persian Gulf. There was a sudden reversal of mood as the Carter administration sought, almost frantically, to reverse the long-term decline of Western basing assets in an area increasingly perceived as an altogether vital U.S. interest. (see Figs. 5.1 and 5.2) The well-known result was the "Carter Doctrine" aimed at protecting U.S. interests in the Brzezinskian "arc of crisis."(173)

Attention – and negotiations – came to be focused on several areas: Somalia, Kenya, Oman, Egypt, and also, in an accelerated way, on Diego Garcia.(174) Not only would the latter's runway be expanded, but also, its new port would deploy on a continuing basis a number of forward supply ships for a Rapid Deployment Force (RDF) being earmarked for the Indian Ocean area. Tanks and other materiel placed aboard these ships could be used for a rapid expansion of U.S. forces in the Persian Gulf area, beyond the some 1,800 Marines to be kept aboard the Indian Ocean fleet. And the great distances involved from the United States and the limitations on U.S. air- and sealift capacity provoked serious discussion about plans for large-scale pre-positioning of war stocks, if secure access for that could be obtained.

The plan to expand Diego Garcia was said to envision "widening the air strip and building ramps to accommodate the long-range B-52's, which must have runways adequate to support outriggers under the tips of their long, drooping wings."(175) The USAF flew some B-52 sorties over the Indian Ocean in 1980, which required several refuelings in air.

During the Iran crisis, the U.S. Navy deployed two carriers, sixteen other combat ships, and six supply vessels in the Indian Ocean, and Diego became vital to their support. C-141 aircraft flew at first all the way from Subic Bay with mail, fresh food, parts, and other equipment; but later, apparently, the problem was eased by use of Omani air bases. Both a destroyer tender and submarine tender were deployed at Diego as further evidence of its growing importance.

Perhaps of equal long-term significance to America's presence in the Indian Ocean-Middle Eastern area (aspirations for demilitarization had been abandoned for the duration) was its seeming success in concluding negotiations with Oman, Somalia, and Kenya for additional facilities. In the first two-named, this apparently required tough bargaining, and in both, the negotiations were nearly aborted.

Kenya, of course, had long allowed the U.S. port visits and P-3 staging rights at Mombasa, and the United States in turn had become a major supplier of arms to Nairobi; additionally, it had mounted a military demonstration when the latter was threatened by Idi Amin's Uganda. In 1980, however, Kenya, in exchange for increased economic and military aid, offered the United States expanded access, apparently to entail greater U.S. use of air and naval facilities, depots for fuel and spare parts, and possibly the use of an aircraft hangar.(176) Mombasa's distance from the Persian Gulf rendered its utility in a crisis there questionable; its main purpose appeared that of acting as a supply point for the U.S. Indian Ocean fleet.

For over a half-year in early 1980, the United States bargained with Somalia over the initiation of American military access, involving repeated visits by high-ranking U.S. military and diplomatic delegations to Siad Barre in Mogadiscio.(177) The U.S. aim, of course, was primarily that of access to the former Soviet naval base at Berbera, which aside from its position outside the Bab El Mandeb, was closer than Mombasa to the Persian Gulf. Primarily it would be intended for Red Sea operations – for ASW patrol craft or to base fighter-bombers flown in from the United States. Initial reports indicated Somalia's demands of up to $2 billion in military and economic aid and also for U.S. diplomatic backing in its quarrel with Ethiopia over the Ogaden. The United States appeared to consider this too high a price, and was also reluctant to risk getting militarily involved in the interminable Horn conflict. The negotiations appeared stalled, perhaps aborted; but then suddenly in August 1980, the United States apparently acquired use of Berbera for only some $25 million in economic and military aid for 1981 on top of some $100 million of other aid.(178) Additionally, the United States appeared to have avoided a commitment to back Somalia over the Ogaden. Perhaps ultimately, Somalia offered the facilities to acquire a U.S. "tripwire" deterrent vis-a-vis Soviet-backed Ethiopia, though the role of Saudi Arabia in these negotiations may also have been important, if unmentioned in press reports. The full extent of future U.S. access to Somalia was not immediately clear; potentially, it could provide extensive naval repair, storage for weapons and fuel, and runways which could accommodate large transports, tankers, tactical fighters, and even B-52 bombers if necessary.

Earlier in 1980, also for a relatively lenient price in economic and military aid, the United States had also achieved enhanced access to Omani bases (it had for several years been staging P-3 flights out of the old British air base on Masirah Island).(179) That would apparently involve use of the airstrip at Masirah, the ports of Muscat and Matrah, and airfields at Seeb and Thumrayt; Muscat might be used to deploy minesweepers if the USSR ever decided to mine the Straits of Hormuz.(180) In the period immediately following the Soviet invasion of Afghanistan, Oman, closely tied to Egypt and a recipient of U.S. weapons, appeared entirely forthcoming about expanded use of its air and naval facilities. But then, U.S. use of one of its airfields for refueling C-130s en route from Egypt during the abortive hostage rescue raid into Iran apparently angered the Omanis, who apparently claimed they had been misinformed about what was going on.(181) Kuwait, Iraq, Saudi Arabia, and other Arab nations also increased pressure on Oman to restrict U.S. access, presumably fearing its implications for the Arab-Israeli conflict. After some remonstrances, however, following the Iran raid, Oman agreed to an expanded use of its facilities. As it is an OPEC state not badly in need of economic aid, the price was a modest one, in the $100-300 million range.(182)

During the tense period of early 1980, with its aura of historical watershed, the possible acquisitions of U.S. facilities in Pakistan, Saudi Arabia, and Egypt were also seriously discussed; as of this writing, the eventual outcomes were not yet clear. After the Soviet invasion of Afghanistan, when Pakistan rejected a U.S. offer of $400 million in aid as "peanuts," former Secretary of State Kissinger and others also looked to the possibility of U.S. bases in Pakistan.(183) A naval base at Gwadar, near the Straits of Hormuz, and perhaps resumption of use of air facilities at Peshawar, or intelligence bases near the Khyber Pass were presumably in mind,(184) the latter of potentially great importance in the wake of America's loss of facilities in Iran and the continuing precariousness of those in Turkey and China. The Pakistan government, however, appeared adamant about not granting the United States access, and the matter appeared to fade even as Soviet involvement in Afghanistan began to acquire all the earmarks of a quagmire. Later, there was a dearth of talk about facilities as the Reagan administration moved forward with a vastly increased military aid program for Pakistan, to include modern F-16 aircraft.

Saudi Arabia, likewise, seemed reluctant to grant the United States increased access, even despite its heightened anxieties about neighboring threats. Since the close-down of the USAF base at Dhahran in 1962, the United States had had no permanent facilities there; Saudi financial preeminence perhaps nearly precluded even minor symbolic infringements of its sovereignty and dignity.(185) Its pronouncements in 1980 appeared to stress the U.S. use of ad hoc facilities on an only case-by-case basis, and its was noted that the U.S. aircraft which stopped at Oman en route to the Iranian desert rendezvous appeared to have skirted around Saudi airspace at the expense of a much longer route. Whether, quietly, the U.S. Navy would in the future receive greater access to Saudi ports such as Jidda remained unclear. Of course, the United States did begin to operate AWACs out of Saudi Arabia, and then the Reagan administration moved ahead with the controversial sale of AWACs and F-15 enhancements, altogether tightening the U.S.-Saudi security tie, but still leaving the question of U.S. access in abeyance.(186) Further unclear was the ultimate impact of the Iraqi debacle in its war with Iran on Saudi strategy in relation to U.S. basing access.

Egypt, by 1981, was moving toward a much closer relationship with the United States, as fully evidenced by massive economic aid, the prospect of vastly expanded acquisitions of U.S. weapons, and joint U.S.-Egyptian military maneuvers. By 1979, some increased U.S. military access had become part of the bargain. U.S. AWACs aircraft (and perhaps also SR-71s) began to operate out of a base at Upper Quena, and some U.S. F-4s, piloted by American fliers, began to rotate in and out of Egyptian air bases, partly for training purposes, but also apparently as a signal of potential future military backing.(187) There was some talk about the U.S. Navy's use of repair facilities, or at least for replenishment purposes, of the former Soviet base at Alexandria;(188) also, more seriously, about pre-positioning of U.S. war materiel in Egypt. Earlier talk about U.S. use of airfields in the Sinai, retained by Israel as part of the Camp David accord, appeared by 1980 to have faded, at least for the time being. Importantly, however, the United States overtly made use of Egypt's airfields for launching the C-130s on the Iran rescue raid, one strong indication of Egypt's new willingness to grant the United States significant use of its facilities.(189) By late 1980, perhaps most importantly, it was reported that the United States would be granted use of an Egyptian base at Ras Banas on the Red Sea, which would require $400 million in improvements and could be used to stage elements of the Rapid Deployment Force into Southwest Asia, and also possibly as a base for B-52s.(190)

During the period 1979-1980, there was also some periodic discussion of possible U.S. use of Israeli facilities, perhaps of limited value
to the United States, however, so long as access to Egypt's bases was
maintained. The Israeli government appeared itself ambivalent on this
score, but on balance, seemed to welcome the possibility of the U.S.
Navy's use of Haifa, if not also Israeli air bases in the Negev.(191) For
the United States, however, there was the prospect of a net loss
regarding relations with Arab oil producers, so that things did not
immediately go beyond a token ship port visit or two to Haifa. In 1981,
the U.S.-Israel strategic cooperation agreement related to the Saudi
AWACs deal seemed to hint at some pre-positioning of U.S. materiel,
but it was quickly rescinded after Israel announced its annexation of the
Golan Heights.

For certain serious contingencies, however, Israeli air and naval
bases would presumably be automatically available to the United States
if desired; perhaps of most potential importance would be the Israeli
Negev air bases, which could stage flights if necessary from the
Mediterranean through to the Red Sea and the Indian Ocean. Apparently
not to become a reality after some discussion was U.S. use of the two
major airbases in Sinai to be abandoned by Israel as part of its final
withdrawal in 1982 to the 1967 lines.(192) Egypt appeared to reject all
U.S. entreaties along these lines.

In early 1982, the Reagan administration moved to enhance the
United States en route access to the Persian Gulf by bargaining with
Morocco over staging points at two airfields. As part of the bargain,
increased military aid was promised, apparently heralding a new tilt in
U.S. policy toward the Western Sahara conflict.

Whether the United States would seek still further points of access
around the Indian Ocean remained unclear. An expanding arms client
relationship with Sudan had appeared to increase the possible use of
Port Sudan for the U.S. Navy. There was some talk about joint use of
Djibouti with the French navy, presumably backed by Saudi and Somali
pressures or entreaties. The Australian Cocos Islands and even, under
some circumstances, resuscitation of a U.S. presence in South Africa
were also subjects of rumors.

The Atlantic and West Africa

Geography and politics, as often noted, have provided the United States
with obvious long-held advantages, relative to the USSR, in operating
throughout the Atlantic region. U.S. bases along its own east coast, and
relatively secure access to the UK for air bases, the submarine base at
Holy Loch, and various technical facilities, have been virtually locked-
in assets. Similar to the western Pacific, overflight routes to the entire
eastern Atlantic littoral are not conceivably at issue. Still, the United
States has had some increasing problems in this area as it has
elsewhere, most notably with respect to the Portuguese Azores and
Iceland. As earlier indicated, both are highly critical to U.S. ocean

surveillance and ASW operations, and in the former case, to the maintenance of an efficient air staging route to the Middle East, certainly pending the development of larger and longer-range transports and/or enhanced refueling capabilities.

In the immediate aftermath of the Portuguese revolution, during its radical interregnum, continued U.S. access to Lajes seemed in jeopardy, particularly so for any future operations on behalf of Israel.(193) Indeed, the Arabs were reported to have offered Portugal substantial financial inducements to eliminate Lajes as a staging facility on Israel's behalf. These events, among others, were related to the retrofitting of the American C-141 transport fleet with air-refueling capability, and also to the improvement of the long-range capabilities of the larger C-5As.(194) The later rightward shift in Portuguese politics left the precise future status of Lajes still unclear, and while U.S. base rights were renewed in 1979, there were new renewal negotiations looming for 1983.(195) In some circumstances, it was envisaged that the United States might forcefully impose its use of Lajes on behalf of Israel, even if that might endanger its overall subsequent future access. Lajes could, of course, be important for resupply operations, not only to Israel, but also for NATO Western Europe in the case of hostilities with the USSR. And of equivalent importance is its value for conducting maritime surveillance and ASW, which enables coverage of critical areas of the ocean with fewer forces than would otherwise be required if operations had to be conducted from the United States. The continued potential volatility of Portuguese politics, and Portugal's full dependence on Arab oil, leave the future use of the Azores by the United States, at least for some purposes, considerably in doubt.

Continued U.S. access to Iceland, particularly to the air base at Keflavik, may also be in some doubt, given the ever-present neutralist tendencies of Icelandic politics, recently exacerbated by the imbroglio over fishing rights with the UK.(196) Less critical for staging operations than are the Azores, it is of at least equivalent importance for ocean surveillance and ASW operations, given its proximity to the exit to the Atlantic of Soviet ships operating out of the Kola Peninsula through the G-I-F-UK (Greenland-Iceland-Faeroes-UK) gaps.

According to Cottrell and Moorer,

> the Azores and Iceland permit their (P-3 Orion aircraft) maximum operational use in terms of hours on station for antisubmarine patrol. Lying 900 to 1,000 miles west of Portugal, the Azores provide an ideal location as a base for surveillance aircraft operating over large portions of the Atlantic which would be extremely difficult to cover from any other available facility. Lajes could also be used as a center for active anti-submarine warfare in the event of hostilities. The location of the Azores with respect to what is known as the Atlantic Ridge provides the U.S. with a vantage point from which to better detect any submarines operating east of the Ridge. Without the Azores and Iceland it could cost the U.S. as much as $6 billion more to provide the same coverage.(197)

U.S. access here, for the long run, is in some doubt, and there was recently a flurry of rumors about contingency plans to move some U.S. facilities to Scotland.(198)

Until recently, U.S. access to Norway had been a rather subdued subject, save for periodic flurries of concern by the Norwegian Left about U.S. Loran and Omega stations there.(199) More recently, however, Norway has become a more prominent military terrain, as attention has focused on NATO's "northern flank."(200) Scenarios of Soviet attacks on Western Europe have focused attention on Soviet naval egress through the Straits between the Kola Peninsula and the northern Atlantic, and on U.S. ASW capabilities there.(201) Then too, the United States has moved to pre-position war materiel in Norway for the possible sending of small Marine or other RDF units in the case of war, whose task it might be to prevent Soviet takeovers of Norwegian airfields which could be used for air missions far into the Atlantic.(202) Spitsbergen and its outer shelf became more contested terrain, too, both because of possible oil resources and because of their strategic proximity – regarding monitoring devices – to the maritime routes leading out from the Kola Peninsula.

Elsewhere in the Atlantic, the United States relies on two key island positions controlled by Britain – Bermuda and Ascension – both of which are favorably located in a vast ocean which, in contrast to the Pacific, has few islands. The United States has a ninety-nine-year lease on its Bermuda facilities, now used only for minor operations, but of potentially greater utility as a fallback position from the Azores. Recent racial problems there, however, may be said to place future American access to Bermuda in some doubt.

Ascension in the South Atlantic (so recently become very prominent in connection with Britain's Falkland Islands operations) appears to be more secure, and may yet become the keystone of an American staging network running to southern Africa and on to the Indian Ocean. It was apparently used, with British permission, in connection with operations in Zaire and Angola. And at least one study envisages Ascension as of secondary importance only to Diego Garcia as a long-range U.S. staging base, albeit with the problem of refueling over a 4,570-mile stretch from Florida.(203) It is also of potential if not present importance for P-3 staging in the South Atlantic, an area of potentially significant Soviet naval activity, and also a possible replacement for satellite tracking and data relay stations lost elsewhere. American access to Brazilian bases could hypothetically mitigate that problem, but that does not now seem to be in the cards, given recently strained U.S.-Brazil relations.

The United States now has only limited access rights along the whole of the west African littoral, either for naval or air operations, a consideration which could become of greater importance in the event of further military contingencies in Zaire or in southern Africa. Naval port calls are made sporadically and ad hoc in several places, but there are no usable permanent facilities. Air staging facilities might be made available in certain circumstances in Liberia (Roberts Field), Ivory

Coast, Gabon, Senegal (which apparently allowed the RAF transit rights en route to Falklands operations), or Cameroon, perhaps for joint Franco-American operations; indeed, some of these were made available to assist U.S. operations in connection with the two Shaba Province crises and in Angola.(204) The impact of the recent Liberian coup on U.S. access there (Omega station, communications, air staging) is not yet clear, nor is the possibility for improved U.S. relations with strategically located Cape Verde. Further north, the United States has now phased out its communications facilities in Morocco (apparently superseded by satellites and alternatives in Rota), though apparently not because of Moroccan pressure at a time of extensive U.S. assistance to its counterinsurgency effort in Spanish Sahara.

Generally, West Africa is one area where one might anticipate a later U.S. push for expanded access. Not unrelated, it is here noted that the West African coast, and not only Nigeria, is gradually becoming a very important oil-producing region with considerable possibilities for further significant expansion.

The Mediterranean

Until the mid- to late 1960s, the Mediterranean was considered virtually an American lake; indeed, it was thought of as virtually incorporated within NATO's southern flank. The United States long had extensive access to air and naval bases all around the Mediterranean – in Spain, Italy, Greece, Turkey, and Morocco – at a time the Soviets were still straining to obtain initial footholds in Egypt and Syria. American naval forces were then easily more than a match for the Soviets throughout the Mediterranean, providing the United States favorable leverage in crises such as those in 1958 (in Lebanon), in 1967, and 1970 (Jordan).(206) But simultaneous with the recent rise of Soviet naval deployments and acquisition of onshore access, the U.S. position in the Mediterranean has suffered from numerous shocks which greatly have reduced the availability of facilities in that area. The Greece-Turkey conflict over Cyprus (plus internal developments in both countries), the rise of Eurocommunism in Italy, and tightened political conditions for the use of bases in Spain have had a significant combined impact. By the late 1970s the Mediterranean had fully become a two-power sea, and American ability to conduct military operations in the Middle East, or, if necessary and desired, on behalf of Yugoslavia, had become somewhat more questionable. Further, the once formidable network of U.S. technical facilities, particularly in the eastern Mediterranean in proximity to the southern USSR, had also been placed in some jeopardy, with a host of ramifications (particularly with respect to intelligence gathering), only perhaps subject to compensation by new technological developments.

Since the signing of an agreement with the Franco government in 1953, Spain has provided a major hub of U.S. basing facilities, at the critical juncture of the western Mediterranean and the eastern

Atlantic, featuring the air bases, the submarine and ASW base at Rota, and a variety of technical facilities. The agreement was renegotiated in 1970 and then again in 1975, resulting in an arrangement whereby the United States would pay Spain about $1.2 billion in military and economic grants and credits over a several-year period. The high price extracted by Spain was feared by the United States as a possible precedent for other base negotiations – Turkey, Greece, Portugal, Philippines – where host nations might raise the ante as they sensed their increased leverage over an increasingly beleaguered United States.

The agreement actually provided for some reduction in the U.S. base complex in Spain; specifically, the United States agreed to withdraw its nuclear Poseidon submarines from Rota by 1979. It agreed to this "denuclearization" of Spain in part because of the coming deployment of the longer-range Trident submarines, which would be based solely in the United States. Otherwise, the United States retained use of the major air bases at Zaragoza and Torrejon, though the treaty also required the withdrawal of a wing of KC-135 tankers from Spain, while allowing for continued stationing of five such tankers at Zaragoza.(207)

At the time of the treaty's signing, there was a brief flurry of unsubstantiated rumors about a "secret" agreement which would allow the United States to use its Spanish facilities to "supply weapons to third countries, including Israel."(208) The rumors were vehemently denied, and the Spanish government insisted that it would maintain a veto over the right to use the bases in specific crises, as it did during the 1973 war. The facts of Arab oil leverage over Spain seemed virtually to ensure that such a veto would again be exercised in the event of a new Middle Eastern war. In the meanwhile, however, the Spanish facilities (due up soon for another renewal negotiation) could remain important for staging aircraft and other materiel to the eastern Mediterranean and Middle East during normal conditions; and for a variety of crises, Torrejon, Rota, and Zaragoza could be used to shuttle fighter aircraft to potential battlefronts. The naval air station at Rota, meanwhile, retained its importance as a hub of U.S. ASW activity in and around the crucial Gibraltar Straits.

For the future, the status of the U.S. bases in Spain remained just a bit uncertain, even despite the treaty renewals. The political situation in post-Franco Spain remained unsettled, and it was apparent that even a nonviolent "liberal" evolution of Spanish politics might put increasing pressures on U.S. basing rights, in parallel with similar trends elsewhere. But Spain's recent entry into NATO reinforces U.S. prospects for continued access, the Gibraltar problem notwithstanding.(209) Looming here too, as elsewhere in Indonesia, was the potential issue of "closure" of maritime straits perhaps subject to new international legal "norms."

By the late 1970s, U.S. access rights in Italy too, despite its membership in NATO, had come to be seen as at least potentially precarious, or at least in certain circumstances. Here, in distinction from Spain, Greece, and Turkey, a price in the form of military and economic aid was not in question. The question was whether Italy would continue to allow the United States full use of its facilities, or for that matter continue its present role in NATO, if the Italian Communist Party (PCI) should acquire a more powerful role in Italian politics, presumably as a partner in a coalition government. PCI leaders denied they would raise the issue of Italy's NATO membership, but there were still doubts that a more powerful PCI could or would refrain from attempting to limit the American military presence and role in the Mediterranean.(210) Short of that, there were increasing public opinion pressures, instigated by the Italian Left, directed against the continued presence of U.S. nuclear submarine facilities at La Maddalena on Sardinia, as well as the hint of restrictions on U.S. staging of aircraft transfers to the Middle East via the air base at Sigonella on Sicily. Finally, U.S. decision makers had also come to worry about the availability of Italian bases for possible military operations in response to a possible Soviet intervention in Yugoslavia.

The implications of a diminution of U.S. basing rights in Italy would be profound for the U.S. position in the Mediterranean. The United States has there almost every kind of military facility conceivable, involving logistics, training, supply, communications, and recreation. According to Cottrell and Moorer, "a loss of access to these facilities would deal a critical blow to the U.S. position in the Mediterranean; in light of the trends in the region, it is highly unlikely that the Sixth Fleet would be able to relocate elsewhere in the Mediterranean."(211) Indeed, as they point out, many U.S. contingency plans for the loss of various other Mediterranean facilities (Greece and Turkey) involve their substitution by Italian facilities.

American access problems have, of course, been more immediately critical in Greece and Turkey in recent years, where the United States has been trapped between its obligations to two mutually and historically hostile NATO allies since the most recent conflict over Cyprus in 1974, after which Turkey clung to its expanded new position. In the wake of an arms embargo (subsequently modified) imposed by the U.S. Congress, Turkey virtually halted all activities at U.S. military installations, including some very important intelligence gathering posts, whose functions apparently were replaced in part by then still available installations in Iran. Greece, meanwhile, accused the United States of favoring Turkey in the dispute, withdrew from NATO's military command, and also threatened to close U.S. bases.

With Greece, there were continued negotiations over a new facilities agreement, which apparently involved some thorny status-of-force issues as well as the level of compensation and America's attitude toward the Greece-Turkey impasse over Cyprus and the Aegean.(212) In April 1974, in a tense period, the United States had agreed to close its air base at Hellenikon and to cease home-porting six destroyers at Elefsis near Athens, for which there was no replacement facility equally accessible to the Turkish Straits area.(213) In the late 1970s, negotiations continued over the future status of the major Sixth Fleet communications and intelligence center at Nea Makri; the Iraklion air base, Souda Bay naval base and anchorage, and NAMFI missile range on Crete; several other communications sites (some associated with NATO's tropospheric scatter network called ACE High, others major nodes and relay points for the Defense Communications System) and a batch of NADGE (NATO Air Defense Ground Environment) radar sites. The Souda Bay facility is used to monitor the movements of ships and aircraft in the Mediterranean by naval aircraft; that at Nea Makri is a major link between communications complexes in Italy and Spain and includes an electronic net that follows the movement of all ships in the area; Iraklion is reported to be "a relay station for all intelligence gathered in Turkey and a major intercept center where all coded radio communications in the area are taped and transmitted to the National Security Agency center in Maryland,"(214) and a communications center for all of the Middle East, North Africa, and the Eastern Mediterranean.

In particular, the future Greek role in U.S. intelligence-gathering operations and Greece's access to their intelligence products were apparently at issue. Greece, meanwhile, was demanding a large infusion of military and economic aid for continued access to the installations, and it was not clear just how the new agreement with Turkey would affect those demands.

By 1981, there were reports indicating that the anti-Americanism exhibited in Greece in previous years had considerably waned. Further, increased U.S. Navy port visits had apparently resumed, and Greece had apparently availed the United States of extensive air transit access during the Iranian hostage crisis.(215) Those trends, and perhaps also the precedent set by the new facilities agreement with Turkey, seemed to augur finalization of a new base agreement. But then, the election of Andreas Papandreou's leftist government dramatically undercut all previous assumptions, and by 1982, the future status of U.S.-Greek installations was very much in doubt. A considerable diminution of U.S. access seemed inevitable.

During the late 1970s, the question of U.S. access to Turkish facilities had received considerably more attention than that of Greece, at a time the once solid U.S.-Turkish alliance came under great strain. Also, after the 1974 Cyprus crisis and the subsequent, albeit partial and temporary, U.S. arms embargo, Turkish relations with the USSR warmed considerably, and Turkey also moved closer to radical Arab states such as Libya and Iraq. At the same time, Turkey's growing internal political chaos, fueled by severe national financial problems, provoked by 1980 expectations that the country would eventually slide into civil war or chaos comparable to that in Iran, albeit for the time being seemingly stalled by the Turkish military takeover and associated restoration of civil order.

The United States, of course, had much to lose if its use of Turkish facilities was eliminated or greatly curtailed. Actually, U.S. naval access to Izmir and Istanbul had earlier been reduced because of friction with the Turkish population, though visits continued to be made to more remote locations. Still at stake, however, were some twenty-three or twenty-four facilities: several air bases including a major one at Incirlik, some headquarters and support groups, NADGE radar sites, POL and nuclear weapons storage sites, some twelve communications installations and, perhaps most importantly, a number of facilities deemed of utmost importance to U.S. intelligence surveillance of the USSR. Regarding the latter, one U.S. congressional report stated:

> Intelligence collection agencies in Turkey have supported U.S. plans, policies, and programs for many years. Electronic and signal intelligence (ELINT and SIGINT) play important roles.... Several installations, for example, are related to strategic nuclear activities. Radars of Samsun, near the Black Sea coasts, have been tracking Soviet missile test shots from Kapustin Yar (east of Volgograd) since 1955 – including SLBM's. Turkey also affords a window on the range at Tyuratam (beside the Aral Sea), where MIRV testing for Moscow's new SS-18 and SS-19 ICBM's is still taking place. Turkish stations tie into the U.S. worldwide seismic network that monitors subterranean nuclear tests in the low kiloton category. Conventional collection efforts cover a wide spectrum, from covert contacts with various sources to sophisticated surveillance of Soviet fleet operations, using detection devices aloft, ashore, afloat, and perhaps on the Black Sea floor.(216)

In 1979, after the Iranian revolution had terminated U.S. use of intelligence facilities somewhat redundant to those in Turkey, the latter's full importance was highlighted during the debate over ratification of SALT II. SALT opponents anxious about U.S. ability to verify adequately its provisions, waxed increasingly concerned about the implications of the loss of U.S. access to Turkish facilities, particularly regarding telemetry monitoring of Soviet tests of MIRVed missiles. The Carter administration tried to reassure critics with the prospect of U-2 flights, which, launched from the Akotiri base on Cyprus (U.S. use of which had been denied by the UK during the 1973 war), could fully substitute for the use of ground facilities if given access to Turkish airspace. Perhaps surprisingly, the Turkish government expressed resistance to such overflights, stating they could be conducted only with Soviet assent, hence "shifting the onus" onto Moscow.(217) A then harried U.S. government sought additional substitute measures which might suffice pending development of new satellite capabilities. Use of Norwegian facilities was bruited,(218) even at a time of growing controversy over various forms of U.S. military access, such as Loran and Omega stations, and pre-positioning of combat materiel for Marines near the Kola Peninsula. Possible use of alternative monitoring facilities either in Pakistan or in China was also publicly discussed; the latter was later revealed to have come to fruition.(219) By 1980, first the stalling of SALT II in the U.S. Senate and then the new U.S.-Turkey Defense Cooperation Agreement (DCA) seemed to have rendered these issues moot for the time being.(219)

The U.S.-Turkey DCA of 1980, a five-year renewal agreement, appeared to reinstate most of the previously existing American access to facilities, even if with more stringent status of forces provisions. There was some reduction in the overall number of facilities, but the key ones at Dyarbakir, Samsun, Belbasi, and Incirlik were retained, apparently retaining for the United States most of its desired intelligence capability. The installations apparently would be operated on the basis of joint control. Aside from a some $450 million infusion of immediate U.S. economic and military aid, there were also quid pro quo provisions for various kinds of "military-industrial cooperation" (U.S. assistance to indigenous arms production capability), apparently involving an ammunition plant, a factory for air defense weapons, and construction of naval frigates. A new trend, perhaps to be duplicated elsewhere, appeared emerging here, whereby the U.S. seemed willing to transfer technology and weapons R&D (also to entertain purchasing arms or components from a near-developing country) in lieu of still more extensive military grant or credit aid.(220)

The Current Basing Networks of America's Western Allies

By the mid-1970s, the major powers' competition for access had been reduced almost to a strictly two-power game. Except for a few scattered enclaves (mostly remnant island possessions where indigenous populations are either meager or non-existent, hence not providing the basis for viable independence movements), the British Empire and its once vaunted accompanying basing system had virtually disappeared. France, however, also having lost an empire, appeared in the late 1970s to be trying to reestablish some outlying strategic military positions in Africa: garrisons, air and naval bases, and connecting staging networks.

During the 1960s and early 1970s, Britain abandoned its remaining positions east of Suez: in Singapore, Malta, Gan in the Maldives Islands, the Seychelles, Bahrain, and Masirah Island. Use of the latter two outposts, along with Diego Garcia, was bequeathed to the United States (only temporarily in the case of Bahrein), as was Ascension, a very important air staging point in the South Atlantic which also houses American technical facilities. Britain also retained Bermuda and some islands in the West Indies, which also remained available for the United States. Despite a few last, spluttering intervention forays in the Caribbean (most notably in connection with the belated independence of Belize), "little England" had abandoned almost all of the final vestiges of its ability to project force overseas. Under some pressure from the United States, it continued to exercise sovereignty in places such as Diego Garcia (its sovereignty here could actually impede U.S. use in some instances), Bermuda, Gibraltar and Ascension, which might prove crucial to later U.S. or western staging and intervention efforts. A continued hold over the Akotiri air base on Cyprus (used for radar monitoring of the eastern Mediterranean and for the staging of U-2 flights) was another such example. But the end of the British naval presence in Malta in 1979 seemed almost a final symbolic step on the long road to full divestiture of a once global basing system.(221)

France, on the other hand, propelled by the Gaullist nationalist ideology of "grandeur," made a more strenuous effort to hold on to some points of access, in Africa in particular. Seemingly dismayed by growing American passivity in the face of Soviet and Cuban inroads, France — manifestly obsessed with raw materials sources — began around 1977-1978 to pursue a more aggressive policy in defending its own as well as Western interests, mostly, where "moderate" African regimes held sway.(222) Fairly extensive French garrisons were maintained in Senegal, Ivory Coast, Gabon, Djibouti, and until recently, in Chad and Niger. French Jaguar fighter-bombers were early on deployed in Senegal for combat missions against Polisario guerrillas in Spanish Sahara in support of Morocco and Mauritania, and they were also used in Chad, where French troops were deployed to impede the southward advance of Libyan-backed insurgents. In both cases, by 1980, France had abandoned these operations, though the conflicts themselves went on.(223)

On the African east coast, France retained a significant Indian Ocean naval task force based in newly independent Djibouti (at least until recently, larger than the U.S. naval presence), along with a moderate garrison of some 4,500 troops.(224) Concerned for a while that its Indian Ocean flotilla might require finding a new home, speculations were floated about the use of the island of Mayotte in the Mozambique Channel, contested by the newly independent Comoros Islands, as well as about enhanced use of Reunion, still a full-fledged French departement. At one point, France apparently also approached North Yemen about building a new naval base.(225)

Meanwhile, French operations in Zaire in response to the two invasions of Shaba from Angola, as well as those in Chad and Spanish Sahara, were assisted by the availability of an air staging network along the West African coast, consisting of Moroccan airfields, Dakar, Abidjan, Libreville, and Kinshasa. Though the assisting nations involved were primarily French arms client states (Zaire a partial exception), joint U.S.-France use of these facilities in support of Zaire appeared to indicate that France's system of aerial access might, in certain circumstances, be available for general western interests, even if France simultaneously resisted its clients' providing the United States access of its own.

To a degree, however, France had developed forward bases outside of the orbit of the American-led NATO security system, in line with its independent foreign policy and its self-defined specific economic and cultural interests in Africa. Some writers pointed to a new, explicitly formulated "indirect strategy," associated particularly with General André Beaufré, which would involve a more forward French "presence" overseas to provide various forms of conventional deterrence.(226) The French navy would be critical to such a strategy, which is crucially propelled by concerns about raw materials access.

Both Britain and France, of course, continued to maintain "forward" garrisons in West Germany as part of the joint NATO shield, in the case of France now to involve tactical nuclear missiles. And though the public data are limited, both also apparently retain some technical facilities overseas to deal with intelligence, communications, weapons testing, and such. Some reports noted an apparently important remaining British intelligence listening facility known as Little Sai Wan on Hong Kong; the UK retained weapons testing installations in Australia. France was reported utilizing an atmospheric research station on remote Kerguelen Island in the Indian Ocean; its nuclear tests continued at Muroroa. Burgeoning European satellite programs would presumably require overseas facilities, as had their American model, perhaps in some cases involving co-use of installations now used by the United States in European-controlled territories such as Ascension and Reunion Islands.(227)

Then too, by 1980, there were some indications that the former European colonial powers, Britain and Germany as well as France, might be returning to the use of extended overseas naval access.(228) This became apparent amidst talk about a European role in aiding the U.S. presence in the Persian Gulf and Indian Ocean. Britain's buildup of its Indian Ocean presence apparently involved resumption of traditional naval access to Singapore en route from Hong Kong to the Indian Ocean. Even West Germany was mentioned as a possible naval participant in Indian Ocean affairs, with what implications regarding onshore access remained to be seen.(229)

NEW ("OLD") ENTRANTS TO THE BASING GAME

Much has been written in recent years about the alleged decline of bipolarity, the increased global diffusion of military power and technology, the rise of new regional centers of power, and so forth.(230) Variously, these trends are said to result from a breakdown of ideological bipolarity, from OPEC's rise to economic if not military power, and from the growth of some indigenous weapons development and production capability in nations such as India, Israel, South Africa, Brazil, and Argentina. Accordingly, some middle-range powers have also begun to acquire extraregional if not global security interests (and some capability for extraregional power projection) which have created needs for external points of military access.

China, despite its rise to the status of near-great power, symbolized by its growing nuclear missile capability, has not yet developed very much ability to project conventional power overseas.(231) But its navy is growing, and it does perceive itself as in competition for influence in the Third World with the USSR, if not the United States, reflected, among other things, by its arms supplies to Zaire, Pakistan, Somalia, and Cambodia to counter Soviet supplies to their rivals. Thus, China also requires some naval ports of call, overseas ship repair facilities, and perhaps, later, air staging points.

To date, China's use of overseas facilities has remained very limited. It has been reported using Malta's drydocking facilities(232) and, earlier, a communications base in Zanzibar, before Soviet arms became dominant in Tanzania. Its merchant ships are also reported to have used repair facilities in Romania, Singapore, and Albania (at least up to the recent political falling out with the latter). It is not here known to what extent China has maintained intelligence listening posts or other technical facilities in countries where its influence is strong and its arms supplies prominent, as in Pakistan, Zaire, Cameroon, Cambodia (earlier under Pol Pot), North Korea, and Albania.(233) Its long-range missile tests into the Indian Ocean may dictate the need for some facilities, if not already present, and it has also been reported that China, like the USSR, has displayed interest in "oceanographic research" in the South Pacific which may have comparable military rationales.

Iran, under the Shah, was apparently bent on building some approximation of a "blue-water" Indian Ocean navy, and was reported to have offered cash to Madagascar for use of the formerly important French naval base at Diego Suarez. And in exercising its fleet around the Indian Ocean on annual cruises, it had been availed of port stops in India and Australia, among other places. India may have similar ambitions.(234) Oil-rich Nigeria, moving to expand its military reach and anxious to contribute to the black cause in southern Africa, is claimed to aspire to use of some other nations' African ports.(235) Japan's still small navy has made some recent port visits to Southeast Asia, despite the still lingering memories of World War II.(236) Australia's navy, now apparently to provide a part of the overall Western presence in the Indian Ocean, is reported to have made use of naval access to Sri Lanka.(237)

Cuba, amidst its heavy and growing military involvement in Africa, has made extensive use of staging facilities en route across the Atlantic, in some but not all cases piggybacking on already established Soviet access. In moving troops and materiel to Angola in 1975 and since, it has been reported using airfields, variously, in Barbados (which appears to have ceased to allow Cuba access under U.S. pressures), Trinidad, Guyana, Cape Verde, Sierra Leone, and perhaps even in Portugal's Azores and in Canada's Newfoundland.(238) Its fishing fleets have also operated out of Angolan ports, perhaps involving some corollary military missions.

For some nations, in the "pariah" category, overseas access even for relatively trivial and not very visible purposes may be very difficult to achieve. Israel's quiet, almost clandestine, military relationships with Ethiopia and Kenya apparently earlier provided some use of Ethiopian-controlled islands in the Red Sea near the Bab El Mandeb and, of course, the use of Nairobi airport on the way home from Entebbe.(239) South Africa is denied access even for its commercial airliners throughout most of Africa. When its former prime minister, Mr. Vorster, visited Israel, his plane apparently was allowed to refuel only in the Seychelles Islands, but that was prior to the latter's subsequent leftist coup.

Increasingly, some aspiring powers may have their forces and equipment stationed overseas, for protection of friends and to earn currency. Thus, one recent article reporting on an agreement which would see Pakistani combat troops stationed on Saudi Arabian soil in return for Saudi financial aid, said "the proposed military deal would also fit an emerging pattern in the Middle East and other regions in which militarily proficient third-world nations, such as Cuba and Pakistan, are ready to provide combat forces for political or financial gain."(240) Pakistani, North Korean, Cuban and North Vietnamese pilots and other personnel had long been scattered among several Arab host nations.

All in all, it appears that the future may see a more complex game involving bases and other forms of access, as aspiring powers try to extend their strategic reach.(241) In the case of some small and middle powers, however, the quest for access of their own may remain secondary to considerations of that available to the major powers which provide arms or other forms of assistance to them. In different situations, this may depend primarily on the leverage of the supplier's access diplomacy, sometimes on the smaller power's, or on both. In the Iran-Iraq war, Iraq's use of Jordanian and Saudi transport points for reception of arms resupplies illustrated the general matter of access leverage.(242)

Israel, for instance, while possessing little clout in oil-dependent countries such as Spain, Portugal, or Germany, has managed to lean on overall American leverage in providing access to facilities such as Lajes in times of crisis. Zaire has counted on other moderate regimes in West Africa to allow staging of materiel from France; but, in part, what is crucial is French leverage for access in countries like Senegal and Ivory Coast.(243) Various Middle Eastern countries other than Israel have had to exercise political influence to assure arms staging via Spain, Italy, Greece, and Turkey, often where diplomatic ties have not been strong, and again where American influence has had to be brought into play. As an illustration of how such matters may work on an intra-Third World basis, Sri Lanka earlier allowed staging of arms supplies from Indonesia to Pakistan during one of the latter's conflicts with India.

Recent bewildering events in the Horn of Africa have demonstrated the complexities of power and influence involved in the diplomacy of access in small power conflicts, where still other minor powers located along staging routes are compelled virtually to choose sides. Ethiopia, having become a Soviet arms client, had its problems not only with Egypt, but also with Soviet ally Iraq, which backed Somalia and resisted the transit of Soviet arms.(244) With Libya backing Ethiopia, but Sudan and Egypt opposed, the Soviets apparently had to resort to unauthorized overflights, banking on the fears of lesser powers that interdicting them would bring on a serious diplomatic crisis or a military response.(245) The tricky diplomacy of Cuba's staging efforts to Angola brought into play some similar complexities. Some nations now find themselves cross-pressured between friends and allies; and between ideology, national interests, and Third World identifications; in deciding whether to provide access in certain crisis situations. Hence, there are resorts to clandestine provision of access or winks at formally unauthorized access, but where in an age of all-seeing satellite reconnaissance, little may be kept secret for long, though vocally denied.

COMPETITIVE BASE DENIAL STRATEGIES AND ACTIVITIES

The geopolitical strategies of each of the superpowers – and of some others as well – have been directed not only at obtaining and hanging on to facilities, but at nudging rivals out of theirs or at preventing them from acquiring them. A variety of diplomatic instruments have been used to that end: economic and security inducements, threats, propaganda, instigation of indigenous political protest movements, preemptive base acquisitions, preemptive arms selling, and so forth.(246) More and more, the United Nations has become a propaganda forum in which efforts have been made to put pressures on rivals' basing presences, in an era of sensitivity by smaller powers to charges that they compromise newly-won sovereignty by a foreign base presence.

The Soviets, in particular, have long mounted an all-out propaganda effort, much of it through foreign language broadcasts, aimed at creating political pressures on U.S. and other Western bases.(247) And as the Soviets were long a revisionist power as measured by basing assets, they were also long enabled a virtually cost-free propaganda denial strategy which characterized foreign bases as an inherently capitalistic phenomenon.

In recent times, the Soviets have placed considerable emphasis on "exposing" what they claim to be developments of new U.S. basing networks and strategies, real or imagined, in a manner often apparently revealing of Moscow's global cognitive map.(248) For instance, warnings have been issued about an alleged, burgeoning South Atlantic alliance which might provide bases for NATO in a southern arc stretching from Chile to South Africa,(249) and also about the ASEAN grouping in Southeast Asia, where the United States has been alleged seeking new bases on Morotai Island in the Molucca's group in Indonesia as part of a new fallback, post-Vietnam Asian periphery strategy.(250) Among the other prominent recent targets of Soviet propaganda have been Oman, Bahrain, Cyprus, Italy, Greece, Thailand, Australia, Japan, and Malta. Australians are subtly warned of the implications of playing host to U.S. Omega facilities and other bases related to nuclear deterrence, lest they end up being targets in a nuclear war;(251) Norway receives similar warnings about Loran and Omega facilities. Propaganda targeted on Japan and Italy harps upon the possible environmental dangers to civilians of U.S. nuclear ships making port calls.(252)

Oman and Bahrain have been targets of propaganda (otherwise deemed "disinformation") which harps upon the possible role of their U.S. facilities in support of Israel.(253) According to one Soviet broadcast, "this decision by Sultan Quabus (to allow the U.S. use of

Masirah) was received in the Arab world as an act of betrayal of the Arab nation, an act which will result in the Americans dominating not only the Arab sea routes but also the entire Arab world and its natural wealth."(254) And in another, Tass crowed that Bahrain's decision to have the U.S. Middle Eastern naval force removed from the base at Jufayr was "the consequence of the Arab countries' mounting discontent with the American 'gunboat diplomacy,' one of the manifestations of which is Washington's support for Israel's expansionist policy with regard to neighboring Arab countries."(255) Broadcasts aimed at Thailand stress issues of sovereignty, and also speak darkly of the lurid activities of American spy planes and other intelligence apparatus.(256) Filipinos are bombarded with data on murders and rapes allegedly committed by U.S. sailors, appealing to their national dignity.

In a subtle but determined fashion, Soviet propagandists play up and attempt to reinforce local demonstrations by indigenous communists against U.S. facilities in countries such as Italy, Greece, and Japan, attempting to create a broader base of public political support for doing away with the bases, and to cement relationships between groupings in a "popular front."(257) Otherwise, Soviet propaganda also highlights statements by various Third World leaders demanding withdrawal of Western bases. In 1976-1977, a great effort was made to amplify complaints from India, Madagascar, Mauritius, and the Seychelles about Diego Garcia, and about the asserted desirability of a neutralized Indian Ocean freed of foreign base presences.

The United Nations has become a particularly useful forum for Soviet political efforts directed at getting U.S. bases removed from the Third World. On the one hand, the Soviets continue to profess their goal of a world totally freed of all foreign bases, but then they have also orchestrated Third World efforts to target specific U.S. bases or countries where military access is now afforded.

In recent years these efforts have particularly been directed at removing various remnant island dependencies from the U.S. and Western orbit. Micronesia, American Samoa, Puerto Rico, St. Helena (owned by the UK), Guam, Bermuda, Turks and Caicos, Diego Garcia, Gibraltar, Tuvalu, Montserrat, the British Virgin Islands, and the Keeling Islands have been among the numerous targets.(250) These efforts have been pursued relentlessly in the UN's "Committee of 24," and in its Subcommittee on Small Territories. The pressures are often meaningfully felt and reacted to; Britain, after one rancorous session, conceded its willingness in principle to give independence to tiny St. Helena. The U.S. position in Micronesia has also been under relentless attack in the UN, apparently to some ultimate effect, as measured by recent independence strivings and the very forthcoming American response.

Propaganda is not, of course, the only Soviet weapon in its effort to reduce the Western basing structure. Fomentation of coups and revolutions have taken care of some (Seychelles, Vietnam, Angola), while in other cases, the promise of massive arms shipments has served to nudge Western interests aside. As Western strength has waned, subtle threats have become more useful to persuade some countries (Thailand, for instance) of the sheer practicality of a more neutral stance.

The United States as well has often used both carrots and sticks in its efforts at blocking expansion of the Soviet basing network. Economic aid (PL 480 food) was earlier dangled in front of Sekou Toure in an effort to stop Soviet Atlantic reconnaissance flights out of Conakry, and it may somewhat have succeeded.(259) Earlier, economic aid and perhaps also the prospect of diplomatic recognition, entered into at least implied U.S. bargaining positions related to Soviet basing hopes in Angola. U.S. arms supplies and economic aid have helped pry Egyptian bases from Soviet control, though a similar effort was unsuccessful in the case of Syria. Threats have long been used to restrict Soviet use of Cuban bases, going back to the 1962 missile crisis, reiterated in 1970 when Soviet intentions to use Cienfuegos as a nuclear submarine base began to emerge. However, the hoary principle of rebus sic standibus (terms of agreements remain valid only so long as the political conditions under which they were signed remain) has gradually eroded the U.S. threat in consonance with a changing balance of power.

In recent times, the United States has made extensive proxy use of Saudi cash, in connection with convergent U.S.-Saudi interests, in keeping the Middle East free of Soviet bases. The Saudis earlier, of course, abetted the U.S. bankrolling of Egypt, prior to the Camp David accords. Beyond that, Saudi money has also helped to drive the Soviet presence from North Yemen and Sudan (now less certain again in the former case), was instrumental in the Soviets being pushed out of Somalia, and has also been dangled in front of radical South Yemen with similar ends in mind.(260)

Oil-rich OPEC nations have also now become factors in the base-denial game in a broader context, often in relation to U.S. desires to maintain the potential for staging arms to Israel in a future crisis. Arab financial leverage has been used to jeopardize U.S. use of the Azores, and also to block use of Spanish air bases for possible refueling of Israel-bound transports. Libyan financial support given Malta was used to ease the withdrawal of the British presence.(261) Arab oil and money has also apparently affected future Greek and Turkish intentions concerning American use of facilities in some possible circumstances. And ironically in light of the above, Saudi Arabia has apparently offered Oman cash inducements to block expanded U.S access there.

In some cases, the timing and pace of Western (particularly British) withdrawals from unwanted or compromised facilities may have been determined by fears of Soviet takeovers. Britain earlier seemed to worry about withdrawing from Malta more because of fears it would soon be replaced there by the USSR than because of the needs of its own naval forces. Similar considerations were in evidence with the withdrawals from the Maldives, Seychelles, and Mauritius, with the memory of the Aden denouement a graphic reminder. France has had similar fears about Djibouti and Mayotte. While the U.S. worries about losing some bases in Micronesia, it perhaps worries even more about possible later Soviet access there.

China's apparent pressures on Vietnam to deny the USSR use of former U.S. bases, and India's (and other littoral states') complaints to the United States about Diego Garcia and other Indian Ocean bases, are still further common examples of base-denial activities not restricted to the superpowers.(262) But in recent times, Iraq, above all, has become identified with such efforts.

Since the fall of the Shah of Iran, and also since Egypt's alienation from most of the remainder of the Arab world because of the Camp David accords, Iraq has been bidding for a new role as Persian Gulf hegemone and leader of the Arab "rejectionist front." It also appears possible it will become the first Arab nuclear weapons state, on the basis of some ongoing transactions with France and Italy, howsoever postponed by the Israeli preemptive air raid in June 1981. Amidst this drive for enhanced status, Baghdad has also worked hard at blocking the development of new (and old) U.S. and other Western basing facilities, particularly those which might allow for intervention on behalf of Israel. It was recently reported trying to block U.S. development of air and naval facilities in Oman, Somalia, and Kenya with threats, cash, and oil diplomacy; also, it has been reported working on Djibouti, Madagascar, and the Seychelles to reduce their commitments to French and/or British naval presences.(263)

On a more general level – though no doubt with Israel and the United States still in mind – Iraq in early 1980 floated a "Pan-Arab Charter" which, among other things, asserted the need to keep all superpower bases out of the region.(264) Echoing similar regional demands periodically made for removal of all major powers' basing presences in Africa (by the OAU), and by groupings of Indian Ocean littoral states, the Iraqi charter might presage a more aggressive organized effort perhaps increasingly to be surfaced in a variety of international forums as part of a "North-South" agenda. To the extent successful, it would raise very serious questions about relative advantaging and disadvantaging for the two superpowers if both were forced significantly to retrench from overseas access by "popular demand."

Perhaps somewhat curiously, the recent past appears to have witnessed at least one example of base-denial activity even within the tattered U.S.-led Western alliance. In late 1980, one report stated that "France dissuaded Senegal from holding further discussions with the United States on the possibility of increased access to military bases."(265) The context was increased French economic aid to a strapped former colony which apparently also had made overtures to the United States for aid. Whether France wished to deny the United States access for its own security reasons, or as part of a broader contest for dominant interest, or whether the denial was on behalf of some other nation(s) – the Arabs, other African states? – was not at all clear.

In returning to the propaganda disinformation activities discussed above, it should be pointed out that base-denial efforts, particularly on the Soviet side, have gone hand in hand with efforts to minimize or to deny one's own access. During 1977-1978, for instance, the Soviet media virtually outdid itself in insisting that the USSR did not have, and did not plan for, bases in Mozambique, despite some evidence to the contrary.(266) There and in Somalia earlier, foreign newsmen (and in the case of the latter, U.S. Congressmen) were taken on "selective" tours of base areas in attempts to prove that nothing untoward was involved. Otherwise, Soviet propaganda attempts to emphasize the peaceful or "scientific" character of efforts to enhance access, particularly regarding the "grey" areas between military and civilian endeavors.(267)

SUMMARY

The foregoing analysis has portrayed what, on the face of it, would appear to be a significant decline in the availability of U.S. overseas facilities, current events in the Indian Ocean area notwithstanding. The implications, particularly in connection with a parallel though uneven improvement in the Soviet global network, are much argued over. Pessimists such as Moorer and Cottrell appear to see the portents of disaster, not only with respect to U.S. capabilities for military intervention on behalf of allies or for full-scale war with the Soviets, but also in relation to others' perceptions of the evolving U.S.-Soviet global balance, with all that may entail for maintaining the credibility of commitments and the forestalling of some dependent nations' moves toward neutralization or "Finlandization."

Those less inclined to pessimism point to the earlier redundancy of the U.S. basing system, seeing it now as more closely matching actual requirements, as well as being economically more feasible. Besides, it is argued, post-Vietnam America is less likely to intervene, or even to threaten to intervene in the Third World, so that many facilities are seen as superfluous, if not expensive and perhaps vulnerable, liabilities. Others strike a position in between, recognizing the potentially serious political import of America's forced withdrawal, yet claiming that what remains of the U.S. basing network provides a solid, lean, and not excessive capability for most foreseeable contingencies.

In a general sense, the very nature of the U.S. overseas basing network, excepting the relatively unchanged circumstances in Western Europe since France's partial defection from NATO, has undergone a considerable shift from a basis in territorial control (either formal or through agreements based on alliances) to one based on minimal "functional network control." Where once access was assured in numerous locales (and where military force was expected to be used if necessary), it must now be bargained for, often ad hoc with respect to specific circumstances. In many areas, the profile of the U.S. presence has become much lower, as the number of major naval and air bases has declined. For military intervention and staging operations, the United States now relies on a surprisingly small network of global facilities, banking on improved aircraft ranges, new refueling techniques, and enhanced at-sea naval logistics to compensate for what has been lost.(268) A small number of very crucial remaining bastions – the Azores, Ascension, Diego Garcia, Subic Bay, Guam – have become vital but nearly irreducible pivots of a now very taut and vulnerable system. In a more subjective vein, the greatly reduced availability of ports for ship visits has reduced the possibilities for "showing the flag," the political consequences of which are difficult to measure.(269)

Of course, one might point out that, almost paradoxically, some aspects of the ongoing military buildup being pursued by the Reagan administration may result in an actual reduction of basing requirements. It has been claimed, for instance, that an increase in the deployed number of U.S. carrier groups – allowing for their frequent rotation while still maintaining a strong posture overseas – would reduce the pressures for utilization of offshore home ports in places like Cockburn Sound.

As its previous bastions of naval and air deployments have withered, the United States has striven to retain control over various networks of technical facilities, necessary for global capabilities in communications, intelligence, satellite data relays and surveillance, ASW and ocean reconnaissance, nuclear test detection, and air and submarine navigation. In many of these areas, new technologies may now be rendering some old facilities obsolete; to what degree is not clearly ascertainable. Satellites are gradually replacing land-based communications facilities and are more and more assuming intelligence functions once performed from land.(270) The same holds true for navigational facilities, including those used for precise positioning of nuclear-armed submarines. Likewise, new technology placed on the ocean floors may be lessening the need for shore-based facilities; to what degree is not clear. The growing difficulties in maintaining access to foreign countries seems itself to be driving ever-increasing technological change so as to reduce the need for such access.

Despite the overall decline in American access to facilities, there seems not yet to have been a degradation of its networks of technical facilities.   Remaining communications facilities in Europe, the Philippines, Diego Garcia, Japan, and Australia, in combination with new satellite technology, appear to have retained a fully functioning global defense and diplomatic communications network. Intelligence operations, though apparently badly hurt by elimination of bases in Iran and Thailand and perhaps also by some restrictions in Turkey and Greece, are now increasingly conducted by esoteric satellite technology; and besides, considerable capability is retained in Western Europe, South Korea, Japan, and now China. Tentatively, the most important U.S. ASW facilities (hydrophonic arrays, SOSUS) remain intact in Iceland and the Azores, as do the P-3 bases located variously in Spain, Kenya, Oman, Bermuda, Japan, and elsewhere. In short, the U.S. still retains a strong basis of global network control and points d'appui commensurate with a global, near-imperial status, but it appears there is now little room for further losses without measurable substantive impacts. There may, in other words, finally be some limits to superseding access to foreign facilities with new technologies.

One point which does stand out, however, in assessing the current trends in the U.S.-Soviet competition for access, is the extent to which the United States has, at least until very recently, virtually denied itself an aggressive search for new points of access, with the exceptions provided by the experiences in Oman, Somalia, Kenya, and Egypt, also with Colombia and Honduras. By contrast, Soviet setbacks in places like Egypt and Somalia have immediately been compensated for by strenuous diplomatic efforts to acquire new bases in nearby locales, usually entailing aggressively applied doses of military aid. The United States has evidenced little similar, competitive, compensatory behavior, though the opportunities may well have been available. Some new or expanded facilities, or lesser forms of access, have been acquired, not only in the aforementioned Indian Ocean area states, but also in Cameroon, Diego Garcia, and Australia. But in other places where increased U.S. arms and general diplomatic support may be strongly desired – Israel, Sudan, Brazil, Indonesia, Pakistan, Taiwan, Tunisia, Liberia, Ghana, Gabon, Dominican Republic, Guatemala, Ivory Coast – and where a price (military access) might well be demanded as a quid pro quo, the United States has remained surprisingly passive. Either that or American leverage in such matters has declined relative to that of the USSR; or is to be measured in a qualitatively different way; or is permanently compromised by the history of Western imperialism.

It remains to be seen whether a newly aggressive U.S. foreign policy may yet act to reverse these trends, in the near or long term, in lieu of what has become an habitual "technological solutionism." By mid-1981, however, it had become apparent that the new Reagan administration – having already abandoned almost all of its predecessor's arms transfer and human rights restrictions – was moving purposefully toward such a reversal.(271)

NOTES

(1) See, among numerous press reports, "CIA Finds Soviet's Arms Outlays Lead U.S. by 50%," New York Times, January 27, 1980, p. A3. More generally, see Francis P. Hoeber and William Schneider, Jr., eds., Arms, Men, and Military Budgets (New York: Crane, Russak, 1977).

(2) Among numerous analyses, see in particular Capt. William H. J. Manthorpe, Jr., "The Soviet Navy in 1979: Part I," Naval Institute Proceedings, April 1980, pp. 113-119; and Part II, pp. 119-123.

(3) Ibid., Part I, p. 114 has a complete breakdown by ship type and class.

(4) See William F. Scott, "The USSR's Growing Global Mobility," Air Force Magazine, March 1977, pp. 57-61. More recently, see Joint Chiefs of Staff, "United States Military Posture for FY 1982" (Washington, D.C.: GPO, 1981).

(5) "The Soviet Navy in 1979: Part I," pp. 115-119; and in greater detail, B. Dismukes and J. McConnell, eds., Soviet Naval Diplomacy (New York: Pergamon, 1979), esp. chaps. 2-3 and appendix D.

(6) This imitative epidemic is often said to have been triggered by the big price the United States was seen willing to pay for renewal of its bases in Spain in the five-year pact signed in 1976. See "The Spanish Connection: A Wider U.S. Commitment in the Making," The Defense Monitor 5, 2 (February 1976). For an overall picture of the increasing costs of U.S. overseas facilities in recent years, one may consult the unclassified data provided by the Pentagon's Office of the Assistant Secretary of Defense, Comptroller's Office, published periodically under the heading of "DOD Annual Operating Costs of Maintaining U.S. Military Forces in Foreign Countries and Areas."

(7) See, for instance, Charles C. Petersen, "Showing the Flag," and Abram N. Shulsky, "Coercive Diplomacy," in Dismukes and McConnell, Soviet Naval Diplomacy. For a comprehensive analysis, involving both aggregated data and case studies spanning the entirety of the postwar period, see Barry M. Blechman and Stephen S. Kaplan, Force Without War (Washington, D.C.: Brookings Institution, 1978).

(8) See Weigert, "Strategic Bases," in H. Weigert, V. Stefansson, and R. Harrison, eds., New Compass of the World (New York: Macmillan, 1949).

(9) For analyses of targeted large Soviet arms transfers during the 1950s and 1960s, see the relevant sections of Amelia C. Leiss et al., Arms Transfers to Less Developed Countries, C/70-1 (Cambridge, Mass.: MIT Center for International Studies, 1970); and Uri Ra'anan, The USSR Arms the Third World: Case Studies in Soviet Foreign Policy (Cambridge, Mass.: MIT Press, 1969).

(10) This little-noticed Soviet allocative dilemma is examined in an unpublished manuscript by Barton Whaley on Soviet and Chinese clandestine arms transfers, which this author was privileged to examine.

(11) Generally, on Soviet naval expansion aims, see Sergei G. Gorschkov, Red Star Rising at Sea (Annapolis, Md.: U.S. Naval Institute, 1974), translated by T. A. Nelly, Jr., particularly the final chapter entitled "Some Problems in Mastering the World Ocean." See also George E. Hudson, "Soviet Naval Doctrine and Soviet Politics, 1953-1975," World Politics 29, 1 (October 1976): 90-109.

(12) See Avigdor Haselkorn, "The Soviet Collective Security System," Orbis 19 (Spring 1975); 231-254; and Haselkorn, The Evolution of Soviet Security Strategy: 1965-1975 (New York: Crane, Russak, 1978).

(13) Ibid., p. 3.

(14) See Michael D. Davidchik and Robert B. Mahoney, Jr., "Soviet Civil Fleets and the Third World," in Dismukes and McConnell, Soviet Naval Diplomacy, appendix A.

(15) Ibid.; and also Ralph Ostrich, "Aeroflot," Armed Forces Journal 118, 9 (May 1981): 38 ff.

(16) In addition to other sources cited herein, see C. Joynt and O. M. Smolansky, "Soviet Naval Policy in the Mediterranean," Research Monograph No. 3, Department of International Relations, Lehigh University, Bethlehem, Pa., 1972; and the chapters by A. Z. Rubinstein, U. Ra'anan, R. O. Freedman, and G. S. Dragnich, in M. MccGwire, K. Booth, and J. McDonnell, eds., Soviet Naval Policy (New York: Praeger, 1975).

(17) See Charles C. Petersen, "Trends in Soviet Naval Operations," Soviet Naval Diplomacy, esp. tables 2.12-2.15, pp. 77-84.

(18) Ibid., pp. 42-44.

(19) See Petersen, "Showing the Flag," pp. 88-114, with an excellent summary data compilation on p. 92 in a table headed "Trends in Diplomatic Port Visits by Deployment Region, 1967-76."

(20) Petersen, "Trends in Soviet Naval Operations," pp. 68-69.

(21) Petersen, "Showing the Flag," p. 88.

(22) Petersen, "Trends in Soviet Naval Operations," pp. 68-69.

(23) Petersen, "Showing the Flag," pp. 103-104.

(24) Ibid., p. 105.

(25) See Petersen, "Trends in Soviet Naval Operations," who notes that these problems were a function not only of a dearth of facilities, but also of the character of the Soviet Navy's capabilities. Thus, from p. 64:

> The Soviet Navy's capabilities and practices are also relatively primitive in the replenishment of consumables other than fuel. For instance, Soviet warships, unlike their U.S. counterparts, are unable completely to satisfy their own fresh water needs because of inadequate water distillation equipment. Although many of the fresh water problems encountered in older Soviet warship designs have been overcome by advances in propulsion technology and improved water distillation plants, many of the newer ships continue to require supplementary fresh water. Supplying fresh water is accordingly an important secondary function for Soviet naval oilers and naval-subordinated merchant tankers

alike. . . . Soviet water replenishment, like fuel replenishment, is time-consuming and rarely effected underway. . . . Replenishment of dry stores (provisions, spare parts, etc.) in the Soviet Navy reflects a similar "make do" philosophy. . . . In contrast to Western navies, the Soviet Navy has not yet used helicopters for dry-stores replenishment.

See also Barry M. Blechman and Robert G. Weinland, "Why Coaling Stations Are Necessary in the Nuclear Age," International Security 2 (1977), who summarize as follows, p. 92:

On the other hand, when the Soviets first deployed forces in the Mediterranean in the 1950s, and even when they returned to establish a permanent presence there in the 1960s, the forces that they sent were drawn from what was essentially an enlarged coastal defense fleet. It was a "day-sailing" navy that had been ordered to "go to sea and stay there." It did not possess the full range of integral combat capabilities – lacking deployable air cover – and had only limited at-sea replenishment and support capabilities."

(26) Petersen, "Trends in Soviet Naval Operations," p. 64, states one Soviet problem, apparently still in force, as follows:

Nor are the Soviet Navy's eleven ammunition transports and seven missile support ships equipped for transferring ordnance while underway. In fact, deployed units have never been observed receiving ordnance at sea. These transports are instead used mainly for ferrying ordnance from the Soviet Union to friendly ports, where resupply is effected.

(27) See, ibid., pp. 69-72; and Soviet Naval Diplomacy (New York: Pergamon, 1979), Richard Remnek, "The Politics of Soviet Access to Naval Support Facilities in the Mediterranean," appendix D, pp. 357-403.

(28) Remnek, ibid.; Robert O. Freedman, "The Soviet Union and Sadat's Egypt," pp. 211-31 in MccGwire, et al., Soviet Naval Policy; and R.G. Weinland, "Land Support for Naval Forces: Egypt and the Soviet Escadra 1962-1976," Survival 20 (1978): 73-79.

(29) See Remnek, "Politics of Soviet Access," pp. 377-386; and Haselkorn, Evolution, pp. 120-21.

(30) See Flora Lewis, "Soviet Navy Loses Right to Use Egyptian Ports," New York Times, April 5, 1976, p. 1; and "Sadat to Oust Soviet Ships, Technicians," Washington Post, March 16, 1976, p. 1. Remnek, "Politics of Soviet Access," p. 376, also notes Moscow's "intransigence" on the arms question.

(31) According to Weinland, "Land Support," p. 77, in 1975, "Although the nucleus of support ships the Soviet Union has stationed in Alexandria was allowed to remain and submarine maintenance and repair operations at the shipyard there were allowed to continue, the Soviet Union lost the 'right' to enter and leave the harbor at will."

(32) See Weinland, "Land Support," p. 79. Remnek, "Politics of Soviet Access," p. 377, ascribes the "final" expulsion of the Soviets from Egypt by President Sadat in 1976 to a Soviet attempt to prevent India from overhauling and providing spare parts for Egyptian aircraft.

(33) See Remnek, "Politics of Soviet Access," p. 370; Weinland, "Land Support," p. 76; Haselkorn, Evolution, p. 107.

(34) Remnek, "Politics of Soviet Access," p. 370; and Haselkorn, Evolution, p. 109.

(35) Haselkorn, Evolution, p. 112; also Weinland, "Land Support," p. 75.

(36) See in particular J.C. Hurewitz, "Weapons Acquisition: Israel and Egypt" (paper presented to the Inter-University Seminar on Armed Forces and Society, Chicago, October 1973), p. 11; and Haselkorn, Evolution, p. 102. Weinland, "Land Support," p. 75, notes these flights by aircraft with Egyptian markings, but where it was "widely assumed that these operations were undertaken both by and for the Soviet Union."

(37) See Haselkorn, Evolution, p. 115, for discussion of Soviet attempts around 1972 at acquiring a naval facility on the Egyptian Red Sea coast, which was to be connected to Aswan by a new road. According to Remnek, "Politics of Soviet Access," p. 373, the USSR did receive permission to build such a facility, but the project was cancelled in Sadat's July 1972 volte face. The latter was said caused by, among other things, Soviet restrictions on Egyptian access to the Mersa Matruh base and because the Soviets were thought to have abused their access to Egyptian airfields in transshipping arms to India during the 1971 Indo-Pakistani war.

(38) See Remnek, "Politics of Soviet Access," pp. 376-382; and Haselkorn, Evolution, pp. 115-116, 118. According to Remnek, "Moreover in the spring of 1976, when the Soviets lost what remained of their access to facilities in Egypt, they were able to shift some naval support operations to Syria, stationing a diving tender, a barracks craft and a small ammunition transport in Tartus."

(39) Remnek, "Politics of Soviet Access," p. 382; and "Syria-USSR: Soviets Asked to Leave Syrian Naval Port," Defense and Foreign Affairs Daily, January 14, 1977.

(40) According to Remnek, "Politics of Soviet Access," pp. 382-83, the

naval technical repair yard at Tivat suffered a major cutback in repair and overhaul activity during the late 1960s, largely as a consequence of the Yugoslav Navy's retiring large numbers of obsolete warships. The Tivat yard's economic prospects became even worse at the end of the decade when it began operating on the basis of profit and loss. In order to save the yard, it was decided to undertake a major and badly-needed modernization program in the early 1970s and to assign the yard responsibility inter alia for the repair and overhaul of Yugoslav patrol submarines, all five of which are outfitted with Soviet sensors and torpedo armament. By the early 1970s then, if not earlier, the Soviet naval high command must have recognized the potential value of the Tivat facility as a supplement to, or even substitute for, Alexandria's Al Gabbari shipyard.

(41) But Yugoslav resistance to more extensive Soviet access, particularly regarding a naval base at Kotor and open-ended overflight rights, is noted in "Yugoslavs Report that Tito Rebuffed Brezhnev on Air and Naval Rights and a Role in the Warsaw Pact," New York Times, January 9, 1977, p. 8.

(42) Ibid.; regarding the Soviet overflights during the 1973 war see, inter alia, Laurence Silberman, "Yugoslavia's 'Old' Communism," Foreign Policy 26 (Spring 1977), p. 15. According to him, "during the 1973 Middle East war, the Yugoslavs openly permitted Soviet military overflights to supply Arab armies, and caused a chill in U.S.-Yugoslav relations in the process, notwithstanding the reluctance of the Eastern European section of the State Department to respond."

(43) Some very recent reports, however, near the outset of the Reagan administration, pointed to cessation by Greece of Soviet access to this shipyard. See "Greece Will Stop Servicing Ships From Soviet Fleet," New York Times, April 9, 1981, p. A6, in which it is said that Greece's agreement to repair support vessels for the Soviet Mediterranean fleet had been heavily criticized by NATO. The Neorian yard had a $2 million contract to repair a Soviet tugboat.

(44) See "Greece Is Said to Offer to Service Soviet Ships," New York Times, January 16, 1982, p. 5.

(45) See Remnek, "Politics of Soviet Access," p. 388, who notes periodic rumors about Soviet use of Mers El Kebir. He also notes that by the Evian accords of 1962, France retained a 15-year lease on the base and a nearby airfield at Bou Sfer, providing Algeria a legal basis to deny other powers the use of these installations.

(46) Ibid., p. 386, refers to "brief replenishment and maintenance stops by diesel submarines and their tenders at the civil port of Annaba, with the frequency of such visits having increased somewhat in late 1976."

Haselkorn, Evolution, pp. 106-107, cites reports of Soviet use of Algerian air bases as early as 1969. He also claims (p. 109) that although a visit in 1970 by Admiral Gorschkov failed to gain Soviet access to Mers El Kebir, it did result in landing rights for naval reconnaissance aircraft. See Abram Shulsky, "Coercive Diplomacy," in Dismukes and McConnell, Soviet Naval Diplomacy, p. 144, who cites Algeria, Mali, Guinea, and Congo-Brazzaville as Third World countries utilized for staging Soviet arms to Angola.

(47) See "Soviet Navy Bears Down on NATO," Christian Science Monitor, August 2, 1977, p. 14, which reported that before the brief fighting between Libya and Egypt, two Soviet Foxtrot submarines were sighted in the port of Tobruk. See also "Libya: Soviets Building up Tobruk," Defense and Foreign Affairs Weekly Report on Strategic Middle Eastern Affairs 2, 33 (August 25, 1976).

(48) See "Soviet Aid to Build Arms Caches in Territory of Its Mideast Allies," New York Times, March 14, 1980, p. A11, in which Israel's Ariel Sharon was quoted as saying that the port of Bardia was being deepened and shore installations expanded.

(49) One report said that Russian pilots were operating MIG-25 and Tu-22 Blinder aircraft from Libyan air bases for intelligence missions over the Mediterranean. See Middle East Intelligence Survey, 1-15 November 1979, vol. 7, no. 15, p. 119. Then, see "NATO Alarmed at Potential Use of Libyan Air Bases by Russians," International Herald Tribune, March 4, 1981, p. 2, wherein it was stated that "a strong probability that the Soviet Air Force would have the use of Libyan bases in the event of a crisis in the Mediterranean is causing growing concern to NATO planners." The article proceeded to discuss the possibility of Soviet deployment of a mixed force of Backfire bombers, Sukhoi fighter-bombers, and MIG fighters in Libya which "would shift the balance of power in the Mediterranean to the Soviet Union."

(50) See "NATO Seen Little Changed, Despite Mediterranean Politics," Washington Post, April 18, 1976, p. A17, A19, wherein increased Soviet ship visits to Tunis are noted.

(51) See "Spain Charges Soviets Monitoring Hot Spots," Washington Post, January 31, 1976, which reports that "Soviet fishing trawlers based at Spain's Canary Islands are ranging as far south as Angola for electronic monitoring of U.S.-backed forces fighting in the former Portuguese colony." Years later, with Spain trying to gain entry to NATO, it appeared prepared to reduce such access. See "Spanish Leader Hoping for Entry to NATO in '81," New York Times, April 14, 1981, p. A8, which refers to "the strategic Canary Islands, where Soviet 'fishing' vessels, laden with sophisticated radar, are known to be engaged in extensive electronic espionage."

(52) Haselkorn, Evolution, p. 106, discusses Soviet designs on Alboran.

(53) The Soviet anchorages in the Mediterranean are mapped out in Petersen, "Trends in Soviet Naval Operations," p. 65. See also "Instability in NATO Examined," Washington Post, April 18, 1976, pp. A17-A18. In "Soviet Navy Bears Down on NATO," Christian Science Monitor, August 2, 1977, p. 14, it is reported that the Soviet Black Sea fleet makes extensive use of an anchorage near Kithera Island (Greece), and "in international waters between the big Western installations on the island of Crete and the bay of Sollum on the Egyptian-Libyan coast."

(54) Petersen, "Trends in Soviet Naval Operations," p. 65.

(55) Remnek, "Politics of Soviet Access," p. 376.

(56) John K. Cooley, "Soviet Ships Prowl for New Havens," Christian Science Monitor, April 7, 1976, pp. 18-19.

(57) For the early phase of this expansion, see, inter alia, MccGwire et al., Soviet Naval Policy; Geoffrey Jukes, The Indian Ocean in Soviet Naval Policy, Adelphi Paper no. 57 (London: IISS, 1969); W. Adie, Oil Politics and Seapower: The Indian Ocean Vortex (New York: Crane, Russak, 1975); and George E. Hudson, "Soviet Naval Doctrine and Soviet Politics, 1953-1975," World Politics 29, 1 (1976). For a more recent perspective, see Richard B. Remnek, "Superpower Security Interests in the Indian Ocean Area," Alexandria, Va.: Center for Naval Analyses, June 1980, Professional Paper No. 285.

(58) Even after the opening of the Suez Canal, however, Soviet ships operating in the Indian Ocean were apparently those based at Vladivostok and Khabarovsk in Siberia. See "Soviet Ships Reportedly Destined to Reinforce Indian Ocean Fleet," New York Times, February 5, 1980, p. A10.

(59) Among numerous items on Soviet facilities in Somalia, see "Somalia-U.S.S.R.: Major Naval Complex Nearly Ready," Defense and Foreign Affairs Daily, January 7, 1977; J. Bowyer Bell, "Strategic Implications of the Soviet Presence in Somalia," Orbis 19, 2 (1975): 402-14; Haselkorn, Evolution, p. 128; Petersen, "Trends in Soviet Naval Operations," pp. 71-72; and Richard Remnek, "Soviet Policy in the Horn of Africa: The Decision to Intervene," Center for Naval Analyses, Alexandria, Va., Professional Paper 270, January 1980.

(60) Haselkorn, Evolution, p. 128; and the Defense and Foreign Affairs Daily article cited in note 59.

(61) "U.S. is Seeking to Mend Fences with South Yemen," Philadelphia Inquirer, June 4, 1978, p. 3A, which notes the pivotal role of Saudi diplomacy in these efforts.

(62) Regarding the evolvement of Soviet access to various facilities in South Yemen, see in particular, "Soviet Activity Found Growing in Aden Region," New York Times, June 10, 1980, p. A13. In "Soviet and Iranian Planes Watch U.S. Navy Moves in Arabian Sea," New York Times, December 5, 1979, p. A20, the monitoring of U.S. ships by Soviet IL-38 aircraft based in Aden during the Iranian hostage crisis is reported. See also "Soviet Increases Mideast Influence in 20-Year Pact with South Yemen," New York Times, October 26, 1979, p. A10; and "U.S. Asserts a Soviet Submarine Has Entered South Yemen Port," New York Times, August 6, 1979, p. A4, which reports on the visit of a Soviet nuclear submarine carrying cruise missiles. "Upheaval in Yemens," Near East Report 22, 26 (June 28, 1978) reports not only on Soviet naval bases at Aden and Socotra, but also a new one said being built at Ash-Sheikh Said at the mouth of the Red Sea.

(63) "Soviet Influence Found Growing in Aden Region," NYT, cited Soviet MIG-23 and MIG-25 and Su-22 deployments at Aden, possible submarine pens on Socotra along with anchorages for surface ships, berthing facilities near Mukalla, east of Aden; air bases at Little Aden, Lahej, and Mukalla; and bunkering facilities on Perim. "Soviets Show Flag in Aden," Washington Post, June 1, 1979, p. A11 reports on Soviet exercises involving air-cushion amphibious vehicles near Aden. See also "U.S. Buildup in Indian Ocean Challenges Soviet Advance," New York Times, April 19, 1981, p. 1. Generally, regarding Soviet strategic perspectives on their switch of clients in the Horn region, see Richard Remnek, "Soviet Policy in the Horn of Africa: The Decision to Intervene," Alexandria, Va., Center for Naval Analyses, January 1980, Professional Paper 270.

(64) Note of Soviet use of an intelligence facility on Socotra is made in "U.S.S.R.:   Intelligence Ship Deployment: Naval Deployment in Mozambique," Defense and Foreign Affairs Daily, August 3, 1976. In the previously cited "U.S. Buildup in Indian Ocean Challenges Soviet Advances," it was claimed that "the large floating dock that the Soviet Union had in Berbera had been towed to Socotra." Other unsubstantiated reports hinted also at Soviet submarine pens on Socotra.

(65) Ibid.; In "Soviet Activity Found Growing in Aden Region," New York Times, June 10, 1980, it is said that "Soviet warships also have bunkering facilities on Perim Island at the entrance to the Red Sea and at nearby Turba."

(66) See in particular "New Soviet Anchorage Reported in Ethiopian Isles in the Red Sea," New York Times, October 28, 1980, p. A6, which quotes Pentagon sources as saying that about half of the Soviet squadron in the Indian Ocean was anchored in the Dahlak Islands, whose support facilities had apparently come somewhat to supplant as well as supplement those on Socotra Island.

(67) See "Iraq: Defense Protocol with U.S.S.R.," <u>Defense and Foreign Affairs Daily</u>, October 13, 1976; "Soviets Consolidate Penetration of Iraq," <u>Afro-Asian Affairs</u>, no. 73, February 1979, p. 2; and Haselkorn, <u>Evolution</u>, p. 127, who reports on Soviet minesweepers said based in Basra.

(68) Haselkorn, <u>Evolution</u>, p. 123.

(69) At the height of the Ethiopia-Somalia war, in which Iraq backed Somalia while the USSR backed Ethiopia, it was reported that the Soviet ambassador was called to the Iraqi foreign ministry and told that Russian planes were not to use Iraqi airfields or overfly its airspace. See "Oil Wealth Causing A Shift in Iraqi Foreign Policy," <u>Washington Post</u>, August 8, 1978, p. A14.

(70) The Soviets apparently lost all or most remaining military access to Iraq during the latter's war with Iran, during which the USSR was not particularly forthcoming with arms replacements and spare parts, though resupply of Soviet-origin equipment did continue from other sources. See in particular "Iraqi Aide in Moscow Again for Arms Talks," <u>New York Times</u>, November 12, 1980, p. A12. In "Iraqi's Said to Get About 100 Tanks," <u>New York Times</u>, February 4, 1981, p. A4, it is reported that Iraq had probably received Soviet tanks from Eastern European countries, of course, virtually implying Soviet connivance. For full detail concerning Iraqi arms acquisitions during the recent war, see "Iraq: Arms Purchased Wherever Possible," <u>Middle-East Intelligence Survey</u>, February 16-28, 1981, vol. 8, no. 22, p. 176.

(71) Haselkorn, <u>Evolution</u>, p. 110; and <u>Time</u> magazine, October 5, 1970, p. 33.

(72) Haselkorn, <u>Evolution</u>, p. 48, wherein various sources are cited around 1967 concerning reported Soviet naval and air access to North Yemen. Egyptian-Soviet collaboration on a naval base at Mocha was therein reported; also an air base near Sa'na.

(73) See "South Africa: A Bet on U.S.?" in <u>New York Times</u>, March 16, 1981, p. 1, wherein Soviet sending of naval vessels into Mozambican ports in response to a South African raid on Mozambique is reported. See also "Southern Africa: Soviet Equipment Entering Through Nacala," <u>Defense and Foreign Affairs Daily</u>, February 17, 1977, vol. 6, no. 32; and "U.S.S.R.: Intelligence Ship Deployment: Naval Deployment in Mozambique," in ibid., August 3, 1976, vol. 5, no. 148; and "Russian Navy: A New Interest in Third World," <u>New York Times</u>, December 10, 1979, p. A19.

(74) See "Marxist Madagascar Seeks Better U.S. Ties," <u>Washington Post</u>, March 22, 1981, p. A22.

(75) Regarding Soviet designs on the Seychelles, see "Soviet May Be Seeking Base in Seychelles," New York Times, June 23, 1980, p. A17.

(76) Petersen, in "Showing the Flag," p. 102, cites Mauritius along with Cuba, Algeria, Yugoslavia, and Iraq as countries where the Soviet navy has "regularly made operational visits." This is noted also in "Indian Ocean: The U.S. and the Soviet Presence," NYT, April 19, 1981, p. 3; and Haselkorn, Evolution, p. 113 and p. 124, which notes reports about Soviet ship repairs on Mauritius.

(77) Regarding Soviet efforts to acquire access to the Maldives, see "Moscow's Growing Interest in the Maldives," Business Week, May 19, 1980; and "Life Goes on Placidly in Maldives After the End of One-Man Rule," New York Times, July 9, 1979, p. A4, wherein it is claimed that the Maldives turned down a Soviet offer of more than $1 million a year to lease the island of Gan, ostensibly for use by the Soviet fishing fleet.

(78) See Haselkorn, Evolution, p. 122. According to "Indian Ocean: The U.S. and the Soviet Presence," NYT, April 19, 1981, p. 3 the Soviet navy does stop at Indian ports, but ships carrying nuclear weapons are barred.

(79) See "Moscow's Spring Offensive: Two Afghan Options?" New York Times, March 10, 1980, p. A12; "In Afghanistan, 2 Soviet Trends Now Emerging," October 30, 1979, p. A6; and "Soviet Units in Afghanistan Dig in as if for a Long Stay," October 9, 1980, p. A20.

(80) "Moscow's Spring Offensive," New York Times, March 10, 1980, discusses the possibility of Soviet deployment of Backfires in Afghanistan, with 5,500 mile ranges.

(81) Haselkorn, Evolution, p. 107.

(82) Ibid., p. 131.

(83) "Singapore: New Contract for Soviet Ship Repair," Defense and Foreign Affairs Daily, March 3, 1977, p. 2, wherein it is reported the Keppel shipyard had routinely repaired Soviet vessels over several years.

(84) Petersen, "Trends in Soviet Naval Operations," p. 66, provides a map of Soviet anchorages in the Indian Ocean.

(85) For basic data, see, inter alia, F.J. West, Jr., "Force Projections: U.S. Maritime Posture in the Indo-Pacific Region" (paper presented for the Fletcher School's conference on "Security and Development in the Indo-Pacific Arena," April 24-26, 1978), p. 6. See also "Japan Planning Sizable Increase in Arms Budget," New York Times, July 4, 1980, p. A4; and "Japan's Press Buzzing a Soviet Carrier," June 26, 1979, p. A12.

250 GREAT POWER COMPETITION FOR OVERSEAS BASES

(86) See, inter alia, "Soviets Pouring Aid into Viet," Pittsburgh Press, September 3, 1978, p. B4; and "China's Lost Chance: No Quick, Easy Victory in Vietnam," New York Times, February 24, 1979, p. 4.

(87) Regarding Soviet access to Camranh Bay and other former U.S. bases in Vietnam, see, inter alia, "U.S. Noninvolvement Defended by President," Washington Post, February 21, 1979, p. A4; "Vietnam Reports Arrival of Soviet Naval Contingent," New York Times, November 6, 1979, p. A8; "Japan's Premier, Wary of Soviet, Favors a Stronger Defense Effort," ibid., April 20, 1979, p. A8; "Soviet Ships Arrive at Camranh Bay," ibid., March 29, 1979, p. A7; and "Japan Planning Sizable Increase in Arms Budget," NYT, July 4, 1980, p. A4. According to the latter, "The Soviet use of former American bases in Vietnam has added to Japan's defense problems. Submarines based on Cam Ranh Bay are now patrolling as far south as the Strait of Malacca between Singapore and Sumatra through which most of Japan's oil imports pass." For a broader analysis, see Tai Sung An, "Soviet Access to Cam Ranh Bay: Political and Military Implications," Naval Institute Proceedings, September 1979, pp. 111-113; and W.H. Walls and E.R. McDaniel, "Soviet Bases in Vietnam: Implications for the Seventh Fleet," ibid., pp. 113-116.

(88) Haselkorn, Evolution, p. 132 cites several sources reporting on Soviet installation in Laos of radar, satellite communication and electronic and communications intercept facilities in addition to several airfields.

(89) Ibid., p. 116.

(90) See "Economic Union Studied by South Pacific Nations," New York Times, August 20, 1979, p. D1, wherein it is stated that "the Soviet Union has approached Tonga to provide it with port facilities, and the Libyan government has offered generous aid for the small island kingdom. These approaches, the perceived post-Vietnam lessening of United States interests in the region, and the withdrawal of the British, had led commentators here to refer to the small South Pacific countries as "the soft underbelly of the West." See also Stephen Ritterbush, "Resources and Changing Perceptions of National Security in the Central and Western Pacific" (paper delivered at the Fletcher School's conference on "Security and Development in the Indo-Pacific Arena," 1978), p. 37.

(91) Ritterbush, "Resources and Changing Perceptions," pp. 33-35.

(92) See "Peru: More Reports of Soviet Deal," Defense and Foreign Affairs Daily, Weekly Report on Strategic Latin American Affairs, January 20, 1977, vol. 3, no. 3, wherein speculations are made about possible Soviet naval access to Peruvian ports at Callao and Trujillo.

(93) See "Self-Rule Granted for Marshall Isles," New York Times, January 15, 1980, p. A5.

(94) See Petersen, "Trends in Soviet Naval Operations," pp. 77-78, table 2.12, "Atlantic Ocean Operations, 1964-1976" for relevant information.

(95) The potential value for the USSR of operating submarines out of Cienfuegos is discussed in "Allies Foresee Wartime Peril in Cuban Base," New York Times, December 3, 1979, p. A5.

(96) "Senate Panel Calls Hearings on Soviet Troops in Cuba," New York Times, September 7, 1979, p. A6.

(97) William Safire, "Brezhnev's Big Ear," New York Times, September 6, 1979, p. A21. See also James Reston, "The Hidden Prices," New York Times, September 23, 1979, p. E19, which describes the Soviet intelligence collection installation at Lourdes in Cuba as "the largest known Soviet intelligence installation outside the U.S.S.R."

(98) "Soviets Deploy Spy Ships off U.S.," Christian Science Monitor, August 1, 1977, p. 15, which notes the Tu-95 routes between Murmansk and an air base in Cuba, running along the U.S. Atlantic coast, with the Soviet base at Conakry in Guinea also part of this reconnaissance network.

(99) George F. Will, "The Defense Gap," Newsweek, October 1, 1979, p. 84, and "Senate Panel Calls Hearings on Soviet Troops in Cuba," NYT, September 7, 1979, p. A6.

(100) See Shulsky, "Coercive Diplomacy," p. 130; James M. McConnell, "The Rules of the Game," in Dismukes and McConnell, Soviet Naval Diplomacy, p. 260; "Russian Navy: A New Interest in Third World," New York Times, December 10, 1979, p. A19; and Haselkorn, Evolution, p. 123.

(101) For a general discussion of Soviet military aid clients in West Africa, see D.R. Smock and H.H. Miller, "Soviet Designs in Africa," American Universities Field Staff Reports, 1980, No. 17 (Hanover, N.H.), pp. 2-5; and "Soviet Tightens Grasp in Africa," New York Times, December 14, 1975, p. 19. Shulsky, "Coercive Diplomacy," cites Guinea, Algeria, Mali, and Congo-Brazzaville as among the countries allowing the Soviets to stage arms en route to Angola during the civil war.

(102) Regarding earlier Soviet access to Nigerian ports, see "New Soviet Role in Africa Alleged," New York Times, December 10, 1975, p. 11, which discusses that access as having been achieved in connection with delivery of MIG-21 fighter aircraft.

(103) The Soviet acquisition but then loss of access to a base at Luba in Equatorial Guinea is discussed in "Caught in Russian Waters," The Russian Report 1, 5 (August 1980): 9; "Spain Rushes to Aid New Regime in Equatorial Guinea," New York Times, September 12, 1979, p. A5; and "Equatorial Guinea Warms Up to Spain," December 26, 1979, p. A5.

(104) See "Soviet Said to Aim for Angola Bases," New York Times, November 28, 1975, p. 5 and the previously cited "Russian Navy: A New Interest in Third World," New York Times, December 10, 1979, p. A19.

(105) See "Radical Grenada Symbolizes Political Shift in Caribbean," New York Times, August 20, 1979, p. A4. Therein, a German publication is noted as contending that a base for Soviet warships was under construction there and that "American spy planes had discovered vast areas of the interior cleared, as they were in Cuba, for the installation of missile bases." See also Tad Szulc, "Radical Winds in the Caribbean," The New York Times Magazine, May 25, 1980, pp. 16ff, wherein Cuban construction of an airport on Grenada – one rumored to have military potential – is discussed.

(106) Michael D. Davidchik and Robert B. Mahoney, "Soviet Civil Fleets and the Third World," in Dismukes and McConnell, Soviet Naval Diplomacy, appendix A, p. 329, claim, however, that fish account for only some 13 percent of all annual protein consumption in the USSR. For comparative data regarding Soviet vs. U.S. vs. W. European, etc. reliance upon fish for protein, see Dennis Pirages, Global Ecopolitics (N. Scituate, Mass.: Duxbury, 1978), p. 80 and pp. 86-7, in a chapter headed "The Politics of Food." See also Geoffrey Kemp, "Scarcity and Strategy," Foreign Affairs, Vol. 56, no. 2 (January 1978), pp. 396-414 who notes that the bulk of the world's major fishing areas is located in less than 10 percent of the oceans.

(107) Davidchik and Mahoney, "Soviet Civil Fleets," p. 324.

(108) Haselkorn, Evolution, p. 106, cites press reports claiming that the Canaries were used as a refueling and supply base for some 200 Soviet trawlers, operating off the coast of West Africa, some of which ranged as far south as Angola for ELINT operations. Regarding this issue, see also "Spain Charges Soviets Monitoring Hot Spots," Washington Post, January 31, 1976, p. A5; and "Spanish Leader Hoping for Entry to NATO in '81," New York Times, April 14, 1981, p. A8, wherein it was said that a new Spanish prime minister, Calvo Sotelo, was anxious to reduce Soviet access to the Canary Islands.

(109) Davidchik and Mahoney, "Soviet Civil Fleets," p. 324.

(110) Ibid., pp. 324-329.

(111) This is discussed in Ritterbush's paper, "Resources and Changing Perceptions," on the Micronesian islands, previously discussed.

(112) See Davidchik and Mahoney, "Soviet Civil Fleets," pp. 328-329.

(113) David Rees, "Soviet Sea Power: The Covert Support Fleet," Conflict Studies, no. 84, June 1977, p. 5.

(114) Davidchik and Mahoney, "Soviet Civil Fleets," p. 323, who note that civilian tankers can be used as needed to support naval operations, but for commercial operations in other periods.

(115) Ibid., p. 321.

(116) Ibid., p. 333.

(117) Ibid., pp. 332-333. A recent and extensive analysis of Aeroflot's global operations is provided in Ralph Ostrich, "Aeroflot: How Russia Uses Its 'Civil' Airline for Covert Activities," Armed Forces Journal 118, 9 (May 1981): 38ff. Ostrich discusses four major functions of Aeroflot, vis-a-vis trooplift (as an adjunct to VTA), intelligence gathering and communications monitoring, transport of clandestine agents, and "showing the flag."

(118) Haselkorn, Evolution, chaps. 1, 2.

(119) Concerning the rarely discussed Soviet presence in and access to Mongolia, see ibid., p. 97, who reports that as early as 1966, some 10,000 Soviet troops were ensconced there; additionally, large numbers of mobile SS-14 and SS-15 IRBMs targeted against China.

(120) Soviet overflights over Yugoslavia are noted in Laurence Silberman, "Yugoslavia's 'Old' Communism," Foreign Policy, no. 26 (Spring 1977); pp. 3-27. Later, the United States apparently protested to Yugoslavia over alleged Soviet stopovers en route to Angola to arm the MPLA. See "Africa Tension Mounts on Angola Meeting," Washington Post, January 10, 1976, p. A6.

(121) The previously cited "Soviet Tightens Grasp in Africa" notes among other things, Soviet use of Pointe Noire and Brazzaville in Congo as "major transshipment points for arms to Angola."

(122) See "U.S. Charges Soviet Mounts big Airlift to Ethiopian Army," New York Times, December 14, 1977, p. 1.

(123) Haselkorn, Evolution, chap. 6.

(124) "Soviet Arms Airlift to Vietnam Hinted as Combat Goes on," New York Times, February 23, 1979, p. 1, which vaguely refers to the likelihood of landing rights somewhere in South Asia. The previously cited September 3, 1978, p. B4 Pittsburgh Press article, "Soviets Pouring Aid Into Viet," claims Soviet air stops both in Pakistan and India.

(125) In "A Soviet Sub-Detection System?" Newsweek, September 8, 1980, p. 15, it is said that "U.S. intelligence sources speculate that the Soviet Union hopes to lay down a massive new grid of underwater hydrophones to detect American submarines," but that "U.S. officials think the Soviets still lack the land-based technology necessary to make a detection system work properly."

(126) "Uganda: Getting 'Satellite Stations' Which Will Aid Soviet Reconn. Effort," Defense and Foreign Affairs Daily 6, 124 (July 6, 1977) refers to stations funded by the UN's International Telecommunications Union which would be used to collect the output of the Soviet Cosmos series of reconnaissance spacecraft. See, in particular, "ASTP Tracking Facilities," in Aviation Week and Space Technology, May 5, 1975, regarding Soviet tracking stations.

(127) See Davidchik and Mahoney, "Soviet Civil Fleets," p. 322; and Rees, "Soviet Sea Power," p. 5, under "Freighters as fleet auxiliaries."

(128) Alvin Cottrell and Thomas H. Moorer, "U.S. Overseas Bases: Problems of Projecting American Military Power Abroad," Washington: Georgetown CSIS, 1977, paper no. 47.

(129) Ibid., p. 9.

(130) The two sides of this argument are presented in U.S. Senate Committee on Foreign Relations, "United States Foreign Policy Objectives, and Overseas Military Installations," prepared by Congressional Research Service, Library of Congress, Washington, 1977 (hereinafter referred to as the SFR Report), "Introduction and Overview," in terms of strategies labeled "containment" and "regional partnership," the latter perhaps somewhat of a euphemism for a substantial degree of American withdrawal.

(131) Cottrell and Moorer, "U.S. Overseas Bases," pp. 6-10.

(132) These trends are summarized in Herbert G. Hagerty, "Forward Deployment in the 1970s and 1980s," Washington: National Defense University, 1977, National Security Affairs Monograph, 77-2, pp. 13-20.

(133) These factors were nowhere more in evidence than with regard to U.S.-Greece negotiations over a base renewal pact, as described in "Greece Gives U.S. a Monday Deadline on Bases Pact," New York Times, June 10, 1981, p. A11. Those negotiations were pre-Papandreou.

(134) Cottrell and Moorer, "U.S. Overseas Bases," p. 9.

(135) These matters are ably discussed in the SFR Report, pp. 134-194, country-by-country, but organized or disaggregated into two regions: Southeast Asia and Southwest Pacific, and Northeast Asia. For each,

the study probes into the effectiveness of the U.S. base structure in meeting U.S. objectives (military, political and economic), and alternative instruments to promote those objectives.

(136) Generally, in recent years, the lingering status of U.S. access to Thai facilities has remained shrouded in silence. In "B-52s to be Used for Indian Ocean Surveillance," Defense/Space Business Daily, vol. 88, no. 37, p. 289, it was averred that U.S. use of Thai air bases was being revived, at least regarding P-3C reconnaissance flight stops and also staging for C-141 transports at Takhli. U.S.-Thai negotiations over the status of the sensitive electronic spy station at Ramasun are discussed in "Bangkok Weighs U.S. Offer on Spy Base," Washington Post, May 15, 1976, p. A14, wherein participation by Thai technicians was apparently a major point of contention. Regarding P-3 flights from Utapao, see Lenny Siegel, "Australia to Patrol Seas for U.S.," Pacific Research and World Empire Telegram, July-August 1975, pp. 14-15.

(137) As indicated in "Carter Orders Weapons to be Sent to Thailand," Centre Daily Times, July 2, 1980, p. 2 (AP Dispatch), escalated U.S. arms shipments to Thailand may also have anticipated increased American military access.   Continued access was further hinted in Peter Navarro, "If Thailand is Periled," New York Times, July 9, 1980, p. A19.

(138) However, as noted in the SFR Report, p. 153, ASEAN nations including Indonesia were active in persuading the Philippines to continue U.S. use of important bases there for the benefit of all the ASEAN nations. Also, the SFR Report, p. 160, indicates Surabaya in Indonesia, along with Malaysia's Penang, as hypothetically a replacement for Subic Bay as a major U.S. naval base, if the United States were to lose use of the Philippine base.

(139) Norman Friedman, "SOSUS and U.S. ASW Tactics," U.S. Naval Institute Proceedings, March 1980, p. 120, provides a map with information developed by SIPRI regarding the presumed locations of U.S. and allied sea-bottom sonar arrays and "their probable maximum submarine detection areas." The Indonesian Straits are not here part of the scheme, though some arrays are pictured covering the gaps between the Philippines, the Halmahera Islands, and Papua/New Guinea.

(140) For a period, the question of U.S. renewal of its Philippines' base agreement seemed seriously in doubt, with the normal strains associated with the basic issue of sovereignty further exacerbated by the Carter administration's pressures on the Marcos regime regarding human rights. Also, the impact of the U.S. withdrawal from S.E. Asia prompted Marcos to question "whether these bases do in fact provide us effective protection or whether they only increase the danger to our country because of the provocation the bases represent to others." See "Philippines Marcos Considering Break in U.S. Military Ties," Washington Post, January 9, 1977, p. A12.

(141) See "U.S. and Filipinos Sign Agreement On the Use of Air and Navy Bases," New York Times, January 8, 1979, p. A2. This article records numerous changes in heretofore extant status of forces provisions in addition to the financial arrangements involving military aid and credit, industrial development, etc.

(142) Early adumbrations of another strenuous round of negotiations with an increasingly pressured – by domestic opponents – President Marcos are discussed in "Reagan Facing Limited Decisions on Southeast Asia," New York Times, February 26, 1981, p. A2.

(143) A plea for reconsideration of Taiwan as an important U.S. basing hub is in William F. Buckley, "Take Another Look at Taiwan," Centre Daily Times, June 11, 1980, p. 4, written in the context of the early months of the Reagan administration.

(144) The ROK more recently was reported the location of one of the five GEODSS (Ground-based electro-optical deep space surveillance) stations about to replace the network of Baker-Nunn telescopic cameras that long had been an integral part of satellite tracking. See "Laser Weapons to be Tested at White Sands Range," New York Times, March 3, 1980, p. A16.

(145) See Friedman, "SOSUS."

(146) Cottrell and Moorer, "U.S. Overseas Bases," p. 52.

(147) For a "mood piece" portraying the social backwash of U.S. withdrawal from bases in Japan, see "U.S. Handing Back to Japan Vast Base That Was Key to Military Operations in Asia," New York Times, November 30, 1977, p. A8. In the spring of 1981, however, there were renewed tensions over the issue of nuclear weapons brought onboard U.S. ships to Japanese ports, and confessions by U.S. officials that this had long been practiced unofficially.

(148) In "U.S. and Australia Reveal Memo On Exchange of Military Support," New York Times, March 26, 1980, p. A17, it is said that "Washington was considering seeking either base or homeport facilities at a naval base near Perth for the United States Indian Ocean fleet." The SFR Report, p. 160, discusses Darwin as well as Cockburn as a possible U.S. naval facility. For recent indications of a downplaying of Cockburn's future see "Political Influence . . . and Importance of Bases," The Western Australian, May 20, 1981; and "Navy Drops Plan for Indian Ocean Port," Washington Star, April 24, 1981.

(149) See "U.S. Halts Australian Talks on Use of Bases by B-52's," New York Times, January 15, 1981, p. A7; and "Wise B-52 Delay," The Sydney Morning Herald, January 15, 1981, p. 6.

(150) According to Cottrell and Moorer, "U.S. Overseas Bases," p. 54, "it could not handle the repair of ships with the tonnage of a cruiser – certainly not carriers."

(151) These matters are discussed in Ritterbush, "Resources and Changing Perceptions," p. 32.

(152) See "Self-Rule Granted for Marshall Isles," New York Times, January 15, 1980, p. A5; whereby it is said "the arrangement gives the islanders all the attributes of sovereignty outside the defense and security sphere, including the right to make treaties with foreign nations and to 'dispose of their resources as they see fit,' except that they will probably be unable to qualify for membership in the United Nations." See also "Fragmentation Threatening New Nation in Pacific," ibid., February 7, 1979, p. A12; "Island Territories Get Economic Plan," ibid., February 24, 1980, p. 19; "Palau Islands in Pacific Become Republic of Belau," ibid., January 3, 1981, p. 4; and "U.S. To Drop Claims on 25 Pacific Isles," ibid., May 19, 1980, p. A7, which reports U.S. transfer of some islands to the brand new nations of Tuvalu and Kiribati.

(153) This is discussed in Ritterbush, "Resources and Changing Perceptions," pp. 23-31, who notes Soviet desires for a facility in this region to service surveillance ships.

(154) Richard G. Toye, "The Projection of U.S. Power by the Air Force in the Western Pacific and Indian Ocean," Paper delivered at Fletcher School Conference on "Security and Development in the Indo-Pacific Arena," Boston, April 1978, p. 22.

(155) These issues are discussed in Ann L. Hollick and Robert E. Osgood, New Era of Ocean Politics (Baltimore: Johns Hopkins University Press, 1974), in a chapter by Osgood, "U.S. Security Interests in Ocean Law," wherein he identifies 16 straits in the world which might be important for the mobility of the U.S. Polaris fleet and which would be overlapped by territorial waters if 12-mile boundaries were agreed to. Most important among these are Gibraltar and the Indonesian Straits of Ombai-Wetar and Lombok. Generally, as Osgood ably demonstrates, the Soviet Navy is perhaps more subject to restrictions by a new LOS than the USA, particularly in the northeast Atlantic and with regard to exits from the Sea of Japan area.

(156) Regarding the supersession of ground-based technical facilities by satellites (or, contrariwise, their continued interdependence), see, inter alia, "Technology is the Key to Arms Verification," New York Times, August 14, 1979, p. C2, which among other things says the United States will in 1983 launch a new satellite which would be able to replace many of the electronic intelligence functions now performed by ground stations.

(157) In "U.S. Plans to Sell a Satellite Ground Station to China," New York Times, January 9, 1980, p. A9, it was announced that "the U.S. was prepared to sell China a ground station for receiving information from the Landsat Earth Resources Satellite, which has possible military applications." By mid-1981, as reported in "The China Policy That Isn't," ibid., June 14, 1981, p. C1, U.S. officials were declining to confirm or deny that the U.S. had monitoring stations in China to watch over Soviet missile launchings. William Safire, in "Inside Deng's Mind," New York Times, June 15, 1981, p. A23 claimed it was an "open secret" that the PRC had replaced Iran as "the world's leading Soviet-watching station"; which secret was verified a few days later in "U.S. and Peking Jointly Monitor Russian Missiles," New York Times, June 18, 1981, p. 1.

(158) Geoffrey Kemp, "The New Strategic Map: Geography, Arms Diffusion and the Southern Seas" (paper prepared for Fletcher School Conference on "Implications of the Military Build-Up in Non-Industrial States," May 6-8, 1976) stressed the growing strategic importance of the South Atlantic region, and particularly of Brazil.

(159) Concerning the complex U.S. strategic dilemma regarding Mexican oil and combatting radical revolutions in Central America and the Caribbean, see Daniel James, "Mexico: America's Newest Problem?" The Washington Quarterly 3, 3 (Summer 1980): 87-105.

(160) Cottrell and Moorer, "U.S. Overseas Bases," p. 39. They ask, empathizing with Castro's presumed perception, "Why should Havana not expect the United States to react favorably to calls for renegotiation since it has already done so in the Panamanian case?" Generally, on the future of U.S. Panama Canal Zone facilities, see Lt. Col. Jack Child, "Military Aspects of the Panama Canal Issue," Naval Institute Proceedings, January 1980, pp. 46-51.

(161) See "Costa Ricans Expel U.S. Air Force Unit," New York Times, July 11, 1979, p. A7.

(162) According to the SFR report, p. 203, although many of these facilities are becoming increasingly outmoded by new technologies (old oceanographic research facilities replaced, for instance, by new buoys which relay data to satellites), the United States will in the future retain a strong interest, particularly in the facilities on Bermuda (important for ASW) and on Andros Island in the Bahamas (research and development on ASW weapons).

(163) For a portrayal of the vast shift in arms acquisition patterns in Latin America, which saw U.S. arms sales in 1977 fall below those of Western Europe and the USSR, see the prepared statement by John A. Bushnell, State Department, before the Subcommittee on Inter-American Affairs, House International Relations Committee, June 27, 1978.

(164) Again, the irreducible necessity of retaining Diego and Ascension for staging operations to the Middle East/Indian Ocean area was stressed in P.M.   Dadant, "Shrinking International Airspace as a Problem for Future Air Movements — A Briefing," Santa Monica, CA: RAND, 1978, Report R-2178-AF, esp. pp. 19-20.

(165) Regarding the U.S. satellite tracking station on Madagascar, used by the U.S. for 12 years, see "Malagasy Ousts 2 U.S. Aides," Washington Post, September 24, 1976, p. A4.

(166) For general information, see Lenny Siegel, "Diego Garcia," Pacific Research, vol. 8, no.3, March/April 1977, pp. 1-11; Joe Stork, "The Carter Doctrine and U.S. Bases in the Middle East," Middle East Report and Information Project, September 1980, pp. 43-44; and "U.S. Studying $1 Billion Expansion of Indian Ocean Base," New York Times, April 6, 1980, p. 16.

(167) Siegel, "Diego Garcia," pp. 6-7.

(168) Ibid., p. 6.

(169) R. Toye, "The Projection of U.S. Power by the Air Force in the Western Pacific and Indian Ocean," p. 31.

(170) Ibid., pp. 25-29, for more extended analysis of this and other routes where refueling capability would be required.

(171) Hence, according to Siegel, "Diego Garcia," p. 3, "currently U.S. subs can project missiles into the heart of the U.S.S.R. from the northwestern reaches of the Indian Ocean, but as the new C-4 missile, with a range of 4,000 miles, goes into service, Poseidon and Trident subs will be able to operate effectively in most of the ocean."

(172) There were also strong Third World pressures on the U.S. presence at Diego, including demands that the island be "returned" to Mauritius. See "OAU Denounces U.S. Over Diego Garcia," New York Times, July 5, 1980, p. A4; and "As Armadas Intrude on 'Zone of Peace,' Region Watches with Mixed Feelings," ibid., April 21, 1981, p. A8.

(173) For general analyses of this reversal of mood towards the latter part of the Carter administration, see "Persian Gulf: Little Debate About Buildup," Washington Post, August 10, 1980, p. 1; "Soviet War in Gulf A Major U.S. Worry," New York Times, December 18, 1980, p. A6; "Have Doctrine, Need Mobility," The Economist, February 9-15, 1980, pp. 15-16; "The U.S. Gets Tough," Newsweek, January 21, 1980, pp. 22-26; "Pentagon Activates Strike Force: Effectiveness Believed Years Off," New York Times, February 19, 1980, p. A1; "The Roadblocks to Mobilizing in the Persian Gulf," Philadelphia Inquirer, January 27, 1980, p. 1G; "How U.S. Strategy Toward Persian Gulf Region Evolved," New

York Times, January 25, 1980, p. A6; and "Is America Strong Enough?" Newsweek, October 27, 1980, p. 48ff.

(174) See "Indian Ocean Lands Reported to Agree To Use of Bases," New York Times, February 12, 1980, p. 1; "U.S. Warily Seeking New Outposts Abroad," Washington Post, February 25, 1980, p. 1; "U.S. Would Link Aid to Access," ibid., February 28, 1980, p. 1; and "Snags Arise in Talks on Access to Bases," New York Times, March 30, 1980, p. 8.

(175) "U.S. Studying $1 Billion Expansion of Indian Ocean Base," NYT, April 6, 1980, p. 16.

(176) See "Kenya Agrees to Expand U.S. Use of Military Bases," New York Times, June 28, 1980, p. 5; "U.S. Warily Seeking New Outposts Abroad," Washington Post, February 25, 1980; and "U.S. Wins Bases in Oman and Kenya," ibid., April 22, 1980, p. A3.

(177) "U.S. is Reported to Study Offer of a Somali Base," New York Times, December 23, 1979, p. 1; "Somalia Asks High Price for U.S. Access to Bases," Washington Post, April 22, 1980, p. A17; "U.S.-Somalia: American Base in Somalia," Middle-East Intelligence Survey, August 16-31, 1980, vol. 8, no. 10, p. 79; and "Muskie Indicates U.S. May Decide Not to Pursue Access to Somalia Base," New York Times, June 25, 1980, p. A4.

(178) See "U.S. and Somalia Expected to Conclude Pact on Bases," New York Times, August 19, 1980, p. A8; "U.S. and Somalia Sign Arms Accord," ibid., August 23, 1980, p. 3; "U.S.-Somalia Pact Drawing Opposition," ibid., August 29, 1980, p. A6; and "House Panel Skeptical on U.S. Pact with Somalia," ibid., September 17, 1980, p. A14.

(179) Earlier U.S. access to Masirah is discussed in "Middle East: U.S. Secretary of State to Visit," Defense and Foreign Affairs Weekly Report on Strategic Middle Eastern Affairs, February 9, 1977, vol. 3, no. 6.

(180) "U.S. May Use Desert Island Airfield As Base for Defense of Persian Gulf," Washington Post, October 11, 1980, p. A21; "U.S. Announces Pact with Oman on Access to Air Bases and Port," New York Times, June 6, 1980, p. A9; "Oman to Be Supply Link for U.S. Fleet," ibid., January 28, 1980, p. A6.

(181) "Oman Says No To Use of Bases," Centre Daily Times, May 3, 1980, p. 21.

(182) See Stork, "Carter Doctrine," p. 42.

(183) "Pakistani Dismisses $400 million in Aid Offered by U.S. as Peanuts," New York Times, January 18, 1980, p. 1; "U.S. Bases in Pakistan Suggested by Kissinger to Fight Soviet Threat," ibid., January 14, 1980.

(184) The potentialities of Gwadar as a U.S. naval base are bruited in T.H. Moorer and A.J. Cottrell, "The Search for U.S. Bases in The Indian Ocean: A Last Chance," Strategic Review, Spring 1980, pp. 36-37. During the debate over U.S. capabilities to monitor SALT II in the wake of the Iranian revolution, resumption of U.S. use of intelligence facilities at Peshawar was speculated upon but considered unlikely; likewise staging of U-2 flights out of Pakistan. See "U.S. May Use Modified U-2 Plane to Monitor Soviet Missile Testing," New York Times, April 4, 1979, p. 1. Regarding the Reagan Administration's move to tighten relations with Pakistan, see "Reagan and the Gulf," New York Times, February 23, 1981, p. A6.

(185) "Saudis Considering Military Tie to U.S.," New York Times, February 6, 1980, p. 1; "U.S. Jets Near Gulf Improve War Data," ibid., October 9, 1980, p. A13; and "Brown Orders a Study of Saudi Request for Equipment to Improve F-15s," ibid., October 22, 1980, p. A17.

(186) For analyses of the Saudi AWACs controversy see, inter alia, the various editions of Near East Report, during May and June 1981. Stork, "Carter Doctrine," p. 41, in discussing possible future U.S. naval access to Saudi Arabia, notes that "when the base and headquarters of Jubayl is turned over to the Saudi Royal Navy in the near future, it will be operated and maintained by Hughes, Bendix, Holmes and Narver, a California firm," perhaps implying the contingency of American access. See also Frank Gervasi, "Island of Instability," Harper's, September 1981, pp. 13-18.

(187) See Stork, "Carter Doctrine," particularly regarding U.S. use of the Egyptian air base at Qena for training exercises with AWACs and for launching the U.S. rescue raid in Iran. See also "U.S. to Deploy F-4 Jets in Egypt to Build Land-Based Air Power," New York Times, June 13, 1980, p. 1; "U.S. Flying Electronics Planes over Persian Gulf," New York Times, March 10, 1980, p. A13; and "Drill in Egypt: Signal by U.S.," New York Times, November 13, 1980, p. A17.

(188) Alexandria's possible use for U.S. ship repairs is discussed in "Cairo's Future and U.S. Aid," New York Times, March 29, 1979, p. A11.

(189) Regarding the use of Omani and Egyptian facilities for the Iran rescue raid, see "Angered by Use in Raid," Philadelphia Bulletin, May 4, 1980, p. 1; and "The Plan: How it Failed," Newsweek, May 5, 1980, pp. 27-28. An Omani base was used to refuel C-130 aircraft which had originated their mission in Egypt.

(190) Regarding Ras Banas, see, inter alia, "Egyptians Welcome Troop Ties with U.S.," NYT, November 12, 1980, p. A10.

(191) "Begin Would Offer Facilities," New York Times, January 5, 1980, p. 7.

(192) In "The National Security Adviser," Near East Report 25, 1 (January 2, 1981), it was noted that Reagan's then national security adviser, Richard Allen, had considered U.S. use of the former Israeli Sinai bases at Eitam and Etzion. See also George E. Gruen's letter to the New York Times, November 28, 1980, p. A21, "Before the U.S. Could Use Two Sinai Bases."

(193) See "High Stakes in the Azores," The Nation, November 8, 1975.

(194) "In-Flight Refueling to Aid C-5 Wing Life," Aviation Week and Space Technology, July 12, 1976, pp. 32-34.

(195) A good summary of the subject is in Stephen S. Kaplan, "The Utility of U.S. Military Bases," Military Review 57, 4 (April 1977): 43-57.

(196) This is discussed in Lothar Ruehl, "Iceland's Vital Value to NATO Strategy," Atlantic Community Quarterly 14, 1 (Spring 1976): 66-68.

(197) Cottrell and Moorer, "U.S. Overseas Bases," p. 14.

(198) See "Scottish Isles Try to Keep Their Distance From Mainland," New York Times, May 23, 1980, p. A15 wherein it is reported that the islanders (the Western Isles in the Outer Hebrides) "have convinced themselves that NATO sees Stornaway as a partial replacement for the huge Keflavik base in Iceland, where there have been severe problems with the local population."

(199) See "Norway: U.S. Base Modernization Request 'Reasonable,' " Defense and Foreign Affairs Daily 6, 140 (July 28, 1977).

(200) See, inter alia, Col. Arthur E. Dewey, "The Nordic Balance," Strategic Review 4, 4 (Fall 1976): 49-61.

(201) In "Mysterious Soviet Ship Movements Worry and Puzzle Norwegians," New York Times, August 4, 1978, p. A2, it is said that

> at Gamvik, on the Nordkinn Peninsula, the Norwegian Government operates a key listening post for the United States. Although theoretically top secret, it has recently been discussed in Norwegian publications as the terminus of a submarine cable linking sonar stations lying on the seabed between Norway and Spitsbergen. According to one account, this sonar system used

principally to monitor Soviet submarine activity, is code-named Caesar.

(202) See "U.S. Arms in Norway Are Topic of Talks," New York Times, February 11, 1980, p. A7, wherein it is noted that the American weapons and vehicles to be stocked in Norway are expected to be in quantities sufficient for use by an American brigade, or about 8,000 men." Norway still barred stationing of foreign troops or nuclear weapons, and subsequent negotiations involved Norwegian insistence that pre-positioned U.S. materiel would not be kept in the northern part of the country where it might be provocative to the Soviets. The possibility of — and implications of — a Soviet takeover of Norwegian airfields is discussed in "Navy Sees Limit on Ability in Atlantic War," New York Times, February 20, 1980, p. A6. See also "Norwegian in Soviet for Touchy Talks," New York Times, December 21, 1980, p. 17.

(203) This is discussed, as previously noted, in the works by Dadant on aerial overflights and by Toye on air staging. Ascension also hosts a U.S. space tracking station (it was the one which discovered that some of Skylab's solar panels were being ripped away on that spaceship's destructive descent) as noted in "Skylab Put Into Tumble by NASA for Splashdown Landing," Centre Daily Times, July 11, 1979, p. 1.

(204) Press reports on this were scant, but Dakar was rumored to have been used for staging U.S. materiel to Zaire, no doubt with French prompting.

(205) The phasing out of U.S. Moroccan facilities, including the Kenitra communications center, is noted in "Hassan Worries About U.S. Support, Wants Envoy Young to Visit Morocco," Washington Post, May 29, 1978, p. A18.

(206) This is noted, in the context of access matters, in William B. Quandt, "Lebanon, 1958, and Jordan, 1970," in B.M. Blechman and S.S. Kaplan, Force Without War (Washington, D.C.: Brookings, 1978), pp. 222-288.

(207) On U.S. Spanish bases, particularly regarding the 1975 pact, see Kaplan, "Spain Pact Has Plusses for Both Sides," Washington Star, March 4, 1976, p. A4; "The Spanish Connection: A Wider U.S. Commitment in the Making," The Defense Monitor 5, 2 (February 1976); and "Spanish Treaty Contains Terms for F-16 Sales," Aviation Week and Space Technology 105, 1 (July 5, 1976): 69-70.

(208) See "Secret U.S.-Spain Airlift Accord Told," Washington Post, October 11, 1976, p. A24; and "No Secret Pact on Bases, Spain Says," ibid., October 14, 1976, p. A25.

(209) See "Carter Urges Spain to Join NATO Allies," New York Times, June 26, 1980, p. 1; and "Spain Leans Toward Bigger Western Defense Role," New York Times, January 27, 1980, p. 5.

(210) This is worried about in Cottrell and Moorer, "U.S. Overseas Bases," pp. 21-22.

(211) Ibid., p. 21.

(212) See "U.S. Hoping to Save Its Bases in Greece," New York Times, October 2, 1980, p. A9; and "Greece Threatens to Close Bases," ibid., August 21, 1980, p. A2.

(213) This is discussed in "Rising Hatred of U.S. in Greece is Imperiling A Vital Defense Flank," Wall Street Journal, January 6, 1976, p. 1.

(214) House of Representatives, Committee on Foreign Relations, "Greece and Turkey: Some Military Implications Related to NATO and the Middle East," Report Prepared by the Congressional Research Service, Library of Congress, February 28, 1975, p. 14.

(215) "Greece Rejoins the Military Wing of NATO After Six-Year Absence," New York Times, October 21, 1980, p. 1.

(216) House Committee on Foreign Affairs Report, "Greece and Turkey: Some Military Implications Related to NATO and the Middle East," p. 13.

(217) See "Turkey Would Let U-2 Use Its Airspace If Soviet Approved," New York Times, May 15, 1979, p. 1. Later, this position was reversed by a new Turk government, as indicated in "Turkey Won't Ask Soviet to Approve Possible U.S. Air Surveillance," ibid., July 5, 1980, p. A3.

(218) See "U.S. Plans New Way to Check Soviet Missile Tests," New York Times, June 29, 1979, p. A3.

(219) For details of the pact, see "U.S. and Turkey Sign Pact on Aid and Bases," New York Times, March 30, 1980, p. 1; and "Defense Cooperation with Turkey," in Gist, Department of State, Bureau of Public Affairs, May 1980.

(220) Gist, Department of State.

(221) See "Malta, an Oft-Conquered Isle, Seeks a Few Good Friends," New York Times, October 10, 1979, p. A2, wherein Malta leader Dom Mintoff's maneuverings and threats to turn his island into a Libyan or Soviet base after the British withdrawal are discussed.

(222) Basic data on French troop deployments in Africa are provided in "Dirty Little Wars Suddenly Get Bigger," New York Times, May 21, 1978, p. D1; and "France's Aid in Chad's Civil War Highlights Its Touchy Police Role," New York Times, May 15, 1978, p. 1.

(223) Ibid.; and "France's Aid in Chad's Civil War Highlights Its Touchy Police Role," New York Times, May 15, 1978, p. 1.

(224) See "Massed Allied Warships: Warning to Iran on Strait," New York Times, October 17, 1980, p. A14, discussing a French squadron of six ships at Djibouti; and "Strategically Situated Djibouti Finds That It Has Many 'Benefactors,' " ibid., June 12, 1980, p. A14 wherein aid to the small country from France, Saudi Arabia, Iraq, and Kuwait is discussed. U.S. naval access there is also noted, as are periodic visits by Soviet "scientific vessels." Also, "Indian Ocean: Focus of Super-power Confrontation," Middle East Intelligence Survey, February 16-29, 1980, vol. 7, no. 22, p. 175. Herein, it is said that "based in Djibouti, Mayotte and Reunion, the French forces usually consist of a helicopter carrier with embarked marines, two or three destroyers, a Polaris-type submarine, minesweepers, landing craft, support ships, and air force units at the land bases."

(225) "YAR: France Interested in Constructing Naval Base," Defense and Foreign Affairs' Weekly Report on Strategic Middle Eastern Affairs, August 10, 1977, vol. 3, no. 32.

(226) This is discussed in Stephen S. Roberts, "French Naval Policy Outside of Europe" (paper delivered at meeting of International Studies Association, Section on Military Studies, Kiawah Island, S.C., November 8, 1978). Roberts draws heavily from Gen. André Beaufré, An Introduction to Strategy (New York: Praeger, 1965). See also "Giscard Gives French Foreign Policy a Gaullist Look," New York Times, March 25, 1980, p. A10, which also discusses France's role in repelling a Libyan-backed incursion into Tunisia in the foregoing context.

(227) The eleven-nation European consortium which has been engaged in the Ariane rocket testing program has utilized a launching base at Kourou in French Guiana (actually a French overseas département), which is favorably located near the Equator to maximize lift-off capability. See "From Jungle Outpost, Europe Readies a Space Age Challenge," New York Times, June 16, 1981, p. C1.

(228) See "Massed Allied Warships: Warning to Iran on Strait," New York Times, October 17, 1980, p. A14.

(229) See "A New Ostpolitik?" The Economist, August 30, 1980, pp. 12-13.

(230) See the introductory and summary chapters of Edward Kolodziej and Robert Harkavy, Security Policies of Developing States (Lexington, Mass.: D.C. Heath, 1981).

(231) For one general analysis of China's growing naval capability, see L. Bruce Swanson, Jr., "China's Navy and Foreign Policy," Survival 21, 4 (July/August 1979): 146-154. He notes the primary focus of China's naval problems as in adjacent waters involving the Tonkin Gulf, and the Spratly and Paracel Islands.

(232) See "Malta, an Oft-Conquered Isle Seeks a Few Good Friends," New York Times, October 10, 1979, p. A2, wherein it is noted that "Peking has built the Red China Dry Dock to handle supertankers."

(233) Chinese access to Pakistan could yet take another, unexpected form, as bruited in "Taking a New Road to China: The Karakorum Highway," New York Times Magazine, December 2, 1979, pp. 38ff. Herein,

> For Peking the KKH is a way around the specter of Russian encirclement. China is locked into a 4,673-mile border with the hostile Soviet Union, and the Russian fleet at Vladivostok could blockade her coasts. To China's south lies Vietnam, a former friend turned new foe, and to the southwest sprawls India, an untrusted neighbor. The KKH opens up a backdoor through Pakistan to the Arabian Sea and the West.

(234) Within its own territorial bailiwick, India has deployed Soviet-supplied warships to the Andaman Islands. See "India: Navy Deploys Seven Vessels to Port Blair," Defense and Foreign Affairs Daily 6, 27 (February 10, 1977).

(235) See John Ostheimer and Gary Buckley, "Nigeria's Security Policy" in Kolodziej and Harkavy, Security Policies.

(236) See "Japan Warships Visiting Singapore," New York Times, October 6, 1969, p. 11.

(237) See again "Massed Allied Warships: Warning to Iran on Strait," NYT, October 17, 1980, p. A14.

(238) See "Barbados Bars Angola Flights," Washington Post, December 19, 1975, p. A20, wherein Trinidad and Tobago, and Barbados are discussed. U.S. pressures were said to have been successful in stopping transits via Barbados and Trinidad and Tobago, but not via Guyana, en route from Havana to Guinea Bissau. In ibid., January 31, 1976, "Canada Bars Cuban Flights to Angola," p. 5, it was reported that Canada had refused use of Gander International Airport in Newfoundland as a stopping-off point en route to Angola, but only following U.S. protests of a couple of transits.

(239) Israel's reported earlier use of Ethiopian-controlled islands in the Red Sea (later to be utilized by the USSR) is reported in "Ethiopia: Israeli Bases in Operation?" Defense and Foreign Affairs' Weekly Report on Strategic Middle Eastern Affairs, January 19, 1977, vol. 2, no. 3.

(240) "Pakistan Said to Offer to Base Troops on Saudi Soil," New York times, August 20, 1980, p. A5.

(241) In some cases, this may also involve traditional types of access, as for cases of "hot pursuit" involving neighboring countries. See, for example, "Thais Letting Pol Pot Forces Pass Through Territory," New York Times, April 26, 1979, p. A2.

(242) See, inter alia, "Saudi Ports Handle Iraqi War Supplies," New York Times, November 21, 1980, p. A14; and "Iraqis Said to Get About 100 Tanks," New York Times, February 4, 1981, p. A4.

(243) See again "Soviet Setbacks: Quiet Diplomacy Brings Advances For U.S., Europe in Western Africa," Washington Post, May 31, 1978, p. A1 wherein Senegal's granting of access for U.S. C-141 transports carrying French Foreign Legion jeeps and some drivers is discussed.

(244) In "Shortcut on Cyprus Overshadows Mideast Peace Efforts," Washington Post, February 24, 1978, p. A19, it is reported there was a small crisis between Kenya and Egypt over the former's seizure of an Egyptian aircraft overflying Kenya en route to Somalia with ammunition.

(245) "U.S. Charges Soviet Mounts Big Airlift to Ethiopian Army," New York Times, December 14, 1977, p. 1.

(246) There is no extant, general analysis of base denial activities, strategies, and rationales. Much of what is involved is covered, however, in Alvin Cottrell, "Soviet Views of U.S. Overseas Bases," Orbis 7, 1 (Spring 1963): 77-95.

(247) Ibid., notes the Soviet emphasis on "neutralizing" U.S. basing hosts and on "disengagement" in Europe and elsewhere, the latter a euphemism for disarmament, i.e., the disappearance of the U.S. basing presence.

(248) The general Soviet perspective on U.S. bases – or at least that for propaganda consumption – is outlined in "Soviet General Comments on U.S. 'Bases Strategy,' " broadcast on Radio Sofia, as reported in FBIS, USSR International Affairs, September 9, 1976, commenting on an article by Soviet Prof. Maj.-Gen. Rayir Simonyan.

(249) FBIS, USSR International Affairs, February 1, 1977, under "World 'Political Climate' Opposes S. Atlantic Bloc."

(250) FBIS, USSR International Affairs/Southeast Asia, reporting on broadcast, Oct. 27, 1976, under "U.S. Interest in Military Base in Indonesia Hit." See also January 12, 1977, under "Attempts to Make ASEAN Military Bloc Denounced."

(251) See, for illustrations, FBIS, USSR International Affairs, March 22, 1977, broadcast under "U.S. Omega System Base in Australia Threat to World Security;" ibid., March 22, 1977, under "U.S. Hopes to Re-open Bases in Thailand," ibid., January 17, 1977, under "Bahrein Reportedly Asks U.S. to Close Naval Base."

(252) See ibid., August 25, 1976, under "Sardinian Protest Over U.S. Base Shows Dissatisfaction," and ibid., October 6, 1976, under "Yokosuka Protests Presence of U.S. Carrier 'Midway.' "

(253) See ibid., January 10, 1977, under "Bahrein Reportedly Asks U.S. to Close Naval Base."

(254) Quoted from ibid., January 26, 1977, under "Oman's Qabus to Allow U.S. to Use Al-Masirah Base."

(255) Ibid., January 10, 1977, "Bahrein Reportedly Asks U.S. to Close Naval Base."

(256) Ibid., January 17, 1977, under "Pravda Comments on Weisner's Visit to Bangkok," and ibid., November 16, 1976, under "U.S. Military Tramples Thailand's National Dignity."

(257) See, for example, FBIS, USSR International Affairs, August 20, 1976, under "Sardinian Protest Over U.S. Base Shows Dissatisfaction."

(258) See FBIS, USSR International Affairs, November 16, 1976, under "U.S. Attempts to 'Annex' Micronesia Contradict Detente," ibid., November 19, 1976, under "Tass Reports on UN Vote on U.S., U.K. Possessions," which focuses on the "right to self-determination of the people of American Samoa." See also ibid., October 22, 1976, under "UNGA Condemns French Occupation of Mayotte Island."

(259) This is discussed in the previously cited Washington Post article, "Soviet Setbacks: Quiet Diplomacy Brings Advances For U.S., Europe in Western Africa," Washington Post, May 31, 1978, p. A1.

(260) For a general analysis, see Adeed Dawisha, "Saudi Arabia's Search for Security" (London: IISS, 1980), Adelphia Paper no. 158, which provides extensive data on Saudi military and economic aid (including the financing of others' arms acquisitions).

(261) See "Mintoff Appears Headed for a Slim Victory in Malta," New York Times, September 20, 1976, p. 2, for a discussion of Libyan attempts to deny the West use of Malta.

(262) See, for instance, FBIS, Southern Africa, December 14, 1976, under "Ratsiraka, Seychelles President Discuss Diego Garcia Base."

(263) See Claudia Wright, "Iraqi Diplomatic Strategy," New York Times, June 5, 1980, p. A23.

(264) This is discussed in Robert G. Weinland, "Superpower Access to Support Facilities in the Third World: Effects and Their Causes" (paper delivered at meeting of International Studies Assoc., Philadelphia, March 18-21, 1981); and in "Iraq: Frustration in the Gulf," Middle-East Intelligence Survey, July 16-31, 1980, vol. 8, no. 8, pp. 60-61.

(265) See "Senegal, Once France's Star Colony, Sees Glory Dim," New York Times, September 17, 1980, p. A2.

(266) See FBIS, USSR International Affairs, January 21, 1977, under "Mozambique Disproves Western Claims of Soviet Base," and ibid., October 15, 1976 under "Soviet Bases in Mozambique Denied as 'Fabrication.' " Another example, this time relating to India, is ibid., January 27, 1977, under "Saxbe Falsely Claims USSR Seeks Base in Indian Ocean."

(267) See, for instance, ibid., January 11, 1977, under "Soviet Research Ship Visits South Pacific Islands," wherein a voyage of a Soviet scientific research ship to various Southwest Pacific Islands and New Zealand is discussed, for instance, involving a project on "ecosystems of islands and their rational utilization."

(268) See "The U.S. Airlift Has Growing Strategic Role," New York Times, November 15, 1975, p. 9. For data on the range and payload capacities of various U.S. transport aircraft, see Toye, "Projection of U.S. Power," pp. 11-12, who discusses the future impact on basing requirements of the C-141 "stretch" and refueling program and the strengthening of C-5 wings.

(269) See Blechman and Kaplan, Force Without War, for an elaborate attempt at quantifying various aspects of coercive diplomacy and the political consequences of "presence."

(270) See "Technology is Essential to Arms Verification," New York Times, August 14, 1979, p. C1; "Soviet Spies Got Data on Satellites Intended for Monitoring Arms Pact," ibid., April 29, 1979, p. 1; and "U.S. Increases Reliance on Intelligence Satellites," ibid., December 18, 1979, p. 1.

(271) For adumbrations of the Reagan Administration's new arms transfer policy, see "The Hardware Store is Open and Customers Come Running," New York Times, June 21, 1981, p. E21.

6 Basing and Geopolitical Theories

Toward the late 1970s, there occurred a somewhat surprising and only partly explicable recrudescence of the almost forgotten term "geopolitics," which had been consigned for over a generation to history's dustbin. Whether the new upsurge in usage reflected mere semantic faddism or whether it presaged some significant, durable new ideological tides in the West remained unclear.

There were clear signs of a growing reaction to the post-Vietnam zeitgeist; to easy assumptions about millenial "new world orders," a revolutionary "global consciousness" and of interdependence (the idyllic "global village") as a positive norm.(1) This trend was earlier partly masked by the outcome of the 1976 U.S. election, but perhaps better reflected by conservative trends in other English-speaking democracies and even in Scandinavia.

Reagan's election seemed somewhat to underscore such a trend (more recent elections in Europe seemed to contradict it), though, of course, domestic economic concerns largely produced his election victory. More fundamentally, one might have sensed an almost unconscious groping for broad conceptualizations of the very nature of the contemporary strategic competition; to encompass variously the nuclear balance, shifting ideological currents, resource shortages and economic warfare, and the changing basis of spatial competition in an era claimed by many to be moving beyond simple bipolarity and "containment."

We shall here discuss the evolving major powers' competition for overseas military access in the context of the traditional corpus of geopolitical theories, and of some of its more contemporary echoes and updatings. The reciprocal link here is not easily established. A mapping of the spatial power relationships between the major contending nations of various eras is, of course, what geopolitics is fundamentally all about. As such, the global or regional systems of basing facilities and other forms of military access constitute an important part of the geopolitical equation, both objectively in terms of real and potential relative military power, and perhaps in a more symbolic sense as well, denoting the more subjective aspects of status, position and "presence." But then, overseas bases may be said to constitute only one aspect of the spatial basis of power, as the size, location, and resources of the home base are obviously also very telling of geopolitical advantage and disadvantage.(2) Bases are an element of a nation's power and one measure of its diplomacy, but then, its power will also determine and be reflected by the extent of its overseas access.   Finally, the geographical locales of the competition for bases may tell us much about the broader basis of the global struggle at any given time.

These matters must, as we shall see, be understood within the context of the fundamental nature of the present international system. Older geopolitical theories rather assumed either or both major power conquests of large land domains (and the aspiration for more such conquests) and a tendency toward uncontested global sea control by the dominant maritime power. Nowadays, the international "norms" which virtually preclude imperial conquest (and the realities of 150-plus sovereign states) and the long-time absence of high-seas naval conflict (which could, after all, easily trigger a nuclear war) have perhaps rendered other geopolitical frameworks anachronistic. Instead, the combination of global ideological conflict, "surrogate" or "local" wars, and seemingly endless arms races, has been superimposed upon a spatial chessboard which has featured constant competition for basing access, related mostly to the future contingency of war, but often both merely symbolic and grimly serious. And, hence, the status of that competition at any given time provides about the best available indicator of the geographical patterns of that conflict.   The aforementioned "norms," virtually precluding outright overseas conquest, assure that competition will be over points d'appui, and "functional network control," rarely involving large-scale conquest. But, of course, there might one day be a major superpower war, in which case basing access might indeed be a crucial determinant of victory or defeat.

DEFINING GEOPOLITICS: THEORY, IDEOLOGY, AND SEMANTIC CONFUSION

In the past few years, the term "geopolitics" has come to be used in such a variety of meanings that it is no longer clear just what it means. Like the heavily belabored terms "imperialism," "colonialism," and "interdependence," it has come to mean almost everything, and there-fore perhaps almost nothing, at least for someone searching for empirically based definitions. But the growing use of the term has become important in another way, for it appears that "geopolitics" and "geopolitical thinking" have become virtual code words, viewed either positively or pejoratively, in the war of words between polarized elements of the U.S. foreign policy establishment. This war of words is of course very important, as it expresses broad, divergent, ideological perspectives on the ends and means of national diplomacy.

By the late 1970s, the term "geopolitics" had become strikingly ubiquitous in the American elite press and in the pronouncements of leading politicians. A hint of what had become involved was illustrated by Newsweek magazine's use of it no less than three times in a single short article entitled "Carter as Arms Merchant," which depicted his administration's difficulties in hewing to the moralistic and restrictive arms-sales policy promised during the 1976 election campaign (subsequently formalized in a Presidential Decision Memorandum) in the face of the usual realities of world politics.(3) The article referred to the "central focus of this new geopolitical attention" in the Horn of Africa,(4) and quoted one Carter aide as saying, almost poetically, that "on all of these things, you have to trim your sails and deal with the geopolitics of the moment."(5) More broadly, in an almost wistful tone, Newsweek also averred that "the arms trade isn't the only field in which geopolitical (emphasis mine) reality has forced Carter to modify his views in recent weeks," and that "most conspicuously, he has lowered his voice on human rights, in response to protests from allies and antagonists alike."(6)

Then, consider the following revealing quotation from the New York Times' financial pages in the wake of American freezing of Iranian assets amid the hostage crisis.

> Analysts here also contend that the United States did not fully appreciate how unsettling the freezing of Iranian deposits was to many overseas investors. Many operators thus did not realize that much of the action on gold reflected this special circumstance, which would not continue to contribute to higher prices in the face of ebbing geopolitical tensions.(7)

Hence it appeared that a concept which in past generations had referred primarily to grand strategy, to the competitive advantages of certain continental or other locations; and to macrolevel theory on a very simplified, almost abstract, global plane, had been brought down to the microlevel of day-to-day diplomatic maneuvering, with essentially geographic distinctions appearing of only incidental importance. There was also some irony in the current tendency to equate geopolitics with "realism" (in the Morgenthauian sense) as a norm of diplomacy, in light of the near-total divorce of the "geopolitical" and "realist" schools reflected in the scholarship of the 1930s and 1940s.(8)

Newsweek was by no means alone in its new-found use of the term. Removed from the toils of office, Henry Kissinger, too, had begun to use it. In criticizing the Carter administration's allegedly tepid response to Soviet-Cuban moves in Africa, he spoke of "the presumption that we are facing a global geopolitical challenge incompatible with any definition of detente."(9) In his wide-ranging and pessimistic testimony on the SALT II pact, he asserted that "the geopolitical equilibrium must be maintained lest radical forces hostile to the West gain such momentum that they appear as the irresistible wave of the future."(10) He later said he could support ratification of the treaty only "if it is accompanied by a vigorous expression of the Senate's view of the linkage between SALT and Soviet geopolitical conduct." In outlining what he claimed was an ominously tilting overall military balance in favor of the Soviets, incidentally, the shrinkage of American access to overseas bases was cited as a major element of American decline, along with the Soviets' expansion of basing access and their establishment of vast arms depots in Libya and Ethiopia "which will enable the Soviet Union to move its own or proxy troops rapidly to their prepositioned weapons."(11)

Press reports further indicated that there was an increasing incidence of debate within the U.S. foreign policy bureaucracy over whether – or to what extent – the United States ought or ought not "play the geopolitical game." The obvious implication was, of course, that it was not the only game in town, if it ever had been. As we have noted in our introduction, rival new games – or perhaps really old games in new rhetorical garb – were in evidence, stressing the primacy of international economics and international income redistribution, human rights, "morality" in diplomacy, and arms control and disarmament.(12) Vietnam had seemed to produce a curious full circle back to the 1930s, though there were serious arguments over whether isolationism or "neoisolationism" adequately described some of the new currents.

In current usage, then, "geopolitics" had actually come to assume several basic but overlapping meanings, either explicitly or implicitly, construed either broadly or narrowly, and sometimes incorporating outright contradictions. Admixed with traditional usage still adhered to by some, and here subsequently to be discussed, these may be broken down as follows:

- A euphemism or code-word denoting the playing of traditional balance-of-power politics; looking back to the classical age of diplomacy, presumed to contain an almost nineteenth-century flavor of amorality in its absence of sentiment.
- A stress on geography or territoriality at the expense of ideology as explanatory of diplomacy and alignments, though as Kissinger may have implied, this does not preclude the use of ideology as an instrument of geopolitical cum territorial goals.
- A stress on short- or long-run maximization of national power and interest (defined in terms of territory and resources) and on total war and diplomacy, a throwback to what is normally assumed to have been characteristic of the post-1945 Cold War. Although the diplomatic norms and practices of twentieth-century total war and those of the classical period (seventeenth to nineteenth centuries) are commonly considered very distinct, near opposites, geopolitics now appears used to describe aspects of both regarding the conduct of diplomacy.
- Related to the above, a mode of waging diplomacy and/or warfare in contrast to – or in conflict with – idealistic, millenial strivings for arms control, universally applied liberal values (human rights), and economic development; to the now familiar "new world order" or "global consciousness" themes.

• In its broadest and perhaps vaguest sense, "geopolitics" becomes merely coterminous with power politics or with all of international relations, and merely denotes the user's verbal concession that such matters are endemically conflict-ridden, hence, a rather simple truism.

Cutting across some of the above definitions – in a way summing them up – is that by Shahram Chubin, centering on the contrasting foreign policy perspectives of the two contending U.S. foreign policy elites of recent years, respectively called the geopolitical and regionalist perspectives.(13)

GEOPOLITICS AND REGIONALISM

The differences between the Carter Administration and the Republican Administration preceding it were less basic than often appeared, but, as was the case with parallel polarization in academia between geopolitical and regionalist approaches to the Third World, the emphases were quite different. The debate about the merits of these two approaches is important because it contains what promises to be a continuing divergence in perspective about the sources of third-world instability and the appropriate responses to that instability.

The primary difference between the two schools lies in their assessments of the centrality of the competition with the USSR and the role of force. While the geopoliticians continue to see the world in these terms, the regionalists point to the expanded agenda of world affairs and to multi-polarity, complexity and diversity. The one therefore focuses on Soviet power, the importance of regional balances and allies and immediate American interests. The other, more relaxed about military power, seeks to avoid open-ended involvements while pursuing long-run world-order interests. The geopolitician seeks to cultivate and reward allies, stressing American dependability and credibility; the regionalist emphasizes the compatibility (or incompatibility) of allies with the values of the United States and advocates dissociation. The former fears an eroding balance, divided allies and set-backs that reverberate to the global disadvantage of the United States; the latter fears entanglement, irrelevance and reflexive linkage. The geopolitician sees the risks of war increasing because of uncertainties created by regional retreat; the regionalist, seeking a more limited definition of security, cringes at muscular machismo and at loose talk of "credibility." The one looks to military security, strong leadership and resilience as the key to world order; the other believes that world order is nurtured by adjustment, restraint, bargaining and moral example.

These views lead to quite different assessments of the function of military power and of its relationship with the exploitation of third-world conflicts. The geopoliticians assert the continuing and inescapable centrality of military power, and they stress its importance in deterring the USSR. They demand American leadership of the Allies and seek to reassure friendly states in the Third World. It follows that regional military balances are therefore seen as especially critical, both because strategic parity encourages probing and because the United States is reluctant to become directly involved in defending her interests. In short, military power still determines the risk calculus of the opportunistic exploitation of third-world instabilities. The regionalists, on the contrary, are impressed by the limited utility of military power (which they expect that the USSR will also eventually understand), and they see regional successes as determined less by power than by local political conditions. The "prevailing local winds" are the principal determinants of influence; the trick of diplomacy is to adjust to them and thus inhibit Soviet advances. The regionalists focus on the constraints operating on Soviet power (which, they emphasize, is one-dimensional), on the intractability of many problems to solution by military power, on the strength of indigenous natinalisms and on the costs of alignment with third-world states which face multiple threats and invariably fail to meet minimal standards on human rights.

In short, the modern use of the term "geopolitics" had come curiously to express what some had come to think of as an almost anachronistic manner of conducting diplomacy, with an emphasis on power, national interest, overseas access, and territorial control. Those who worried about its rise used the term almost in irony, with a tinge of sarcasm, almost as if "the resort to geopolitics" represented an unwanted concession to reality under pressure, something one resorted to when ideals failed or had to be compromised. Hence the reference to the "geopolitics of the moment" implies a temporary aberration and a desire to move it out of the way to allow for unhindered pursuit of the new Wilsonianism. What is most reminiscent, of course, is the dualism of "realism" and "idealism" ably portrayed for the interwar period by E.H. Carr, and also the kinds of grudging concessions to the necessity for the (after World War I) disgraced balance-of-power politics arrived at on the eve of another world war.(14)

Aside from the growth of Soviet military might and overseas access, the growing use of an old concept was caused by anxieties over the ominous specter of world resource shortages, by the late 1970s a dominant concern in the West, all the more so because it promised to be a near-permanent and intractable problem. Again, almost subconscious public rhetoric may offer some clues. In 1977, roughly coincident with the Newsweek article, a New York Times interview with South African Prime Minister Vorster, primarily devoted to southern African racial problems, began with the following question: "Would you give me your view, in the world context, of the geopolitical position of South Africa and how it relates to the East-West competition in terms of resources?"(15) Vorster's reflexive response was to state statistics on South Africa's relative role as an industrial power within Africa, comparing it with America's share of world industrial production. As the response was devoid of any military-geographic context, the reader was left to wonder whether it merely constituted a non sequitur or whether it involved a new interpretation of geopolitics with a primarily economic cast.

There are, of course, more traditional and more formal definitions of geopolitics, much argued over, but which generally stress the nexus between geography, strategy, and politics (or political science). Saul Cohen, for instance, one of the several major chroniclers of geopolitical theory, states that "the essence of geopolitical analysis is the relation of international political power to geographical setting," and also repeats the obvious truism that geopolitical views vary with the changing setting and with man's interpretation of the nature of this change.(16) Central to such a definition, as he sees it, are the geographical "realities" which consist of landform distributions and patterns of movement, with population distributions and resources complementary. Cohen was writing at an earlier point when resource distributions may not have been perceived as so utterly crucial as they are today. He asserts that geopolitical analysis, to the extent "value-free," has two major aspects: (1) the description of geographic settings as they relate to power, and (2) the laying out of spatial frameworks that embrace interacting power units.(17)

Peltier and Pearcy, coauthors of a work on military geography, write of the art or science of geopolitics as "utilizing geography as guidelines for political purposes," which is said to provide a "common meeting ground of military geography, strategy, and diplomacy."(18) Richard Hartshorne, compiler of perhaps the best short bibliographical review of the field, stresses the necessity for defining political geography as separate and distinct from political science and/or international relations, and defines geopolitics as "simply the application of the knowledge and techniques of political geography to the problems of international relations."(19)

Some writers, earlier convinced that the history of interwar German geopolitics had given the term a permanent and false pseudo-scientific mystique, prefer not to use the term at all, or if so, to carefully qualify and denature it. Harold and Margaret Sprout, therefore, prefer merely to discuss "geopolitical hypotheses." According to them, there have historically been three basic types, alternating in primacy: (1) "Those where the distribution of political power and influence in the world are explained or predicted mainly as a function of geopolitical configurations, i.e., the layout of continents, oceans, and connecting seas;" (2) "Those in which political distributions are explained or predicted as functions of variations among nations in security of access to useful earth material, especially non-human sources of energy;" and (3) "Those which see power and influence as functions of variations of climate."(20) As we shall discuss, present hypotheses, in contrast to those purveyed earlier in the century, have tended to shift attention from the first to the second of these, though they are by no means unconnected or mutually exclusive. Both can, of course, be related to basing access.

It would appear, nonetheless, that the present vernacular use of the term "geopolitics," defined primarily in terms of the practice of traditional balance-of-power politics, has strayed somewhat from the earlier emphases of political geography, albeit with the retention of basic common concerns. To the extent this is more than superficially meaningful (this writer for one suspects that it is), the reasons would appear to lie in the previously discussed groping for new conceptualizations of grand strategy, involving both substance and style.

The earlier geopolitical writings were clearly underpinned by an essentially Hobbesian world view, an acceptance of global power struggle as endemic. With that as a given, students of geopolitics then sought answers about who might then prevail and why. The newer, recent vogue of geopolitics in the United States appears representative of a return to a widespread concession of struggle as endemic, and is then also a philosophical basis for a program of action. The growing prominence of basing and access problems, meanwhile, has highlighted the visibly geographic nature of the contemporary global struggle for power, if for no other reason than that press reporting of such matters is often accompanied by maps.

THE GEOPOLITICAL TRADITION, POSITIONING, AND OVERSEAS ACCESS

Although geopolitics as a "science," pseudo-science, or discipline (or merely a shorthand term for the cross-discipline of political geography) is a relatively new development, dating back only a century or so, some scholars have traced the evolvement of recognizable geopolitical perspectives well back into history. Such perspectives have long been reflective of the dominant political currents and power configurations of the times, though much earlier, of course, they necessarily also reflected the limited knowledge of global geography imposed by states of the art in transportation and cartography. It is now sometimes easy to forget that it is only in the last few centuries that one could speak of a truly global political system qua system which might form the basis for truly global political cognitions.

Saul Cohen, for one, sees a consistent tendency on the part of theorists from the ancients to the present to hold geopolitical perspectives which have reflected "the world that matters" – the essence of spatial and power relationships among the dominant powers.(21) Earlier, of course, this was a merely regional, subglobal matter, and such perspectives seem inevitably always to have been self-centered, "Ptolemaic." Over a long period, Cohen traces explanations and images devised to explain disparities of strength through the Old Testament, the various Nile and Euphrates civilizations, Greece, Rome, and the bipolar division in the Middle Ages between Christian Europe and Muslim Asia.(22)

According to Cohen, the Portuguese efforts to circumnavigate Africa in the fourteenth and fifteenth centuries produced the first major attempt at breaking the continentally oriented geopolitical thinking of Christian Europe, and a "revolutionary strategy freed of older insular concepts."(23) This view, he claims, "matured into a truly global strategic view as Europe's national states began to carve out colonial empires, acquiring key islands and coastal enclaves in their drives to unite ocean basins."(24)

It is now easy to forget just how primitive the geopolitical imagery of fifteenth-century Europe actually was. As Boxer notes,

> Most medieval maps reflected either the Ptolemaic belief that the Indian Ocean was a landlocked sea or else the Macrobian conception of an open seaway to the Indian Ocean round a (highly distorted) southern Africa. South of what is now the contested Spanish Saharan coast, there were tales of a "Green Sea of Darkness" from which it was thought there was no possibility of return.(25)

Portugal's stress then on maintenance of dispersed points d'appui rather than large-scale territorial control, of course, is strikingly resonant with contemporary access diplomacy and in contrast to the subsequent lengthy interregnum of western colonialism.(26) Its manpower resources could not, at any rate, have allowed for much beyond control of coastal trade entrepots and scattered fortified points.

Between the Middle Ages and the nineteenth-century origins of modern geopolitical theory, there was gradual evolvement of the now familiar themes of overlapping global views. Kant's universalism, the hierarchical systems of regional divisions within a unified globe of Humboldt and Ritter, and Ratzel's analogy of the state as an "organism" lent particular uniqueness by the space it occupied, all antedated later themes.(27) Raum and Lage, Blut and Boden, and also theories variously stressing seapower and landpower all emerged during the nineteenth century. There was also an increasing tendency to perceive a correlation of large continental areas with political power. Ratzel early saw the future in the large continental land formations of North America, Russia, Australia, and South America, even despite the caveats imposed by qualitative bases of power and possibly asymmetric advantages resulting from location.(28) The assumptions related to power and dominance were, of course, defined primarily in terms of strictly military geography.

The progression of premodern geopolitical theory during the twentieth century can be analyzed for the most part according to varying attributions of primacy to landpower, seapower, and airpower — and their relation to strategic location — though most are sufficiently sophisticated so as to take into account a multiplicity of factors even if a single one came to be deemed dominant.

Halford Mackinder, an Englishman first coming to prominence around the turn of the twentieth century, is perhaps the most famous of the twentieth-century geopolitical theorists. His "The Geographical Pivot of History," written in 1904, forms a point of departure for all subsequent writings, has apparently heavily influenced the strategic perceptions of major nations, and in turn spawned some important countertheories, albeit all focused in one way or another on the preeminence of the Eurasian continental heartland and the natural rivalry between it and the rimland (or, in Mackinder's terminology, "marginal crescent").(29)

Basic to Mackinder's theory, subsequently altered and evolved over some forty years, was the perception of the inner area of Eurasia as the pivot region of world politics, and of the control of this heartland as the potential basis for world domination, assuming the will as well as the capacity to conquer (see Fig. 6.1 and Fig. 6.2). Somewhat vaguely, control of the heartland was said to provide the basis for "outflanking" the maritime world, whether through outright conquest or through an earlier anticipated form of political or economic "Finlandization" was not clear.(30) Meanwhile, others such as James Fairgrieve, utilizing a less Eurocentered perspective, pointed out that China's location (and population) also provided the possible basis for such domination from the eastern side of the Eurasian heartland.(31) Again, what exactly was meant by "domination" was not entirely clear; whether it ultimately pointed to a hegemonic or hierarchical world system as per one of Morton Kaplan's ideal-types, or short of that, a more effective, autarkic "continental" system patterned after Napoleon's strategy against Britain, which could deny the heartland's resources and markets to peripheral naval powers.(32)

Mackinder's views evolved, with time and the unfolding of additional events, to allow for an expansion of the earlier demarcations of the heartland pivot area, which had originally included that part of Eastern Europe and North Asia characterized by polar drainage, and which stressed defensive depth, potential resources, and invulnerability to seaborne attack. The image was that of a large and presumed autarkic fortress, defended to the south by mountainous ramparts and to the north by nearly unapproachable, icebound sea routes. The heartland power would not, of course, require overseas bases as a major element of its power, though Mackinder was aware that the resource base of a dominant heartland power might ultimately enable it to mount a naval challenge to the rival maritime powers if it could develop the requisite shipbuilding capacity and an "oceanic frontage."(33) If that occurred, the latter could be beaten or at least stalemated at their own game, while continuing to labor under severe disadvantages with respect to projection of land military power onto the Eurasian continent.

Although the heartland concept was later revised to include the Tibetan and Mongolian upland courses of the great rivers of India and China, more centrally, it came to a focus on the military importance of the north-south belt of Eastern Europe running between the Baltic and Black Seas, from Estonia to Bulgaria. Summing up his theory in relation to the basis for global domination, Mackinder enunciated in 1919 his famous dictum: "Who rules East Europe commands the Heartland: Who rules the Heartland commands the World-Island: Who rules the World-Island commands the world."(34)

The prospect of an upcoming struggle between Russia and Germany for domination of Eastern Europe and hence the heartland had a powerful impact on Mackinder, whose ideas, after all, reflected centuries-old British fears about a continental land-power coalition

Fig. 6.1. Mackinder's World – 1904.

Source: Saul B. Cohen, Geography and Politics in a World Divided, 2nd edition, Oxford University Press, New York, 1983.

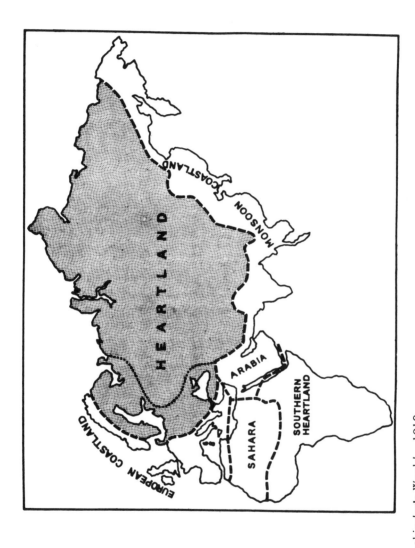

Fig. 6.2. Mackinder's World – 1919.

Source: Saul B. Cohen, Geography and Politics in a World Divided, 2nd edition, Oxford University Press, New York, 1983.

which could dominate Europe and hence negate traditional British balancing politics on the continent. The possibility of a dominant German-Russian condominium over the heartland was also contemplated as an alternative to the physical dominance of the one over the other.

Over the past sixty years, Mackinder's basic thesis, in its several forms, has been subjected to extensive exegesis and revision. One way or another, however, its basic substance has dominated geostrategic thought, reflected in theoretical German geopolitics and Nazi foreign policy, in Soviet foreign policy with its long-held spatial cognition of "capitalist encirclement," and, of course, most graphically in the postwar U.S. containment policy.(35) Some writers, Robert Walters for instance, claim that the heartland thesis has formed the basis for the U.S. postwar strategic nuclear doctrine(s), albeit not explicitly stated, with its perceived necessity for the balancing of the (earlier) Sino-Soviet population and land army advantage with a mass destruction equalizer.(36) Still others, Colin Gray for instance, assert ironically that now well beyond the interwar heyday of geopolitics, Mackinder has never been more relevant, particularly given the Soviet achievement of nuclear strategic "rough equivalence" or better, which removes the hitherto American "equalizer" of its geographical disadvantage.(37)

There are, however, some views to the contrary. Alan Henrikson, for instance, in a well-researched study replete with considerable evidence from maps, has related the corpus of geopolitical writings and its heartland/rimland imagery to the more contemporary vogue of "center" and "periphery."(38) In doing so, he has demonstrated how throughout much of the post-1945 era, both U.S. and European images had come to acquire an "America-centric" world view, one even frequently reflected in North Pole-centered azimuthal map projections as well as 0° meridians running through Washington rather than Greenwich. There was a sense of a new reconstellation of forces brought about by Europe's collapse, and of the onset of an American century as trumpeted by Henry Luce and others. New technological developments in weapons and logistics, meanwhile, were thought to have eroded the long-held military-geographic basis of the traditional Eurasia-centered heartland thesis, producing a new and fundamental geopolitical "paradigm shift."(39) By 1973, however, Vietnam, "detente," the decline of U.S. economic primacy, and above all, the oil crisis of 1973 itself had diluted the American sense of global centralness, resulting according to Henrikson, for many Americans, in a sense of "geopolitical flux."(40) After this brief interregnum, some were to claim that the inherent basis of traditional geopolitics in the Eurasian heartland had reasserted itself after all, and for all of the traditionally stated reasons.

Mackinder's ideas were absorbed by and integrated into the main body of German geopolitics during the interwar period, represented most notably in the work of Haushofer. The emphasis there was on autarky and lebensraum, Social Darwinism and the assumption of constant struggle, Clausewitzian military theory, Ratzel's devolvement of the world into large states, and Mackinder's pivot in the world island.(41) There were also assumptions about the assumed "naturalness" of north-south combinations of continents, reflected in predictions about the inevitability of a world divided into "pan regions" laid out in longitudinal belts, representing Pan-America, Pan-Asia, and Eur-Africa. Geopolitik represented a virtual apotheosis of geographic determinism (its map distortions aside), leavened with an exaggerated view of states as analogies to struggling organisms. On a more mundane policy level, its central assumptions were those of inevitable conflict over the heartland, the necessity for either dominating or coopting Russia, and also for destroying or neutralizing the encircling British seapower.

To the extent, incidentally, that German geopolitik was hinged on Mackinder's landpower thesis, it tended to denigrate the importance of rimland air and naval bases; or, rather, perceived them as vulnerable to attack from the land. Thus, according to Strausz-Hupé, "Several Geopolitikers, among them Haushofer himself, pointed repeatedly to the fact that Britain's naval bases at Hong Kong and Singapore, though magnificently suited for serving as fleet bases, did not possess adequate defenses against a land attack by a modern army."(42) In these instances at least, they were right.

In the 1940s, Haushofer's German school of geopolitics was fully discredited, morally and practically, and was retrospectively shrugged off as a propaganda rationalization for naked German expansionism.(43) Aside from the crude militarism and racism involved, the "theories" were found wanting in their faulty map perceptions about north-south continental combinations and particularly in their underestimation of the strength of the United States, earlier cavalierly consigned to a role as satellite of the World Island.(44)

Mackinder's was not the only macrolevel, geopolitical world view vying for attention during the early part of the century. Its obverse and rival (in some senses) was Mahan's thesis about the historical primacy of seapower.(45) Mahan stressed the indivisibility of seapower and the long-term military and economic dominance of hegemonic seaborne powers, and above all, the cost advantages of long-distance projection of power by sea by comparison with overland transport. Mahan's thesis, like Mackinder's, was also centered on the crucial Eurasian landmass. Both saw it as the key to global power.   And while stressing total, indivisible control of the sea, Mahan also emphasized that such control could only be achieved by controlling land bases having the advantages of strategic location and defensive depth to hinterlands.

Like Mackinder, Mahan was (with prescience, from today's perspective) obsessed with the spectre of potential Russian power, and he too saw it as unassailable by contrast with the "rim" of the heartland, considered highly vulnerable to control by long-range seapower. At the time he wrote, however, long-range land transport and communications were at a technical and cost disadvantage relative to those by sea (aircraft had not yet entered the equation as a possible balancing factor); indeed, they had been for centuries during the "Columbian Age." Russia, hence, was seen to have had disadvantages as well as the advantage of invulnerability to seaborne attack, resulting from the combination of its weak Central Asian logistical system and the formidable natural barriers along its long southern border. Its later development of a global navy was but dimly perceived, though both Mahan and Mackinder were concerned (on behalf of the Anglo-Saxon powers) about the possibilities of a dominant heartland power becoming a great naval power as well – Napoleon had given a hint of that possibility, even if not consummated. The zone between the 30° and 40° parallels was seen as that of future decisive competition between Britain and Russia. In Mahan's view, Anglo-American naval power (assumed collaborative) would achieve dominance from key land bases surrounding Eurasia because of the inherent advantages of sea-movement over land-movement, which would allow for favorable concentrations of force at decisive, chosen points of conflict. Looked at another way, seapower was claimed to allow for more advantageous use of "indirect" strategies, in the sense later proclaimed by B. Liddell-Hart.(46)

In contrast to Mackinder, and with an almost uncanny prescience for what unfolded in the 1950s, Mahan looked to an alliance between the United States, UK, Germany, and Japan, faced off against Russia and China,(47) perfectly reflective of a heartland-versus-rimland spatial confrontation. But his basic thesis about "the world that mattered," while quite similar to Mackinder's, came to a diametrically opposite conclusion about who and what would dominate. Where Mackinder saw control over Eastern Europe as crucial, Mahan saw as crucial dominance of the rimland littoral, no doubt influenced by the then surprising ability of the colonial powers to control huge populations and areas in India, China, and elsewhere by coercive naval diplomacy and sea-supported outpost garrisons. That, of course, was before Japan exploded the myth of Western military superiority, first in 1905 and then in 1941, and before modern guerrilla warfare and mass-based national liberation movements had rendered such colonial control too costly to sustain.

The rimland naval dominance posited by Mahan, then inspired by the history of several centuries of respective Portuguese, Spanish, Dutch, and British sea control, was heavily dependent on overseas, or "secondary," naval bases.   And from the perspective of the early twentieth century, it was not easy to foresee the end of colonial control and the kind of symmetrical bargaining between naval powers and basing hosts which would later emerge. Indeed, bases were then not so much seen as ingredients of naval dominance, but rather as the natural and near-automatic result of it. During the previous centuries, Britain's control of the seas had allowed it, in wars with its various European rivals, easily to pick off the latter's overseas bases once victories on the high seas had been won, for instance, against France in the eighteenth century in the Caribbean and the Indian Ocean. Only later on, post-decolonization, would a nation such as the United States have a preeminent global navy, but with its access to bases determined far more by quid pro quo bargaining and alliance diplomacy than by the raw facts of naval strength.

The American Nicholas Spykman, writing during the Second World War, produced a variant of Mahan's seapower/rimland thesis – really, a more sophisticated, complex and then current version – then heavily influenced by the fear of Germany and the need to balance her with a combination of Anglo-Saxon seapower and Soviet landpower.(48) His concession of the necessity of a strong landpower to be added to the maritime powers' side of the balance would one day later be reflected in assumptions about America's need to ally with China for analogous reasons. Spykman also perceived Mackinder's marginal crescent as a crucial cockpit of decision, involving Maritime Europe, the Middle East, India, Southeast Asia, and China, with their combined resources, populations, and interior sea lines. (See Fig. 6.3). Reversing Mackinder's famous dictum, he produced the paraphrase: "Who controls the Rimland rules Eurasia; who rules Eurasia controls the destinies of the world."(49)

Spykman was earlier relatively optimistic, with Mahan, about sea and air power control of the rimland, and insistent about the necessity for overseas bases; but with the passage of years and technical developments, he also foresaw that improved land communications were improving the power potential of the heartland power(s). He was not then, of course, able to foresee the future developments of Soviet air and sea power which would alter the basis for contemporary geopolitical perspectives, though he had insisted, somewhat distinct from Mackinder and others, that control of the rimland rarely had been – and was not likely to be – indivisible.

Most fundamentally, Spykman saw seapower around the rimland and in the marginal seas having become crucially reliant on complementary land-based airpower. He did not, however, see this as necessarily meaning that heartland airpower would control the rimlands. Rather, he envisaged a future of intra-rimland conflict,(50) one in which the extra-rimland naval powers might find allies along the rimland as well, perhaps, as in the heartland. The basic Mahan/Mackinder paradigm was here made more complex.

Some political geographers of the last generation were, in pursuing the rimland naval thesis, still more specific about the crucial points of contention in the geopolitical "zones of decision." Hans Weigert, for instance, writing after World War II, placed central emphasis on the "marginal seas" around the Eurasian land mass and their associated outlets and chokepoints.(51) These, he noted, had long been subject to almost uncontested control by Anglo-American naval power, with a few exceptions such as the Sea of Okhotsk. He emphasized the importance, particularly, of maritime highways between the oceans, access to enclosed seas, and channels between insular areas and mainlands.

In the first category, that of maritime highways between two oceans, attention was directed to the Mediterranean system (the Straits of Gibraltar, Sicilian Straits, Suez Canal, Mediterranean Sea, Bab El Mandeb), to the Panama Canal, and to the waterways linking the Indian and Pacific Oceans (Straits of Malacca, Sunda, Singapore, San Bernadino, Suragao, Lombok, Makassar, Torres).(52) Among the important points of access to enclosed seas he found crucial were the

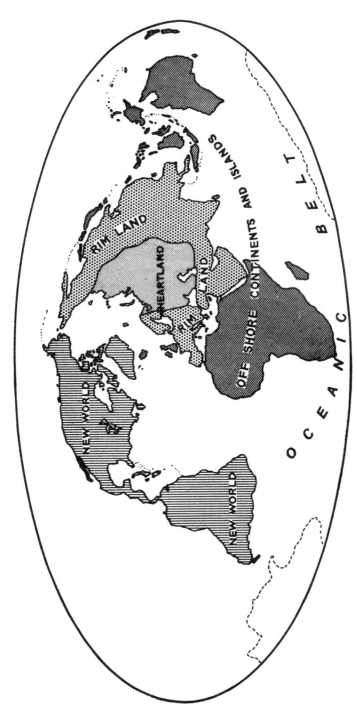

Fig. 6.3. The World of Spykman.

Source: Saul B. Cohen, Geography and Politics in a World Divided, 2nd edition, Oxford University Press, New York, 1983.

Turkish Straits system (Dardanelles, Sea of Marmara, Bosporus), the Baltic Straits system (Kattegat, Skaggerak, the Sound, the Great Belt, Kiel Canal), the St. George's and Irish Channels controlling the southern and northern entrances to the Irish Sea, the various entrances to the Sea of Japan (Tartary, La Pérousse, Tsugaru, Tsushima, and Shimonoseki Straits), and the Straits of Hormuz at the entrance to the Persian Gulf.(53) Important channels cited between insular areas and the mainland were the English Channel, Straits of Formosa, Hainan Strait, Palk Strait, and the straits of Messina, Bonifacio, and Otranto.(54)

Many of the above-listed chokepoints had been foci of military contention during World War II, and thus it is not surprising that perceptions of their importance were retained in its immediate aftermath, even despite what then seemed an assured long-term dominance of Anglo-American naval power. Only later, expanding Soviet naval strength and accompanying basing access, the rise of newer sovereignties and military powers, and even the prospective new Law of the Seas' maritime regime would bring some of these locales to renewed prominence, in a greatly altered context. The Straits of Hormuz, for instance, were to acquire a military/strategic importance hardly foreseen in the 1950s. And one recent article, in espousing a more active forward posture for the U.S. Marine Corps, identified seven chokepoints at which the Soviet navy would have to be denied egress at the outset of war: the G-I-UK Gap, Skaggerak, Straits of Gibraltar, the Turkish Straits, Suez Canal, and the Tartar, La Pérousse, Tsugaru, and Korean Straits.(55) But then, commentators such as Weigert viewed these strategic locations primarily in terms of all-out wartime contingencies, and much less in terms of the kinds of coercive diplomacy, posturing, and "balance of perceptions" which would characterize the recent era.

Theories of airpower dominance formed the third leg of the triangle of traditional geopolitical theory, emerging only during the interwar period after the advent of long-range bombers and aircraft carriers. Its major spokesmen, Douhet and Seversky, foresaw a new pivot area (in Mackinder's terms) in the North Pole region and stressed the mutual vulnerability of the Eurasian and Anglo-Saxon portions of the northern land mass across the Arctic.(56) A future of land, sea, and air routes across the polar world was envisaged. There developed an "airman's global view," which was featured on maps as an azimuthal equidistant projection (replacing the traditional imagery associated with transverse mercator maps) centered on the North Pole, but which also portrayed a distorted sharp division between the Western and Eastern hemispheres, the more so as one moved south toward the equator.(57) Also newly highlighted were the trans-Arctic "great circle routes" which provided the shortest flight distances between the United States and USSR.

The airspace within the Arctic Circle, centered on the North Pole, became perceived as the "central area of decision," where if air supremacy (by air superiority fighters) were achieved, would then allow for full, unhindered destruction of the enemy's homeland. The legacy of Clausewitz was here in evidence, with its emphasis on the destruction of the enemy on the field of battle, as well as an analogy to Mahan's insistence upon the indivisibility of sea control.(58) There is also here an emphasis on one "critical force," the heavy bomber, which now replaced the role of the pre-World War I dreadnought as the ultimate arbiter of battle.(59) Douhet and Seversky wrote, however, before the mixed conclusions of the U.S. Strategic Bombing Survey from World War II raised serious questions about the crucial role of strategic bombing.(60) Even the moderate airpower advocates who recognized that total victory must ultimately be won on the ground, however, perceived the need for first controlling the air to destroy the enemy's war-making potential. All of that, of course, preceded the advent of mutual nuclear deterrence.(61)

Regarding the nexus here of geopolitical frameworks and the importance of overseas bases, the airpower theories appeared even more than land power theories (and in contrast to seapower theories) to deemphasize the necessity for overseas bases. As Seversky wanted the United States to avoid surface combat, he regarded overseas bases as undesirable and unnecessary, except perhaps in the UK.(62) To the extent, however, airpower theories had really been viable (that is, not overtaken eventually by the reality of intercontinental missiles), a considerable premium would still have been placed on fighter bases for airfighting and bomber interception over the polar regions and for long-distance escorting of bombers. Refueling bases for the latter would also be crucial (or bases for tankers), as would early-warning radar installations around the Arctic rim. Canada (particularly Newfoundland and Labrador), Greenland, Iceland, Alaska, and Spitsbergen would become critical areas of access and contention, as indeed some of these areas had been in the early stages of World War II for ferrying materiel from the United States to Britain.

The airpower global view appeared also to disagree with both the landpower and seapower theories about potential dominance by a heartland power, the USSR. John Slessor, one of its advocates, saw the air age actually conferring a disadvantage on the USSR despite its central position. According to him, "air power has turned the vast spaces that were her prime defense against Napoleon and Hindenburg and Hitler into a source of weakness."(63) Further, he stated that "in these days of nearsonic speeds, the depth of penetration necessary to reach some of her vital centres is offset by the area to be defended and the fact that it can be attacked from almost all round the compass."(64) In short, what had normally been thought of as Soviet advantages – size, centrality, and inaccessability – were now thought of as either of no advantage or as disadvantageous, though it was not entirely clear just how the USSR could be attacked from "all round the compass" in the heavy bomber age without the use of bases.

Some geopolitical theorists, for instance George Cressey, actually concluded that "the Heartland" might actually lie in North America rather than in Eurasia, with the former's adequate size, compact shape, central location, good boundaries, access to two oceans, favorable topography and resources, and technological dynamism.(65) Generally,

Cressey's view merely inferred from the power measurements following World War II that technology had transcended location as a determinant of dominant global power.

After 1945 there was a lengthy moratorium on macrolevel geopolitical theorizing; at best, the field became an almost obscure adjunct to that of international relations. The reasons for this have already been noted. The advent of long-range nuclear delivery systems had even given rise to some easy assertions that the territorial foundations of the nation-state had been undermined, that nations' traditional protective shells had become "permeable," and that in the process, factors of size and distance had been rendered relatively marginal.

Furthermore, the fantastic World War II production effort by the United States and the then expected indefinite superiority of U.S. technology had produced a somewhat different interpretation of the relationships between size, location, and power than that familiar to readers of Ratzel and Mackinder. Technological dynamism came to be viewed as the key element of power, in an era of potentially destabilizing qualitative arms races.(66) National power came to be indexed simply and graphically by GNP figures, assumed strongly correlated with technological capacity through the multiplier of per capita GNP.(67) Indeed, industrial and scientific development came to be perceived as the essential end goal of world politics.

During the 1950s and 1960s, little was produced in the West in the way of macrolevel geopolitical theory or global views stressing locational advantages. Geopolitics was submerged beneath the behavioral revolution in international relations scholarship, and strategists were primarily devoted to theories of nuclear deterrence and of limited warfare and counterinsurgency.

One exception was Robert Walters, a maverick who exhumed Mackinder in depicting the American Cold War strategy as essentially based on the old heartland-rimland pattern.(68) Walters was also critical of the total American reliance on nuclear deterrence, and considered sea control and submarine warfare (underseas control) the really crucial future foci of superpower competition. He had no really new global theory to espouse, and was essentially reiterating Spykman's, but with an emphasis now shifted from the rimlands to the high seas and underseas.(69) As such, Walters also anticipated the more diffuse global spatial nature of big-power rivalry which was to emerge in the 1970s when the Soviets leapfrogged the rimland. The conflicts he envisaged, particularly given assumptions about nuclear naval developments, would not necessarily have put a premium on traditional naval bases, but might have focused attention on some new access requirements – land-based ASW hydrophone arrays, land-based ASW aircraft, and perhaps satellite data relay facilities related to ocean surveillance, communications, and navigation.(70)

During the 1970s, the initial stirrings of a resurgent interest in explicitly geopolitical theory was evidenced in the writings of Geoffrey Kemp and Colin Gray, both Britishers long resident in the United States, and both of whom had dealt extensively with nuclear strategy. Their emphases were somewhat different.

Kemp, in a series of papers outlining a "new strategic map," asserted that "during the late 1950s and the 1960s Western strategists lost touch with the keen 'geographic sense' which had been developed during World War II," attributing this to developments in military technology, the taking for granted of Western overseas access networks, the (baneful) influence of scientists and economists on strategy, the primacy of ideological conflict, and the rise of the "space ship earth" concept.(71) He proceeded to point to changes in the 1970s which had reasserted the importance of geography (and of access questions): widespread global diffusion of conventional arms, nuclear proliferation, the spectre of diffusion of cruise missile technology, the erosion of Western base rights, increasing dependence by the West for raw materials, and the creeping closure of the world's oceans. Most uniquely, however, Kemp asserted the growing geostrategic importance of the "southern seas" and of the sea lines of communication (SLOCs) from that region's sources of raw materials. Concerning resources, the emphasis was on peacetime logistics, but where a threat to SLOC's was presented either through superpower (Soviet) interdiction or by the new menace of small nations' navies wielding seaborne precision-guided munitions. Oil, above all, was central to Kemp's writings, but the older emphasis on mineral raw materials was broadened to one which included fish (for protein), fresh water, and other agricultural products.

In reintroducing the old critique of transverse mercator maps, and by utilizing azimuthal projections from a variety of new centers, particularly in the Southern hemisphere, Kemp came to stand Seversky nearly on his head. (See Figs. 6.4 and 6.5). The possibility of a new "pivot area" in South Africa was bruited, and the strategic importance of Brazil and India highlighted.(72)

Kemp's analyses (which preceded the Falklands crisis of 1982), and others as well, pointed to the growing crucial importance of numerous small islands throughout the world, many of which, in an era which has seen most former Western possessions decolonized, would not appear to have the "critical population mass" requisite for independent status. Diego Garcia, the Cocos Islands, Mayotte, Ascension, St. Helena, the Falklands, the Spratlys, and various islands in the Pacific have now become vital pieces of strategic terrain, as they may allow for global staging and technical functions no longer easily available from newly independent developing states. For that very reason, the USSR has mounted a continuing, massive political effort within the UN's "Committee of 24" to have them divested from Western control, usually aided in such efforts by most radical developing states.

This was not, of course, a new theme, as witness the nineteenth-century British advantageous use of small oceanic islands for coaling stations and telegraphic cable terminals. But now, numerous heretofore rather obscure islands in the South Atlantic and southern Indian Oceans were pointed to as potentially vital points of basing access, astride sea and air routes related to resource logistics, particularly the oil route around the Cape of Good Hope. Kemp concluded that the Western maritime powers should improve their ability to deploy forces in the southern seas and emphasized the relationship of basing access to resources in those regions.

In contrast to Mackinder, Mahan, Spykman, Seversky, et al., Kemp's global view was more multilayered, with varying emphasis depending upon somewhat separate aspects of contemporary strategy. His focus on the southern seas was matched by azimuthal projections centered on Moscow (the strategic view of the world from the USSR), which highlighted the USSR's potentially ominous long-term vulnerability to new nuclear powers all around its periphery, a vulnerability not symmetrically faced by the United States. This assumption of an imputed new Soviet geopolitical perspective resonated oddly from the earlier airpower theorists' (Seversky, Slessor) notions about Soviet vulnerability, but in a greatly altered and unexpected way. The Soviets' lengthy rimland exposure to numerous hitherto weak (but potentially nuclear) states was now conceived to be a potential source of threat, but not one caused by a Spykmanian seapower containment strategy.(73)

Colin Gray, meanwhile, produced a short book on geopolitics in the mid-1970s which, among other things, entailed a wholesale onslaught upon American "arms controllers," behavioralism in American scholarship, and the "legalistic," "engineering" approach to American diplomacy and strategy.(74) In depicting the American underestimation of the Soviet drive for global hegemony, Gray also harked back to Mackinder. His emphasis, in some contrast to Kemp's, was perhaps somewhat more Eurocentered, crucially assuming a Soviet strategy of "hemispheric denial," through a European blitzkrieg and control of the North Atlantic from the naval complex on the Kola Peninsula.(75) The extension of this denial strategy to African and Asian resources was, however, also anticipated, amounting to a reaffirmation of Mackinder's thesis about the potential for global dominance, but extended by Gray to the concept of a "Eurasian-African World-Island."(76) Critical here was the concern about the Anglo-Saxon countries' loss of unquestioned naval superiority and undivided sea control which had allowed for rimland containment and uninterrupted transatlantic logistics.

TOWARD A NEW, COMPLEX GLOBAL VIEW

The recent attempts by Kemp, Gray, and others to refocus attention on strategic geography and on the crucial relationships between size, location, and power can, as noted, be interpreted as lineal descendants of the geopolitical tradition of the early twentieth century. In combination, they remind us of the lingering hold of the heartland/rimland, landpower/seapower dichotomy which has long dominated geopolitical imagery, albeit now modified by the circumstances of the superpower nuclear balance, nuclear proliferation, peacetime economic warfare, the mix of ideological and balance-of-power diplomacy in the developing world, the vast expansion of the world's independent nations, and so forth. What further, then, might be provided as new global views, and how might they be related to the competition for access?

One reason, of course, for the postwar unpopularity of broad global, geopolitical theories is their inability to do justice to the sheer

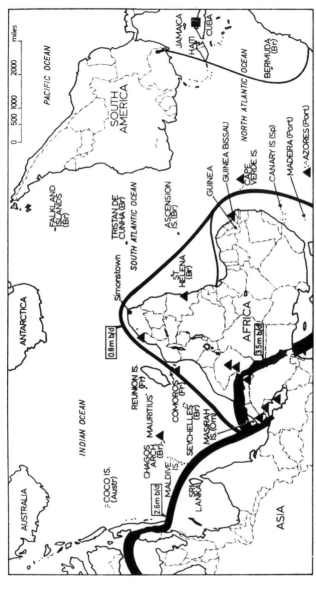

Azimuthal Equidistant Projection centred on Cape Town, South Africa. All distances from the centre of the projection are correct.

▲ Western military facility
◼ Soviet military facility
m b/d Million barrels of oil a day
─── Oil sea lines of communication

Fig. 6.4. The Southern Seas, 1965.

Source: Geoffrey Kemp, "The New Strategic Map in Survival," IISS, March/April 1977, p. 51.

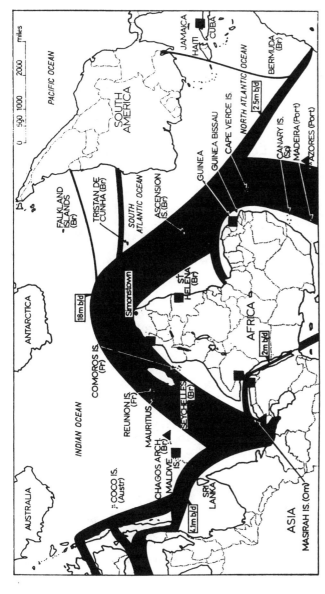

Azimuthal Equidistant Projection centred on **Cape Town, South Africa.** All distances from the centre of the projection are correct.

Fig. 6.5. The Southern Seas, 1976.

Source: Geoffrey Kemp, "The New Strategic Map in Survival," <u>IISS</u>, March/April 1977, p. 51.

complexity of what is involved. For that reason, Jones and other critics had warned that such overarching global views could provide little more than vague aids to understanding, could act merely as filters for the channeling of information.(77) The lack of clarity involved was demonstrated by the difficulties in defining "the heartland" and explaining its meaning, and by the pitfalls inherent in speaking of "control of the rimland," when the latter was comprised of numerous states rarely all aligned with one or another major power. Then too, the very meaning of geopolitical advantage and "dominance" was called into question in circumstances short of war, particularly when all of the major land, sea, and airpower theories were predicated on its eventuality. Still, with all of these caveats, many contemporary theorists continued to attribute a central, critical reality to what has been at stake between the respective followers of Mahan and Mackinder. And whatever the empirical validity of such global views, it is important to note that they have been utilized as practical frameworks of evaluation by decision makers.

Surely, the essential acceptance of Mackinder's heartland thesis (and of the appropriate counter-responses provided by Mahan and Spykman) constituted the first premise of the U.S. postwar containment policy which evolved after 1945. The most basic fact of life was that of the huge negative Western military manpower disparity, as measured by land troop divisions, vis-a-vis the combined forces of the USSR and China, exacerbated by the power-over-distance deflator inherent in America's geographical position, requiring that relatively disproportionate resources be allocated to naval and air logistics forces. The situation was, of course, somewhat analogous in a larger sense to that labored under by Britain for centuries vis-a-vis the European continent. As a result, containment – if not the hope of "roll-back" – took on the nature of a very structured and comprehensive cognition, emphasizing rimland defense of the marginal lands and seas with the hope of fencing in the Soviets and denying them access to the Mediterranean, Indian Ocean, and points along the Atlantic and Pacific littorals.

The West could not, of course, even contemplate an amphibious assault upon the northern Soviet drainage lands, nor an armored assault across the northern European plains – Napoleon and Hitler had failed at that against much weaker earlier Russias. It could, however, concentrate on rimming the USSR with forward bases – for the Strategic Air Command, intelligence listening posts, and forward troop deployments – and could also attempt to make credible a threat to apply force at a place of its own choosing in response to aggression or provocation. After Korea, however, Dulles's enunciation of the short-lived massive retaliation doctrine was an implicit tip of the hat to Mackinder, despite continuing assertions by some analysts that modern technology could compensate for the power-over-distance gradient faced by the United States in projecting power around the Eurasian rim.(78) But at least for a time, the Soviets were themselves denied military access and client states outside of the central heartland area.

Some analysts with a longer-range historical view have actually focused on the dichotomy of landpower and seapower (or rivalrous seapowers) in the absence of the heartland/rimland imagery. George Modelski, for instance, has encapsulated the global struggle for power since the advent of a truly global system around 1500 in terms of alternating "long cycles" which have marked the dominance and decay of hegemonic powers and which have been ended and reborn with major wars.(79) In portraying the succession of Portugal, Spain, Holland, Britain, and the United States, Modelski subsumes Mahan under "a tradition of writing on international affairs that might best be described as 'oceanic,' mostly because sea power, the implications of an island position, and the importance of international trade are its distinguishing characteristics."(80) Reaching back even further, he cites Alexander Hamilton's perception of the histories of the "commercial republics" of Athens, Carthage, and Venice, as well as Holland and Britain, as models for the recent American military and commercial dominance based on seapower.(81) At any rate, the oceanic model, to the extent valid, reminds us that the dichotomy of heartland and rimland is but a twentieth-century construction, based primarily on fears of potential Russian power going back to the turn of the century.

Modelski's long cycle model also entails the generalization that long periods between major wars have normally witnessed the devolvement of the system from near unipolarity (a world order dominated by one seapower) to growing multipolarity, with the latter always anticipating a new decisive war from which a new hegemonic power would emerge, or an old one emerge newly strengthened. As such, Mahan's thesis about the indivisibility of sea control (and its attendant ramifications regarding global access networks) is seen as merely descriptive of the early phases of a long cycle where unipolarity in seapower prevails.

One other point emphasized by Modelski in the context of long cycles bears mention, and it is one closely related to the matter of access diplomacy. He notes that a successful, dominant oceanic strategy has historically relied merely on the utilization of global points of access, and has failed when falling into the trap of "imperial presumption," overextension through attempts at large-scale territorial control or excessive management or manipulation of client states. Athens, Venice, and later Britain are recorded as having fallen into that trap. Rather, a preferred strategy, according to Modelski, would best be modeled after that of Pericles' Athens: "an attitude of watchful waiting, no conquests or interventions; protecting the security of the home base through invulnerable deterrents; and cultivating the 'command' of sea, air and space as the elements most 'strategic' to a global position."(82)

The theory of the long cycles, in conjunction with the geopolitical tradition of Mahan and Mackinder, may provide some insights into the evolving spatial U.S.-Soviet global competition, particularly as applied to access diplomacy. Primarily, it points to the current period as one characterized by a shift from global U.S. dominance, in the "oceanic" tradition, to one of greater multipolarity and instability evidenced by indicators encompassing all aspects of military and economic strength, and also diplomatic alignments.(83)

As Modelski has described it, such periods of decline of a heretofore dominant oceanic and commercial power have, in the past, resulted in wars which realigned power relations and brought forth new patterns of dominance. But at present, the facts of the nuclear standoff appear to preclude such a denouement, and that has resulted in a rather novel form of geopolitical competition.

While Gray and others continue to perceive Mackinder's imagery as aptly descriptive of the current global struggle (and certainly it retains considerable validity), it might be argued that the present spatial configurations of that struggle have acquired a much more dispersed and diffused pattern. The U.S. containment ring around Eurasia, formed by the multilateral alliance structures erected in the 1950s, has long since been leapfrogged and breached. As such, the assumptions of Mahan, Spykman, et al. about Anglo-Saxon rimland naval control are no longer valid. The USSR has acquired client states (and hence various forms of actual or potential military access) in all areas of the globe, including some twenty states in Africa, plus numerous others such as Syria, Iraq, (earlier) South Yemen, India, Cuba, Vietnam, and so forth.(84) That, in conjunction with the Soviet development of a large blue water navy and long-range air transport logistics network, has now moved the locus of the global struggle from one along a definable line or "front" around Eurasia to one of a much more dispersed nature. Among other things, the spatial assumptions behind the domino theory, as applied to Vietnam, have been exploded, all the more so because of China's defection from the Soviet bloc.

The diffusion of spatial competition can also be seen in its extension from what had been, only a half century ago, one involving only a surface plane extending across both land and sea (the advent of underwater communications had actually preceded deployment of submarines). As we have pointed out, the contemporary struggle for access has now fully been extended to three dimensions, involving the underseas as well as outer space, giving rise to new terminology and to new imagery, for instance, a "geopolitics of outer space."(85) And as also pointed out, the development of new technologies in communications, surveillance, and navigation have resulted in intricate webs of connections between the three domains, even as applied to specific military operations such as locating or positioning submarines or warning of an impending nuclear attack. The result has been the emergence of new crucial access requirements in ways not anticipated by the traditional heartland/rimland imagery nor by the assumptions about indivisible sea control.

Mackinder's fears about a heartland landpower developing into a seapower as well, one further blessed with a network of global access, are indeed coming to pass. Whether, in addition, this must lead to a form of "dominance" or "hegemony" — to a successful war — remains to be seen. Nowadays, the competition for access appears conducted with the assumption of continuing nuclear standoff, so that its implications must be gauged according to a welter of essentially subjective and ever-shifting criteria, ranging across resource control and their possible peacetime denial, coercive diplomacy short of war, prestige and related global perceptions of power, support of ideologically linked clients in surrogate wars, and so forth. It is noteworthy that the already lengthy U.S.-Soviet competition for basing access – and here in some contrast to the past struggles involving Britain against Portugal, Spain, Holland, and France – has been conducted with hardly a shot having been fired. So far, it has been a battle fought with the tools of diplomacy. Its ultimate meaning, hence, remains yet obscure and uncertain.

As a postscript to this discussion, it might be noted that some of the doctrinal pronouncements and budgeting decisions of the Reagan administration's first year appeared, if only implicitly, to represent a revival of the classical Mahan thesis. The United States openly announced the aspirations for clear maritime dominance and the threat to respond to Soviet provocations at points of Soviet vulnerability, even if geographically removed from that provocation. According to one source, the program would substitute a more offensively oriented approach, centered on a greatly expanded navy that would be able to intervene anywhere in the world to wage long multiple wars against forces of the "Soviet military empire." Reminiscent of the rimland strategy advocated by Mahan and inspired by British practice, the emphasis was on undivided sea control. A new element involved extensive reliance on qualitative superiority in high-technology naval weaponry to offset a still large Soviet quantitative advantage in ships. The search for expanded basing access was part of this strategy,[86] which by 1982 had come explicitly to be designated a "maritime strategy" most closely associated with Secretary of the Navy John Lehman.

GEOPOLITICS, ACCESS, MAP IMAGES, AND COGNITIVE DISTORTIONS

As skeptical critics have never tired of pointing out, the long history of attempts at filtering geographical reality through geopolitical "theories" or "global views" has consistently been marred by the resort to map and/or more comprehensive cognitive distortions. In some cases, this has resulted from an almost unavoidable tendency to caricature reality in attempting to produce broad generalizations. In others, what Hans Speier once called "magic geography" has deliberately been used for propaganda purposes, either as an element of wartime strategy or an aspect of diplomacy by intimidation.[87]

Basically, the problem of cognitive distortions may be perceived at two related levels. On the one hand, as discussed interminably in political geography textbooks, there are perceptual distortions produced by two-dimensional maps in lieu of spherical globes, which may take any number of forms, depending upon the negative trade-offs conceded. Secondly, one can speak of distortions produced in the minds of decision makers, or of the general public, by various internalized images or caricatures of geographical "reality," even aside from the map distortions.

The problems produced by two-dimensional maps inhere in the specific purposes of various map projections, each of which is intended to highlight some aspects of reality at the unavoidable expense of others. The most commonly used map, the transverse mercator, for instance, diminishes in accuracy as one moves from the equator toward the poles, producing exaggeratedly outsized land masses in Greenland, Canada, the USSR, and Antarctica.(88) Some analysts have also noted that such maps tend to reinforce fears about the Russians being "ten feet tall."(89) Then too, depending upon how the mercator map is laid out – where it is divided at its ends – different "vertical" slices of the world (Europe, the Americas, East Asia) can be placed at its center, with a certain psychological impact on the viewer.(90) Such things may cumulate to a practical impact on the minds of decision makers, not to mention scholars, even sophisticated ones.

Some scholars – Weigert, for instance – were to claim that some geopolitical theories, specifically Mackinder's, were heavily influenced by use of Mercator maps.(91) Use of the Mercator may actually have shaped perceptions of the strategic utility of some overseas bases. Some have even queried whether Japan's emphasis on attacking Pearl Harbor at the outset of World War II may not have been misplaced, what with Hawaii's peripheral, flanking position regarding a direct attack route toward the United States. They further assert that more attention to great circle routes – and less to Mercator – might have directed Japan's attention to the possibilities of concentrating more heavily on an axis leading through Dutch Harbor and British Columbia.(92)

To compensate somewhat for the shortcomings of the transverse mercator, polar azimuthal projections helped usher in the "air age," but they in turn produced their own distortions (the further one moved from the North Pole), exaggerating the size of Africa and South America, as well as the distances between the latter two continents.(93) Such a projection was also claimed to promote support for a "hemispheric defense" strategy.(94) (In a related sense, we have noted the odd notions of German geopolitik about "pan-regions" and longitudinal groupings of continents, such as the assumed "naturalness" of a close tie between North and South America.)(95)

More recently – and actually intended as aids to empathizing with others' strategic cognitions – there has been a newer vogue of centering map projections at a variety of places to depict the "view of the world" from Moscow, or Buenos Aires, or Peking, or Capetown. Such maps can, for instance, despite their inherent distortions, help one to comprehend the anxiety felt about encirclement and nuclear proliferation by the Soviets, or the strategic isolation of South Africa, or the encirclement feared by Peking of alleged Soviet making.(96)

There has also recently been considerable attention to cognitive mapping in a more comprehensive sense, involving a variety of economic, political, and cultural factors, including social distance.(97) These have demonstrated, among other things, sheer ignorance of some of the demographic complexity of some areas, and the impact of traumatic historical memories. Much has been written, for instance, about the stated fears of some U.S. national security managers during the Vietnam War that its (Vietnam's) loss would produce a Communist flotilla in San Francisco Bay (dominoes with a vengeance!). Likewise, Richard Barnet has discerned the manner in which 1950s U.S. Cold Warriors habitually encapsulated the entirety of the Third World as "the grey areas."(98) Concerning distance, there is the well-worn memory of Chamberlain's lament about why the British should be made to worry about such a "far-away land" as Czechoslovakia.

Sometimes, even fairly sophisticated students of international rela- tions may be dismayed by learning of their own ignorance of geography. How many would be aware, for instance, as German pre-World War II strategists were, that the narrowest part of the Atlantic Ocean in which to utilize aircraft for interdicting shipping lies on a line between Newfoundland and the West African coast from Morocco to Guinea Bissau?

The foregoing brings us to the question of how certain kinds of imagery, or cognitive maps, of varying subjectivity, are applied to the problems of access and bases. There are no easy answers here, for much of such imagery involves predictions, one way or the other, about how the acquisition of this or that base by the Soviets (or losses of same by the United States) will affect future diplomatic alignments, global perceptions, or perhaps the course of a general war. The perceptions involved tend, that is, strongly to be ideologically determined, from right to left, depending upon degrees of concern about future Soviet global designs.

Among those in the United States inclined to view the unfavorable trends in the "base race" vis-a-vis the USSR with great concern, the dominant imagery seems to revolve about graphic metaphorical terms (called idle cliches by opponents) such as "blocked chokepoints" and "outflanked" geographic positions, begging in the minds of critics the specification of more precise scenarios. Hence, Soviet naval outposts at Aden, Berbera (earlier), and Umm Quasr raise the prospect of the sea-based oil pipeline being "choked" near its source, either at the Straits of Hormuz or the Bab El Mandeb. Possible future Soviet access to Mauritius, the Seychelles, or the Maldives provokes the spectre of interdicted SLOCs in the Indian Ocean; the prospect of Soviet naval bases in Vietnam is viewed as a potential "dagger" at the Japanese oil lifeline running through the South China Sea. Soviet access to Mozambique and Angola (and the possibility of its future extension to a black-controlled South Africa or "Azania") raises the spectre of Soviet "control" over sea lanes around the Cape to Europe and the United States.(99) Soviet use of bases in Vietnam and India (also the vague possibility of its facilities in Taiwan) is portrayed as "outflanking" China, just as Soviet access in Libya and Algeria (in connection with menacing Soviet activity off Norway and Svalbard) is claimed to "outflank" NATO. Saudi Arabia is increasingly depicted, sometimes with the aid of maps and heavy arrows, as having been "outflanked" by a Soviet pincer movement directed through Iraq (earlier), South Yemen, and Ethiopia. Soviet moves toward South Pacific bases are said to represent the beginnings of an "outflanking" of the whole U.S. position in the Far East and the Pacific. The terminology is clearly drawn from military operational tactics, projected onto a global screen, and is treated with sarcasm by those who wonder, for instance, why the United States ought to worry about Soviet interdiction of oil routes around southern Africa, when such an interdiction would be so much easier at the exit of the Persian Gulf.

That is one view. On the other side, even short of subnuclear warfare scenarios, it is claimed that there is an important, less measurable impact of the tide of basing access trends (what Moorer and Cottrell call "geopolitical momentum"), that its cumulative impact will indeed count, and that it already has.(100) Here, one is drawn into analyses of the political impact of a military presence, of "Finlandization" and intimidation in numerous contexts. Soviet access to Angola and Mozambique is perceived as important in affecting South African behavior. Saudi Arabia's policies are seen as certainly having been altered by the changing facts of military access around its periphery. The U.S. NATO allies in the Mediterranean are seen as gradually and subtly having shifted toward neutralization by the proliferating Soviet presence in the Mediterranean and North Africa. China is, rightly or wrongly, seen worried about the prospect of Soviet naval access to Vietnam, and to be warily viewing its new relationship with the United States with that in mind. Though military scenarios are paramount in many cognitions, the elusive relationship of all of this to "hemispheric denial" and resource control looms large.(101)

At some levels, the practical meaning of the contemporary competition for bases is less obscure, less arguable. Primarily, this refers to arms transfers for surrogate wars, and to technical facilities. Soviet forward positioning of war materiel in Ethiopia, South Yemen, and Libya unquestionably affords more rapid, massive, and efficient arms assistance for potential conflicts in the Horn and throughout Africa; likewise, its arms caches in the Middle East serve similar purposes with respect to South Asia and the Far East. The United States has long taken advantage of forward-located materiel in Europe, including Turkey, for contingencies in neighboring regions. And, as earlier noted, both superpowers have almost open-ended requirements for intelligence, surveillance, and communications facilities, even if redundant, anywhere they can obtain them.

GEOPOLITICS, BALANCE OF PAYMENTS, AND OVERSEAS FACILITIES

As is discussed at great length in the current literature on international political economy, it is only in the more recent part of the postwar period – subsequent to the collapse of the vaunted American-constructed Bretton Woods international economic system and the fall of the dollar – that the financing of American overseas military commitments, including bases, has come to pose a serious problem. During the early part of the postwar period, the U.S. "dollar surplus," derived from a very favorable balance of trade, allowed for easy financing of overseas installations, as well as for extensive aid to allies along the old containment rim.(102) Indeed, even if not explicitly stated as such, U.S. expenditures on overseas military commitments became a deliberate mechanism for assisting various allies, particularly in recuperating Europe, to rectify their own payments imbalances. Among other things, during this period, the United States also accrued a large fraction of the world's monetary gold reserves, a horde which has now largely been dissipated.(103)

Beginning in the late 1950s and accelerating thereafter, the U.S. dollar glut turned into a dollar drain, as the rebuilding European and Japanese economies became more competitive. But, as the latter remained under the U.S. security umbrella, a bargain was struck whereby Western Europe (primarily West Germany) and Japan agreed to finance the American balance-of-payments deficit. The willingness of these countries to pile up dollars and not to insist upon payment in gold long masked the fundamental shift in economic power which was undermining the previously dominant U.S. role. But France began to revolt during the 1960s, and then the early 1970s witnessed the U.S. devaluations and withdrawal from the gold standard which effectively marked the end of the Bretton Woods system.(104)

Hence, again by about 1970, the United States was faced with the inherent disadvantage of its geographical position regarding the costs of overseas installations and deployments. Robert Gilpin has ably stated the dilemma as follows:

> The fundamental problem posed for the United States during this period was the asymmetry of the American and Soviet geostrategic positions. The resulting monetary burden of maintaining global hegemony and balancing Soviet power on the rimlands of Europe and Asia was (and is) substantial. Consequently, the balance of payments issue was a central one for the United States. How is it possible to pay for the maintenance of large military establishments abroad, to finance and support allies, and generally to cover the costs of far-flung overseas commitments? Such a balance of payments problem is not crucial to a strategically well-placed continental power, such as Germany prior to World War I and the Soviet Union since 1945; such continental powers are able to radiate influence from within their own boundaries. But it is of the essence for a sea power trying to balance such a land power. How this problem was resolved is of critical importance for understanding American foreign economic policy in the 1960s and early 1970s.(105)

Further, it appeared that the burden of U.S. overseas commitments was proportionately greater than that earlier faced by Great Britain at the height of Pax Britannica. Gilpin thus quotes Harold and Margaret Sprout as follows, illustrating a dilemma which by 1980 had become still more pronounced.

> At the peak of British power and influence, the decade of the 1860s, total expenditures for military purposes averaged less than 30 million per year. Adjusting for inflation and changes in the dollar price of sterling, this works out to something in the range of 1 to 2 percent of average U.S. military expenditures in the 1950s and early 1960s. In short, mid-nineteenth century British governments policed a worldwide empire . . . and exerted on other nations an influence as great as, if not considerably greater than, the United States can achieve today at a real cost fifty to one hundred times larger.(106)

Gilpin, in pursuing this argument further, points out that as the U.S. trade position worsened in the 1960s and 1970s, it was only the then growing, massive dividend remittances from the overseas operations of the U.S. multinational corporations (MNCs) which allowed for balancing the costs of overseas military deployments.(107) That, of course, caused De Gaulle and other Europeans to carp about their being compelled in effect to abet the expansion of an American overseas economic and military empire.(108) Actually, in the early 1960s, U.S. direct investment outflows had greatly exceeded the return of dividends to the United States, prompting the U.S. government to some restrictions on the former. That situation had changed drastically by 1980. However, the then vastly increasing European, Japanese, and OPEC investments in the United States (by then in excess of the outflow of U.S. investments) promised a later flood of dividend remittances out of the United States, in a manner which might later provide serious problems for the financing of U.S. overseas military commitments, unless other vehicles for rectifying payments imbalances could be found.(109)

As it is, a rigorous or even remotely comprehensive analysis of the relationship, for the United States, between balance of payments and the costs of overseas military commitments is not easily come by – it is well beyond the scope of this work. The Pentagon's Comptroller Office does, however, provide annual data on U.S. forces' overseas operating costs, which can be obtained going back to 1970.(110) However, the year-to-year data entail some serious problems of comparability, particularly regarding what is and is not included. Table 6.1 displays the DOD's data for FY 1970; table 6.2, for FYs 1978, 1979, and 1980, which are at least revealing of the spread of costs by countries and regions, and roughly indicative of what, overall, is involved. As all figures are current, the approximate doubling of most prices during the 1970s must be taken into account in discounting long-term changes.

Table 6.1. Department of Defense Estimated
U.S. Costs and Foreign Country
Contributions by Country (a)
FY 1970
(Thousands of Dollars)

Countries	Annual U.S. Operating Cost (b)	Dollar Equivalent of Host Country Contributions
Australia	$ 7,000	$ -
Bahamas	3,000	-
Belgium	22,000	383
Bermuda	20,000	-
Brazil	2,000	-
Canada	47,000	-
Chile	1,000	-
Cyprus	2,000	-
Denmark	8,000	246
Ethiopia	16,000	74
Germany	2,200,000	41,023
Greece	29,000	337
Iceland	31,000	-
Iran	7,000	1,862
Italy	116,000	408
Japan	550,000	336
Korea	680,000	79
Leeward Islands	1,000	-
Libya	20,000	-
Netherlands	19,000	313
New Zealand	2,000	-
Pakistan	2,000	-
Portugal	19,000	88
Philippines	280,000	233
Ryukyus	538,000	-
Saudi Arabia	1,000	1,244
South Vietnam	6,700,000	41,800
Spain	90,000	35
Taiwan	85,000	762
Thailand	455,000	481
Turkey	90,000	1,340
United Kingdom	224,000	2

(a)   All countries with over 100 U.S. military personnel as of December 31, 1969. Two countries omitted for security purposes.
(b)   DoD accounting records are not maintained to reflect total U.S. costs on an area basis. Operating costs for FY 1970, therefore, were estimated by using appropriate factors. Included are the costs of all military and civilian personnel located overseas and the cost of operating and maintaining facilities overseas. These estimates do not include indirect logistic and administrative costs for support from U.S.
Source: Comptroller's Office, U.S. Department of Defense.

Table 6.2. DoD Annual Operating Costs of
Maintaining U.S. Military Forces in
Foreign Countries & Areas

Country	FY 1978	($ Millions) FY 1979	FY 1980
Western and Southern Europe			
Belgium	39	42	45
Denmark (Incl. Greenland)	73	76	94
Germany	4,592	5,001	5,588
Greece (Incl. Crete)	70	76	81
Iceland	72	84	91
Italy (Incl. Sicily and Sardinia)	233	259	282
Netherlands	36	37	39
Portugal (Incl. Azores)	35	37	39
Spain	179	193	209
Turkey	170	204	286
United Kingdom	452	514	553
Forces Afloat	270	330	334
Other	8	7	11
Total Western & Southern Europe	6,229	6,860	7,652
Eastern Europe	3	3	3
Africa, Near East and South Asia			
Bahrain Islands	4	5	6
British Indian Ocean (Incl. Diego Garcia)	21	26	28
Egypt	1	1	1
Iran	4		
Israel	2	2	2
Saudi Arabia	10	12	13
Afloat	19	14	14
Other	6	8	7
Total Africa, Near East & South Asia	67	68	71
East Asia and Pacific			
Australia	21	22	28
Japan (Incl. Okinawa)	938	1,000	1,050
Philippines	257	271	292
South Korea	838	927	973
Thailand	5	2	3
Afloat	311	353	358
Other	6	7	4
Total East Asia and Pacific	2,426	2,582	2,708

Table 6.2. (Cont.)

Country	FY 1978	($ Millions) FY 1979	FY 1980
Western Hemisphere			
Bermuda	28	31	33
Canada	46	54	56
Cuba (Guantanamo)	47	51	55
Panama	10	126	175
Afloat	22		
Other	11	11	12
Total Western Hemisphere	164	273	331
Grand Total	8,889	9,786	10,765

Notes

DoD accounting records are not maintained to reflect total U.S. costs on an area basis. Operating costs for all years therefore include estimates developed by the use of appropriate factors. Included are the salary costs of all military and civilian personnel located overseas and the cost of operating and maintaining facilities overseas. These estimates do not include indirect logistic and administrative costs for support from outside of the country, nor do they include major procurement or military construction costs.

Estimates include military and civilian salary rates in effect on 1 October 1979.

Here, it is seen that the total annual operating costs of U.S. overseas military commitments (including forces afloat as well as on-land installations) are near $11 billion, excluding "indirect logistic and administrative costs for support from outside of the country" and "major procurement or military construction costs." These, however, apparently do not include the (in some cases at least) rather massive amounts of economic and military aid the United States has been compelled to grant some of its base hosts as indirect rental for the use of facilities. For some countries — Spain, Philippines, Turkey, Greece Portugal — these costs have run into hundreds of millions of dollars annually, together adding into the billions. But then, offset payments by Germany and others militate in the opposite direction. Still, the overall net outflows for balance-of-payments purposes must amount to somewhere in the $10-15 billion range. Those are not trivial figures relative to the facts of recent U.S. payments imbalances nor to the overall size of the defense budget. However, the real (deflated) costs may actually now be somewhat lower than they were in the late 1960s and early 1970s when the financial burden of maintaining U.S. forces in Vietnam ($6.7 billion) exceeded the combined operating costs of all other overseas commitments (about $5.6 billion, roughly equal in real terms to the 1980 figure of $10.7 billion).

The U.S. has apparently achieved some "savings" in its overseas military costs over the past decade because of the phasing out of facilities in Iran, Taiwan, Ethiopia, Pakistan, Libya, and several other countries. But in some cases – Spain, Italy, Netherlands, Portugal, Turkey, Australia, Denmark, Iceland, Germany – the base operating costs appear to have escalated even in real terms. Those for Europe and Japan account, of course, for the vast bulk of overseas expenditures, even if in the future, those related to the new commitments in Egypt, Oman, Somalia, Kenya, and Diego Garcia are likely to loom much larger, as are perhaps those for the category "afloat." And, some of the press reports on the costs to the United States of some symbolic or training-purpose rotations of army and air force units to Egypt bespoke of nearly fantastic fuel costs for such deployments, perhaps a sign that the logistics expenses for maintaining overseas facilities were becoming a major burden.

On the flip side of this rather indistinct coin, it is to be noted that a strictly <u>financial</u> assessment of the cost to the USSR of its growing overseas basing network would be even harder to come by. The USSR, like the United States, utilizes a variety of quid pro quo for use of basing facilities – arms sales and aid; low-priced sales of oil, natural gas, cotton; subsidized purchases of clients' raw materials. One recent article, for instance, in attempting to cost out the Soviets' "unsinkable aircraft carrier just ninety miles off the Florida coast," explained how the Soviets prop up Cuba's economy through purchases of sugar and nickel, despite the USSR's being the world's largest producer of both commodities.(111) Earlier, they had bought up much of Egypt's and Sudan's cotton crops, often for resale elsewhere. The same article claims that Vietnam has not only been given markets in the USSR for a variety of light industrial goods, but also for Vietnamese vodka: "It's believed the stuff is used for domestic Soviet consumption, thus freeing Russian vodka for export to hard-currency markets."(112) The article concluded that the USSR is paying an increasingly burdensome price for its overseas ventures and access, raising the traditional arguments – familiar to students of "theories" of imperialism – about whether empires were worth the financial cost. Of course, to the extent the Soviets planned upon more global military deployments – in Latin America, southern Africa, southwest Pacific – the economic advantages accruing to it from a heartland position would dissipate somewhat. This apparently does not, however, always apply so much in the Soviet as the American case to balance-of-payments problems. Hence, according to Gilpin:

> The Soviet Union, on the other hand, has been generally free of this balance-of-payments problem. The bulk of Soviet military forces have remained within the Soviet Union proper, and foreign aid has been in the form of goods or military equipment. But where the Soviet Union has stationed large military contingents outside the country as in Eastern Europe, it has created a monetary and payments system to support this extension of

power. By creating the ruble bloc, manipulating the value of the ruble, and keeping the ruble inconvertible, the Russians have forced the East Europeans to finance their military presence in Eastern Europe. Thus, the extent of Russian influence has been largely determined by the scope of their military rather than their economic power.(113)

Most critical to an analysis of the costs of Soviet overseas facilities, however, would be an assessment of the "aid" component to its arms transfers, at least for non-OPEC clients. Such data are very hard to come by.

However, it should be pointed out that simply looking at trends in the costs of overseas bases, without reference to overall defense costs and deployments, may capture only one aspect of a complex and interrelated problem. Indeed, in some respects, an inverse relationship may exist between base costs and some areas of defense procurement. Hence, the Reagan administration's planned increase in the number of U.S. carrier groups is said to presage a diminished requirement for foreign naval facilities, which would appear also to suggest a favorable net balance of payments impact. Then too, enhanced air transport capacity (new longer range transports, more refueling tankers) is expected to reduce somewhat the need for overseas staging facilities. In short, the economics of overseas bases – regarding defense expenditures and payments balances – is a more complex matter than it appears on the surface.

BASES, GEOPOLITICS AND RAW MATERIALS DEPENDENCE

The past few years have witnessed escalating alarms about expected future shortages of raw materials and about dangerously increasing American, European, and Japanese dependence upon resources – fuels and non-fuel minerals – from developing nations thought increasingly prone to waging economic warfare against "the North." The alarms, begun seriously with OPEC's success and also the 1973 oil embargo, have arisen in response to ominous projections which juxtapose an assumed finite world resource base to rising global population and consumption trends. Near the extremes of worst-case doomsday scenarios, analysts such as Dennis and Donella Meadows, authors of the celebrated Limits to Growth, have predicted a virtual collapse of the world economy (as we have come to know it) during the twenty-first century, with attendant mass deaths caused by starvation, pollution, and disappearing energy resources.(114) Even more sanguine such projections, however, point to massive economic dislocations resulting from resource shortfalls.(115)

Even aside from aggregate global problems, however, numerous analyses point to the increasing vulnerability of the United States and the remainder of the West from rising dependence upon Third World fuel and mineral sources. Some highlight the possibilities for proliferation of OPEC-like cartels to other commodities such as bauxite and phosphates, which might greatly shift the overall terms of trade to the disadvantage of Western industrialized countries.(116) Others point to the possibilities for disruption by the USSR of sea lines of communication along which Western resource imports must travel, either in connection with a major war or in various circumstances short of that.(117) Then too, various LDCs are seen capable – at various times and for various reasons – of disrupting the flow of resources to the West, a specter illustrated by the war between Iran and Iraq in 1980-1982.

These pessimistic though debatable projections lend themselves to speculation about impacts on the international system; specifically, with respect to changing patterns of power and alliances and to the prospects for either greater conflict or more cooperative behavior under duress. Will the strong react by using military muscle on the weak to grab up dwindling resources, including those under new international ocean waters, perhaps even unexpectedly ushering in a new era of "territorial imperialism?" Or will a really "new world order" be ushered in, featuring more cooperative norms, perhaps built upon new international institutions or at least "regimes," for instance, those to deal with the Law of the Sea, extended economic zones, and with the activities of multinational corporations? Or, more likely, will trends develop between those extremes, featuring very hard bargaining between the developed and developing worlds, as adumbrated by Cancun, perhaps with continuous and fitful economic warfare, embargoes, and occasional desultory military interventions to secure access to raw materials in emergencies? In any case, international "legal" norms which have haltingly developed over the past several decades, along with the rough balancing of superpower military might, have made it increasingly difficult for the industrial nations to use military force for ensuring flows even of desperately needed resources, even aside from the high economic costs of intervention as demonstrated, for instance, in Vietnam.(119) As a result, even very weak nations may come to feel free to conduct economic warfare with impunity, constrained only by the fear of some form of economic retaliation.

Space does not here permit a full analysis of these problems which, at any rate, have been the subject of some exhaustive recent studies, including one by Arthur D. Little (A.D.L.) for the U.S. Navy's Year 2000 project, and another published under the auspices of the International Economic Studies Institute (IESI).(120) The conclusions of these and other such analyses are highly complex, subject to varying interpretations (particularly in contrast with one another) and also to changes in the light of ever-new developments. For the United States, present dependence on external sources for petroleum and for some key non-fuel minerals is summarized, respectively, in tables 6.3 and 6.4.(121) The USSR is far less dependent on overseas raw materials.(122) It is relatively self-sufficient in energy; among the non-fuel minerals, only bauxite and fluorspar stand out as areas of dependence. Food is, of course, another story.(123) For Japan and Western Europe, meanwhile, massive raw materials dependence is a presumably permanent and increasingly expensive reality.

Table 6.3. U.S. Reliance on Imports for
Strategic Materials in 1980

U.S. Net Import Reliance*	Material	Major Foreign Sources**	Uses
100%	Columbium	Brazil, Canada, Thailand	Alloy steels, cutting tools
100%	Titanium (Rutile)	Australia, India, others	Titanium sponge products
97%	Manganese	Gabon, Brazil, Australia, South Africa, France	Steel and iron making
97%	Tantalite	Thailand, Canada, Malaysia	Electronics
93%	Cobalt	Zaire, Belgium, Luxembourg, Zambia	Jet engine manufacture
91%	Chromium	South Africa, Philippines, U.S.S.R.	Stainless steel
87%	Platinum Group metals	South Africa, U.S.S.R., Britain	Coatings, catalytic converters
62%	Cadmium	Canada, Australia, Mexico	Electroplating, electrodes
54%	Tungsten	Canada, Bolivia, South Korea	Machine tools, alloys
53%	Antimony	China, Mexico, Bolivia	Batteries, solders, flameproofing

*Imports as a percent of apparent consumption. 1980 data are estimates, and where not available, 1979 data are presented.
**Leading sources of imports, 1976-79.
Source: U.S. Bureau of Mines. Reprinted in the New York Times, June 15, 1981.

Table 6.4. U.S. Petroleum Imports from OPEC Nations, 1960–1980
(in Thousands of Barrels per Day)

Year	Saudi Arabia	Iran	Vene-zuela	Libya	Indo-nesia	United Arab Emirates	Algeria	Nigeria	Total OPEC	Arab Members of OPEC(1)
1960	84	34	911	0	77	0	1	0	1,314	292
1961	73	61	879	0	62	0	0	0	1,286	284
1962	74	49	906	18	69	0	0	0	1,265	241
1963	108	62	900	19	63	0	1	0	1,283	258
1964	131	66	933	39	68	3	6	0	1,361	293
1965	158	80	994	42	63	14	9	15	1,476	324
1966	147	89	1,018	69	53	13	4	11	1,471	300
1967	92	71	938	42	66	5	5	5	1,259	177
1968	74	61	886	114	73	16	6	9	1,302	272
1969	65	46	875	135	88	14	2	49	1,336	276
1970	30	38	989	47	70	63	8	50	1,343	291
1971	128	112	1,020	58	111	80	15	102	1,673	327
1972	190	142	959	123	164	73	92	251	2,063	530
1973	486	223	1,135	164	213	71	136	459	2,993	915
1974	461	469	979	4	300	74	190	713	3,280	752
1975	715	280	702	232	390	117	282	762	3,601	1,383
1976	1,230	298	700	453	539	254	432	1,025	5,066	2,424
1977	1,380	535	690	723	541	335	559	1,143	6,193	3,185
1978	1,144	555	645	654	573	385	649	919	5,751	2,963
1979	1,356	304	690	658	420	281	636	1,080	5,637	3,056
1980(2)	1,252	8	460	550	337	179	481	846	4,233	2,523

(1) Saudi Arabia, Iraq, Qatar, Libya, United Arab Emirates, Algeria and Kuwait.
(2) Preliminary.

Note: The total OPEC column includes imports from nations not separately listed on the chart: Ecuador, Gabon, Iraq, Kuwait, and Qatar.

Source: Department of Energy.

The foregoing brings us to the basic and arguable meaning of the anxieties over raw materials cutoffs, in the context of present and future access strategies and the converse strategies, such as they are, of resource denial. The basic dividing line here – and the subject of considerable confusion in the literature – is that between wartime and peacetime conditions. We have noted the preparations of the major powers for the contingency of cutoffs at the outset of World War II; similar contingencies were faced before World War I. But in earlier times, and this includes the interwar period, the prospect of raw materials shutoffs under normal peaceful conditions was hardly considered (even the autarkic policies of Nazi Germany and the USSR during the interwar period were directed primarily at expected wartime contingencies). The fact of colonial control over resources in the developing regions, the relative absence of ideological struggle, and the then strongly prevailing norms of business laissez-faire which gave almost complete latitude to corporations in selling to whomever they pleased, practically precluded purposive, serious economic warfare during peacetime.(124) (The situation of blocked currencies and of "imperial preference" during the depression was not an exception here; it was of essentially economic and not political derivation.)

Nowadays, of course, economic warfare has increasingly become an aspect of contemporary total war diplomacy during peacetime, entering not only the domains of superpower rivalry and the overall conflict between north and south, but also conflicts between small nations. Arab use of the oil weapon against Israel is familiar enough; likewise, Nigeria's veiled threats to cut off oil shipments to nations which continue to supply arms to South Africa or which even refuse to apply stiffer economic pressures against Pretoria. Earlier African pressures on Iran to halt oil shipments to South Africa, and similar Arab threats against countries which hint at buying arms from Israel (Thailand, Taiwan, Austria) or which threaten to establish diplomatic relations with her (Portugal) are other examples of the use of leverage through resource diplomacy, as is, of course, the at least implied threat of embargo of U.S. grain, however lacking in practicality or credibility.(125) American and other nations' earlier embargoing of Rhodesian chrome demonstrated that commodities other than oil may be used as instruments of economic warfare.

The Soviet strategic literature is not very expressive of a resource denial strategy vis-a-vis the United States as a key component of a grand strategy, but there are hints that such considerations are gradually acquiring an enhanced status in high Soviet political circles, perhaps only now in the wake of OPEC's demonstrated success. Marshall Sokolovsky's classic and presumably almost official strategic primer mentions the subject only twice. In the first instance, under "general concepts," it is pointed out that "in order to attack the enemy's economy according to strategic plans, special operations are often carried out to capture or destroy strategically important regions and sources of raw materials."(126) That, of course, referred to wartime strategy. Later, however, in discussing the "military strategy of imperialist states," Sokolovsky points out that "since the principal capitalist countries are dependent upon the import of many strategic raw materials, fuels, and foodstuffs (sic), and because many strategic raw material sources are quite distant from metropolitan areas, and maritime communications vulnerable, the economically strong countries have been compelled to stockpile large quantities of strategic materials."(127) There is a hint of a strategy there, though with no overt policy prescriptions.

More recently, however, there have been hints that the Soviets take seriously a raw-materials-denial strategy even during peacetime. Soviet goading of the Arabs into an oil embargo on the West in 1973 is well known, and it must be stressed that the subsequently maintained higher oil prices, while certainly not the result of Soviet activity, have seriously hurt Western defense efforts as oil import payments have strained Western economies to the limit. The success of OPEC has, however, now engendered open Soviet aspirations to use raw materials cutoffs or price gouging as a strategy. According to one recent article, "the OPEC oil boycott of 1973-74 was acclaimed by Moscow as confirming its long-held belief in the acute dependence of the 'imperialist' world on the raw material resources of the Third World."(128) At the time, Soviet commentators noted both the economic and political ramifications of the boycott, especially the 'crisis of capitalism' that it helped precipitate.

> "The energy and raw material crisis," Pravda said in 1975, "which has affected the capitalist world in the first half of the 1970s has sharply intensified the role of materials in the world economy and given the problem of raw materials an unprecedently acute international character." "The oil boycott," commented another official Soviet publication "serves as a good example for other developing countries producing mineral raw materials and agricultural export crops." Particular attention was paid to Africa, which is becoming increasingly important in the world capitalist production of the most vital raw materials.(129)

Some of the same themes are touched upon in Admiral Gorschkov's writings on Soviet naval strategy. Commentators such as Colin Gray have warned of the resource implications of a Soviet strategy of "hemispheric denial," but which is envisaged as an actual military onslaught.(130)

The full extent to which peacetime raw materials denial has become central to Soviet grand strategy is not at all clear, though the recent Soviet moves regarding cornering of the cobalt and titanium markets have caused a few stirs.(131) However, as we have indicated, the recent patterns of the Soviet drive for basing access in Africa and elsewhere seems at least to hint at such a strategy, or the building of a basis for it. Western fears of such a strategy (in addition to fears about Third World economic warfare, not necessarily involving the Soviets except indirectly in the sense that Soviet military strength may deter western temptations for military intervention) are now rampant, so that whether it is for real or not, it has entered the mutual perceptions of all concerned. Hence, in part, the new vogue of geopolitics, with its attention to sea lanes, chokepoints, and forward positions of strength.

Many of the Western fears about raw materials cutoffs, of course, are based on still hypothetical situations in between peacetime economic warfare and all-out superpower total war. Hence, there are discussions about subnuclear wars or escalating local crises in which the Soviets might interdict oil supplies at the mouth of the Persian Gulf or en route around the Cape of Good Hope (also about "local" powers obstructing the exit from the Persian Gulf). The possibilities are taken seriously, despite critics who wonder how such activities, defined as casus belli by international law, could be carried out without escalation to nuclear war. It is such scenarios, however, in addition to those involving embargoes by Third World nations, with or without open Soviet connivance, which have impelled increased attention to matters of bases and other forms of military access, most notably in a wide arc around the Persian Gulf, but also in proximity to southern Africa.

NOTES

(1) Regarding the cleavage between the polarized left and right wings of the U.S. foreign policy establishment, and the waxing and waning of the power of the former with the Carter administration, see Carl Gershman, "The Rise and Fall of the New Foreign Policy Establishment," Commentary 70 (July 1980): 13-24.

(2) For traditional analyses – and measurements – of national power, see Hans Morgenthau, Power Among Nations, 5th ed. (New York: Knopf, 1968), chaps. 3-6; and Kenneth Organski, World Politics, 2nd ed. (New York: Knopf, 1968), chaps. 6-9. More recently, see Organski and Jack Kugler, The War Ledger (Chicago: University of Chicago Press, 1980).

(3) Newsweek, August 8, 1977, pp. 31-32, under "Carter as Arms Merchant."

(4) Ibid., p. 31.

(5) Ibid., p. 32.

(6) Ibid., p. 31.

(7) "Gold's Sharp Drop: Many Factors Cited," New York Times, March 25, 1980, p. D5.

(8) Many from the "realist" school of that era were quite hostile to geopolitical theory, as evidenced in Robert Strausz-Hupé, Geopolitics:

The Struggle for Space and Power (New York: G.P. Putnam's, 1942). Hans Morgenthau, Politics Among Nations, 5th edition (New York: Knopf, 1973), p. 158 discusses geopolitics under "the fallacy of the single factor ," dismissing it as a "pseudo-science erecting the factor of geography into an absolute that is supposed to determine power, and hence the fate, of nations." He is highly critical not only of Haushofer, but Mackinder and Mahan as well. But by the late 1970s, in the U.S. press, Realpolitik and geopolitics had become virtually synonymous. Hence, Peter Berger, "Now, 'Boat People' From Taiwan?": "The logic of the abandonment of Taiwan is, once again, the logic of Real-politik. . . . Poring over the ivory chessboard of geopolitics, they have now concluded that Taiwan is expendable in some grand strategy of triangulation, in which they play off Peking against Moscow," in Washington Post, February 14, 1978, p. 37.

(9) "Kissinger Urges Successor to Caution Soviets on Moves," Washington Post, April 21, 1978, p. A26.

(10) "Excerpts from Kissinger's Testimony on Arms Pact," New York Times, August 1, 1979, p. A6. A fuller list of Kissinger's statements incorporating the term "geopolitics" is in Richard Eaton, "Probing Strategic Images: A New Approach to Geopolitical Analysis" (paper delivered at International Studies Association meeting, Philadelphia, March 21, 1981).

(11) "Excerpts from Kissinger's Testimony on Arms Pact," New York Times, August 1, 1979.

(12) For scholarly expressions of this view, which one must be careful not to exaggerate or caricature, see Robert Keohane and Joseph Nye, Transnational Relations and World Politics (Cambridge, Mass.: Harvard University Press, 1970); Keohane and Nye, Power and Interdependence (Boston: Little, Brown, 1977); and Dennis Pirages, Global Ecopolitics (North Scituate, Mass.: Duxbury Press, 1978).

(13) Shahram Chubin. "The United States and the Third World: Motives, Objectives, Policies," in Third World Conflict and International Security, Part II Adelphi Paper No. 167 (London: IISS), p. 22.

(14) E.H. Carr, The Twenty Years Crisis, 1917-1939 (London: MacMillan, 1939).

(15) "Excerpts from Interview with Prime Minister Vorster on South African Policy," New York Times, September 17, 1977, p. 4.

(16) Saul Cohen, Geography and Politics in a World Divided (New York: Random House, 1963), p. 24.

(17) Ibid., p. 25.

(18) Lewis C. Peltier and G. Etzel Pearcy, Military Geography (New York: Van Nostrand, 1966), p. 138.

(19) Richard Hartshorne, "What is Political Geography?" in W.A. Douglas Jackson, Politics and Geographic Relationships (Englewood Cliffs, N.J.: Prentice-Hall, 1964), pp. 52-60, quotation from p. 54. Additionally, perhaps a classic statement defining the importance of political geography and/or geopolitics is in Nicholas Spykman, The Geography of the Peace (New York: Harcourt, Brace, 1944), "Introduction: Geography in War and Peace," pp. 3-7.

(20) See "Geography and International Politics in an Era of Revolutionary Change," in W.A. Douglas Jackson, Politics and Geographic Relationships: Readings on the Nature of Political Geography (Englewood Cliffs, N.J.: Prentice-Hall, 1964), chap. 4, quote from p. 42. As the Sprouts note, geopolitical hypotheses involving climatic distinctions are most identified with Ellsworth Huntington — see, for example, his "The Influence of Geography and Climate Upon History," in Hans W. Weigert and V. Stefansson, Compass of the World: A Symposium on Political Geography (New York: Macmillan, 1944), chap. 13.

(21) Cohen, Geography and Politics, p. 26.

(22) Ibid., pp. 28-33. Another brief review is in Roger E. Kasperson and Julian V. Minghi, eds., The Structure of Political Geography (Chicago: Aldine, 1969), Introduction by editors.

(23) Cohen, Geography and Politics, p. 32.

(24) Ibid., pp. 32-33.

(25) C.R. Boxer, The Portuguese Seaborne Empire, 1415-1825 (New York: Knopf, 1969), p. 26.

(26) This point, in long-range historical perspective, is discussed by Modelski, "The Theory of Long Cycles," in R. Harkavy and E. Kolodziej, eds., American Security Policy and Policy-Making (Lexington, Mass.: D.C. Heath, 1980).

(27) These are discussed by Cohen, Geography and Politics, pp. 33-36, under "Early Global Geopolitical Perspectives," and in Kasperson and Minghi, Structure, Introduction.

(28) Cohen, Geography and Politics, p. 36.

(29) See, among others, ibid., pp. 38-40; Colin S. Gray, The Geopolitics of the Nuclear Era (New York: Crane, Russak, 1977), chap. 2. The primary source is, of course, Halford Mackinder, "The Geographical Pivot of History," which is published along with some other articles by

Mackinder in his Democratic Ideals and Reality (New York: Norton, 1962), pp. 241-264. Other works which analyze or interpret Mackinder include Nicholas Spykman, "Heartland and Rimland," in his The Geography of the Peace (New York: Harcourt, Brace and World, 1944), pp. 38-41; a number of contributions in Hans W. Weigert and V. Stefansson, eds., Compass of the World: A Symposium on Political Geography (New York: Macmillan, 1944); and H. Weigert et al., eds., Principles of Political Geography (New York: Appleton-Century-Crofts, 1957), esp. part 1.

(30) Thus, according to Weigert et al., Principles, p. 213:

> For it is exactly Mahan's exaltation of sea power which was challenged by Mackinder who, viewing the growing strength of Russia and Germany on the continents, became more and more alarmed by the challenge to sea power in a new age in which land power could outflank it and in which the mushrooming growth of industrialization and the extension of railroad nets on the continent were successfully competing with Britain's economic position in the world.

(31) See Cohen, Geography and Politics, pp. 40, 72; James Fairgrieve, "Geography and World Power," in Weigert and Stefansson, eds., Compass of the World, chap. 14, esp. p. 193, where it is claimed that "again like Germany, to an even greater extent than Germany, China is in a position to dominate the heartland with little possibility of interference from others." Further concerning China as a heartland-oriented power, see W.A. Douglas Jackson, The Russo-Chinese Border-lands (Princeton, N.J.: Van Nostrand, 1962).

(32) See Morton Kaplan, System and Process in International Politics (New York: John Wiley, 1957), chap. 3.

(33) Mackinder, Democratic Ideals, pp. 62, 70. In the latter: "What if the Great Continent, the whole World-Island or a large part of it, were at some future time to become a single and united base of sea-power? Would not the other insular bases be outbuilt as regards ships and out-manned as regards seamen?"

(34) Mackinder, Democratic Ideals, p. 150.

(35) The impact of Mackinder on German geopolitik is discussed in Derwent Whittlesey, "Haushofer: The Geopoliticians," in E.M. Earle, Makers of Modern Strategy (Princeton, N.J.: Princeton University Press, 1941), chap. 16; and in Cohen, Geography and Politics, pp. 40-44. For one imputed Western view of Soviet geopolitical perspectives in the context of Mackinder's framework, see David J.M. Hooson, A New Soviet Heartland? (Princeton, N.J.: Van Nostrand, 1964), esp. pp. 117-120 under "The Ghost of Mackinder." Discussing the relation of the

heartland theory to the lessons of World War II, Hooson claims the military significance of "defense in depth" may have been overstated, and that "the decisive contribution of the newly developed lands of the Volga-Baykal zone to the eventual victory was at bottom economic rather than strategic."

(36) Robert E. Walters, The Nuclear Trap (Baltimore: Penguin, 1974), chap. 2, under "The Fortress." Herein, p. 43:

> In the West, particularly in the United States, the ideas of Mackinder had great meaning after the war. Mackinder's Heartland Theory had been given great publicity in the United States in the 1940s, even on the popular level. The fear of Russia was double-barrelled — fear that the Red Army would sweep over Western Europe and a morbid fear of an international communist conspiracy. The Heartland theory gave an intellectual basis for the first fear and the subsequent triumph of Mao Tse-tung in China reinforced the belief that the Heartland could take over the World Island.

(37) Gray, Geopolitics of Nuclear Era, pp. 31-32, 53, 64-67, under "The Lessons of Geopolitics."

(38) Alan K. Henrikson, "America's Changing Place in the World: From 'Periphery to Centre'," in Jean Gottmann, ed., Centre and Periphery: Spatial Variation in Politics (Beverly Hills, Calif.: Sage, 1980), pp. 73-100.

(39) Ibid., p. 75.

(40) Ibid., p. 93.

(41) Cohen, Geography and Politics, p. 41 discusses this amalgam. For a summary analysis, see also inter alia, Derwent Whittlesey, "Haushofer"; regarding the claimed "besmirching" of the discipline of political geography by the racist and Social Darwinist doctrines of German geopolitik, see inter alia, Strausz-Hupé, Geopolitics; Isaiah Bowman, "Geography vs. Geopolitics," in Weigert and Stefansson, Compass, chap. 3; and in great detail, Derwent Whittlesey, German Strategy of World Conquest (New York: Farrar and Rinehart, 1942).

(42) Strausz-Hupé, Geopolitics, pp. 263-264.

(43) It should be noted that some serious early devotees of geopolitics defended it in the face of charges that it had been discredited by Haushofer and his like. Spykman, p. 7, in Geography of Peace, goes to great lengths to distinguish between geopolitics and geopolitik, in particular, attacking the latter for its attraction to analogies between the state and "organisms." Hence, Spykman: "The fact that certain

writers have distorted the meaning of the term geopolitics is no valid reason for condemning its method and material. It is, actually, an appropriate name for a type of analysis and a body of data which are indispensable to the process of reaching intelligent decisions on certain aspects of foreign policy."

(44) Cohen, Geography and Politics, pp. 40-44.

(45) In the original, see Alfred T. Mahan, The Influence of Seapower Upon History, 1669-1783 (Boston: Little, Brown, 1980).

(46) For a discussion of "indirect" strategies in a broad sense, see B.H. Liddell Hart, Strategy (New York: Praeger, 1954), esp. chap. 21 under "National Object and Military Aim."

(47) Noted by Cohen, Geography and Politics, p. 45, drawing from discussion in Alfred T. Mahan, The Problem of Asia and its Effects upon International Policies (Boston: Little, Brown, 1900).

(48) Spykman, Geography of Peace; and Nicholas Spykman, America's Strategy in World Politics (New York: Harcourt, Brace, 1942).

(49) Spykman, Geography of Peace, p. 43. Cohen, Geography and Politics, p. 46, discusses this reversed dictum and with it, Spykman's fears of German control of the European rimland.

(50) Spykman, Geography of Peace, pp. 53-54, discusses intra-rimland conflict.

(51) See Weigert et al., Principles, esp. chap. 8, under "The Impact of Location on Strategy and Power Politics."

(52) Ibid., pp. 233-234.

(53) Ibid., p. 234. See also Gray, Geopolitics of Nuclear Era, p. 43, for a related discussion of current Soviet problems in the Far East regarding access to the open ocean from the major Siberian naval base complexes. See also Michael MccGwire, "The Geopolitical Importance of Strategic Waterways in the Asian-Pacific Region," Orbis 19, 3 (Fall 1975): 1058-1076.

(54) Weigert et al., Principles, p. 234.

(55) See Captain Gary W. Anderson, "A Marine Corps Choke-Point Strategy," Naval Institute Proceedings, April 1980, pp. 103-104, who discusses the possible viable use of marine amphibious units as part of such a strategy utilizing the "Old Advanced Base Force Concept."

(56) See Cohen, Geography and Politics, pp. 49-51; Stephen Jones, "Global Strategic Views," The Geographical Review, 45, 4 (July 1955): 492-508; Alexander P. de Seversky, Air Power: Key to Survival (New York: Simon and Schuster, 1950); and Edward Warner, "Douhet, Mitchell, Seversky: Theories of Air Warfare," in Earle, Makers, chap. 20.

(57) See inter alia, the several selections in Weigert and Stefansson, Compass, chap. 2, under "New Directions and Skyways"; and see Jones, "Global Views," p. 501.

(58) For discussions of much-argued interpretations over Clausewitz's view on total war, decisive battles, etc., see, inter alia, H. Rothfels, "Clausewitz," in Earle, Makers, pp. 93-113.

(59) This concept is developed, historically, in Leonard Wainstein, "The Dreadnought Gap," in R. Art and K. Waltz, eds., The Use of Force (Boston: Little, Brown, 1971), pp. 153-169.

(60) United States, Strategic Bombing Survey, The Effects of Strategic Bombing on the German War Economy/The United States Strategic Bombing Survey, J. Kenneth Galbraith, Director (Washington: Overall Economic Effects Division, 1945).

(61) This is discussed in Jones, "Global Views," and in John Slessor, The Great Deterrent (New York: Praeger, 1957).

(62) See Jones, "Global Views," pp. 502-503: "Since he (Seversky) wishes the United States to avoid surface, and particularly ground, combat, he regards overseas bases as undesirable, probably untenable, and in an age of intercontinental flight, unnecessary."

(63) Ibid., p. 500: "In Slessor's view, the virtues of the Heartland – size, centrality, and inaccessibility – have become either of no advantage or disadvantageous. Have Raum and Lage gone into reverse, so to speak, in the air age?"

(64) Ibid.

(65) George Cressey, The Basis of Soviet Strength (New York: McGraw-Hill, 1945), pp. 245-246, whose writings are discussed in Henrikson, "America's Changing Place," p. 86, and in Jones, "Global Views," p. 497.

(66) This theme is expounded upon in Sprout and Sprout, "Geography and International Politics in an Era of Revolutionary Change," in W.A. Douglas Jackson, Politics and Geographic Relationships: Readings on the Nature of Political Geography (Englewood Cliffs, N.J.: Prentice-Hall, 1964), p. 47, as follows:

Every country has "natural" advantages and disadvantages in comparison with any other. Technological advances may narrow these differences, provided certain other conditions prevail. In any case, the consequences of achieving a higher level of productivity per capita is that this enables a people to pay a higher price for overcoming "natural" obstacles which, at a lowest economic and technological level, were insurmountable. . . . From this perspective, one queries writings which attribute a certain absoluteness to the limitations set by the non-human environment." In an era prior to that of the development of contemporary technical facilities, the Sprouts also saw technology gradually declining the need for overseas bases.

(67) For a comprehensive treatment of the variegated objective and subjective measures of power, see Klaus Knorr, The Power of Nations (New York: Basic Books, 1975). For one statement asserting the extreme difficulties involved in objectifying national power, see Stanley Hoffmann, "Notes on the Elusiveness of Power," International Journal 30 (Spring 1975): 183-206.

(68) Walters, Nuclear Trap, whose book Gray, Geopolitics of Nuclear Era (footnote 39, p. 27) says is "noteworthy for the attention that it pays to geopolitical concepts."

(69) Walters, Nuclear Trap, as evidenced in his chap. 8, contributes to geopolitical theory the prediction of a future focus on the underseas in Arctic regions. He envisages future importance in large submarine cargo carriers; also sees Mackinder finally superseded in that the heretofore invulnerable Soviet Arctic coastline might become a region of military confrontation.

(70) In addition to the other sources cited above, see Thomas S. Burns, The Secret War for the Ocean Depths: Soviet-American Rivalry for Mastery of the Seas (New York: Rawson Associates, 1978).

(71) See the introductory summary to Geoffrey Kemp, "The New Strategic Map: Geography, Arms Diffusion and the Southern Seas" (paper prepared for conference on Implications of the Military Build-Up in Non-Industrial States, Fletcher School, May 6-8, 1976). Additionally see a shorter version, "The New Strategic Map," Survival 19, 2 (March/April 1977): 50-59; "Scarcity and Strategy" in Foreign Affairs 56, 2 (January 1978): 396-414; and (with Harlan K. Ullman), "Towards a New Order of U.S. Maritime Policy," Naval War College Review, Summer 1977, pp. 99-113.

(72) See Kemp, "The New Strategic Map," maps on p. 51, utilizing an Azimuthal Equidistant Projection centered on Capetown. Concerning the new emphasis on the Southern hemisphere, see also Patrick Wall,

"The Vulnerability of the West in the Southern Hemisphere," Strategic Review 41, 1 (Winter 1976): 44-50; and Wall, ed., The Southern Oceans and the Security of the Free World (London: Stacy International, 1978). Noteworthy also, by the early 1980s, was the upsurge in explicitly geopolitical writings concerning Brazil and the South American southern cone, particularly those emanating from Brazil itself and associated with its General Golbery do Couto e Silva. The latter's works accord Brazil a central position in the world, arguing that its dominant geographical position in South America and along the South Atlantic Ocean makes it a prime factor in the politics of both South America and Africa. See Howard T. Pittman, "Geopolitics in the Southern Cone" (paper prepared for the panel on "Geopolitical Theory Revisited," International Studies Association, Philadelphia, March 21, 1981).

(73) Kemp, "New Strategic Map," p. 56.

(74) Gray, Geopolitics of Nuclear Era, pp. 1-7; and Colin Gray, "Arms Control 'the American Way,' " The Wilson Quarterly 1, 5 (Autumn 1977): 94-99.

(75) Gray, Geopolitics of Nuclear Era, chap. 3.

(76) Ibid., p. 40.

(77) Jones, "Global Strategic Views," p. 505, who makes a plea for "a series of filters, a composite or an eclectic global view." See also, Brig. Gen. Richard Eaton, "Probing Strategic Images: A New Approach to Geopolitical Analysis," paper delivered at meeting of International Studies Association, Philadelphia, March 21, 1981.

(78) For this argument, see Albert Wohlstetter, "Illusions of Distance," Foreign Affairs 46, 2 (January 1968): 242-255.

(79) See George Modelski, "The Theory of Long Cycles and U.S. Strategic Policy," in R. Harkavy and E. Kolodziej, eds., American Security Policy and Policy-Making (Lexington, Mass.: D.C. Heath, 1980), pp. 3-19.

(80) Ibid., p. 12.

(81) Ibid.

(82) Ibid.

(83) Ibid., p. 16.

(84) For basic information, see the annual, The Military Balance (London: IISS), which provides orders of battle for most of the world's nations; and also Michael Mihalka, "Supplier-Client Patterns in Arms

Transfers: The Developing Countries, 1967-76," in S. Neuman and R. Harkavy, Arms Transfers in the Modern World (New York: Praeger, 1979), pp. 49-76.

(85) See Geoffrey Kemp, "Defense Innovation and Geopolitics: From the Persian Gulf to Outer Space," in Scott Thompson, ed., From Weakness to Strength (San Francisco: Institute for Contemporary Studies, 1980). This chapter anticipates, in the early 1980s, an impending strategic milieu featuring space-based laser ABMs, anti-satellite weapons, etc.

(86) "Reagan Five Year Program Stresses More Offensive Stance, Larger Navy," Wall Street Journal, February 8, 1982, p. 6.

(87) See Hans Speier, "Magic Geography," Social Research, September 1941, pp. 310-330; Spykman, Geography of Peace, chap. 2; and Strausz-Hupé, Geopolitics, chap. 12.

(88) The distortions produced by Mercator maps are discussed in, inter alia, Harold and Margaret Sprout, "Geography and International Politics in an Era of Revolutionary Change," pp. 39-41. According to them, "The Mercator map was designed as a chart for mariners . . . as a chart for navigating ships across the ocean, the Mercator map was nearly ideal. . . . As long as European states dominated the world, and ships provided the only links connecting continents, the Mercator map was also fairly satisfactory for depicting commercial and military phenomena." See also Jones, "Global Strategic Views"; and Richard E. Harrison and Hans W. Weigert, "World View and Strategy," in Weigert and Stefansson, Compass, chap. 6.

(89) Jones, "Global Strategic Views," pp. 495-6, notes that "on a small-scale map the central position of the Heartland, or of the Soviet Union, in Eurasia looks terrifying. The Rimland seems such a narrow margin that it might be overwhelmed in a night."

(90) Henrikson, "America's Changing Place," discusses in great detail the relationship between meridians, "centeredness" on maps, and perceptions of power, cores, peripheries, etc. Specifically, he discusses the rising and falling tendencies to utilize U.S.-centered maps as reflections of the U.S. power position, in its own and others' eyes. This is also discussed in Spykman, Geography of Peace, chap. 2.

(91) Weigert et al., Principles, p. 217.

(92) On this point — and aided by a map — see Harrison and Weigert, "World View," in Weigert and Stefannson, Compass, pp. 84-85.

(93) Jones, "Global Strategic Views," pp. 502-503.

(94) Ibid., p. 503. Spykman, Geography of Peace, under "Mapping the World," pp. 8-18, claims that the polar azimuthal projection, all things considered, is the most valuable for depicting current political realities.

(95) Cohen, "Geography and Politics," pp. 41-42.

(96) Kemp, "New Strategic Map."

(97) See, for instance, the various selections in R. Axelrod, Structure of Decision: The Cognitive Maps of Political Elites (Princeton, N.J.: Princeton University Press, 1976); Jeffrey Hart, "Geopolitics and Dependency: Cognitive Maps of Latin American Foreign Policy Elites" (paper delivered at annual meeting of American Political Science Association, Chicago, September 25, 1976); and Joseph de Rivera, The Psychological Dimension of Foreign Policy (Columbus, Ohio: Chas. Merrill, 1968), esp. chap. 2 under "The Construction of Reality."

(98) Richard Barnet, Intervention and Revolution (Cleveland: World Publishing Co., 1968), chaps. 1, 2.

(99) Regarding control of southern Africa, for instance, see Wall, "Vulnerability of the West," replete with data regarding freighter and tanker traffic passing the Cape of Good Hope.

(100) Thomas Moorer and Alvin Cottrell, "The Search for U.S. Bases in the Indian Ocean: A Last Chance," Strategic Review, Spring 1980, p. 32.

(101) For one attempt at a wide-ranging analysis, see Michael MccGwire, "Changing Naval Operations and Military Intervention," Naval War College Review 15, 526 (Spring 1977): 3-25.

(102) This theme is most ably discussed in Robert Gilpin, U.S. Power and the Multinational Corporation (New York: Basic Books, 1975), esp. chap. 6, under "Corporate Expansionism and American Hegemony."

(103) See David H. Blake and Robert Walters, The Politics of Global Economic Relations (Englewood Cliffs, N.J.: Prentice-Hall, 1976), chap. 2; and Joan Spero, The Politics of International Economic Relations, 2nd ed. (New York: St. Martin's Press, 1981), parts 1, 2.

(104) See Blake and Walters, chap. 3; Spero, Politics of International Economic Relations, chaps. 1, 2; and John S. Odell, "Bretton Woods and International Political Disintegration: Implications for Monetary Diplomacy," in R. Lombra and W. Witte, eds., The Political Economy of Domestic and International Monetary Relations (Ames, Iowa: Iowa State University Press, 1982).

(105) Gilpin, U.S. Power, p. 152.

(106) Quoted in ibid., p. 151.

(107) See his data in ibid., tables 10 and 11, pp. 159-160.

(108) This point is discussed in several contributions to James Chace and Earl C. Ravenal, eds., Atlantis Lost (New York: New York University Press, 1976).

(109) Adumbrations of this dilemma may be gleaned from Richard J. Whalen, "Negotiable Instruments," Harpers 260 (March 1980): 24-27; and Norman Gall, "How Much More Can the System Take?" Forbes 125 (June 23, 1980): 91-98.

(110) For 1977, 1978, and 1979 data, see U.S. Senate, Committee on Foreign Relations, "United States Foreign Policy Objectives and Overseas Military Installations," prepared by Congressional Research Service, Library of Congress, Washington, 1979, p. 207. Data for other years can be obtained from DOD's Office of the Assistant Secretary of Defense, Comptroller.

(111) See "Soviet Imperialism is in the Red," Fortune, July 13, 1981, pp. 107-108.

(112) Ibid., p. 108.

(113) Gilpin, U.S. Power, footnote 14, pp. 273-274.

(114) Donella H. Meadows et al., The Limits to Growth (New York: Universe Books, 1972). For a critique, see H.S.D. Cole et al., eds., Models of Doom: A Critique of the Limits to Growth (New York: Universe Books, 1973).

(115) Among numerous works surveying the contemporary neo-Malthusian theme, see in particular Dennis Pirages, Global Ecopolitics (N. Scituate, Mass.: Duxbury, 1978), esp. chaps. 1-2, which invoke a new Dominant Social Paradigm (DSP) centered on permanent resource scarcity and hence zero sum international politics; and William Ophuls, Ecology and the Politics of Scarcity (San Francisco: W.H. Freeman, 1977).

(116) For an excellent theoretical analysis of further commodity cartel possibilities, see Pirages, Global Ecopolitics, chap. 5, under "Nonfuel Minerals: The New Cartels?" Therein, the iron, copper, and aluminum markets are analyzed in some detail. See also Zuhayr Mikdashi, The International Politics of Natural Resources (Ithaca, N.Y.: Cornell University Press, 1976), chap. 3.

(117) This specter underpins analyses such as that by Wall, "Vulnerability of the West."

(118) The now ubiquitous and perhaps often abused term "regime," associated with Joseph Nye, is defined by him in "Maintaining a Nonproliferation Regime," in George Quester, ed., Nuclear Proliferation: Breaking the Chain (Madison: University of Wisconsin Press, 1981), p. 16: "International regimes are the sets of rules, norms and procedures that regulate behavior and control its effects in international affairs. Regimes are seldom perfect. They vary in coherence and degree of adherence. We measure their existence in the acceptance of normative influences and constraints on international behavior."

(119) In general, such "norms" are discussed in William Coplin, "Law and International Politics," in Robert L. Pfaltzgraff, ed., Politics and the International System (Philadelphia: Lippincott, 1972).

(120) The author was privileged to see draft copies of the Arthur D. Little Company's study concerning major powers' raw materials vulnerabilities, compiled for the U.S. Navy's Project 2000 (hereinafter cited as "The ADL Report"). Two other major recent works are International Economic Studies Institute, Raw Materials and Foreign Policy (Washington, D.C.: 1976) – hereinafter referred to as "IESI Study; and Yuan-li Wu, Raw Material Supply in a Multipolar World, 2nd ed. (New York: Crane Russak, 1979).

(121) Concerning raw materials, there are somewhat varying opinions on what is or should be of greatest concern. See "Now the Squeeze on Metals," Business Week, July 2, 1979, pp. 48-51; "Allure of Risky Deals in Metals," New York Times, June 5, 1981, p. D1 (which focuses on cobalt, manganese, tantalum, columbium, and chromium); Fred Warshofsky, "Strategic Minerals: The Invisible War," Readers Digest, February 1981, pp. 81-85; and "World Political Climate Could Endanger U.S. Metal Supplies," Centre Daily Times, February 25, 1980, p. 3 (which pinpoints chromium, manganese, and cobalt, with a second echelon consisting of zinc, tin, aluminum, titanium, tungsten, and nickel). IESI, table 2, p. 95, lists bauxite, chromium, copper, platinum group, and petroleum as of "major" U.S. policy concern. Analyses of the world petroleum problem include Pirages, Global Ecopolitics chap. 4; Raymond Vernon, ed., The Oil Crisis (New York: W.W. Norton, 1976); Congressional Quarterly, The Middle East: U.S. Policy, Israel, Oil and the Arabs, 4th ed. (Washington, D.C.: 1979), pp. 70-88; Peter Odell, Oil and World Power (Baltimore: Penguin, 1975).

(122) On Soviet non-fuel raw materials dependence, see Daniel S. Papp, "Soviet Non-Fuel Mineral Resources: Surplus or Scarcity?" (unpublished paper, May 1981). Concerning Soviet petroleum imports, see U.S. Central Intelligence Agency, Soviet Economy: Problems and Prospects (Washington, D.C.: GPO, 1977); and in particular, The World Oil Market in the Years Ahead, (Washington, D.C.: GPO, 1979).

(123) See, in particular, Pirages, Global Ecopolitics, chap. 3; and G. Kemp, "Scarcity and Strategy," Foreign Affairs, 56, 2 (January 1978): 396-414. Regarding the evolving international politics of food, see Raymond F. Hopkins and Donald J. Puchala, Global Food Interdependence: Challenge to American Foreign Policy (New York: Columbia University Press, 1980).

(124) The impact of such laissez-faire practices on arms transfers – or international diplomacy in general – is discussed in R. Harkavy, The Arms Trade and International Systems (Cambridge, Mass.: Ballinger, 1975), chap. 2. For long-term historical perspective, see John Fred Bell, A History of Economic Thought, 2nd ed. (New York: Ronald Press, 1967); also, various writings of Jacob Viner.

(125) Pirages, Global Ecopolitics, discusses the possibilities for U.S. use of the "grain weapon" for political purposes. See also Dan Morgan, Merchants of Grain (New York: Viking Press, 1979).

(126) V.D. Sokolovskii, Soviet Military Strategy, translated by H.S. Dinerstein, Leon Goure, and Thomas W. Wolfe (Englewood Cliffs, N.J.: Prentice-Hall, 1963), p. 115.

(127) Ibid., p. 204.

(128) Bayard Rustin and Carl Gershman, "Africa, Soviet Imperialism and the Retreat of American Power," Commentary 64, 4 (October 1977): 38.

(129) Ibid.; see also "Moscow Believed Unlikely to Shift in Push for Greater Role in Africa," Washington Post, May 30, 1978, p. A10: "Writing last month in the theoretical journal International Affairs, G. Roschin enumerated a long list of U.S. raw material imports from Africa and went on to say that the Soviets give their 'complete support' to a vigorous international struggle to obliterate capitalist exploiters from the African countries."

(130) Gray, Geopolitics of Nuclear Era, chap. 3.

(131) See "Soviets Reportedly Bought Up Cobalt Before Zaire Invasion," Washington Post, May 24, 1978, p. A15. "Zaire has 65 percent of the world's cobalt supply, used in so-called super-alloys required for jet engines, missiles, and submarines." Before the abortive invasion of Shaba Province, the USSR was reported having bought up a major share of the world's available supply of cobalt. See also Warshofsky, "Strategic Minerals."

7 Conclusion

Our preceding discussion has in great measure been devoted to an historical and roughly chronological review of the major powers' basing diplomacy throughout much of the twentieth century, in an attempt to relate that history to a broader sweep of political and military problems. Cutting across such a longitudinal framework – and with an eye to the future – some attention may be due, first, to the relationship of basing problems to a number of streams of modern international relations theory, and second, to several critical, related domains of security policy.

Concerning theory, the previous discussion of geopolitical frameworks may be abetted by attention to such as "systems theory," dependency paradigms, and various quasi-theoretical assumptions connected to the hoary concept of "the national interest." Concerning related security domains, those of arms transfers, arms resupply during conflict, and nuclear proliferation stand out as worthy of contextual discussion.

BASING ACCESS AND INTERNATIONAL RELATIONS
THEORIES OR PARADIGMS

One of the arguably more prominent areas of developing macrolevel international relations theory is that of "systems" theory. The attribution of "theory" here is admittedly rather pretentious; rather one refers to a very flexible framework for comparative history with a long-term historical dimension. Generally, systems theory involves the division of diplomatic history into more or less discrete eras (the interwar period, early postwar period, and such) demarcated by major wars or by other significant watershed events, such as waves of major revolutions or the kind of global power reversal apparently inaugurated by OPEC in 1973. Bracketed by such watersheds, historical epochs can then be compared according to a variety of general characteristics ("variables," if in a strict empirical sense) which in one way or another would be applicable or germane to any period.

Most basically, such systems or epochal characteristics encompass the dual factors of structure, and of behavior or process, corresponding to, first, a "sociology" of the system's power structure and second, the prevailing activities of – and transactions between – the major actor states. Accordingly, scholars such as Morton Kaplan and Richard Rosecrance have devised some rough criteria for comparing historical epochs(1) which, ignoring what would obviously be a somewhat futile concern for precision, can be listed as follows:

- The spectrum running from bipolarity ("loose" or "tight," depending upon what proportion of other nations are closely aligned with the superpowers) to multipolarity, which essentially describes the hierarchy of power and pattern of alliance combinations among major nations.
- The extent of ideological basis of conflict among major powers (including here religion and perhaps even ethnicity or race) in contrast to sheer "balance-of-power" bases for alignments perhaps more strictly geopolitical in nature; these factors in turn will normally drive tendencies toward or against stability and longevity of alignments.
- The tendency to all-out maximization pursued in diplomacy and warfare; contrariwise, converged-upon widespread "norms" about constraints on competition (at another extreme, chivalry).
- If applicable, the "regulator" of the system, be it a form of international law ("mere" custom, balance of power as a norm, etc.) or international organization (of varying degrees of formality or inclusiveness).
- The primary ends of international politics – accrual of wealth, status, territorial expansion, industrial growth, propagation of political values, ideology, religion.
- Dominant modes of economic production and of international economic intercourse – mercantilism, laissez-faire, state capitalism and/or socialism.
- The rate, nature, and diffusion of technological change, particularly regarding major weapons systems.
- Dominant forms of interaction – trade, direct investment, military intervention, emigration flows.
- Trends toward integration and disintegration, autarky and interdependence, convergence (social, cultural, political) or divergence.

In assessing the connection between such a panoply of general systems variables on the one hand, and patterns of strategic basing access on the other, what generalizations can be offered, at least as seemingly divulged by the recent history of the twentieth century? This involves, of course, daunting complexities, but perhaps certain trends or patterns may tentatively be surmised. And, of course, a certain almost tautological reciprocity is here involved; patterns of access serve somewhat to define the structure of the system and its nations' behavior, while the particular mix of the above-listed factors existing at any given point may strongly determine who has strategic basing access to what or where, under what conditions, and at what cost.

Concerning polarity, it is commonly generalized that the interwar period saw a modified form of multipolarity (approaching bipolarity on the eve of World War II as on the eve of World War I); that the immediate postwar period was characterized by a fairly tight bipolarity (with a relatively small unaligned neutral periphery); and that the recent period has tended toward a layered mix of loose bipolarity (in a politico-military sense – with an extensive nonaligned periphery, but with nuclear bipolarity) and economic multipolarity (accounting for the outsized economic strengths of Japan, Western Europe, and OPEC devoid of comparable military power).(2) Further, whereas the interwar period saw a less significant role for ideology as a determinant of alignments (at least until its close) and a greater tendency for shifting alliances, the immediate postwar period witnessed somewhat rigid, ideologically based alignments.(3) More recently, that pattern has been loosened by China's defection from the Soviet bloc, the fragmentation of NATO, and numerous unexpected developments in the Third World, indicating some overall reversal toward the traditional balance-of-power basis for diplomacy.

The patterns of overseas basing seem only partly explicable in the light of the structural characteristics of the several identifiable systems of the past sixty years or so. In the interwar period (as throughout a lengthy period preceding World War I), as noted, the extensiveness of major power access was not strongly correlated with the overall hierarchy of power. Then, the extent of colonial holdings almost entirely determined the possession of bases – Germany, Austria-Hungary (earlier), Japan, Russia, and the United States all had only nugatory regular access to facilities by comparison with Britain and France. Further, the greater tendency to shifting diplomatic alignments in a relatively nonideological context seems to have precluded the mutual granting of "permanent" or routine access within what were then often only weak and tenuous alliances – those conditions began to change only in the late 1930s.(4) This paralleled similar manifestations regarding arms transfers, the patterns of which appeared almost divorced from prevailing alignments.

After 1945, and increasingly as the immediate postwar period progressed, there developed a closer correlation between national power (as measured roughly by GNP and/or military budgets and orders of battle) and global networks of access, all the more so as former colonial empires gradually dissolved. The competition for facilities became virtually a two-nation game and has remained so even as the structure of the system, in some important senses, has shifted toward partial multipolarity. The primary basis for access has remained throughout one of ideological affinity, as that in turn is transmitted through the patterns of arms transfers, military training, and economic aid. But the recently reported use of a Jordanian port and overland logistics by the Soviet bloc for resupplying arms to Iraq, and also the PRC's granting of access to the United States for intelligence facilities, indicate that there are exceptions, perhaps now to become more frequent as national conflicts within the Third World increasingly cut across the lines of ideology as defined by the superpower competition.(5)

The concept of system "regulator" (in Rosecrance's terminology), in the twentieth century has primarily applied to the role of global international organization.(6) The League was, of course, responsible for some initial wedges into the Western colonial structure, if only through the Mandate System and its (ultimately futile) prohibitions on Japanese use of the Pacific islands for military bases, even if violated. In some vague but telling sense, however, the League may have begun a long process of delegitimizing the presence of major powers' overseas bases, the skein of which may be pursued to the present.

The UN, in a number of ways, has had a perhaps major impact on the major powers' access to facilities. It has, of course, been an important facilitator of the entire postwar decolonization process, which itself has greatly altered the global basis for military access. Then too, the UN's "Committee of 24," dominated by a combination of Soviet and radical Third World nations, has been an instrument of constant pressure on the Western powers concerning divestiture of remaining strategic holdings, nowadays for the most part primarily involving small islands such as Ascension, St. Helena, Guam, and Gibraltar. The overall practical impact, while difficult to gauge, may have been somewhat to "delegitimize" the Western powers' continuing control in some places.(7) On the whole, developing "norms" within the UN respecting undiluted sovereignty, and the demilitarization of certain regions such as the Indian Ocean have appeared to place some greater pressures on big powers' access to facilities, possibly disproportionately to the disadvantage of the West. Perhaps also, developing norms concerning an evolving new Law of the Sea regime — which has also emerged out of the UN milieu have also created such pressures, applicable also to overflights and ship passages outside the once traditional three-mile limit. Ironically, despite much talk about growing interdependence, sovereignty seems increasingly both more jealously guarded and territorially more extended.

The shift away from laissez-faire international economics since the 1920s (involving, for instance, earlier, far more unrestricted private corporate roles in transportation, communications, weapons production and trade) has also seen removal of nongovernmental actors (NGOs) from military or quasi-military roles.(8) In the interwar period, private shipping lines and airlines operated somewhat outside the control of their governments in seeking and acquiring access; private German and Italian airlines dominated air routes in South America and the Near East, while western shipping interests operated repair dockyards in China and elsewhere which serviced warships for all comers on a strictly business basis, divorced from prevailing patterns of diplomatic alignment. This began to change in the late 1930s, as some of these private organizations, for instance, America's Pan-Am and Germany's Condor Airline became increasingly entangled in national military and intelligence operations.

Most notably, earlier periods saw little of the linkage politics which dominates contemporary access diplomacy. Nowadays – witness the recent Soviet-Libya relationship – basing diplomacy is enmeshed in a web of interlocking quid pro quo transactions, often spanning arms transfers, economic aid, oil and other raw materials supplies, provision of nuclear technology "sweeteners" and so forth.(9) That, of course, is a function of the near-complete dominance of coordinated government-to-government diplomacy, of a dirigisme which no longer leaves many loose ends for private endeavor.

Overall, one can say that over a lengthy period now, basing diplomacy by the major powers has come to be pursued in an increasingly less permissive international environment. Before 1940, the facts of colonial control and the then existing vast scope for private activities made for a highly controlled environment, and this was one assumption underpinning the analyses of Mahan and Mackinder (easy Western naval access around the "rimlands"). In the two decades after 1945, the very nature of the international system (tight bipolarity, rigid alliances, ideological conflict) retained a still relatively permissive environment for basing access, as reflected for instance in the very relaxed status-of-forces arrangements within which the United States and other Western powers operated.(10) In recent years, however, significant systemic change (decolonization, trends toward multi-polarity, de-coupling of alliances, more symmetrical power relation-ships between north and south) has produced a far less permissive environment for the big power's base acquisition drives.

The United States has been relatively disadvantaged in the bargain thus far, but as witness its experiences in Indonesia, Egypt, Somalia, Iraq, and Sudan, the Soviets have not been completely immune from its effects. But then too, increasing intra-Third World conflict, as in the African Horn and Persian Gulf of late, may serve to provide newly enhanced leverage for basing access to major powers, as quid pro quo for desperately needed military support. And a more desperate global struggle over raw materials, if combined with increased levels of conflict among smaller states requiring protectors and arms suppliers, could militate again toward increased big-power penetration for military access, if only as a result of hard bargaining.

BASES AND DEPENDENCY THEORY: A SWING OF THE PENDULUM?

In recent years, dependency paradigms in their various manifestations, have come almost to dominate mid-level conceptualization in inter-national relations scholarship.(11) They are really lineal descendants of the hoary theories of imperialism developed back near the turn of the century by the likes of Hobson, Lenin, Kautsky, and Schumpeter, which were themselves fundamentally divided along a basic divide between basically economic and more political explanations.   Whereas these theories, however, dealt mostly with trade, investment, and raw materials problems, the more recent dependency models have tended toward a much broader perspective, taking into account the entirety of relationships and transactions between the developed and developing worlds, not excluding the more subjective cultural and psychological dimensions. A whole new terminology has been developed in the process, featuring the vivid imagery of "core" and "periphery," "semi-periphery" and so forth.

Fundamental to such paradigms is a root historical explanation based on assumptions about a "head start" for the West back at the onset of the modern age which, gradually consolidated and made near-permanent by the subsequent "automatic" workings of comparative advantage, is claimed very difficult for the LDCs to reverse. Their situations are considered virtually to have become "structured in," on the wrong end of a lineal and not easily reversed historical momentum.(12)

However, the conjunction of Vietnam and OPEC is now commonly considered to have been a great divide in the 1970s, which did reverse the long tide of historical momentum. More recent analyses, even some from the Left, concede a new view of dependency, as old cores wane and old peripheries move toward the center. There is an at least implicit nod here to the more cyclical views of history, which see endless "rise and fall."

Along with arms transfers, overall terms of trade, cooptation of "comprador" elites, rigidified and inescapable one-crop export econ-omies, and the power exercised by industrial nations in the IMF — the symbolic as well as practical meaning of major power bases on the LDCs' soil had long been a staple of the first, imperialism, and then, dependency literature. If you needed advanced weapons, economic aid, some technology transfer, a loan from the World Bank, or a little "infrastructure," you got it by providing an air staging facility or a locale for a satellite tracking station. Not without reason, a foreign base presence came to symbolize continued post-colonial dependence on big-power protection, the price that had to be paid to keep open the flow of conventional arms, or World Bank loans.

More recently, however, some vast changes have appeared to occur. In a post-colonial world, with bipolarity giving way to a more diffuse global power structure, with the facts of existing and feared raw materials shortages, and with the seeming inhibitions on big power military interventions in the Third World, many smaller nations increasingly seemed able to call some of the shots, acquiring consider-able surprising leverage over major powers. Indeed, where the latter need access badly enough, dependent powers have often been able to demand a very stiff price, and to make it stick. The price is often extensive military and/or economic aid, often too the promise of qualitatively more sophisticated weapons transfers or of nuclear tech-nology which could open the weapons option, and sometimes the assurance of military protection or support.

These more recent trends have been amply illustrated by recent events in the Middle East-Indian Ocean area. There, still contingent American access to Egyptian air and naval facilities has been bought only by massive, multibillion dollar commitments of economic and military aid, plus commitments for the rearming and retraining of Egyptian forces. Oman too, even if an oil power, demanded military aid as well as protection, and the facts about who held the most cards in the bargain were well advertised when Oman temporarily appeared to withdraw from the arrangement because of the nature of U.S. use of its air bases for the abortive Iranian hostage rescue raid. Somalia too demanded and received extensive aid, but sought also a broader U.S. commitment to its side of the Ogaden dispute in exchange for use of Berbera and other facilities. Meanwhile, while the Iran-Iraq war raged, it was announced that the Soviets had achieved a higher level of military access to Syria in exchange for more arms and also a formal defense security treaty. And the "LDC" with the most leverage of all, Saudi Arabia, succeeded in acquiring AWACs and advanced F-15 technology without budging at all toward giving the United States significant access to bases near the Persian Gulf.

None of these bargains at all smacked of the one-sided dependency so dear to the images of radical theorists. Indeed, the clearly changing leverage relationships between the developed and the developing nations concerning provision of military facilities, seemed very accurately indicative of trends in overall leverage relationships between the previously dependent and the erstwhile manipulators of their strings.(13) As in other relationships in other areas of human endeavor and conflict, it often came down to the question of who needed whom more and for what.

BASES AND THEORIZING ABOUT THE NATIONAL INTEREST

Defining and describing national security interests (or the national interest) down a descending hierarchy from primary to secondary to tertiary levels has long been a staple of foreign policy analyses.(14) And such analyses have been central to general paradigms such as Morgenthau's, which contain a core emphasis on raw power and endemic national conflict. Such formulations stress the normalcy of constant, dogged, watchful pursuit of interests, but only up to the practical point beyond which aspirations exceed capabilities. Within that rather vague no man's land, scholars and policymakers argue along a spectrum running from "interventionism" to "isolationism," each claiming to embody prudence, wisdom, and balance. Such differences of opinion over national interests – which have often conflicting long- and short-run considerations – are evidenced virtually in all countries.

The evolving nature of basing-access diplomacy raises some interesting questions about definitions of national interest, all the more so as such access must now increasingly be pursued by tangible quid pro quo and various forms of leverage to a degree not witnessed at least for several centuries during the long age of Western colonialism. In the past, one nation might have viewed another's value – as a reflection of its own interests – according to its potential for weighing in on one side of an alliance, something to be measured by sheer population and its translation into orders of battle. That was particularly the case when earlier, population and land area were perhaps more closely correlated than they are today.(15)

Geopolitical theorists in the 1920s and 1930s did give some attention to the locational aspects of strategic value and hence of rival national interests, paying heed to nations astride chokepoints or traditional invasion routes, or those consigned to the still potentially vulnerable role of "buffer state."(16) But the advent of postwar bipolarity seemed to put a high premium on virtually all territories, as the assumed lessons of the 1930s appeasement period dictated holding firm at all points lest one's credibility slip and the momentum of power shift. Even so, some theorists such as George Kennan were to insist upon retention of a hierarchy from primary to lesser interests, with primary ones being defined by those industrial areas – Europe and Japan particularly – which contained the capacity for producing the "sinews of war."(17) All else was to be considered secondary, that is, relatively more expendable, and such considerations transcended even those of geographical propinquity, which had long defined "spheres of influence" and core interests.

Nowadays, while the relevance of traditional measures of strategic value and national interest – population, military production, geographic positioning in relation to possible avenues of invasion – remain largely intact, two other factors are now increasingly accorded pride of place: raw materials resource location and military access.

What is increasingly apparent is that a nation's value as an access point need not depend upon its size, power, or other traditionally assumed measures of importance. Location astride a vital naval passage or along a transcontinental air corridor is important, but particularly so where for one or another major power, there is no substitute. Hence, critical national interests can often become virtually situational, and also ephemeral.

Somalia was earlier of high value to the Soviet national interest, but only so long as Ethiopia was not available as a substitute. Oman and Kenya have become of near primary interest to the United States, largely for lack of regional alternatives. Turkey becomes more important to the U.S. national interest when Iran defects from the U.S. alliance system, and still more so when Greece really looks precarious; China's role as a U.S. basing host, however, may diminish a bit the importance of Turkey. Israel counts for much less in the U.S. interest calculus so long as Egypt is forthcoming with access for forward prepositioning of materiel, and so forth.

But then, changing international norms and evolving military technology have worked to alter long-held traditional conceptions of value and interest. Iceland and the Azores have apparently acquired much greater value because of the advent of ground-linked hydrophone ASW technology. And the increasing trend toward closure of international air space (including a less relaxed view of military overflights) has put a premium on the air spaces over Zaire, Sudan, Turkey, Yugoslavia, Iran, Pakistan, India, and others, altering in the process perceptions of national interest elsewhere. And we have already noted how previously obscure ocean islands – Diego Garcia, Ascension, Mauritius, Gan, Kerguelen, Pelelieu – have come to be perceived in some cases as vital interests of major powers, no better illustrated than by the efforts made in the UN's "Committee of 24" to bring about their "decolonization."(18) All in all, the imperatives of modern access diplomacy appear to have shifted somewhat the locus of strategic value and of primary interests away from a basis in population and industrial location, and toward an ever-shifting basis in strategic geographical location.

BASING ACCESS AND SOME RELATED SECURITY DOMAINS

A major theme of this book is that of the long-term shifts in the diplomacy of basing access, that is, the changing basis of how or with what facilities are acquired and retained. In that vein, we have portrayed a secular trend throughout this century, whereby the basis of access first shifted from colonial control to military alliances, and then somewhat from the latter to various forms of quid pro quo, often in the absence of formal alliances. Though it is by no means the entire story, the evolving nexus between arms transfers and access to facilities has been central to the more recent changes. It is apparent that this nexus has become tighter, though only a generation ago, it had hardly existed; most certainly, it was not then a significant factor in international diplomacy.

The preceding analysis has appeared to demonstrate that there is a significant and growing correlation between arms transfers and strategic access. Of course, given the current importance of the former as an instrument of diplomacy, it may really be described as an intervening variable measuring overall political association, usually supported by the facts of alliances and/or obvious ideological affinity. The precise nature of the correlation involved (it is the subject of considerable dispute) requires further (rigorous, quantitative) analysis, and is beyond the scope of this work.(19)

Most basing and/or facilities arrangements do appear to coexist nowadays with sole – or predominant – supplier acquisition styles, that is, where a recipient acquires all or most of its arms from one supplier. Conversely, the multiple-source acquisition of arms, particularly if across the major power blocs (the recipient receives both Western and Soviet-bloc arms simultaneously), more often than not occurs where no major power has significant strategic access, indicating a degree of neutrality or ideological "evenhandedness."

Virtually all of the dependent nations which have granted the Soviet Union major basing facilities have received most of their arms from them: Syria, South Yemen, Somalia (earlier), Angola, Vietnam, Guinea,

Cuba, and Iraq (earlier). Iraq, however, even before its war with Iran, had begun to acquire some French weapons (including Mirage F-1 fighters) while still vastly increasing its acquisitions from the USSR, and had apparently put fairly strict limits on Soviet access to air and naval facilities. It is also noteworthy that those major Soviet clients which have maintained significantly diversified arms sources across the major blocs — Libya, Nigeria, India, Sri Lanka, and Algeria to a lesser extent — have demonstrated visible reluctance to grant the USSR major "permanent" facilities. This may in some cases have had less to do with diluted ideological affinity than with the availability of alternative sources of arms; but size, wealth, or both may be other factors. The contrast between Libya and India, on the one hand, and Ethiopia, South Yemen, and Angola, on the other, may be instructive, although the impact of a Soviet presence in deterring external threats may also have played a role in the latter cases. But in no case does the Soviet Union have major basing facilities where U.S. or other Western arms supply predominates.

The same generalizations hold for the hosts to major U.S. facilities. Greece, Turkey, Spain, Portugal, the Philippines, Japan, and so on, have all relied primarily on U.S. arms. Many U.S. facilities, however, are located in nations tied in one way or another to the U.S. security orbit, but where arms-market leverage is not critical. This is true of Australia and Iceland, for instance, and also for numerous facilities located in British possessions or lingering spheres of influence: the Caribbean, the Bahamas, Bermuda, Ascension, and Diego Garcia. There have been only a few cases where U.S. and other Western basing rights have coexisted with some (though not predominant) Soviet arms supplies to the host, most notably Iran (under the Shah), Cyprus, and Morocco.

The above is not meant to convey the impression that arms transfers can always be a sufficient inducement to bring about the granting of access, and the latter once granted, to retain it. The USSR has not, for instance, acquired major permanent naval bases either in Algeria or India, even with heavy weapons transfers, though that has obviously been one intent. And arms shipments were not sufficient to maintain Soviet access in Egypt, though it might be argued that denial to the latter of still more advanced arms than were being shipped was one major reason for Sadat's rupture of what had seemed a solid relationship. Likewise, U.S. arms sales, including the likes of F-15 and AWACs aircraft, have not sufficed to acquire the U.S. permanent facilities in Saudi Arabia; nor have supplies to Indonesia. These exceptions do not, however, invalidate what is clearly a strong and perhaps growing trend, one recently underscored by the U.S./PRC relationship spanning arms supplies (potentially) and facilities access.

Concerning the arms transfer/base nexus, it is apparent this has been, heretofore, primarily a two-nation game, corresponding to the SIPRI typology of arms supply policy styles which characterized U.S. and Soviet motives as "hegemonic" — primarily military-political.(20) The arms supply policies of Britain and France, to the contrary, were characterized as basically "commercial," devoid of such political purposes as the acquisition of bases. Recent French arms sales and base acquisition policies in West Africa, however, may blur such distinctions to an extent.

Generally, the growing connection of arms supply to the acquisition of access may be perceived as part of a broader trend toward linked transactions, in an era witnessing increasingly coordinated security and economic policies spanning a variety of domains or "regimes." Hence, France can ensure oil supplies from Iraq not only via arms transfers, but also through provision of nuclear technology (a nuclear "sweetener") and a national color TV network; Germany's nuclear deal with Brazil involved not only raw uranium sales to the former in return, but apparently also some significant sales of warships to Brazil. The Soviet-Libya relationship has evidenced similarly linked transactions. And, in many cases, bases have obviously entered such bargains, as witness the recent U.S.-Somalia and U.S.-Kenya negotiations, or those involving the USSR with Syria and Vietnam – the precise, actual linkages are often left publicly obscure.

Further regarding the arms-transfer-basing nexus, it should be pointed out that whatever correlations exist are to be measured not only by quantitative arms data, whether utilizing monetary values (for combinations of cash sales, credit sales, or aid) or discrete numbers of weapons systems (so many aircraft or tanks), but by the qualitative component of the transfers.(21) For between suppliers and recipients, and particularly where the latter are not lacking in political clout nor for alternative arms suppliers, what may be at issue regarding quid pro quo is whether the transfer of a given sophisticated system will be allowed. Very often, this will involve not only questions about destabilization of regional arms balances, but perhaps also the potential jeopardization of technical secrets should the systems later fall into the wrong hands. The U.S. dilemma – and its outcome – regarding sales of AWACs and the Phoenix missiles accompanying the F-14 fighter to Iran were fully illustrative of this problem, as was later the U.S. dilemma regarding AWACs for Saudi Arabia.

Such considerations have affected the basing diplomacies of both the United States and USSR in recent years. The level of sophistication of arms to be supplied by the United States to Egypt – and also Saudi Arabia – has become closely bound up with the degree of facilities access to be granted the United States. The United States apparently had to agree to the transfer of advanced attack aircraft in order to expedite its base negotiations with the Philippines. The recent Soviet pact with Syria which clearly increased Soviet air and naval access to that country (perhaps to involve permanent billeting of Soviet pilots) appears hinged not only on security assurances, but also on still more advanced weapons sales to a country which does not lack older ones in massive quantity. Hence, too, the competing U.S. and Soviet access imperatives are not at all conducive to the aspirations by some for regional supplier arms control arrangements which might ban the transfer of certain types of weapons, or of those beyond certain levels of capability.

Arms transfers are not, of course, the only element of quid pro quo for the major powers' overseas facilities, though they appear increasingly central, near ubiquitous. In a related vein, diplomatic and/or military support is often involved, as witness the aforementioned Soviet-Syria relationship, or the force demonstrations by the United States on behalf of Kenya in some recent periods of trouble.

Trade concessions have not, apparently, significantly been used as quid pro quo for bases, though they have come under discussion. The United States has apparently used such concessions only once, with the granting in the 1950s of landing rights to an Icelandic airline, in order to ease Iceland's willingness to continue the provision of U.S. facilities. Trade concessions also run into various collateral considerations, for instance, conflicts with the obligations of GATT agreements such as the recent Tokyo Round. Whether the Soviets have explicitly greased basing deals with trade concessions – such as purchasing Egyptian or Sudanese cotton exports – is not here known.

Explicit rental agreements may, however, be becoming more frequent as quid pro quo in an era witnessing the withering of convergent security perspectives between hosts and users, if not also of formal alliances. Rentals can be relatively advantageous to other forms of "quid" in that they can allow for a clearer picture of cost (an annual unambiguous budget line-item) and hence encourage a more rigorous cost-benefit evaluation of facilities requirements. That has more or less come to characterize the U.S.-Philippines arrangement (though it is more complicated than that), and may well be the wave of the future, looking forward to later U.S. negotiations with Spain, Turkey, Greece, Portugal, and Iceland. More and more, at least for the United States, the matter of basing access may be put on a somewhat bloodless business basis, but hence also subject to questions about why such payments should be made to countries the United States protects in the bargain.

Of course, the attribution of the term "rent" to many basing agreements, if not explicitly stated as such, would be more or less accurate where economic or military aid is involved. For the United States in recent years, this has involved a confusing mix of instruments: Security Supporting Assistance (SSA), the Military Assistance Program (MAP), and the loans involved in Foreign Military Sales (FMS) financing.(22) The old MAP program, once crucial to the U.S. "forward" support system, has recently been whittled down to some eight recipients, for several of whom – Greece, Portugal, Spain, Turkey, Philippines, Thailand – it has acted in large part as rental payment for facilities. FMS financing has similarly been used in several of the above cases, and in South Korea as well. Other forms of economic assistance – AID loans and grants, Food for Peace, the Peace Corps – have had a less frequent and visible connection to basing access, and involve numerous nations with no military ties to the United States (still, South Korea, Portugal, Morocco and other facilities hosts were prominent recipients of Food for Peace assistance.) The same could be said for Export-Import Bank loans, though here too, key base hosts such as Spain and the Philippines have been heavy ExIm loan recipients.

The details of many Soviet base agreements are hard to ascertain. Presumably, similar to the U.S. experience, a plethora of quid pro quo have been utilized: arms transfers, various forms of military and economic aid qua rentals, trade concessions, and diplomatic-military support. There is some evidence that the Soviets have been able, disproportionately, to utilize the first- and last-named instruments more frequently than the United States. The future, however, may yet see a trend toward greater balance between the experiences of the superpowers, as the memories of Western, capitalist imperialism fade.

The evolving access diplomacy, and the quid pro quo offered developing nations for facilities, brings us to the impact of the latter's sensitivities to sovereignty in this context. It is a matter we have touched upon before, but only indirectly.

For long, of course, many developing nations have reluctantly suffered a foreign basing presence, if not imposed by force majeure, because it was needed for their protection either against a rival (to the user) superpower or a regional foe. When the LDCs' leverage was low, it virtually had to concede a permissive basing environment; when high, it could set some terms in status of forces treaties regarding external military uses, extraterritoriality (police and court jurisdictions) access by local officials, and so forth. As noted, however, in recent years, systemic factors have appeared in many ways to be shifting the weight of leverage toward the host countries, with some few exceptions – for instance, perhaps that of the present U.S.-Somalia relationship.

In 1980 the Iraqi "charter" may have foreshadowed a wholesale new trend, perhaps yet to become analogous to the wave of expropriations visited upon many MNCs in recent years. Such a trend might evidence a very heightened sensitivity in the Third World to foreign basing presences – any presence – and might militate toward their extensive withdrawal.(23) If so, and assuming a continuation nevertheless of superpower military rivalry throughout the developing areas, it might direct attention to the surrogate role of new technologies in superseding territorial access.

In particular, it is the conjunction of evolving technology with changing patterns of diplomacy and national interests which is so central to the future of basing access, and which defies more than very speculative prediction.   As previously noted, increased transport aircraft ranges (in great measure due to improved tanker refueling), greater utilization of nuclear engines for ships, and perhaps also enhanced at-sea fleet support capabilities (at a cost) all should act to reduce the major powers' facilities requirements. But those developments are counterbalanced by the enhanced requirements for access related to technical functions (surveillance, satellite-tracking, ASW), which themselves, however, may later be reduced by still newer satellite capabilities, at least in some areas.

However, recent developments surrounding the looming superpower competition for access to Persian Gulf oil seem to augur more rather than fewer needs for basing access. Here, not only actual war scenarios, but also deterrence, and reinforcement or menacing of friendly or unfriendly regimes, all come into play, engendering grimly purposeful jockeying for superiority of <u>potential</u> force projection to a specific area. Hence, the United States looks to access for its Rapid Deployment Force and associated naval and air support in Egypt, Oman, Saudi Arabia, Kenya, and Diego Garcia; the Soviets counter in Syria, South Yemen, and Afghanistan, as well as with overtures to Turkey, whose airspace is critical to them. Will the future see similar jockeying in adjacent arcs surrounding new locales of competition for resources, in West Africa, South Africa, Southeast Asia, or in as yet unsuspected places where oil pools or titanium mines might be found?

BASES, ARMS RESUPPLY AND "SURROGATE CONFLICTS" IN THE THIRD WORLD

Increasingly, as the specter of actual head-to-head superpower military conflict has become relatively remote, attention has come to focus on the role of facilities and other access problems with regard to "surrogate wars" in the Third World. Central here is arms resupply during conflict, an element of contemporary diplomacy brought to prominence in 1973 and 1980, respectively, with the Arab-Israeli and Iraq-Iran wars.(24)

In recent years, of course, numerous Third World nations have amassed impressive and growing weapons inventories acquired from the several major suppliers; the arms buildups have been most accelerated in the Middle East and in Africa, particularly where piled-up petrodollars have been available for "recycle." Overall, such arms buildups – measured both by arms acquisitions and by defense expenditures – have been more marked in recent years in the Third World than they have been in the advanced countries. The frequency of armed conflict has also been higher, a fact probably not unconnected to the previous point.(25) In 1981, for instance, fighting at one level or another raged on along the Iraq-Iran border, in Lebanon, Chad, Western Sahara, Namibia, the Ogaden, and El Salvador, among other places.

Further, in recent years, much discussion has centered on the allegedly escalating trend toward indigenous arms production in the Third World, with some scholars even extrapolating toward a future which might see lessened arms dependence on the part of numerous middle- and small-range nations.(26) India, South Africa, Israel, Brazil, Taiwan, South Korea, Argentina, and Pakistan, among others, have figured in such discussions. Not accidentally, many of the same nations are most prominent in lists of those most likely to cross the nuclear weapons threshold.

But along with increasing capability for arms production among some LDCs, the ever-escalating pace of weapons development – increasingly hinged on modern electronics and computers – has made entry into the lists of arms producers an ever more formidable challenge. Hence, whether there is a long-range trend toward lessened overall dependence (less oligopolistic arms supplier markets) remains yet unclear.

None of the developing countries – for that matter, none but the superpowers plus perhaps France, Britain, and China – are really independent of external arms supply to any meaningful degree, nor could any really aspire to such status anytime soon. Israel's determined efforts, for instance, have resulted only in about 40 percent of its arms needs being produced domestically, and critical residual dependence remains for crucial advanced systems such as missiles, advanced aircraft, tank engines, heavy artillery, and helicopters. And much of the "indigenous" production – in Israel, India, Brazil – is at any rate dependent on technology transfer in the form of licenses from major powers.

Where this continued reality of arms dependence by the whole of the Third World is most evident is in the ever-present contingency of conflict which may require arms resupply – spare parts, ammunition, and replacement systems. The importance of such resupply has repeatedly been demonstrated in all of the recent, major intra-LDC conflicts, with the possible exception of the unusually quick 1967 Middle Eastern war. 1973 was another story, of course, as were both the 1965 and 1971 Indo-Pakistan conflicts, the Iran-Iraq war, the Horn war and, that in Spanish Sahara, not to mention the numerous civil or revolutionary wars such as the recent ones in Guatemala and Salvador. In an era where virtually all arms supplies need the approval of supplier governments, arms resupply has become perhaps the crucial determinant of the outcomes of wars. When the spigot has been shut – as it was for Nicaragua's Somoza regime – defeat has followed rapidly. Or, where the flow has been restricted on both sides – Iran and Iraq, and earlier with Salvador and Honduras – conflicts have tended to peter out into mutual futility because of materiel attrition.

Following from the above, it is clear that the access routes, air and sea, for arms resupply have become a very crucial element of contemporary diplomacy, again all the more so as once private control over arms shipments has virtually disappeared, and as the globe has filled up in the aftermath of decolonization with over 150 jealous sovereignties, even the smallest of which sometimes controls crucial air and/or sea lanes of communications. This arms resupply/access nexus has been demonstrated again and again – in the 1973 war, in the PRC-Vietnam conflict, in the wars in Zaire's Shaba Province, or in Angola, Mozambique, and the Horn of Africa.

For short, intense conflicts requiring massive concentration of power (Arab-Israel war of 1973, PRC-Vietnam conflict), airlifts have been crucial determinants of outcomes; hence, overflight routes and air staging points have been of premium value. But air staging has also been crucial even in less sophisticated contexts, as demonstrated by the repelling of the two invasions of Shaba by forces coming from Angola. In some more protracted conflicts (the Horn, Iran-Iraq), seaborne resupply was more important in lieu of hurried airlifts, and here, naval refueling access may have been important, as well as in some cases, overland transport routes through third countries. As the superpowers have shadowboxed throughout the Third World under their nuclear umbrella; in a dim world of surrogate conflict, arms supplies, and coercive diplomacy, various forms of access for arms resupply have appeared increasingly the very hallmark of modern security diplomacy.

As was well demonstrated by the 1973 war (to a lesser degree by the PRC-Vietnam and Iraq-Iran conflicts), some degree of weapons-producing independence may not at all suffice for a war of attrition where quantitative factors become important. And the costs of maintaining huge inventories of spare parts and ammunition to circumvent the need for resupply can be very high. Israel needed an American transfusion in 1973 after only about eight to ten days of war. Afterward, with a determined effort, its war stocks were reported to have grown to the point of anticipating a thirty-day war, but at a high cost. Generally, and more so with the materiel attrition associated with PGM warfare, virtually all LDC's have had to envisage virtually permanent and unresolvable vulnerability to arms cutoffs during conflict.(27) Each too has had to plan for access routes from the United States, USSR, or other arms suppliers even when conflict has not immediately loomed, and this increasingly has become an important if not very visible aspect of diplomacy among the smaller powers.

SUMMARY – THE FUTURE OF BASING DIPLOMACY

We have attempted in these pages to illustrate the evolvement of basing-access diplomacy throughout much of the twentieth century, tracing it from the wake of World War I to the present. In closing, we are tempted to look foward.   Such prognostications are, of course, fraught with the usual pitfalls. There is, moreover, a natural, almost unavoidable tendency to extrapolate the future from the trends of the recent past. Political history, however, rarely extrapolates for very long; indeed, the unexpected is more the norm than the exception.

With those caveats in mind, we may at least attempt to chart what would appear to be the important questions, that set of imponderables which would appear to define the essential parameters of future basing diplomacy. In a loose sense, that brings us back to a "systems" approach. On the one hand, one can set forth those areas of emerging international diplomacy which would appear to be most critical for the future of basing diplomacy, recognizing, of course, that the specific constellation or mix of those factors which does emerge will count in the aggregate. On the other, one can pinpoint certain areas of basing-access diplomacy likely to be both important and subject to the impact of whatever constellation of epochal characteristics should emerge.

Regarding such epochal characteristics, here viewed acting almost as "independent variables" upon the "dependent variables" characterizing the essentials of basing diplomacy, the following might be watched:

- A variety of trends in the development of military technology; longer-range aircraft abetted by refueling, nuclear-powered surface navies and merchant fleets, "around-the-bend" or "over-the-horizon" satellite communications to home facilities, new types of ASW technology (whether or not dependent on shore terminals).

- Levels of global conflict, and the basis for such conflicts as north-south, east-west, intra-south; in turn, how such loci of conflict shape alliances, alignments, arms-transfer patterns, etc.
- Evolving "norms," partly "psychological" in nature, regarding sovereignty, and how that applies to the granting of access, and possible Third World "peer pressures" in that context. Some might refer here to a possible "regime" determining access diplomacy.
- Developments in arms-transfer diplomacy — indigenous production, evolving oligopolistic structure of supplier markets.
- Evolving "norms," perhaps involving implicit bargaining among the major powers, about spheres of influence and the "permissibility" of rivals' military access in propinquitous regions.
- The evolving relative military capabilities of LDCs and DCs.
- The future state of nuclear proliferation: Will extensive proliferation cause "de-coupling" of some existing large/small power client relationships?
- The future of arms control, as pertains variously to SALT and test ban verification, proliferation, nuclear weapons free zones, and perhaps regional demilitarization such as earlier envisioned for the Indian Ocean area.
- Future superpower behavior regarding, for example, military interventions or coercive diplomacy.

Regarding the seemingly important areas of basing diplomacy which would appear subject to heavy influence from the above combination of factors, some of the following matters would appear to bear watching:

- What will be the future mix of types of bases or facilities required by large powers? Critically, what mix of technical and "traditional" facilities? Will there be an extension of the trend toward increasing importance for the former?
- What will be the nature — and the amount — of quid pro quo asked in exchange for access (military and economic aid, protection, markets for raw materials and manufactures, Security Council votes or vetoes, pressures on regional foes, technology transfer)? Generally, what will be the emerging balance of overall leverage between the large and small nations, and more specifically, regarding numerous bilateral combinations?
- Will the quest for bases remain primarily a two-nation game, or will multipolarity be reflected in this domain as it is, allegedly, in others?
- What will be the nature of access, along the continuum from bases to facilities, as earlier defined?
- How much validity will a heartland/rimland paradigm for global conflict — and for basing diplomacy — retain? In that context, what does the future portend for the economics of big-power competition for overseas access?

● How will future rivalries over raw materials access – and future shifts in the geography of such rivalries – affect basing diplomacy?

If one merely extrapolates, one can speculate with disarming ease about some emerging trends concerning these two sets of variables and questions. Emerging technology, for instance, seems to be <u>diminishing</u> but not eliminating the <u>quantitative</u> requirements for naval and air bases; rather, retention of a small but critical number of access points remains essential. There do appear growing requirements, however, for global networks of technical facilities, which may be lessened in the future by still newer technological developments, mostly involving expanded use of improved satellites. Then, the balance of leverage regarding access diplomacy does seem to be shifting toward the Third World hosts, mitigated somewhat by the latter's dependence for arms, particularly where multiple sources of supply are not readily available. All in all, one might foresee a coming basing "regime" characterized by tough bargaining between, on the one hand, developing countries increasingly reluctant to absorb the infringements on sovereignty and dignity associated with a foreign military presence, but on the other, superpowers which can crucially determine the security of dependent nations via arms transfers both in peace and in war.

Surprises could, of course, greatly alter expectations based on such extrapolations. A tenser, more ideological bipolar struggle (return to the Cold War) could make for a more permissive basing environment, for one or both superpowers. Raw materials rivalries could also, in some circumstances, have the same impact, as witness currently expanded U.S. access near the Persian Gulf. Then too, although not likely, a new era of imperial conquest – perhaps impelled by a struggle for resources – cannot altogether be ruled out. If it occurred, more extensive big-power basing networks would presumably automatically follow. But, a world which saw twenty or thirty new nuclear powers might also be one where large powers disengaged from some areas to avoid being dragged into conflict. Such a world might also see much more restricted big power basing access. It might also see intra-LDC basing diplomacy related to possible small powers' nuclear deterrence vis-a-vis superpowers to compensate for the striking ranges of the former's delivery systems.

Finally, contrary to present trends, new technological developments resulting in vastly increased access requirements are not necessarily to be ruled out, though that is at present not foreseen. It is hard to say what impact on future basing requirements might be wrought by space-based laser stations, massive proliferation of cruise missiles by many nations, or enormous strides in ASW capabilities. Quite probably, one way or another, basing matters will remain, as they have long been, a crucial feature of global diplomacy.

NOTES

(1) See Morton Kaplan, System and Process in International Politics (New York: Wiley, 1957); and Richard Rosecrance, Action and Reaction in World Politics (Boston: Little, Brown, 1963). A recent excellent critique of past efforts at systems theory is in Kenneth Waltz, Theory of International Politics (Reading, Mass.: Addison-Wesley, 1979), esp. chap. 3. See also R. Harkavy, The Arms Trade and International Systems (Cambridge, Mass.: Ballinger, 1975) for a somewhat analogous attempt at applying systems theory to arms transfers.

(2) Regarding bipolarity and multipolarity – and attempts to apply those concepts to recent epochs, see Richard Rosecrance, "Bipolarity, Multipolarity and the Future," The Journal of Conflict Resolution 10 (1966): 314-327; Kaplan, System and Process; and Wolfram Hanrieder, Foreign Policies and the International System: A Theoretical Introduction (New York: General Learning Press, 1971).

(3) The alternating relative presence and/or absence of ideology as a major factor defining historical epochs is discussed in, inter alia, J.F.C. Fuller, Armaments and History (New York: Chas. Scribner's Sons, 1945), chaps. 2, 3; Robert E. Osgood, "The Expansion of Force," in Robert Art and Kenneth Waltz, eds., The Use of Force (Boston: Little, Brown, 1971), pp. 29-55; Hans Morgenthau, Politics Among Nations, 5th edition (New York: Knopf, 1973), chap. 7; and with specific reference to the interwar period, utilizing the idea of homogeneous vs. heterogeneous systems, see S. Michalak, "The United Nations and the League," in L. Gordenker, ed., The U.N. in International Politics (Princeton, N.J.: Princeton University Press, 1971), pp. 60-105.

(4) However, some of the political problems which were increasingly to arise in connection with overhead airspace were already being anticipated near the outset of World War II. See the various selections in chapter 4 of H. Weigert and V. Stefansson, Compass of the World (New York: Macmillan, 1944), esp. Stefansson, "Arctic Supply Line," pp. 295-311, and Graham B. Grosvenor, "The Northward Course of Aviation," pp. 312-335.

(5) The actual "facts" of the resupply of arms to Iraq during its war with Iran in 1980-1981 remain somewhat obscure. Many reports spoke of Soviet denial of resupply, but pointed to East European supplies which, presumably, would occur only with a Soviet imprimatur. But, in "Saddam Hussein Builds on the Rubble," Newsweek, June 29, 1981, p. 42, it is said that "Moscow has re-equipped Iraq with weaponry lost during the past nine months."

(6) Discussed in Rosecrance, Action and Reaction, pp. 220-232.

(7) On the legitimization function of international organizations (as easily, delegitimization), see Inis Claude, "Collective Legitimization as a Political Function of the United Nations," International Organization 20, 3 (Summer 1966): 367-379.

(8) This thesis, oddly ignored in much of the literature, is discussed in Harkavy, Arms Trade, chap. 2.

(9) In mid-1981, there were numerous examples of this growing type of linkage. The Mexican government, responding to French oil companies' refusal to continue to purchase high-priced oil as world prices declined, threatened to cancel a number of French investment ventures and construction projects in Mexico. And, in the context of the Israeli raid, there were reports of Brazilian transfer of German-origin nuclear technology to Iraq, enmeshed in Brazilian supply of armored systems to Iraq and the latter's assurances of oil flows to Brazil.

(10) For a wide-ranging discussion of status-of-forces matters, as applied to one case, see Joseph W. Dodd, Criminal Jurisdiction under the U.S.-Philippine Military Bases Agreement: A Study in Conjurisdictional Law (The Hague: M. Nijhoff, 1968).

(11) Amid a vast and growing literature, see Pirages, op. cit., Alex Inkeles, "The Emerging Social Structure of the World," World Politics 27, 4 (July 1975): 467-495; Ernest Haas, The Web of Interdependence (Englewood Cliffs, N.J.: Prentice-Hall, 1970); Oran R. Young, "Interdependencies in World Politics," International Journal 24, 4 (Autumn 1969): 726-750; and Joseph Nye, "Independence and Interdependence," Foreign Policy no. 22 (Spring 1976): 129-161.

(12) See in particular T. Baumgartner, "The Structuring of International Economic Relations" (paper delivered at International Studies Association, Washington, D.C., February 1975).

(13) This is discussed, generally and theoretically, in Ilan Peleg, "Arms Supply to the Third World: Models and Explanations," The Journal of Modern African Studies 15, 1 (1977): 91-103.

(14) For definitions and general analyses of the national interest, see, inter alia, Fred A. Sondermann, "The Concept of the National Interest," Orbis 21, 1 (Spring 1977): 121-138; Alexander George and Robert Keohane, "The Concept of National Interest: Uses and Limitations," in Commission on the Organization of the Government for the Conduct of Foreign Policy, Appendices, vol. 2, pp. 67-68; Joseph Frankel, National Interest (New York: Praeger, 1970); James Rosenau, "National Interest," International Encyclopedia of the Social Sciences (New York: Macmillan, Free Press, 1968), vol. 2, p. 35.

(15) This is discussed in Samuel Huntington, "Arms Races: Prerequisites and Results," in Art and Waltz, eds., The Use of Force, pp. 369-377.

(16) See Hans Weigert, Principles of Political Geography (New York: Appleton-Century-Crofts, 1957), pp. 176-179. For one recent attempt at analysis of a contemporary buffer state example, see Stephen Cohen, "Pakistan's Security Policies," in E. Kolodziej and R. Harkavy, Security Policies of Developing States (Lexington, Mass.: D.C. Heath, 1982).

(17) See Marvin Kalb, "The Vital Interests of Mr. Kennan," New York Times Magazine, March 27, 1966, pp. 31ff.

(18) Richard Toye, "The Projection of U.S. Power by the Air Force in the Western Pacific and Indian Ocean," paper delivered at Fletcher School conference on "Security and Development in the Indo-Pacific Arena," Boston, April, 1978; and Kemp, "The New Strategic Map," Survival 19, 2 (March/April 1977), pp. 50-59. In the earlier, lengthier version of the latter presented as a paper at the Fletcher School Conference previously noted, extensive data on various (often obscure) islands in the southern seas was compiled.

(19) No really rigorous analysis in the open literature has been done regarding the arms transfer/base correlation, nor regarding time lags which might indicate causation. The author was privileged to review some work along these lines by Michael Squires at the Center for Naval Analyses, in-house.

(20) See Stockholm International Peace Research Institute, The Arms Trade and the Third World (New York: Humanities Press, 1971), pp. 17-18.

(21) For a framework for such an analysis, see A. Leiss et al., Arms Transfers to Less Developed Countries, C/70-1 (Cambridge, Mass.: MIT Center for International Studies, 1970), as discussed in Harkavy, Arms Trade, pp. 92-97.

(22) For a picture of the various kinds of U.S. military aid instruments, see the DOD's "Foreign Military Sales and Military Assistance Facts," (Washington, D.C.: GPO, December 1979).

(23) See the previously cited paper by Richard Remnek, "Foreign Military Access and Host-Nation Sovereignty," unpublished paper delivered at annual meeting of International Studies Association, Philadelphia, March 4, 1981.

(24) A framework for the study of arms resupply diplomacy is offered in R. Harkavy, "Arms Resupply During Conflict" (paper delivered at meeting of International Studies Association, Los Angeles, March 18-21, 1980).

(25) See E. Kolodziej and R. Harkavy, "Developing States and the International Security System," in their Security Policies.

(26) See, in particular, M. Moodie, "Defense Industries in the Third World: Problems and Promises," in S. Neuman and R. Harkavy, eds., Arms Transfers in the Modern World (New York: Praeger, 1979), pp. 294-312; and S. Neuman, "Into the Crystal Ball: Indigenous Defense Production and the Future of the International Arms Trade" (paper delivered at meeting of International Studies Association, Los Angeles, March 19-22, 1980).

(27) See Steven Rosen, "The Proliferation of New Land-Based Technologies: Implications for Local Military Balances," in Neuman and Harkavy, Arms Transfers, pp. 109-130; and Martin van Creveld, Military Lessons of the Yom Kippur War, The Washington Papers, no. 24 (Washington, D.C.: Georgetown University CSIS, 1975).

Selected
Bibliography

PRE-1919 BASING DIPLOMACY

Boxer, C.R. The Dutch Seaborne Empire: 1600-1800. New York: Knopf, 1965.
Boxer, C.R. The Portuguese Seaborne Empire, 1415-1825. New York: Knopf, 1969.
Cole, D.H. Imperial Military Geography, 12th ed. London: Sifton Praed, 1956.
Kennedy, P.M. "Imperial Cable Communications and Strategy, 1870-1914. The English Historical Review, 86, 141 (1971), pp. 728-752.
Modelski, George. "The Theory of the Long Cycles," in R. Harkavy and E. Kolodziej, American Security Policy and Policy-Making. Lexington, MA: D.C. Heath, 1980.
Wallerstein, Immanuel. The Modern World-System. New York: Academic Press, 1974.

BASES IN THE INTERWAR PERIOD AND DURING
WORLD WAR II

Collier, Basil. The Airshop: A History. New York: Putnam, 1974.
DuPuy, Ernest R. World in Arms. Harrisburg, PA: The Military Service Publishing Co., 1939.
Gormley, James L. "Keeping the Door Open in Saudi Arabia: The United States and the Dhahran Airfield, 1945-46," Diplomatic History, Vol. 4, No. 2 (Spring 1980), pp. 189-205.
Millett, Richard. "The State Department's Navy: A History of the Special Service Squadron, 1920-1940." The American Neptune, XXXV (1975), pp. 118-138.
Patch, Buel W. "American Naval and Air Bases." Editorial Research Report, Vol. 1, No. 7, Feb. 16, 1939.

Patch, Buel W. "Overseas Bases." Editorial Research Report, Vol. II, No. 2, July 14, 1951, pp. 441-2.

Roberts, Stephen S. "The Decline of the Overseas Station Fleets: The United States Asiatic Fleet and the Shanghai Crisis, 1932." Arlington, VA: Center for Naval Analyses, Nov. 1977, Professional Paper No. 208.

Roskill, Stephen. Naval Policy Between the Wars, Vol. I, 1919-1929. New York: Walker & Co., 1969.

Weiss, Kenneth G. "The Azores in Diplomacy and Strategy, 1940-1945." Alexandria, VA: Center for Naval Analyses, March 1980, Professional Paper 272.

Weller, George A. Bases Overseas: An American Trusteeship in Power. New York: Harcourt, Brace, 1944.

BASES IN THE POSTWAR PERIOD

Barnet, Corelli. Britain and Her Army: 1509-1970. New York: William Morrow, Co., 1970.

Blaxland, Gregory. The Regiments Depart. London: William Klimber, 1971.

Blechman, Barry and Robert Weinland. "Why Coaling Stations are Necessary in the Nuclear Age." International Security, 2 (1977), pp. 88-99.

Cottrell, Alvin. "Soviet Views of U.S. Overseas Bases." Orbis Vol. VII, No. 1 (Spring 1963), pp. 77-95.

Cottrell, Alvin and Thomas H. Moorer. "U.S. Overseas Bases: Problems of Projecting American Military Power Abroad." Washington: Georgetown CSIS, 1977, paper No. 47.

Dadant, P.M. "Shrinking International Airspace as a Problem for Future Air Movements – A Briefing." Santa Monica, CA: RAND, 1978, Report R-2178-AF.

Dodd, Joseph W. Criminal Jurisdiction under the U.S.-Philippine Military Bases Agreement: A Study in Conjurisdictional Law. The Hague: M. Nijhoff, 1968.

Goodie, Clifford B. Strategic Air Command. New York: Simon and Schuster, 1965.

Hagerty, Herbert G. Forward Deployment in the 1970's and 1980's. Washington: National Defense University, 1977. National Security Affairs Monograph 77-2.

Harkavy, Robert. "The New Geopolitics: Arms Transfers and the Major Powers' Competition for Overseas Bases," in S. Neuman and R. Harkavy, eds., Arms Transfers in the Modern World. New York: Praeger, 1979, pp. 131-151.

Haselkorn, Avigdor. The Evolution of Soviet Security Strategy: 1965-1975. New York: Crane, Russak, 1978.

Infield, Glenn B. Unarmed and Unafraid. New York: Macmillan, 1970.

Kaplan, Stephen. "The Utility of U.S. Military Bases." Military Review, Vol. 57, No. 4, April 1977, pp. 43-57.

Lewis, William H. "How a Defense Planner Looks at Africa," in Helen Kitchen, ed., Africa: From Mystery to Maze. Lexington, MA: Lexington Books, 1976.

Moorer, Thomas and Alvin Cottrell. "The Search for U.S. Bases in the Indian Ocean: A Last Chance." Strategic Review, Spring 1980, pp. 36-37.

Ostrich, Ralph. "Aeroflot." Armed Forces Journal, Vol. 118, No. 9, May 1981, pp. 38ff.

Paul, Roland. American Military Commitments Abroad. New Brunswick, N.J.: Rutgers Univ. Press, 1973.

Philips, Heidi. "Host Press Coverage of Soviet Naval Visits to Islamic Countries, 1968-1973." Arlington, VA: Center for Naval Analyses, June 1976.

Roberts, Stephen S. "French Naval Policy Outside of Europe." Paper delivered at meeting of International Studies Association, Section on Military Studies, Kiawah Island, S.C., Nov. 8, 1978.

Thompson, Scott. "The Projection of Soviet Power." Santa Monica, CA: RAND, August 1977, P-5988.

Toye, Richard G. "The Projection of U.S. Power by the Air Force in the Western Pacific and Indian Ocean." Paper delivered at Fletcher School conference on "Security and Development in the Indo-Pacific Arena," Boston, April 1978.

U.S. Department of Defense, Comptroller's Office, "DOD Annual Operating Costs of Maintaining U.S. Military Forces in Foreign Countries and Areas, Washington, U.S.G.P.O., annual.

U.S. House of Representatives, Committee on Foreign Relations. "Greece and Turkey: Some Military Implications Related to NATO and the Middle East," report prepared by Congressional Research Service, Library of Congress, Washington, U.S.G.P.O., February 28, 1975.

U.S. Senate, Committee on Foreign Relations, "United States Security Agreements and Commitments Abroad, Hearings Before the Subcommittee on U.S. Security Agreements and Commitments Abroad, 91st Congress, Volumes I and II, U.S.G.P.O., 1971.

U.S. Senate, Committee on Foreign Relations, "United States Foreign Policy Objectives and Overseas Military Installations," prepared by Congressional Research Service, Library of Congress, Washington, 1979.

Weinland, Robert G. "Land Support for Naval Forces: Egypt and the Soviet Escadra 1962-1976." Survival 20 (1978), pp. 73-79.

NAVAL STRATEGY, GENERAL, RELATED TO BASES

Brodie, Bernard. Sea Power in the Machine Age. Princeton: Princeton University Press, 1941.

Burns, Thomas S. The Secret War for the Ocean Depths. New York: Rawson, 1978.

Dismukes, Bradford and James McConnell, eds. Soviet Naval Diplomacy. New York: Pergamon, 1979.

Friedman, Norman. "SOSUS and U.S. ASW Tactics." U.S. Naval Institute Proceedings, March 1980, pp. 120-122.

Garwin, Richard. "Anti-Submarine Warfare and National Security," in Arms Control: Readings from Scientific American. San Francisco: W.H. Freeman, 1973, chapter 26.

Gorschkov, Sergei, G. The Sea Power of the State. Annapolis: U.S. Naval Institute Press, 1979.

Graham, Gerald. The Politics of Naval Supremacy. Cambridge: Cambridge University Press, 1965.

Kemp, Geoffrey and John Maurer. "The Logistics of Pax Britannica: Lessons for America." Paper presented at Fletcher School conference on "Projection of Power," April 23-25, 1980, Boston.

Kennedy, Paul M. The Rise and Fall of British Naval Mastery. New York: Scribner, 1976.

MccGwire, M., K. Booth and J. McDonnell, eds. Soviet Naval Policy. New York: Praeger, 1975.

Manthorpe, William H.J., Jr. "The Soviet Navy in 1979: Part I." Naval Institute Proceedings, April 1980.

Rosinski, Herbert. The Development of Naval Thought. Newport, R.I.: Naval War College Press, 1977.

GEOPOLITICAL THEORY, GRAND STRATEGY, MAP IMAGERY

Axelrod, Robert, ed. The Structure of Decision: The Cognitive Maps of Political Elites. Princeton: Princeton University Press, 1976.

Cohen, Saul. Geography and Politics in a World Divided. New York: Random House, 1963.

Collins, John. Grand Strategy: Practices and Principles. Annapolis: Naval Institute Press, 1973.

Cressey, George. The Basis of Soviet Strength. New York: McGraw-Hill, 1945.

Gilpin, Robert. U.S. Power and Multinational Corporations. New York: Basic Books, 1975.

Gray, Colin. The Geopolitics of the Nuclear Era. New York: Crane Russak, 1977.

Henrikson, Alan K. "America's Changing Place in the World: From 'Periphery' to 'Centre'"? in Jean Gottmann, ed., Centre and Periphery: Spatial Variation in Politics. Beverly Hills, CA: Sage, 1980.

Hooson, David J.M. A New Soviet Heartland? Princeton: Van Nostrand, 1964.

Jackson, W.A. Douglas. Politics and Geographic Relationships. Englewood Cliffs, NJ: Prentice-Hall, 1964.

Jones, Stephen. "Global Strategic Views." The Geographical Review, XLV, No. 4 (July 1955), pp. 492-508.

Kasperson, Roger and Julian Minghi, eds. The Structure of Political Geography. Chicago: Aldine, 1969.
Kemp, Geoffrey. "The New Strategic Map." Survival, 19, 2 (March/April 1977), pp. 50-59.
Mackinder, Halford. Democratic Ideals and Reality. New York: Norton, 1962.
Mahan, Alfred T. The Influence of Seapower Upon History, 1660-1783. Boston: Little, Brown, 1980.
Peltier, Lewis and G. Etzel Pearcy. Military Geography. New York: Van Nostrand, 1966.
Speier, Hans. "Magic Geography." Social Research, Sept. 1941, pp. 310-330.
Spykman, Nicholas. America's Strategy in World Politics. New York: Harcourt, Brace, 1942.
Spykman, Nicholas. The Geography of the Peace. New York: Harcourt, Brace, 1944.
Strausz-Hupé, Robert. Geopolitics: The Struggle for Space and Power. New York: G.P. Putnam, 1942.
Walters, Robert E. The Nuclear Trap. Baltimore: Penguin, 1974.
Weigert, Hans W., V. Stefansson, and R. Harrison, eds. New Compass of the World. New York: Macmillan, 1949.
Weigert, Hans et al., eds. Principles of Political Geography. New York: Appleton-Century-Crofts, 1957.

DEVELOPMENT OF TECHNICAL FACILITIES

Carroll, John M. Secrets of Electronic Espionage. New York: Dutton, 1966.
Barnaby, Frank. "On Target With an Omega Station?" New Scientist, Vol. 109, No. 993 (March 25, 1976), pp. 671-672.
Klass, Philip. Secret Sentries in Space. New York: Random House, 1971.
Langer, Albert, Owen Wilkes, and N.P. Gleditsch. The Military Functions of Omega and Loran-C. Oslo: Peace Research Institute, 1976.
McGarvey, Patrick. CIA: The Myth and the Madness. Baltimore: Penguin, 1972.
Siegel, Lenny. "Diego Garcia." Pacific Research. Vol. VIII, No. 3, March-April, 1977.
Stockholm International Peace Research Institute. Outer Space - Battlefield of the Future? New York: Crane, Russak, 1978.

RAW MATERIALS' SOURCES AND BASES

Hahn, Walter F. and Alvin Cottrell. Soviet Shadow Over Africa. Washington: Miami University Center for Advanced International Studies, 1976.
International Economic Studies Institute. Raw Materials and Foreign Policy. Washington: 1976.

Kemp, Geoffrey. "Scarcity and Strategy." Foreign Affairs, Vol. 56, No. 2 (January 1978), pp. 396-414.

Papp, Daniel S. "Soviet Non-Fuel Mineral Resources: Surplus or Scarcity?" Unpublished paper, May 1981.

MISCELLANEOUS

Blechman, Barry and Stephen Kaplan. Force Without War. Washington: Brookings, 1978.

Creveld, Martin, van. Supplying War: Logistics from Wallerstein to Patton. New York: Cambridge University Press, 1977.

Earle, Edward, ed. Makers of Modern Strategy. Princeton: Princeton University Press, 1941.

Howard, Michael. The Continental Commitment. London: Temple, Smith, 1972.

Sokolovskii, V.D. Soviet Military Strategy. Englewood Cliffs, N.J.: Prentice-Hall, 1963.

Index

About the Author

ROBERT E. HARKAVY is an Associate Professor of Political Science at Pennsylvania State University. He earlier served with the US Atomic Energy Commission and the US Arms Control and Disarmament Agency, taught at Kalamazoo College, and was a Senior Research Associate at the Cornell University Center for International Studies. He is the author of The Arms Trade and International Systems, and monographs on the Israeli nuclear weapons program and preemption in conventional warfare; also co-editor and contributor to Arms Transfers in the Modern World, American Security Policy and Policymaking and Security Policies of Developing States. He has published in Orbis, International Organization, Journal of International Affairs, and Policy Studies Journal. During 1982-83 he is a Visiting Research Professor at the US Army War College, Strategic Studies Institute, following which he will be an Alexander von Humboldt fellow at the Christian-Albrechts University, Kiel, Germany.